50637

PN
6725
.T5
1974

Thompson, Don.

The comic-book book

DATE			

THE
COMIC-BOOK BOOK

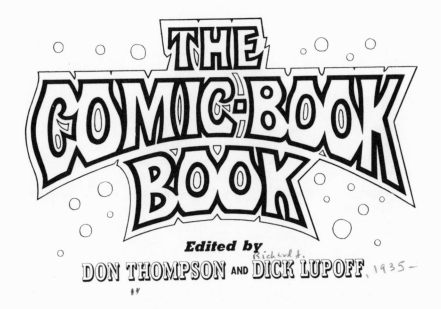

THE COMIC-BOOK BOOK

Edited by
DON THOMPSON AND DICK LUPOFF

Richard t.
1935-

ARLINGTON HOUSE New Rochelle, N. Y.

Acknowledgments

Our thanks and appreciation to Carl Barks; Edgar Rice Burroughs, Inc.; Will Eisner; Famous Funnies, Inc.; Hillman Periodicals, Inc.; King Features Syndicate; Marvel Comics Group; National Periodical Publications, Inc.; William M. Gaines; and Holt, Rinehart and Winston, Inc., publishers of *Seduction of the Innocent* by Dr. Frederic Wertham, © 1954, Frederic Wertham.

Manufactured in the United States of America

Library of Congress Cataloging in Publication Data

Thompson, Don.
    The comic-book book.

    Sequel to All in color for a dime edited by D. Lupoff and D. Thompson.
    1. Comic books, strips, etc.--American--History and criticism. I. Lupoff, Richard A., 1935-   joint author. II. Lupoff, Richard A., 1935-   All in color for a dime. III. Title.
PN6725.T5 1974   741.5'973   73-22448
ISBN 0-87000-193-0

For CARL BARKS

"The Good Artist"

CONTENTS

INTRODUCTION

THE past decade has been marked by a great increase in the interest shown in popular culture. Both popular and academic scholars seem to have discovered that while both the classic arts and contemporary "fine arts" have their place and are worthy of attention, so too have the popular, or mass, arts.

Thus both the media and the individual creators who brought pleasure to audiences in the millions—but were long ignored by the chronicles and critics of the arts—have begun to achieve recognition.

Numerous articles and reviews, and even full magazines and books, have begun to appear on such popular authors, for instance, as H. P. Lovecraft (creator of the horrific Cthulhu Mythos), Sax Rohmer (author of the *Fu Manchu* books), Edgar Rice Burroughs (mastermind of *Tarzan*), and Robert E. Howard (creator of Conan and of King Kull).

There have been books and magazines devoted to old radio and television personalities and shows, to films—including the long-despised serials and "B" programmers—to popular music ranging from jazz and blues through the artists and sounds of the "big band" era, and the modern folk singers and rock and roll musicians of the 1950s and since.

Formal recognition of the importance of "pop" culture has come in several forms. The "pop art" craze of the 1960s led to shows in many museums on images and forms derived from the "mass" rather than the "class" culture. Many universities have begun to offer courses in popular films, music, and literature as topics for serious study. As a single example of this phenomenon, science fiction, which was once regarded as a trashy excrescence of literature at its worst, has achieved recognition on many campuses.

Over 400 colleges and universities were offering regular, credit-bearing courses in science fiction, according to a recent survey by the Science Fiction Writers of America. And that number was increasing annually by leaps and bounds. Simultaneously, a smaller but growing number of colleges were offering special concentrated summer programs for would-be science-fiction *writers*—whether this kind of hot-house treatment will actually yield any serious talents remains to be seen, but early evidence is encouraging.

The comics, while not that far along, have also been gaining in recognition. And well they might!

There is statistical evidence that even in this latter day of domination by television, well over 90 percent of American children still read comic books, and—perhaps more surprisingly—approximately 50 percent of American *adults* do the same. In the case of newspaper comic strips, although the proportions are different (fewer children read them but more adults do) the overall saturation figures are similarly impressive.

Living in or near cities with large university populations, as both your editors do (Dick in Berkeley, California, and Don near Cleveland, Ohio), we are each reminded frequently of the popular campus craze for *Spider-Man* and other contemporary classics. The same stories that small children read as simple, colorful adventures, the college crowd often regard as modern myths with all of the serious though perhaps unconscious significance possessed by the stories of Ulysses, Siegfried, Bilbo Baggins, and other characters of similar "imagic" power.

This growing attention to and appreciation of the comics as a very important element of popular culture goes back somewhat over ten years. We ourselves lay some claim to credit as pioneers for the *All in Color for a Dime* feature, which began as a series of magazine articles as far back as 1960, emerged in collected (and much revised) form as a book in 1970, and has continued its lineal descent into *The Comic-Book Book*.

An increasing number of other books have appeared in this same field. Some, like *The Comic-Book Book* and *All in Color for a Dime*, have been essentially nostalgic, historical, or critical examinations of the comics and their creators, while others have concentrated mainly on reprinting classic examples of comic art along with a lesser amount of commentary and bibliographic data.

Reprint albums of the latter sort have included books devoted to Buck Rogers, Dick Tracy, Little Orphan Annie, Superman, Batman, Wonder Woman, Krazy Kat, Mandrake the Magician, the Phantom, *Little Nemo*, Popeye the Sailor, and others, with special mention due a magnificent volume of reprinted horror classics from the EC comics of the fifties and another volume (at this writing still in the planning stages) on the brilliant *Minute Movies* by the late Ed Wheelan.

In the critical-historical-nostalgic category, books have begun to appear on such specialized topics as the Canadian comic-book industry, which sprang up and flowered briefly during World War II, when import restrictions cut the flow of U.S.-produced comic books almost to the zero point. Sometime comic artist Jim Steranko has issued two volumes in his projected multivolume history of the comic book, with particular value in the many reproductions of classic comic covers and the ferreting out of long-obscure credits for writers, artists, and editors.

Other ambitious projects which, it is hoped, will someday see print, are histories of the comics by Larry Ivie, Jerry Robinson, and Bill Blackbeard.

Although all of these historians tend at times to cover the same ground, none of their books seems to render the others superfluous. Even though specific historical data may overlap, the differences in approach, opinion, and style of presentation have given each such book a unique character, and all are worthwhile.

An immense boon to the would-be collector, scholar, or simple nostalgic reminiscer, would be a comprehensive index to the comics. Such an index would also be an immense project, and although a number of such efforts are under way, the closest available book to that ideal index is a volume prepared for a wholly different purpose!

This is *The Comic Book Price Guide* by Robert M. Overstreet (sometimes referred to as "The Overpriced Guide" but that's

11

another matter). This book, as its name indicates, was created as an aid to dealers and collectors in establishing some sort of reasonably stable price structure for collector's items. But, as a by-product of this effort, the *Guide* has come to include issue numbers, dates, cover reproductions, and a growing amount of bibliographic annotation with each passing edition.

Michael Fleisher, an occasional writer for comic books himself, is working on an encyclopedia of comic-book heroes to be published by Dial Press. Fleisher set himself the not always enjoyable task of reading *every one* of the published stories of Captain America, the Human Torch, Batman, Superman, and a vast horde of other costumed crimefighters. Difficulty in locating copies of each adventure—the publishers themselves do not have complete files of their publications and the gaps in the Library of Congress files would appall the staunchest-hearted bibliophile—has delayed publication, but the task is nearly completed now.

Bowling Green University in Ohio has set up a Popular Culture Center with vast stocks of material once considered unworthy of scholarship, and is publishing scholarly works about, among other things, comic books and comic strips. Despite an unfortunate tendency to be pedantic, these works perform valuable functions. Like most self-consciously scholarly publications, however, they sometimes lose sight of the fact that the product under discussion was intended to be entertaining.

Bowling Green has also given some attention to another recent comic-book phenomenon, "underground comix."

Underground *comix* (the spelling has become so entrenched that some would-be with-it Establishment comic-book publishers have started using it instead of *comics*) are an adjunct of under-ground newspapers, themselves an outgrowth of what has been called the "counterculture" or "hippie" movement. Underground comix and newspapers are sold primarily in "hippie" stores. Underground comix are comic books published by small, privately owned printers such as Print Mint, Rip-Off Press, Krupp Comic Works, and Last Gasp Eco-Funnies. They are usually black-and-white, usually cost $.50, usually contain amateurish or downright awful art, and usually deal with material of a sexual and / or anti-Establishment nature.

All those "usuallys" are to alert you that there are exceptions. Some underground comix are in full color, some cost more or less than $.50, some contain really good art, and some do not involve sex or dope or revolution, though all are, with reason, marked "adults only."

Underground comix artists are making an impression upon the mass media and are appearing in a larger arena than is afforded by the average underground comic book with a circulation of a few thousand copies.

Robert Crumb, the Leonardo da Vinci of the underground, has had at least two collections of his comix books from major publishers (*Head Comix*, Viking Press; *Fritz the Cat*, Ballantine) and was the source of a major movie, the world's first X-rated animated cartoon feature, *Fritz the Cat*.

Skip Williamson has done several illustrations for *Playboy*, including a comic-book rendering of an Arthur C. Clarke short story. Still others are surfacing in the "straight" world.

Aboveground cartoonists and writers have reversed the trend, doing occasional underground comix work for the freedom from censorship it affords. Underground artists also have the advantage of owning their work; most comic-book publishing companies buy all rights to stories—and characters, including ones which may be worth millions of dollars—for one (low) flat fee. Only rarely does a "straight" (aboveground) comics writer or artist collect royalties, no matter how well his work sells or how often it is reprinted. Even if it sells to the movies.

The biggest names attracted to underground comix are Will Eisner and Harvey Kurtzman. Eisner has authorized an underground comic book reprinting his *Spirit* stories and has done new covers and stories for it. Kurtzman has devoted considerable space to underground comix in his book *Comic Books from Aargh to Zap!*, which has often been delayed and is still forthcoming at this writing.

It remains to be seen, whether the underground comix will last and whether they will produce anything of real lasting merit—but it looks as if much of the work of Crumb, Williamson, Gilbert Shelton, Jay Lynch, and Richard Corben, to name a few, will have a permanent impact.

It also remains to be seen whether comic books can ever break into the larger magazine field. An attempt to break out of the 32-page format into 48 pages for a quarter failed recently and comic books appear to be stuck at 32 pages for $.20, with occasional 48-page reprint issues for $.35 and 100-page reprint issues for $.50. This comparatively low price for a four-color comic book—color printing is *expensive*—means that a comic book has to sell well over 100,000 copies of each issue to survive. Couple that with increased distribution problems in recent years and the red ink soon starts flowing. Comic books take up as much newsstand space as more expensive magazines; since the retailer does not make as much money from them as he does from the more expensive magazines, he stops carrying comic books. One solution might be switching to publishing black-and-white comic magazines with higher cover prices.

Easier said than done.

There have been many attempts to break into the magazines, not only for profit but to become free of the censorship of the Comics Code Authority and maybe also to escape the kiddie-fodder stigma comic books have. There have been nearly as many failures as there have been attempts. Such comic-book publishers as EC, Marvel, and DC have tried and failed to make a success of black-and-white comic magazines. Prior to 1973, at least, only Warren Publications (*Creepy, Eerie, Vampirella*) had made much of a success of it. Several imitators of Warren's books have managed to survive but they do not appear to be thriving.

In 1973, Marvel Comics launched the most ambitious foray yet against the magazine barrier with a fleet of bimonthly $.75 titles making their debut at the rate of one a month for most of the year: *Dracula Lives!, Monsters Unleashed, Tales of the Zombie, Vampire Tales, Crazy, Savage Tales*...

Since this book's function is hindsight, not foresight, we shall not venture a guess as to how these publications will fare. If they are still appearing by the time you read this book, you may assume they have made it. If they are not, they did not.

Within the comic-book field, the past few years have been marked by a number of interesting trends, one being a growing awareness of and willingness to address serious contemporary problems such as youthful alienation, political unrest, the peace movement, and the menace of drug addiction. The difficulty of integrating such serious themes into a basically entertainment-oriented medium was exemplified by the sad case of DC's *Green Lantern–Green Arrow* comic. At the very same time that comic was achieving wide notice and high praise for its courageous approaches to such topics as racial prejudice and the menace of pollution, its sales plummeted to the point where it had to be suspended!

Another interesting trend has been the growth in interest in classic heroes—both those revived from earlier eras of the comics, and those newly adapted from other media. These have included more-or-less experimental (although in some cases very successful) revivals or adaptations of Doc Savage, Conan, Kull, Dracula, the Frankenstein monster, many 1940s superheroes including Plastic Man and (most amazingly) the original Captain Marvel, several Edgar Rice Burroughs characters in addition to the perennially popular Tarzan, and that classic mystery man, the Shadow.

If a time machine could scoop up a devotee of the comic books and pulp magazines of the 1930s and 1940s and deliver him to a neighborhood newsstand today, he would be delighted to find dozens of his old friends still around—or around all over again.

What this means, pretty obviously, is that the writers and artists of that classic era had a whole lot on the ball. Their work may at times have been crude and their fictional "logic" sometimes less than rigorous, but they were in touch with certain powerful forces in the personalities of us all that permitted them to conjure up images which have never lost their appeal, and which are today attracting an audience as large and as loyal as ever they did in those decades when we were eager, youthful readers—or our parents were!

And so here is *The Comic-Book Book*. Like its predecessor *All in Color for a Dime* it is partly nostalgic, partly scholarly, partly analytical. (And we should mention that, while *The Comic-Book Book* is a sequel to the earlier volume, it is complete in itself and each chapter can stand independently of anything in the earlier book.) Last time out we concentrated on comic books, and especially on the superheroes who dominated the publications of the 1940s.

In *The Comic-Book Book* we branch out somewhat farther. The superheroes are still here—see Don's chapter on Plastic Man, Juanita Coulson's chapter on Wonder Woman and other distaff superdoers, Ron Goulart's continuing examination of the short-lived and often-forgotten but always-fascinating "second bananas."

But there were dozens of kinds of comic books and comic-book features, and various authors in *The Comic-Book Book* devote their chapters to such themes as detectives (the Spirit), horror comics (Frankenstein, the ECs), aviators (Captain Wings, Airboy,

Blackhawk), jungle men (Tarzan and others of his ilk), magicians (Mandrake, Ibis, Zatara, the Spectre, Dr. Fate, Zatanna), and even classic funny animals (the Duck and the Mouse).

Chris Steinbrunner, our old friend and multimedia expert, is back this time too: from superheroes on the screen in *All in Color for a Dime*, Chris turns his attention in *The Comic-Book Book* to those same larger-than-human figures as they were manifested across the airwaves when we were all much smaller and radios much bigger than they are today.

We're sure that you'll meet many an old friend in the pages of *The Comic-Book Book*, and relive many a thrilling, happy moment of past years as you read through chapters prepared by a dozen of your fellow enthusiasts.

But the end is not yet, not by any means! Not only do there remain many individual characters, features, and comic series to be covered, but whole categories of comic books, each worthy of at least a chapter if not a full volume of its own. These include westerns, crime, true-fact, love, sports, "little kids," great-literature adaptations, teenage-fun, and the so-called underground comics.

We closed our introduction to *All in Color for a Dime* by expressing our hope that enough readers would respond to that book to justify the publication of a sequel someday. The readers did respond, and they—you—receive our heartfelt thanks for that support. And here, as promised, is *The Comic-Book Book*.

We express the same hope now, and pledge once again that if the response to *The Comic-Book Book* justifies our doing so, we shall assemble a crew of scholars, critics, and misty-eyed nostalgiacs for a third time. With that hope uppermost in our minds, we do not say "Good-bye," but merely, in the words of the old radio show announcers, "So long till next time!"

But in the meanwhile, there lie ahead of you a baker's dozen of fond journeys into yesteryear, each of them a chapter of this book. We hope you enjoy them, each and every one!

Dick Lupoff
Don Thompson

INTRODUCTION TO

THE REHABILITATION OF EEL O'BRIAN

THERE'S a thin line in the comics—or in any other art form, for that matter—between that which is *funny* and that which is merely *silly*. As the artist moves through various forms and devices of humor he approaches closer and closer to that line, and when he reaches farce the line is like the proverbial razor's edge.

To mix colorful superheroic adventure with humor is one of the toughest tests ever essayed by the comics—it was so tough a challenge that it wasn't really attempted very often, and when it was, the result was seldom a great success. Twice the trick was pulled off to near-perfection: by Otto Binder and C. C. Beck with the original Captain Marvel ... and by Jack Cole with Plastic Man. Little kids could read Plas's exploits as straight-out adventure yarns, older and more sophisticated audiences could see them as masterpieces of humor ranging from satire to slapstick.

Plas is gone now, as is his creator Jack Cole. The feature, which disappeared almost two decades ago when Everett Arnold's Quality Comics Group left the field, is little more than a fond memory; a short-lived attempt to revive Plas in the 1960s was a dismal failure. But Don Thompson has both a vivid memory and an extensive research file of classic comic books from the 1930s onward, and in "The Rehabilitation of Eel O'Brian" he takes us into the wacky universe of Jack Cole and his crazy india rubber creation.

Don Thompson himself is an editor of the *Cleveland Press* and occasional science-fiction writer, co-editor of *The Comic-Book Book* and the earlier *All in Color for a Dime*, husband of Maggie Thompson ("Blue Suit, Blue Mask, etc." in this volume), and son-in-law of science-fiction writer Betsy Curtis. He also has the oddest mannerism: when he wants to pick something up he just s-t-r-e-t-c-h-e-s out his arm and ...

CHAPTER 1

THE REHABILITATION OF EEL O'BRIAN

by DON THOMPSON

THE people who write and draw comic books seem to have a great deal of faith in the maxim that power tends to corrupt. Hardly anybody in comics is improved in character by being granted increased power. The best that can be hoped for is maintenance of a status quo.

Billy Batson was totally good before he became Captain Marvel; as Captain Marvel he was no better, just stronger.

Some characters became less good with the addition of super-powers. The Hulk, for instance, who has been stomping around in the pages of *Marvel Comics* since the early sixties, was once a quiet, respectable scientist. Now he is a not-so-jolly green giant who beats up anyone and anything that he thinks might interfere with him.

And if the person getting superpowers was a petty crook to begin with, well, sir, those superpowers just made him into a major crook, a supercrook. Shoot the jaw off a nasty German soldier and replace it with a powerfully hinged steel trap and he doesn't reform—far from it. He becomes a super-Nazi who goes around biting people's arms off and, as Iron Jaw, making life dangerous for Crimebuster in dozens of issues of *Boy Comics*, even reappearing years after being declared dead. Permanently graft artificial

19

tentacles on Dr. Otto Octavius in an atomic accident and he stops being meek and mild and becomes the terrible-tempered Dr. Octopus, who goes out and beats up Spider-Man.

Even the good guys have their lapses when feedback from their superpowers renders them temporarily insane or when they misuse their powers because they are in a hurry—as when Green Lantern used his power ring to control the minds of some suspects and forced them to go into the police station and confess all and never mind their Constitutional rights.

However, there was one petty criminal who suddenly acquired superpowers and did not use them for evil at all, but immediately became a force for good in the community, going so far as to join the FBI and even to help arrest his criminal self. What's more, he took on a petty thief and pickpocket as his partner and reformed him too.

The petty crook in question was Eel O'Brian, also known simply as the Eel. While helping three other crooks rob the Crawford Chemical Works one night in 1941 (in *Police Comics* No. 1, August, 1941, to be precise), he was shot by a guard and fell against a huge vat of some unspecified acid, which spilled all over his black-and-red pinstripe suit.

His friends took this calamity with equanimity ("He got The Eel!" "So what? C'mon!") and deserted him ("Adios, Eel!").

This made Eel pretty mad but he had other problems, such as eluding the police, to occupy his immediate attention. He fled through swamps and up a mountainside, where he collapsed and lay unconscious under the full moon. He awoke in that factory for comic-book superheroes, a monastery. A monk turned the police away and cared for Eel. Eel asked why and was told, "Because something told me that here is a man who could become a valuable citizen if he only had the chance."

Eel told his story to the friendly monk, how his folks had died when he was ten, leaving him alone in a world where he tried to work hard but people kept pushing him around, how he finally grew tired of it and started pushing them back. He credited the monk with restoring his faith in mankind.

After the monk left, Eel stretched his arms—a good five feet each. His face was rubbery and he could stretch himself completely out of shape. He immediately deduced it was caused by the acid getting into his bloodstream through the bullet wound.

To his eternal credit, it must be recorded that onetime petty

Plastic Man was seldom at rest; he was always distorting his body, usually into a ridiculous shape. This cover is typical, including the blurb with the minor pun. The profusely perspiring fat fellow in the polka-dot shirt is Woozy Winks, sidekick and comic foil. Copyright © 1948, Comic Magazines, and reprinted by its permission.

crook and robber Eel O'Brian's first thought on learning of his newfound powers was: "What a powerful weapon this would be AGAINST crime! I've been FOR it long enough! Here's my chance to atone for all the evil I've done!"

There was perhaps a touch of personal malice in his first job as a crimefighter: he went after "the rats who deserted me on that Crawford job."

First, from an unspecified source, he obtained a costume made of rubber. (More than 20 years later, in the sixties, Julius Schwartz, editor of *Flash Comics*, conceived a criminal tailor named Paul Gambi who earned his living supplying costumes to superpowered criminals; it is possible that Gambi has an honest counterpart who supplies costumes in confidence to those crime-fighters whose superpowers do not include skill with needle and thread—or, in the case of Eel O'Brian, with a vulcanizing kit.)

Eel joined his former buddies on a caper, stayed outside as lookout and driver, then put on the red-black-and-yellow costume, altered his face, and went after them. He stretched his arms down an elevator shaft at them to terrify them, lay flat on the floor disguised as a rug and rolled up on them, was pushed off a 20-story building and bounced back unharmed, dressed as Eel and drove them off while his left arm stretched out the window and around the car and snatched the crooks out and thrust them through a police station window, then he drove off grinning over how much fun it was to fight for the law.

It was one of the crooks he caught who named him: "He was a man of rubber! . . . a PLASTIC MAN!!"

Plastic Man he was. His career stretched (sorry!) from that first issue of *Police Comics* through issue No. 102 and also included 64 issues of his own comic book and a revival in the late sixties.

He was the creation of Jack Cole, an enormously talented cartoonist whose imagination knew no bounds. Plastic Man turned himself into snakes, furniture, and bizarre animals. He covered great distances quickly by using his arms as wheels or his legs as stilts or springs. He rarely used the same gimmick twice. No matter what he turned into, however, he retained his striking red body shirt with long sleeves, a shoelaced plunging neckline, and a black-and-yellow-striped belt with a yellow, diamond-shaped buckle. He also wore white goggles with black lenses, presumably as a mask, though he dropped the Eel O'Brian identity entirely after a couple of years and was always Plastic

Man, always "on."

When he turned into a rug, it was a red rug with a yellow-and-black stripe. When he turned into a dragon, it was a red dragon with a yellow-and-black stripe. Usually the criminals he approached never noticed this odd coloration and were taken in by his disguise. Once, however, some unusually wary criminals were on the watch for him, and when a red pig with a black-and-yellow stripe around his middle came to the door, they all pointed their guns at it. Unfortunately for them, the pig was a real one which Plastic Man had painted and sent in as a decoy. While they were all watching it, he came up from behind and clobbered them.

For the first couple of years, he operated as an unpaid undercover agent. As Eel O'Brian, a known and wanted petty crook, he joined various gangs and learned their plans. As Plastic Man, he caught them and turned them over to the police. Eventually, he was accepted by the police—why not?—and worked more closely with them. As Plastic Man. As Eel, he was still a wanted criminal; not very badly wanted because he was a petty criminal, but wanted, nevertheless.

Plas ran in *Police Comics* (as the cover-featured character and in the lead spot after the first couple of issues) from 1941 through October, 1950. His own book ran from Spring, 1943, through November, 1956. His publisher was Quality Comics, but the first two issues of his own book were published by Vital Publications Inc. Neither of those first two issues was numbered. The first cover showed him battling four crooks from inside a huge gray skull. The second, much truer to what was to become the spirit of the strip, showed him in a Gay Nineties pose and costume with his buddy, Woozy Winks. He is sedately seated, but his left arm extends clear around Woozy's plump body and his hand is resting on Woozy's left ear as a photographer's clamp.

This difference between issue No. 1 and issue No. 2 is indicative of the change that quickly overcame Plastic Man. Let's face it, friends, it is hard to maintain any dignity while you are contorting your entire body into fantastic and ridiculous shapes. A cartoonist with a sense of humor—and Jack Cole was certainly that—would have put such a character in a funny strip.

And that's exactly what Cole did. He turned "Plastic Man" into a funny strip. Slapstick humor, broad and fast-moving. Plas would walk along the street with his elongated legs startling drunks, absentmindedly stretching an arm back to drag the ogling Woozy away from a startlingly pretty girl or to slap his wrist as he backslid into picking pockets.

For Woozy was a crook, too. He first appeared in *Police Comics* No. 13, November, 1942, as "The Man Who Can't be Harmed." He wore bright green slacks, a pale green shirt with black polka dots, a straw hat, and brown shoes. He wore that outfit throughout his entire career, which included a series of *Woozy Winks* solo stories in *Plastic Man*. He was fat and jowly, with a nose like a casaba melon. He saved the life of Zambi the soothsayer because he happened to be boating near where Zambi was drowning and had only to reach out a hand to rescue him. In gratitude, Zambi bestowed upon him the protection of Nature, which assured absolute invulnerability to harm. When Woozy embarked upon a life of crime, Plastic Man tried to stop him and was nearly killed by lightning and hailstones—he had to take shelter in a culvert ditch. As Eel O'Brian, he approached Woozy with the idea of becoming partners but had to commit a series of robberies to win Woozy's confidence and be allowed to join him. (Said the police captain after this two-week confidence-gaining crime spree, "And where were *you* when Eel O'Brian was tearing the city apart, *Mister Plastic Man?*")

Plastic Man reformed Woozy by asking him what his mother would say if she knew of his crime career and persuaded him to turn himself in. But the police no longer cared about Woozy—in fact, they let him go to help Plastic Man nail the crook they really wanted—Eel O'Brian, who had just committed more crimes in a fortnight than Woozy had ever perpetrated.

In the next issue, Plas and Woozy set out to capture Eel and, with Plas setting up a meeting, Woozy arrested him. Eel was put in jail and promptly escaped by stretching through the bars. After that, everybody pretty much gave up on catching him.

Much later, when Plastic Man had been working with the FBI for some years, his chief revealed that Plas had been identified through his fingerprints as Eel O'Brian, but that the FBI was willing to overlook this, since Plastic Man was obviously completely reformed and an invaluable crimefighter.

Eel, now pardoned, was never heard from again. His rehabilitation completed, he vanished and only Plastic Man remained.

Jack Cole worked on Plastic Man through 1950, although a number of other artists also drew him during that period. The main artist after Cole left was Russ Heath, still active in the sixties

PLASTIC MAN

Plastic Man's creator, Jack Cole, was unable to take his character seriously, which was the strip's greatest charm. Try to imagine your typical straightlaced comic-book character (Superman or Batman, for instance) appearing in such a disgraceful condition and being used as girdle, garters and suspenders. This sort of thing always happened to Plastic Man. Copyright © 1971, National Periodical Publications, Inc., and reprinted by its permission.

and seventies primarily as a war-comics artist for DC. Heath also did a *Plastic Sam* lampoon in the comic-book *Mad*.

Cole later appeared as a gag cartoonist in *Playboy*, doing remarkably fine watercolor cartoons and a series of 52 "Females" cartoons that have been collected in book form and reprinted on cocktail napkins and highball glasses by the bunny empire. His cartoons still are frequently featured in Playboy Press cartoon collections. Reportedly, *Playboy*-publisher Hugh Hefner is a devoted Cole fan and has a collection of Cole's comic-book work, particularly *Plastic Man*.

In 1958, at the peak of his popular acceptance and his success as a *Playboy* cartoonist, Jack Cole died, apparently by suicide. Besides his cartoons, which had appeared in every issue of *Playboy* from the fifth issue in 1954 until the supply was used up after his death, Cole was doing a comic strip called *Betsy and Me*, which was syndicated in 46 papers. He was 43 at the time of his death.

In addition to *Plastic Man*, his comic-book work included drawing some of the early adventures of Daredevil in *Silver Streak Comics*. Daredevil first appeared as one in a string of heroic antagonists of the Claw, a giant-fanged Oriental who was that rarity, a villain with his own strip. Though a man might battle the Claw for several issues, he eventually perished and another took his place. Daredevil not only survived his battles with the Claw, he got his own book and the Claw became a supporting feature in it. By that time, though, Cole was no longer involved with the strip.

Plastic Man was Cole's major achievement, but Plas was not the only memorable character in *Police Comics*. The other great strip in *Police* was Will Eisner's *The Spirit*, which featured the supposedly dead criminologist Denny Colt in a blue suit, hat, mask, and gloves battling crime with no superpowers except an incredible ability to recover from beatings that would have made hash of ordinary men. More on *The Spirit* elsewhere in this book.

Before Plastic Man took over the cover of *Police*, the cover and lead spot were held by *Firebrand*, a strip drawn by the extremely talented Reed Crandall, later to become one of the artists associated with EC comics in the fifties. Firebrand, in reality Rod Reilly, millionaire idol of glamour girls, wore red ballet tights, a red cowl and mask with a flowing scarf in back, and a shirt apparently made of Saran Wrap. The shirt was almost completely transparent, showing off his manly muscles to best advantage.

Looked at dispassionately it was a silly costume, but it was effective. He lasted only the first 13 issues of *Police* and not all of his adventures were drawn by Crandall: S. M. Iger and Alex Blum did a couple of stories toward the end.

The oddest character in those early *Police* issues was the hero of George E. Brenner's *No. 711*—he was a convict in Westwood Prison who slipped out at night to battle crime. His real name was Dan Dyce but when he fought crime in purple—tights, boots, hat, and cape—he called himself No. 711. This was his prison serial number and he also wore it on the chest of his crimefighting togs. He became one of those comic-book heroes who got killed. He appeared in the first 15 issues, dying in No. 15 and being avenged by Destiny (who, though a crimefighter, was not a costumed hero) in No. 16.

Chic Carter, police reporter, was in the first 18 issues of *Police*, sometimes as the Sword, drawn in a humorous cartoon style by Vernon Henkel but apparently meant seriously.

As you may gather, there was a pretty general change of lineup in *Police* after about three years. Other casualties included Arthur Peddy's *Phantom Lady*, some miscellaneous noncostumed characters such as pilot Eagle Evans, and Steele Kerrigan, a crimefighter in mufti, by Al Bryant.

Also perishing was Fred Guardineer's *The Mouthpiece*, District Attorney Bill Perkins wearing a blue suit and a mask. Quality Comics had an affinity for crimefighters who wore blue suits and masks. The most famous was the Spirit, who appeared in most issues of *Police* from No. 11 through No. 102, but there also was the Mouthpiece (first 13 issues of *Police*) and Midnight, who wore a blue suit and mask in *Smash Comics* from issue No. 18 to No. 85. Only Eisner's Spirit had any, well, spirit.

The longest-lived character from the first issue of *Police*, next to Plastic Man, was Roy Lincoln, who operated as the Human Bomb. He wore his white deep-sea diving suit in every one of the first 58 issues. You see, Roy had swallowed a capsule of 27-QRX, a deadly new explosive, to keep it from getting into the hands of Axis agents. This made him a human bomb whose barehanded touch meant release of a powerful explosion. He wore the diving suit to protect himself from the blast; out of costume, he wore gloves. He later got a partner named Hustace Throckmorton—allegedly as comic relief—who had the same power, but in his feet. It was supposed to be funny to see him take off his shoes and kick his way through walls.

There also was *Flatfoot Burns*, a supposedly funny strip about a big-nosed private detective. It ran in an awful lot of issues for a lot of years. Too many issues and too many years.

Manhunter, one of those strips about a policeman who does the bulk of his crimefighting masked and in costume—saving himself a lot of that red tape about search warrants and Constitutional rights—appeared in almost every issue of *Police* from No. 8 to No. 101, from 1942 to 1950. There have been a few "Manhunters" in comics, a couple of them in costume. This is the one who wore blue tights and a blue mask; he also had a savage dog named Thor. He usually stumbled across crimes as Patrolman Dan Richards but fought it as Manhunter.

Except for *The Spirit*, which was begun in 1940 as a weekly comic-book supplement in Sunday newspapers and reprinted in *Police Comics*, the book's only real strip of merit was *Plastic Man*.

Plastic Man fought villains as bizarre as he was, if not more so. He fought gangsters with names like Snout Sniggers; nutty doctors called Dr. Doser and Dr. Slicer; Needles Noggle, who used needles as weapons; Mime the master of makeup; Dr. Ameeba, who could become twins; Stretcho the India Rubber Man, who could stretch *almost* as much as Plas; and a host of others.

Cole included himself in the *Plastic Man* story in *Police* No. 20 (July, 1943). Woozy needed someone to draw a picture of the villains from his description and went to see Cole, who drew himself as blond, chinless, big-eyed, potbellied, and slopeshouldered. Much of that was exaggeration for humorous effect, of course. He also showed himself stuttering badly, apparently a real affliction of his. In all, Cole made considerable fun of himself. When the villains, Abba and Dabba, overwhelmed Woozy and tied him up, Cole took notes, asking them to slow down the fight ("R-r-remember, I s-st-stutter when I w-wr-write!"). When Woozy is tied up, the villains turn to Cole and this dialog—which quickly becomes a monolog—ensued:

> *Abba*: And who might YOU be?
> *Cole*: I muh-might be Ga-Ga-Greta Ga-Ga-Garbo, but I am Jack Cole . . . Heh, heh.
> *Dabba*: So what?
> *Cole*: So *I* was b-bu-born in N-N-New Castle, P-Pa., on D-D-D-December 14, 1914. *I'M* twenty-eight . . . M-m-my wife s-says *I'M* the

buh-best c-c-c-c-ca-cart-t-toonist afoot! P-p-p-publishers *B-BEG* for *MY* s-services! *I* write *MY* own stories, t-too! *I'M* super! ... *I'M* s-swell! I'M, I'M, I'M, I'M etc. etc ...

Abba and Dabba, who were holding their ears by this time, tied—and gagged—Cole. Woozy wryly remarked, "For once I agree with Abba and Dabba!"

When Woozy and Cole were to be killed, trapped where no one could find them, Cole was "rescued" by his publisher, who dragged him off and forced him back to his drawing board. The whole story turned out to have been a dream.

Basically, the data Cole provided about himself seems to be accurate. That he was born in New Castle gave rise to tiresome jokes about carrying Cole to New Castle, which may have been a factor in his moving to Illinois to be near *Playboy* shortly before his death. The birthdate is also correct. I do not know about the ego.

He made another sort-of appearance in *Police* No. 77, (April, 1948) as a statue brought to life. The statue depicts the god of mischief, Eloc. There is no resemblance to the earlier self-caricature; only the backward spelling of his name, which apparently was just a sneaky way of signing the story.

Plastic Man's degree of invulnerability kind of varied. Sometimes he would stretch and twist his way out of the path of bullets; sometimes it was stated flatly that the bullets could kill him. Other times the bullets just stretched his body and snapped back—on at least one occasion a bullet rebounded from Plastic Man's elongated body and killed the would-be assassin. Sometimes he was adversely affected by high temperatures, which brought him dangerously close to melting. But, basically, the worst the crooks were able to do to him was to inconvenience him, delay him long enough for them to escape temporarily. He always (forgive me) bounced back.

Woozy was one of the best hero's flunkies in the comic-book business and he got the publicity he deserved. He was on the cover of virtually every issue of every comic in which he and Plas starred. (Before he came along, Plas frequently shared cover scenes with the Spirit, but unfortunately they never met in a story—what a team-up that would have been!) Woozy frequently was mentioned on the cover as well ("Plastic Man brings you thrills—Woozy, the laughs!") and, as noted, he had his own series. The *Woozy* stories generally ran six or eight pages while Plastic

Man had two or three stories of ten or more pages each. *Woozy* was often not drawn by Cole but by one of a number of lesser artists. The stories usually involved Woozy in a quest for a large sum of money, for a chance to catch some big crook and make Plastic Man respect him (Plastic Man usually didn't appear in the *Woozy* solo stories but was often referred to) or to win some fantastically pretty girl. The only thing he ever succeeded in doing was catching crooks—well, one out of three isn't bad.

Plas chased some pretty strange crooks. There was Phony Fink, who counterfeited counterfeit stamps and was caught because he ran Plas through his printing press and printed evidence on Plas's chest.

My own favorite villain was Clarence Skidd, the King of Zing. Clarence had invented the slipperiest oil on earth—one squirt and you were unable to stand up or hold on to your valuables. He was not formidable in appearance (he was about two feet tall, wore a tuxedo, top hat, and spats) but not even Plastic Man could harm him. Skidd squirted oil on the floor and neither Plastic Man nor Woozy could stand up—with his usual swift thinking Plas had Woozy take off his shoes so he could chase Skidd in his stockinged feet while Plas, who never wore shoes (he never had any toes, either; oh, well, the Spirit never wore socks—there was something odd about many of Quality's heroes), bent his legs forward in the middle and ran on the backs of his knees. Plas finally got his hands on Skidd by guessing the secret of the "friction powder" that Skidd used to keep himself from falling and to enable him to pick up the valuables he had oiled. The secret was a newfangled washing product—the story was published in 1947—called detergent, a chemical that cuts grease.

In one story, Plastic Man battled a creature from outer space, Amorpho, a shapeless blob who assumed other shapes—a squirrel, a dog, a shovel, Woozy—to steal salt. Eventually, he turned himself into Plastic Man and Plas promptly and literally tied him into a knot, then sent him off in his spaceship again. For some reason, virtually all comic-book superheroes sooner or later find themselves fighting someone who has copied their powers and appearance—Plastic Man took this with far more aplomb than the customary superhero did and does: when he answered a policeman's whistle for help and was told that he, Plas, had just stolen a few crates of "imported salt" (!) from the Exotic Foods Importing Company, Plas responded: "I did, eh? Don't worry,

officer! In that case, I'll bring myself to justice!" Then he went off and whipped up on Amorpho.

Despite a certain amount of violence (usually so farfetched that you couldn't think of it as violence) and a number of relatively sexy females, Plastic Man was a clean and wholesome comic strip. By my standards, at least. But the Comics Code Authority, those self-appointed and industry-paid censors of the comics, found a lot of things to change. In *Plastic Man* No. 24 (July, 1950—before the Code) appeared a story—not by Cole—about twins with bottomless gullets who caused a famine by gulping down enormous quantities of food before Plastic Man (disguised as a red roast turkey with a yellow-and-black stripe) caught them. The story was pretty funny, mostly for the drawings of the two skinny gluttons stuffing whole suckling pigs and entire stalks of bananas into their mouths, and harmless. But the Comics Code Authority struck when the story was reprinted in *Plastic Man* No. 63 (July, 1956—after the Code). Besides taking out pictures of starving people biting Plas, the Code removed "FBI" from the nameplate on the desk of Plas's boss, "FBI Chief Branner"—did the Code think the FBI was dangerous to small children?—and had one of the gluttons eat a candy bar whole instead of a can of peas (but they didn't change the text which said he ate a can of peas, can and all). It seems to me that, if they feared the innocent kiddies would imitate the baddies, there would be more danger of kids eating entire candy bars in one gulp than of their eating peas, can and all, but what do I know of the minds of censors? There were other changes. Original: man breaks into pet store and eats goldfish; censored version: he eats fishfood. Original: man is stuffing loaf of French bread into his mouth; censored version: bread is gone and man is pointing with the hand he had been using to hold the bread. Original: X-ray shows human skeletons with huge quantities of packaged foods in the stomach areas; censored version; the X-ray is held so you can't see it. Other reprinted stories had similar alterations—in one, Mr. Aqua, a villain who turned into water, was spilled by Woozy; in the original, Woozy *drank* Mr. Aqua.

Plastic Man could survive bullets and beatings and meltings but he couldn't survive the nit-pickers. He quit after one more issue. He ran another six years in *Police Comics* before that title was entirely turned over to uncostumed crimefighters such as Treasury agents who tracked down Hitler in Egypt. Then he faded into

31

limbo for ten years (except for an issue or so of a reprint published by Super Comics, a short-lived New York publisher which reprinted comics from a number of different comics publishing firms).

Then, in 1966, Plastic Man returned. Sort of.

When the Quality line went out of business, most of the characters it had published were bought by Superman–National Periodicals–DC. The Spirit, Lady Luck, and Mr. Mystic belonged and belong to Will Eisner; these were the three that appeared in the *Spirit* Sunday comic supplements. DC published more than 100 issues of *Blackhawk* but did nothing with most of the other Quality heroes.

In *House of Mystery*, which was born as a supernatural story book and was to become one again, there briefly ran a superhero strip called *Dial H for Hero*. This was about a boy named Robby Reed, who had a magic dial like a telephone dial and a tiresome habit of saying "Sockamagee!" all the time. *All* the time. When he dialed the letters *H-E-R-O* on his magic *H* dial he would become a superhero, until he dialed *O-R-E-H* and became Robby Reed again. Most of the time, he turned into total losers like Giantboy and King Kandy—you should have seen King Kandy; he wore a peppermint-striped suit and a hat full of lollipops and he used a licorice lariat and, well, you just would have had to see him, that's all.

But in *House of Mystery* No. 160 (July, 1966) he also turned into Plastic Man, "that famous crime-fighting hero of years ago." This Plastic Man, drawn by Jim Mooney, was not too imaginative. He slingshot himself after the villains, slapped them with giant hands, bounced after one hood in the shape of a ball, and stretched out of the reach of a cloud of gas. Nothing like what Jack Cole had done with him, but Cole was then eight years dead. That considered, the new Plas wasn't bad—and he was light-years ahead of King Kandy or any of the other flop-oriented "heroes" Robby Reed dialed up.

This was a test, as it turned out. That same year, DC issued *Plastic Man* No. 1 (November–December, 1966). The new Plastic Man was written by Arnold Drake, edited by Murray Boltinoff, and illustrated by Winslow Mortimer. (The first issue, which was mildly promising, was drawn by Gil Kane; the promise left when he did.) This series was not funny, it was silly; childish, even. In a sloppily researched origin story—our original Plastic Man was

32

referred to as "Eels O'Brien," for heaven's sake—this travesty was revealed as the son of the original and the original was presented as an old man who, with Woozy, operated an old folks' home. Considering that he was young and active a mere decade before (to say nothing of being childless and unmarried), one heck of a lot must have happened between 1956 and 1966.

Some editor at DC stated in answer to a letter-writer in 1972 that the revival of Plastic Man—which ran a mere ten issues—was a conceptual mistake. Except for some team-ups of that travesty with Batman in *The Brave and the Bold* (in the second team-up, which an indignant Jack Cole fan sent to me with a "Would you look at this garbage!" letter of outrage, he was said to be the original Eel O'Brian Plastic Man but he sure didn't act like him), DC has since presented Plastic Man only in reprints of the Jack Cole stories. In 1971, an entire issue (the last issue) of *DC Special* (48 pages for a quarter and a real bargain) was devoted to Plastic Man. Included were the origins of Plastic Man and of Woozy Winks, plus three other stories. Reprints also appeared in DC's series of 100-page comics for half a buck (actually, it had 96 pages, but it has long been the custom to count the covers as four pages and who am I to argue with tradition?) and in two issues (No. 149 and No. 150) of a comic book devoted to *Superman's Pal Jimmy Olsen*.

While Plastic Man was in limbo, several imitators appeared. DC, overlooking the original, which it owned, turned Jimmy Olsen (Superman's pal) into Elastic Lad in several stories. He wore a ghastly pair of purple longjohns and drank some potion that temporarily gave him elastic powers. The stories were devoid of humor or imagination, but there were several of them.

DC has another imitation, *The Elongated Man*, which tries to be humorous but doesn't make it. Ralph Dibny drank so much of a soft drink called Gingold that an ingredient in it made him elastic. He first appeared in a *Flash* story in the sixties and has since had a series in *Detective Comics* and membership in the Justice League of America, DC's club of superheroes. He still wore a costume, though his identity was no secret; he also was one of the growing number of married superheroes. His stories were more whimsy than humor. Whenever he encountered some mystery his nose twitched, actually waved from side to side. Someone apparently found this funny but it is certainly not funny enough to warrant doing it in every story, though he did it in every story just the same. There also was a distressing tendency to refer to him as the "Ductile Detective" and the "Stretchable Sleuth" and a little of that goes a heck of a long way. He appeared in very short stories of his own and as a guest in other characters' longer stories. He was born a minor-leaguer and a minor-leaguer he remained, despite some not-bad outings.

Marvel Comics, DC's biggest rival in the sixties and seventies, created its own Plastic Man imitation in 1961 with the first issue of *The Fantastic Four*. The Four were intrepid types who rode up in a rocket and were exposed to cosmic radiation which transformed them into super-types. Johnny Storm became the Human Torch, who could burst into flame and blaze unharmed; his sister Sue became the Invisible Girl; Ben Grimm became the superstrong but monstrously ugly Thing—and Reed Richards became Mister Fantastic.

Mister Fantastic could stretch like Plastic Man but the resemblance ended there. Reed Richards was a sobersided scientist who could whip up a weapon to wipe out an intergalactic menace if you gave him five minutes in his workshop. He lectured and he talked and talked and talked. He was, in short, a crashing bore.

He reserved his stretching for reaching out and catching people, for shielding the bodies of others with his own, for serious and talk-filled battles with evil forces. He never would turn into a red whale with a black-and-yellow stripe or do any of the undignified things Plastic Man did as a matter of course. Apparently neither Jack Kirby, who drew the first 100-plus issues of *Fantastic Four*, or Stan Lee, who wrote them, could see how ridiculous the idea of a man stretching himself to fantastic limits could be. Often as not, when Reed stretched himself he got hurt—like he would stretch out and grab the Human Torch, burning his silly self in the process. *Fantastic Four* had humor (and many, many other merits) but the humor came mostly from the Thing and the Human Torch, most assuredly not from Mister Fantastic or from the equally depressing Invisible Girl, who eventually married him.

None of these imitations is up to the original, but without Cole they hardly could be. The best hope for the future of *Plastic Man* lies in reprints. DC has reprinted *Superman, Wonder Woman*, and *Batman* in hardcover book form. They likely will have a *Captain Marvel* hardcover, since DC acquired all rights to the fabled Big Red Cheese in 1972 and revived him in *Shazam Comics*. Possibly sales of that *Plastic Man* issue of *DC Special* or reader requests or just plain good fortune will result in a hardcover collection of *Plastic Man*.

Or, while we are hoping for miracles, maybe DC will find someone good enough to follow Jack Cole and revive *Plastic Man*. It could happen. If a crook like Eel O'Brian can become one of the FBI's best agents, anything is possible.

INTRODUCTION TO

MICKEY MOUSE AND
THE PHANTOM ARTIST

IN this latter-day of Disneyland in California and Disney World in Florida, *The Wonderful World of Disney* on the tube, and the very name Walt Disney associated with a sweetness and gentility and purity that some of us find a bit too much to take, it's hard to think of a Disney creation as a tough, feisty, brawling daredevil. Least of all Disney's Mickey Mouse, whose very name has come to symbolize a set of values rejected by many folks.

But things were not always thus with the Mouse, and it is not the Mouse of this latter day that concerns us in *The Comic-Book Book*. It is the Mouse of another era; one might say, almost another Mouse. In the words of the poet Joseph Sanders, this rodent was "Not Mickey Mouse, cute TV star / Not Mickey Mouse, suburban slob / But the Mickey Mouse of 'Mickey Fights the Phantom Blot' ... " Indeed, this is the Mouse who concerns us—and Bill Blackbeard.

Bill Blackbeard brought a lifetime of interest in the comic strip to fruition with the founding, in 1967, of the San Francisco Academy of Comic Art. By 1971 that institution had evolved into the National Newspaper Archive and Academy of Comic Art—a wonderland hidden inside an unprepossessing old building. Within the Academy are shelves, stacks, and cabinets filled with one of the outstanding collections of comic art in the world—including huge volumes, bound files of major newspapers dating back to the turn of the century and earlier. All of this material is used in research that will lead, ultimately, to a massive, definitive history of the comic strip, by Bill Blackbeard.

But that project will require several more years—if not decades—of effort. In the meanwhile there emerge from the Academy such tantalizing bits of work-in-progress as "The First (Arf, Arf!) Superhero of Them All" in *All in Color for a Dime*—and "Mickey Mouse and the Phantom Artist" in *The Comic-Book Book*.

CHAPTER 2

MICKEY MOUSE AND THE PHANTOM ARTIST

by BILL BLACKBEARD

FLAT against the cold, mossy stones above the green-jawed depths of the crocodile pit, arms outstretched to either side of his wall-clinging body, edging cautiously along a narrow ledge away from the trapdoor entrance, the little guy calculated his chances of making it to the distant end of the ledge before one of the lunging saurians just below his inching feet snapped its hungry jaws about an ankle and jerked him down into the black, threshing waters.

It was 1933, and a hundred-thousand readers of the daily funnies had turned to the comic page to find out what would happen next in the crocodile-pit episode of one of the great daily adventure strips of the thirties. Nothing in *Tailspin Tommy*, *Dick Tracy*, *Bobby Thatcher*, *Wash Tubbs*, *Little Orphan Annie*, *Tarzan*, or *Buck Rogers* was quite as gripping that week. In fact, few of the still-new adventure strips (it was only nine years since the first highly tentative serious action strips had appeared) was able to equal—let alone surpass—the comic narrative about the nervy guy now in the crocodile pit for day-to-day suspense and fascination.

Yet few comic-page readers over 18 in the year of 1933 were aware of this. The older people of the time were not paying any attention at all to the sweating hero on the ledge. The same adult-strip addicts who would thumb through their freshly opened daily paper to find out if Junior Steele's father had been done in by Steve the Tramp in *Dick Tracy*, or whether the bleakly aged Captain Folly had thwarted his hook-handed mate's attempt to drown him in *Wash Tubbs*, dropped unseeing eyes past the equally grim hazards of the youth spread-eagled above the crocodiles.

After all, how much serious attention could a grown human being give to the impossible perils of a *mouse*?

For it was the Mickey Mouse of the 1930s newspaper strip who had lowered himself to the perilous ledge attempting to find the trapdoor through which the mad scientists of Blaggard Mansion, Professors Ecks, Doublex, and Triplex, had dropped their victims to the crocs. It was a death-defying, tough, steel-gutted Mickey Mouse, quite unlike the mild, blandly benign Mouse of contemporary Disney Studio usage, who held the kids of 1933 rapt with his adventures on pirate dirigibles, cannibal islands and bullet-tattered fighter planes—just as he would have held adult adventure-strip readers if it were not for their stereotyped reaction to an animal hero.

In the adults' remembered experience (in 1933, pretty much as now), animal narratives were for kids. Most had never even heard of, let alone read, such thoroughly mature works of fiction or poetry as Algernon Blackwood's *Dudley and Gilderoy*, or Don Marquis's *archy and mehitabel*. In strips, they were then familiar with the popular but juvenile *Felix the Cat* of Pat Sullivan from the 1920s, the equally child-slanted Harrison Cady *Peter Rabbit* and Lang Campbell *Uncle Wiggily* of the same decade, and—if their memories cast back far enough—Jimmy Swinnerton's kid-focused *Boner's Ark* prototype of the 1910s, *In The Good Old Days*, and C. M. Payne's pre-*Pogo* swampland fantasy, *The Possum Gang* of the same period. There had simply not been many humanized animal strips before the mid-1930s, and virtually all of these—with the marked exception of Sidney Smith's *sui generis* innovation, *Old Doc Yak* of 1912–19—were aimed primarily at children. (The only "animal" strip that appealed solely to a mature viewpoint, regardless of age, was George Herriman's *Krazy Kat* of 1909–44, but since this brick ballet was over the heads of most readers, it received the same blank eye from the general public as the juvenile strips.)

The Mickey Mouse image on a theatrical poster of the 1930s was something else, however. Like that of Felix the Cat ten years earlier, the cinematic symbol of the mouse was a beacon to adults. It drew them by the millions into movie theaters everywhere, kids in tow. Yet not even the vast enjoyment these people derived from the Mouse's animated antics led many of them to give much time to his escapades in newsprint. An animated slapstick romp for five minutes was one thing. Even an animal gag strip built around a film character like Felix might be worth a glance, if the daily point could be picked up without concentration. But a *serious*, cliff-hanging, continued daily strip devoted to a funny animal? Where was the relevance, the empathy? How, they wanted to know, can you *care* if a mouse gets bopped on the head or shot?

But for the kids of the time (as well as for a few perceptive adults, of course), there was plenty of relevance and empathy in the daily *Mickey Mouse* strip. The imaginative maturity of the art and the story-line, the sound, sustained characterization of the *dramatis animalis*, the unfailing wit and narrative point of the dialogue, above all the episode-to-episode excitement and comedy of the graphic continuity, riveted the reader of those days to the fast but superbly paced adventures of the strip's stunningly portrayed cast.

The refusal of so many adult-strip readers to see what was right under their noses, thanks to their blinkered preconceptions about subject matter, was not at all unusual. Many well-read individuals of education and intelligence, after all, have consistently ignored a number of prose works of high wit and imagination because they had the look, subject matter, and imprimatur of "children's books." The Frank Baum *Oz* novels, the *Finn Family Moomintroll* series, the *Jerry Todd and Sekatary Hawkins* opera, and such fine individual works of fantasy and adventure as E. Nesbit's *Enchanted Castle*, William Bowen's *Old Tobacco Shop*, and Karle Wilson Baker's *Garden of the Plynck* have long gone ignored by adults quite capable of enjoying them, because of their assumption that books focusing on children and fanciful creatures could not possess the same poetry, characterization, and narrative force as the finest "adult" fiction. It is not a very far step from such a self-frustrating attitude to that of the comic-strip reader serenely certain that a strip about a mouse fighting, say, mutineers at sea could not possibly be as gripping as one about a human being doing the same thing.

Above Mickey's speeding monoplane, an immense and menacing

cloud moved to blot out the sky and sun from his sight—and moved *against* the strongly blowing tail wind which buoyed his thundering craft forward. He remembered now what the crazed pilot had told him and Captain Doberman back at the airport, and gulped. Perhaps what the terrified flyer had tried to tell them *was* true, after all. If so, in a minute there would be ... *and there it was!* Dropping hideously down from the massed cloud into his flight path perhaps half a mile ahead was the thing he had already anticipated—*the monster spider the pilot had raved about!* Automatically, he tried to miss the bulbous, black-bodied horror—and realized with dismay that there would *be* no escape. For a ghastly web of glittering, thickly viscous cords had dropped from the cloud beyond the spider—a web a thousand feet across!

So it was that the daily *Mickey Mouse* became the only major comic-page adventure strip of first-rate art and imagination to run virtually the whole of its creative course unappreciated by any sizable number of the adult readers of the medium. Not even such a motley lot of formal chroniclers and historians as the field has had to date have indicated the least awareness of the status and character of the Mouse strip; most, in fact—from Martin Sheridan in his 1944 *Comics and Their Creators* to Gerard Blanchard with his *La bande dessinée* of 1973—pass blithely by the comic-strip Mickey to discuss the Mouse only as an animated cartoon figure, if at all. Occasionally, a text may acknowledge that the movie Mouse got on the comic page—but no more.

The blade of chain-reaction blindness was unfortunately double-edged. If hundreds of thousands of strip fans have gone to their graves since 1930 unknowingly the sadder for having missed the *Mickey Mouse* daily strip, the same adamant disinterest, reflected in the attitudes of newspaper feature editors across the country (abetted by the prevailing economic depression, of course), curtailed the distribution of the strip itself. In many large cities—San Francisco, New Orleans, Detroit, St. Louis, for instance—the daily *Mickey* never appeared at all; in several others—Los Angeles, Chicago, Oakland, New York, among them—the strip ran only in the local afternoon race-result dailies, or in the most blatantly sensational morning tabloids: the sort of papers bought and thrown away by city workers, but not widely read by home subscribers. As a result, millions of potentially interested kids never had a chance to read the strip regularly at all. For many of these kids, the only vestiges of the strip they ever saw were the sharply altered Big Little Book reprints of 1933 and later (all dialog balloons and many crucial panels were omitted), the short-lived David McKay episodic selections of the early 1930s (a single, fine Sunday-page collection was their only worthwhile publication), and the cut, often extensively altered and redrawn continuity republished in *Mickey Mouse Magazine* and *Walt Disney's Comics and Stories* between 1938 and the early 1940s—all without a single hint to the book and magazine readers that an independent daily-strip source existed.

Among strip buffs, then, those of us who remember reading the actual daily *Mickey Mouse* in the newspapers of the time probably comprise something of an exceedingly lucky elite. But *what* we remember!

There were the struggling, inchoate beginnings of the strip (imagine the sheer nerve involved in launching so shapeless a new comic feature on the nation's newspapers—even one based on a smash cinema hit—in January, 1930, amid the belt-tightening aftershocks of the 1929 Stock Market Crash): Mickey doing makeshift Mack Sennett things with cannibals on a desert island at the outset, antics almost as inept as the stuff in *Charlie Chaplin's Comic Capers* of the 1910s—yet becoming involved a bare month later with the first sinister machinations of his strip-long archenemies, Pegleg Pete and Sylvester Shyster (the latter an attorney, of course), and introducing us in the process to the earliest of the strip regulars, Horace Horsecollar, Clarabelle Cow, and Minnie Mouse (herself already seen briefly in the first week of the strip)—blundering in short order through his first full suspense adventure, half animated cartoon, half serious strip continuity, in a gangster-haunted old mansion—extending the range of his escapades, with Minnie at his side, to a rattling passenger train where he meets Pete and Shyster for the second time (with his first rendition of the flabbergasted dismay that was to become his classic response in their subsequent encounters)—attempting suicide when faced by the apparent success of his first rival for Minnie's tail-curling attention—desperately combing the rural countryside trying to recover money stolen from a bank in order to save Minnie's father's farm—all this and much more before the end of 1930, drawn and narrated with an increasingly evident verve and zest found at similarly full pitch in only one other daily adventure strip of the year: Roy Crane's brilliant seriocomic thriller, *Wash Tubbs*. (The dull, plodding story-illustrations of the 1930 *Tarzan*; the silly, gymnastic tumbling-about of the early, juvenile *Buck Rogers*

41

of that period; the gray, gritty art and obsession with aircraft technology which slowed the pace of the contemporary *Tailspin Tommy* to a shuddering konkout—to glance at the most popular adventure strips then on the nation's comic pages—seem forced and contrived against the ceaseless inventive freshness and pace of the fast-developing *Mickey Mouse* strip of that first fine year.)

What *Mickey* had going for it from the very beginning, of course, was the conceptual image of the pint-sized hero himself. This was nothing less than a work of simple genius on someone's part—although precisely who, among those early Disney Studio employees of 1928, sketching the opening frames of the initial *Mickey Mouse* film, *Plane Crazy*, first pinned down all the essential elements of the sliced-pie black eyes, round black ears, uptilted and jellybean-tipped nose, face-framing black carapace (this, of course, borrowed from Felix), the widely grinning mouth (*oh*, that grin of the mid-1930s, when Mickey's full, beaming face on a Saturday matinee screen would proclaim the beginning of a Disney cartoon!), and compact, shorts-clad, tail-balanced black body perkily active with gloved hands and bulbous brogans at the ends of licorice-stick arms and legs—precisely *who* assembled this disparate array of odd parts into its brilliant whole, looked at it, and said "*This is it—this is the Mouse!*," we don't actually know. (There was, remember, no preceding film or strip cartoon figure at all like Mickey, although aspects of the popular Felix—the round black nose, the all-black body, both so convenient for animation needs—can be discerned in the first shaping of the Mouse; certainly he didn't in the least resemble any preceding comic rendering of a *mus musculus*: even Herriman's outré Ignatz looked more effectively mouselike than Mickey.) The promotional necessity of centering credit from the beginning on one organizational individual at the Disney Studio has obscured the credit likely due other persons involved in this crucial moment of creation. (Recently published material suggests animator Ub Iwerks's hand as central in shaping the classic Mouse.)

Mickey's name we know a bit more about. Walt Disney, we are told from numerous sources, initially wanted to call his new film hero Mortimer the Mouse, rather unimaginatively echoing the nomenclatural structure used for several previous movie-cartoon animal stars, such as Felix *the* Cat, and Disney's own, now abandoned, Oswald *the* Rabbit (and later continued by Iwerks with his Flip *the* Frog). His wife, Lillian B. Disney, however, suggested the useless article be dropped, and that a sprightlier name be used—like *Mickey* Mouse. She also suggested Minnie as the name of Mickey's girl friend. Mrs. Disney, it now appears, may not have been particularly inspired, but may only have had a tenacious memory, since Johnny Gruelle, of *Raggedy Ann and Andy* fame, had featured an earlier Mickey and Minnie Mouse team as regular characters in a children's fiction series he wrote in 1921 for *Good Housekeeping* (the most widely read women's magazine of its time, and certainly seen by Mrs. Disney). Both Gruelle characters (brought to my attention by writer Martin Williams) were cartoonized mice, traditionally rendered in Gruelle's art, while Mickey was Minnie's rather young son instead of her paramour, but the names may have stuck in Mrs. Disney's head, to reemerge eight years later in their new and immortal application.

> Her open mouth turned down in a black crescent moon of horror, Minnie Mouse screamed her fear as the heavy mass of the nether millstone to which she was tied hand and foot shuddered with the grinding pulse of the old mill machinery which brought the upper millstone humming and spinning down to pulverize her. In a minute—two at the most—the slick, whirling stone surface would touch the tip of her upturned nose, and then it would be the end. At the lever which controlled the speeding mill mechanism, the black-bearded gypsy grinned his terrible delight at Minnie's peril, while outside, Mickey Mouse realized there was only one way to stop the doom that whirled toward Minnie. Seizing a saw which leaned against the mill wall . . .

The first *Mickey Mouse* daily-strip episode, actually drawn in late 1929, appeared on January 13, 1930. According to Disney Studio records crediting the artists and writers who have worked on the various Disney newspaper strips over the years, this first, rather elaborately drawn episode (which opened with Mickey daydreaming on a barnyard haystack about becoming a great aviator like Lindbergh) was scripted by Disney himself, penciled by a key studio animator, Ub Iwerks, and inked by another artist named Win Smith. Through some mixup in King Features' distribution of this and other early strip episodes, Ub Iwerks received byline credit for the feature in several subscribing papers, probably to the surprise of Mouse movie fans who had already come to associate their favorite with Disney, and to the undoubted dismay of Disney himself. The correction was soon

43

made, and the byline changed to a rather staid "Walter Disney" (which belied the less formal "Walt Disney" already being signed to the episodes, although echoing the copyright line, "Walter E. Disney," which also appeared with each day's strip).

The new comic strip, in a studio fast gearing itself to meet the rising public demand for more Disney films, was not a prime concern, and artists assigned to it tended to regard it as a ghetto job. Iwerks left the initial strip triumvirate in less than a month, turning the penciling over to Smith. For three months Smith followed Disney's daily outline, turning out a loosely formed, slapdash pratfall strip which reflected the rapid-fire visual gags of the Disney cartoons, then he shifted gears abruptly into semiserious narrative when King Features Syndicate (at whose request the strip was begun) felt it was time to introduce the daily suspense continuity then increasingly popular in newspaper comic strips. Finally Smith seems to have felt he wanted something else to do. Disney himself had reportedly become weary of having to guide the story details along from day to day (animation gags of the sort he was used to were one thing; an involved story-line was something else again), and wanted out of the chore. Fresh blood seemed called for, and Disney apparently remembered a young cartoonist who had joined the studio a short time before, expressing interest in working on the new strip. At the time, since he obviously felt Win Smith was doing a good job, Disney had put the new man in animation and had temporarily forgotten his strip interest. Now he decided to see how the ambitious youngster would do with the strip, and he turned both penciling and inking over to the 24-year-old, five-years-married, Utah newcomer named Floyd Gottfredson.

In this quiet, almost happenstance way, comic-strip history was made. A happy combination of factors had assigned a man with a still undeveloped but fundamentally first-rate creative story imagination and graphic genius to a still formless and ill-directed new comic strip. The enthusiastic young Gottfredson (who, however, had reportedly come to enjoy his animation work and was a bit disgruntled to be handed the strip at last) found that unexpected reserves of imagination and artistry within himself took wing as he worked on the still-primitive *Mickey Mouse* adventure panels, and he cottoned to the new job almost at once. Disney was clearly pleased with Gottfredson's fresh, ready flow of suggestions and innovations for the story as well as with his obvious ability to handle the whole show ... for, after the new man had served a week's apprenticeship, Disney gave him control of the strip narrative as well.

For the next two and a half years, from April of 1930 until late 1932, Gottfredson was in full charge of *Mickey Mouse*, although his penciling was now faithfully and closely inked by a number of young artists, including Al Taliaferro (who later went on to draw the famed *Donald Duck* newspaper strip), and the gifted Ted Thwaites, who painstakingly rendered Gottfredson's sketched action from the early 1930s until the 1940s. Aside from giving more point, spice, and prominence to the dialog, and firming up Win Smith's uncertain strip style, which hovered indecisively between the necessarily realistic consistency of newspaper-strip art and the more free-floating animation-frame techniques (in one early haunted-house sequence, Mickey is depicted in a suddenly dark room in an Al Jolson blackface pose, crying, "Minnie!" instead of "Mammy!"; in another, Pegleg Pete suddenly looms much larger than his normal size when he has Mickey cornered), Gottfredson made no immediately perceptible changes in the tenor of the strip he had inherited. The big changes came, but they developed surely and subtly.

As soon as he had shaped the style of the *Mickey Mouse* strip into a mold capable of containing his own intense graphic visualization of the new, developing world of Mickey and his friends, Gottfredson gradually began to clothe the brazen, capering, one-dimensional movie Mouse of those slapstick days with the close-woven fabric of consistent character, background, chronology, friends and enemies, and *raison d'être* that was to make Mickey one of the great comic-strip characters of all time. This substantive Mickey of circa 1932 and later, derived from and retaining the bouncy ebullience and inventive ingenuity of the early screen figure (who is able, in a 1931 short called *The Castaway*, to wrap the tail of a swallowed lion around the engulfing jaws of the alligator who has devoured it, and so dispose of both adversaries), with his Gottfredson-detailed personal history and complex relationships with the multitude of characters who appeared and reappeared in the strip, had and has a far greater reality as an individual creation for those of us who followed him faithfully through the years than the bland, stodgy, gelded studio personality known today to most people as Mickey Mouse. As one old fan of the Gottfredson strip remarked recently, in speaking of the compared demeanor of the Disney screen character over the past three decades, "It's as if *our* Mickey had had a lobectomy."

The differences between the screen and strip Mickey were by no means so marked in the early 1930s. By mid-1932, when a cartoon called *The Klondike Kid* was released, the Disney animators had edged away from the almost total surrealism of the earlier Mouse films into a realistic adventure framework approximating the Gottfredson strip of the period. In *The Klondike Kid*, a humorous suspense-chase film with overtones of Chaplin's *The Gold Rush*, Mickey pursued a heavily bearded Pegleg Pete (named Pierre Jambedebois in this short) to rescue the mousenaped Minnie from a cliff-perched house crushed at the climax by a huge, snowballing avalanche gathered around a tumbling dog sled, Mickey, and Pluto (his strip pet being here utilized as a single sled dog). Subsequent films of the same semiserious realistic-action genre were *The Mail Pilot* (1933), *Two-Gun Mickey* (1934), *Shanghaied* (1934), and *The Mad Doctor* (1933: this last title was recently held by Disney executives to be so gruesome, according to a 1972 *Variety* report, that it has been permanently withdrawn from international release). Unfortunately for this promising development in the Mouse films (which might conceivably have led to an experimental short feature or two based on the newspaper adventures, much along the line of an abortive feature-film project later planned for Donald Duck and Pegleg Pete, to have been handled in part by animator Carl Barks, the story-line for which can be found in the first Barks *Donald Duck* comic book, *Donald Duck Finds Pirate Gold*: Dell, 1942), it was out short by a completely unexpected event, when a supporting actor in a 1934 Disney Silly Symphony titled *The Wise Little Hen* made such an overnight hit with the public that most studio energies were turned to promoting this new star. (Who? Nobody else but Donald Duck!) In the course of this promotion, the studio Mickey was reshaped into a straight mouse for the comic duck, while films featuring Mickey alone were sharply reduced in number. In a surprisingly short time, the film Mouse acquired the narrow dimensions of the mild-mannered, much-put-upon Mickey who generally represents the character for most people today, while the new Donald took over much of the Jimmy Cagney ebullience and energetic inventiveness that had been integral to the Mouse of the adventure films. Mickey's drab starring films of 1935, such as *On*

Ice, Mickey's Kangaroo, and *Mickey's Garden,* reflect the staid, stay-at-home figure the movies were to feature from that time on: grave markers for what might have been.

This alteration in Mickey's film character was a sharp blow to the kids who were following the Gottfredson strip, of course. I can recall how a number of us fans of those days, catching one of the new, bland *Mickey Mouse* cartoons at a Saturday matinee, liked to pretend that *our* Mickey, the Mickey of the strip, was only an actor in these films, playing roles quite apart from his real character. We would joke a bit after the show about how Mickey had better start complaining to his agent about these stuffy character parts Disney kept giving him, a make-believe attitude which took some of the immediate edge off our irritation. (We wanted Mickey exchanging potshots with Arabs from desert oases on the screen—*à la* Victor McLaglen in *The Lost Patrol*—not minding obnoxious twin nephews or acting as twittery straight man to a duck.)

There were some rough edges to this kid idea of the adventurer-actor Mickey, of course—how, for example, could the Mouse receive a star's income and still be forced to take the kind of odd jobs (bellhop, plumber, etc.) that kept the strip narrative going? How could the Disney Studio manage to get an active criminal and killer like Pegleg Pete to act in such films as *Mickey's Service Station*?—but these problems could be resolved with a bit of thought in an afternoon's backyard conversation. Mickey and his pals, obviously, were all actors for a very small-time, nearly bankrupt Burbank studio (Burbank had been established as Mickey's home town in the 1938 daily strip; earlier, Gottfredson had called it Homeville), run by someone named Walt Disney, which was able to operate only a few weeks a year, and which paid its hapless actors just enough to enable them to survive while at work. It wasn't Pete in the films at all, but a law-abiding double, possibly Pete's twin brother, who played Mickey's mortal enemy for the flicks. (Interestingly, Mickey was shown to be an active film actor at the Disney Studio twice in the strip in the late 1930s, so it would seem that Gottfredson and his associates had been thinking along the same line as us kids in relating the screen Mouse to his strip counterpart.)

Although the studio fortunately permitted Gottfredson to follow his own course with regard to the Mouse's character, someone at an executive level did insist that the strip reflect the changes the

47

animators chose to make from time to time in the physical appearance of Mickey and his fellow actors, as well as in their implicit residential background. The strip hero's frequent and prolonged adventures away from home enabled Gottfredson to manage the domestic changes by degrees, so that readers hardly noticed them, but from a rural setting in the early days of the strip (and the film cartoons), in which Mickey could call on a dozen nonhumanized farm animals to help him set up a miniature golf course in 1930, he has been shifted to a suburban city background (Homeville-Burbank) by 1933, and is running a big city newspaper by early 1935. Gottfredson also managed the physical changes in Mickey and the other strip regulars almost unnoticeably, which in Mickey's case included the omission of the extra eyebrow lines above his eyes, the elimination of the soles and heels of his shoes, and the filling-in of the narrow pie-slice gaps in his eyes themselves, changes primarily made to simplify the animation of the studio puppet. So subtly handled were Gottfredson's incorporation of these changes into the strip that it is difficult even today, looking back over a full file of the strip, to remember just where to pinpoint the introduction of each of them.

> Flattening himself on the thick leather breadth of the conveyor belt, Mickey looked down at the brightly-lit figures of Pegleg Pete and the German scientist whom the fat-jowled thug had employed to make his desert fortress impregnable. Pete's narrowed, shaggy-browed eyes darted here and there about the machinery-crammed laboratory, looking for the intruder he was sure was there. Inadvertently, as he swung his huge posterior about in his irritated search, he bumped a switch, to the scientist's alarm—and the belt to which Mickey clung began to move ... swiftly! Before the lean, bald scientist could move to turn off the great, door-raising machine Pete had jarred into action, Mickey was flying with horror off a sharp curve in the speeding, vibrating belt, backwards, helpless, to land with terrible impact in the middle of a group of power coils! Sparks spewed, electricity arced and flashed—and the lights suddenly dimmed as Mickey caromed off the coils into the laboratory's thermic infrequency cabinet, swinging the heavy metal door that sealed it off shut after him. He was trapped!

When serious adventure continuity entered the comic strips in 1925, via J. R. Williams's *Out Our Way*, Roy Crane's *Wash Tubbs*, and Harold Gray's *Little Orphan Annie* (the first corpses ever seen in a comic strip appeared in an *Out Our Way* narrative on December 4, 1925), stories rambled on without any particular time limit. Later, faced with the burgeoning popularity of suspense continuity in strips, syndicates decided common sense dictated the need for a uniform narrative length and as a general rule settled for three months as the time a strip story should normally run. This enabled newspapers ordering a new strip to open it in their pages with a fresh story within a reasonable period of time, and prevented duller readers losing track of characters and point in overlong stories. (Nevertheless, some strips, such as Clarence Gray's *Brick Bradford*, spun out narratives of a year or more in length again and again; others, such as Milton Caniff's *Dickie Dare*, wrapped up stories in a month or less at a crack.) Gottfredson's *Mickey Mouse*, under King Features syndication, adopted the three-month story pattern from the outset (experimenting with a few shorter narratives along the way), and this length seemed ideal for the generality of Mouse adventures, although some daily Gottfredson narratives of the late 1930s, such as those in which Mickey became King of Medioka, or made a movie based on *Robinson Crusoe*, ran much longer than three months. (It is interesting to note that the Whitman Publishing Company, which reprinted hundreds of strip adventures in truncated Big Little Book form in the 1930s and 1940s, was able to cut normal publishing costs by printing all its titles in uniform page length, thanks to the general syndicate policy on story duration: a strip story ran three months; the Big Little Book reprinting it ran 294–314 pages—and, later, 424 pages by dint of simply adding more panels from the original strip story than before. The two later *Mickey Mouse* adventures mentioned, however, never made Big Little Book reprint because of their inordinate length.)

Readily adapting his creative scope to the variety of backgrounds and experiences this handy allotment of story space permitted him, Gottfredson began to shape the series of hazardous comic adventures that would flex and develop the muscles and mind of the callow, easily frightened, but impudently plucky little Mouse left him by Disney, Iwerks, and Smith. Almost at once, in mid-1930, Gottfredson hurried Mickey off to the grimmest part of the arid West in a frantic pursuit of Pete and Shyster that took him to Death Valley and several close brushes with doom, following this sufficiently exhausting stint with a brutal emotional crisis for Mickey caused by Minnie's alienated affections, which carried the distraught Mouse to the extremity of attempted suicide. (Shotguns, bridge leaps, gas, drowning, and hanging are all tried, with distressing futility: Mickey's gargantuan luck and deep-seated urge to survive were too much for his short-lived despair in this bleak sequence.) Already, before the end of his first six months on the strip, Gottfredson had harrowed his hero fearfully, toughening him for the rough times ahead, and already Mickey was nervier and more aggressive in confronting the problems the strip posed for him. The seasoned, rough-and-ready adventurer of the Arabian desert, the Klondike, and the weird insides of a cloud-concealed pirate dirigible, was visibly shaping up.

The times ahead called for a tough Mouse—Gottfredson saw to that. Faced with repeated attempts to kill or cripple him by the burly, shaggy-pelted, tombstone-toothed Pegleg Pete (a wooden-legged thug endowed with a kind of criminal genius, an endless enthusiasm for new projects, and a miserable streak of bad luck which brings Mickey athwart his path repeatedly), the embattled Mouse survived by nerve, fortune, quick thinking, and plain dogged endurance. Mickey encountered the boisterously murderous Pete at least 18 times over the prime 20 years of the adventure strip, in the course of which lethal brushes, Pete—who is physically four times Mickey's size—tried to shoot, strangle, drown, blow up, crush, eviscerate, and otherwise destroy him. And Pete (with or without his two murderous and recurrent colleagues, Sylvester Shyster: a lean, grim, bespectacled rodent in courtroom black, and Eli Squinch: a gruff, whiskery New England miser determinedly after the main chance) was only one among many fearsome adversaries Mickey had to face down in the course of his hectic career of solving mysteries, saving another character, seeking hidden treasure, or undertaking secret government missions. Even Pete might have boggled at the sight of the gaunt, hooded, rubbery–winged Bat Bandit, who rode the night trails of the West, or the tall, ebon-cloaked stalker of the city shadows called the Blot, both of whom—particularly the Blot—brought Mickey close to a bloody demise many times over. Then there were the criminally insane trio of professors who had developed a horrible hypnotic ray in the crocodile-pitted Blaggard Mansion; the madly ambitious Dr. Vultur and his seemingly invincible pirate submarine; the Einsteinian eccentric, Dr. Einmug, who had literally built an island in the sky; and the seven mocking ghosts who haunted the villa of the beleaguered Colonel Bassett. Beside such grim bogies as these, the petty counterfeiters who hide out in an abandoned house and give Mickey a brisk tussle, or the night-flitting jewel thief named the Gleam, provide only routine menaces.

It was in the fierce business of facing and defeating these schemers and killers that Mickey learned how to pilot a plane, skipper a ship, ride a camel, run a newspaper, race a horse, an ostrich, and a dog, match a kangaroo against a gorilla, deep-sea dive, hunt whales, manage a prizefighter, play a saloon piano, parachute jump, train an elephant, fly a blimp, rule a country, make a movie, control a genie, adopt a cannibal, capture a dinosaur and generally qualify as a mouse of all conceivable trades.

Even as he fought his way gamely from peril to peril in the daily strip, Mickey was tumbled headlong into a fresh newspaper arena: the Sunday comic page. Toward the close of the Gottfredson strip's second year, King Features suggested the Disney Studio prepare a Sunday *Mickey Mouse* page for distribution in January, 1932. An initial page was penciled and inked by a studio artist named Earl Duvall, and appeared on January 10, 1932, after which the new Sunday feature was turned over to Gottfredson for story and penciling, and to Taliaferro and Thwaites for inking. The Sunday *Mickey* page (which was divided between a lower two-thirds of 16 panels devoted to Mickey himself, and an upper third framing a new feature called *Silly Symphonies*, initially starring a bouncy little fellow named Bucky Bug) was primarily a gag strip, which only occasionally turned to adventure continuity in the vein of the daily strip. The gags usually featured violent action and were often rib-crackingly funny: Mickey riding an automatic lawn-mower gone wild; Pluto pulling Mickey through a gallery of statues in pursuit of a cat (with a resultant "reconstruction" of the broken statues that is visually one of the funniest payoffs in strip history); Mickey trying to make out as a milkman with a horse (not imprecisely named Tanglefoot) who applies a newly learned ability to hand Mickey a bottle of milk from the wagon with his teeth at every stop—and similarly hands a bottle to any passerby who will stand still long enough to take it. There was a nutty kind of happy-go-lucky gaiety in these early Sunday pages of Gottfredson's, which is perhaps best reflected in print by the songs that ran through the gag sequences like a lyric thread; one of the best—written by Carl Stalling for the animated cartoons—larruped along like this:

OH, th' old tom cat, with his meow, meow, meow,
Old houn' dog, with his bow, wow, wow;
The crow's caw caw, an' the mule's hee haw—
Gosh! What a racket, like an old buzz saw!
   I have listened to th' cuckoo cuck his coo coo,
   An' I've heard th' rooster cock his doodle doo-ooo;
   But the cows an' th' chickens, they all sound like th' Dickens,
   When I hear my little Minnie's YOO-HOO!

Rendition by Mickey, of course, painting a backyard shed while his paint-sodden nephews, freshly scrubbed and dripping, are hung up by their pants on a clothes-line to dry—and keep them out of further mischief. (Donald Duck—*vide* Mike Barrier's piece elsewhere in this book—was the *second* Disney character to be plagued with annoying nephews; the first comic character of all to be beset with nephews—three of them, like Donald's—was Happy Hooligan, back in the 1900s.)

The infrequent adventure continuity in the Sunday strip, when it appeared, was quite as good as anything in Gottfredson's daily narrative. The best of all the Sunday stories was probably the first, which ran from January 29 to June 13, 1933, involving cattle rustling on Minnie's Uncle Mortimer's ranch. This yarn, outlined for Gottfredson by studio story man Ted Osbourne, featured the full *Mickey Mouse* cast of the time, aside from Pete and Shyster (Pete appeared only once, later, in the Sunday strip; Shyster, never): Mickey, Minnie, Horace, Clarabelle, and—just added to the roster—the lean, gawky buffoon with the matched buck teeth who was to be Mickey's closest buddy through dozens of later adventures: Dippy Dawg (later, Dippy the Goof, then just plain Goofy, all being awesomely appropriate names). The cattle ranch story, soundly structured in both both gag and suspense sequences, is a major *Mickey Mouse* classic (the episode in which Mickey and other ranch hands disguise themselves as cattle inside old cowhides to trap the rustlers—a notion apparently borrowed by Osbourne from an identical Sol Hess *Nebbs* Sunday sequence of 1926—is particularly hilarious), and deserves full-color reproduction in book form, together with the dozen or so other Sunday narratives spread over the run of the strip into the mid-1940s: the few of these drawn by studio artist Manuel Gonzales after he relieved the overworked Gottfredson on the Sunday page in mid-1938—or by artist Bill Wright after he relieved Gonzales in turn by mid-1942—proving quite as entertaining as those handled by Gottfredson himself. Wright later was assigned to redraw Gottfredson's strip for comic books and was ordered to change every panel, usually by facing everyone in another direction.

> Seated at the giddily swaying junctures of the fronds of the great fern up which they had just shinnied a tailsbreadth ahead of the swiping claws and ripping fangs of a saber-toothed tiger, Mickey and Goofy looked worriedly down at the fern's furry green bole, where the great cat snarled and lunged upward at them. It was pleasantly obvious that the prehistoric saber-tooth couldn't climb effectively— but that was suddenly a matter of no consequence. Goofy saw the new horror veering toward them out of the tropical sun first. "Mickey!" he gasped. "L-look! Whut's—" "Omigosh!" cried Mickey, almost tumbling from his precarious perch in shock as he looked in the direction Goofy pointed—looked at the wide and hungry beak, the tiny, gristly eyes fixed on them as the spread, leathery wings carried the creature on his determined path at express train speed. It was a pterodactyl—and Mickey and Goofy were so much clustered fruit for its razor-toothed jaws!

There's no doubt that the comic-strip Mickey—scrappy, tough, inquisitive, Quixotic, enduring, at once heroic and hilarious (a kind of combination Jimmy Cagney and Harold Lloyd)—was an important and central figure in the imagination of the kids who read the newspaper comics of the 1930s and were lucky enough to have run across the Gottfredson creation. So real was he to us that we invented wild and wonderful adventures of our own for him, flying him to Mars and the Moon in rockets invented by a mad Professor Triplex, who had survived the Blaggard Mansion blast; sending him in search of a surviving Chinese dragon in the hills beyond Peking; matching him against a terrible new Pegleg Pete who can appear in several places at once, committing crimes with simultaneous alibis; having him assigned by the Secret Service to a circus, where the only way he can get the needed confidence of a high-wire man is by pretending to be a professional tight-rope walker himself, *ad delirium*—and we devoured our clipped files of the strip, our tatterdemalion *Mickey Mouse* Big Little Books over and over. There were plenty of other top-quality imaginative idols for kids in the entertainment media of those days, needless to say—Doc Savage, the Spider, Conan, the Cthulhu Mythos, Kimball Kinnison, Laurel and Hardy, W. C. Fields, Humphrey Bogart, Popeye, Wash Tubbs, the Spirit, Poppy Ott—but the strip Mickey reigned paramount among those for many of us. (It is worth noting, too, that the extreme popularity of the screen

Mouse in the 1930s made it possible for those of us fortunate enough to have parents with decently paying jobs in that grim era to surround ourselves cheaply with Mickey's image: on wallpaper, rugs, lampshades, drinking glasses, watches, cereal boxes, nearly everything we used or touched at home—and on pencils, pencil-boxes and writing pads at school, for that matter. There were even Mickey Mouse Cookies, in little animal-cracker boxes with white carrying cords, filled with crispy images of Mickey, Minnie, Horace, Clarabelle, Goofy, Donald, and the others. It was literally a Mickey Mouse world then.)

All of this ardent response resulted, of course, from the compelling strength of Floyd Gottfredson's graphic and narrative imagination in the strip medium. Although shrouded in complete anonymity behind the bland "Walt Disney" signature affixed to each strip episode, he reached us kids with as great a unique and individual personality as Roy Crane, E. C. Segar, Cliff Sterrett, Warren Tufts or any of those other top-echelon strip artists who, like Gottfredson, seemed to be born to express themselves in the panel medium. We *knew* Gottfredson, although we didn't know who he was, and we loved him as much as people ever loved Charles Dickens, Will Rogers, or Charlie Chaplin. It wasn't the plots or story-lines of *Mickey Mouse* (some of which were pretty hackneyed in general structure, and prepared for Gottfredson in part by studio writers after mid-1932) that kindled and maintained this deep affection and fascination we felt for the strip artist and his creations; it was, rather, the panel-by-panel manner in which Gottfredson's inspired pen picked out the characteristic responses of his figures to each fresh situation in graphic delineation. They were *his* people; his art made them his, and he shared them superbly with us during those lush, lovely years of the adventure strip. (That the fine genius of the strip lay in its art is demonstrated by the result when another staff artist was assigned to *redraw* some of the Gottfredson stories for *Walt Disney's Comics and Stories*—Lord knows why—with the same dialog and panel content. The second artist's work lay dead on the page from the outset, imbecile and unbelievable, where Gottfredson's had moved like lightning and shone like day from start to finish.)

It is hard to guess how much Gottfredson had to reshape the plots and story ideas tossed at him in the warmly informal studio get-togethers of story-men and artists with the *Mickey Mouse* artist, where such able writers as Merrill de Maris, Ted Osbourne,

Dick Shaw, Webb Smith, and Bill Walsh contributed to the narrative structure of the strip over the years. The intense unity of viewpoint, theme, and character in the story-lines of the strip from the start in 1930 onward, despite the preparation of nominal scripts by different writers, certainly suggests, however, that Gottfredson simply organized such material as he received into a matrix that suited his creative attitude and took the story ball from there. That was, after all, almost certainly the reason Disney had assigned him the strip and kept him on it permanently thereafter. It is, accordingly, all the sadder to face the fact that this brilliant phantom artist was left so wholly unidentified to his readers. One wonders why the "problem" involved (of confusing a simple-minded public with another man's byline on a strip starring a character associated by them with Walt Disney's film cartoons) couldn't have been solved as Edgar Rice Burroughs, Inc., so thoughtfully handled it with that company's Sunday and daily *Tarzan* strips of the same period: by maintaining Burroughs's commercially vital name on the printed byline of the strips while allowing the individual artists who worked on the strips over the years to sign their names in the panels below. The general public never noticed this and so was not "confused," while the really interested readers were not kept in the frustrated dark about a given artist's identity. (Of course, there was—and is—a further level of difficulty at Disney Studios, where a myth is maintained about the creative equality and nonirreplaceability of all the artists on the payroll, and nothing is apparently feared more than an individual artist of real worth being singled out for praise by letter and published comment among his lesser fellows. Such an artist might even—horrors—get the idea that he was worth more than his brethren and ask for *more money*, as well as create dissatisfaction in the ranks by his individual slice of fame and credit, however deserved. Worse, and most unthinkable, of course, is the possibility that such a talent, rising to public recognition and celebration from within the studio, might come to eclipse even the mighty Walt himself . . . No, the possibilities are too ugly and complex to be faced; it is better to be blatantly unfair and limit the identification of artists to screen credits at most, which very few of the public note, and an industry award or two, which even fewer of the public heed. A great strip artist is, obviously, pretty small potatoes around a thriving animation and live-action film studio—and there is no doubt that the Disney strip artists have been made to feel the impact of this view ever since 1930.)

Virtually the pioneer among these Disney strip artists, and certainly the longest-lasting in a single position, Floyd Gottfredson was possessed of a hard-earned and well-utilized knowledge of panel narrative technique that seems to have been sparked by the close attention he gave many of the classic comics of his Utah childhood and adolescence in the early decades of this century. Among his recalled favorites of that time were Walter Hoban's *Jerry on the Job* (his particular delight, and a wide favorite among his fellow strip artists in general), Herriman's *Krazy Kat*, Billy De Beck's *Barney Google*, Cliff Sterrett's *Polly and Her Pals*, Fontaine Fox's *Toonerville Folks*, the various works of Russell Patterson, and Roy Crane's *Wash Tubbs*. Of all these strips, interestingly, the only one with a strong, regular, daily story-line was Crane's rollicking, knockabout adventure strip, which flung its hand-to-mouth soldier-of-fortune heroes, Wash Tubbs and Gozy Gallup (and later, of course, Captain Easy), from one side of the wide, mysteriously exciting world of the 1920s to the other. It is also the one strip, before or after, which bears any real resemblance to Gottfredson's own *Mickey Mouse*. The resemblance is considerable. Its cocky, trouble-ridden shrimp of an adventurer-hero, Wash, often seems a ringer for Mickey in behavior, character, and even appearance (and this years before Mickey existed), while Wash's taller, slightly loony sidekick of the 1920s, Gozy, functions in Crane's strip much as Horace, and later Goofy, did in Gottfredson's. Wash and Gozy, too, were recurrently faced with a rough, tough, lowbrow archenemy named Bull Dawson, whose character and behavior paralleled Pegleg Pete's in virtually every rotten detail. Even the exotic *Treasure Island* innocence so characteristic of Mickey's early strip adventures around the world is much the same as that to be found in Wash's and Gozy's 1920 strip escapades in the snowy and salty corners of the earth. These similarities, of course, are as accidental as they are fortunate, and both *Mickey Mouse* and *Wash Tubbs* were among the finest adventure-thriller strips ever to blazon a comic page—equally extraordinary sets of magic casements opening daily on the foam of perilous seas, in faery lands newborn.

Gottfredson still draws the daily Mouse strip today, 43 years after its inception, and 20 years after the last vestige of adventure continuity was dropped from it: an incredible and remarkable record of fine work. To see his skilled hand pencil in the action of the daily panels in his tiny office—the same office he has occupied at the studio since starting work on the strip in 1930—is a major pleasure; curiously, the penciled work seems much more striking, more like the old, forceful graphic work of the adventure strip of 1930–50, than the inked and printed panels made of it for publication in the postage-stamp-sized strips prevailing in newspapers today. One hesitates to blame Gottfredson's present inker; possibly it is the marked reduction in size, as well as the generally poor reproduction of the strip in the source available to me, that makes the printed strip seem so alien, so different from the grand old strip of the past. More likely, however, a good part of this depressing difference lies in the content, for *Mickey Mouse* is today just another gag strip like so many, many others crowding the comic pages for attention. It is, certainly, far superior to the terrible *Donald Duck* gag newspaper strip the studio is currently fielding (in which Donald and his companions look like rejects from the cast of Tod Browning's *Freaks*), but it is not sufficiently different from the general competition to stand out. That this should be the present status of a strip that once pulled the eye away from everything else on the page, by virtue of the stunning adventure action in panel after panel and the graphic freshness with which it was limned, is a sad thing to see. It is not, I think, Gottfredson's choice.

The gag orientation is, of course, a fate shared by all humorously styled strips distributed by King Features today, and apparently not much can be done about it. Any formal continuity beyond a thematic linking of gags seems to have been forbidden to the nonrealistic strips in King Features' roster (*Thimble Theatre* being the only apparent exception) since at least the early 1950s. Other major syndicates have generally followed suit, although a few maverick strips—*Gordo, Pogo, Peanuts*—still feature continuity a good bit of the time. The argument runs that modern newspaper readers have barely enough patience to tolerate continuity in "serious" strips (which are themselves said to be falling off regularly in reader appeal), and that the simplest sort of one-glance gags are preferred. People who used to sit and read the paper now, it seems, skim through it in order to turn to the panacea of TV as soon as possible. This may very well be the case (although one wonders if the present jam-packed comic page isn't part of the trouble, and whether the cutting-back of strip content in most papers to a few of the very best, all run as large as possible in the resulting space, might not restore the old public fascination with comics), but it is a tragic truth to face if it means (as it appears to) that it would be disastrous strip policy to permit, say, Beetle Bailey and his buddies to undertake a prolonged strip escapade, to send Snuffy Smith back to the city in a fresh, continued encounter with Barney Google and (why not?) Spark Plug, or to simply return Gottfredson's long and unnecessarily demeaned Mouse to his old paths of glory.

We cannot even, unfortunately, return ourselves to the original Gottfredson narratives in any extant printed version in this country, although the majority of his stories are kept regularly in print in fine editions for readers of all ages in many European countries, notably Italy and France. The logical source for such reprints, Western Publishing Company's series of Disney-character feature books and magazines, has long had an incomprehensible policy of assigning staff artists to *redraw* the old Gottfredson stories when they are used at all, although the equally fine Carl Barks Duck strips are regularly reprinted in full as first published. This policy, at least in part, appears to derive from a notion that what the parents of today's children managed to enjoy with great gusto and no apparent harm on the comic pages of the 1930s and 1940s is somehow too strong for today's delicate toddlers. Accordingly, the Pegleg Pete of the old newspaper strip is changed in the Disney comic books to "Black Pete," a softened and less menacing version of the Gottfredson villain, minus—of course—the wooden leg. Threats and dangers in the older newspaper strip are omitted or unrecognizably altered to creampuff equivalents in the redrawn versions (the most notable destruction of this sort was wrought by a Western artist on a comic-book version of Gottfredson's "Phantom Blot" story of 1939, in which the whole point—the recurrent deadly traps set by the Blot for Mickey—was reshaped to make it appear the Blot was just kidding around with the Mouse, not really intending to *hurt* him or anything like that), while all the character, substance, and beauty in Gottfredson's original art are thrown out with the bath water. Thus millions of comic-book readers of the 1950s and 1960s, who had never seen the Gottfredson strip, were presented with a Mickey Mouse who had been redrawn with inept hands, matched against idiot perils, and generally made to conform with the present studio image of the priggish, proper Mouse: a pathetic figure whose handling contrasted starkly in absurdity of story and art with the brilliant *Donald Duck* stories then being turned out by Carl Barks in the pages of the same publisher.

Easily ranking with the half-dozen finest new comic-strip artists to emerge from the 1930s—the five others being Milton Caniff, Al Capp, Will Eisner, Walt Kelly, and Alex Raymond—Gottfredson came close to being the forgotten genius of his most productive period. For decades from the 1930s forward, many of us *Mickey Mouse* devotees wondered whose hand, or hands, worked with such superb and sustained magic behind the obviously meaningless "Walt Disney" signature maddeningly present in the lower-right-hand corner of every daily strip. No one was ever able to find out until Mal Willits, a Hollywood writer and book dealer, penetrating the veil of secrecy at last some six years ago, sought out and identified the extraordinary Floyd Gottfredson.

We are all in Willits's debt.

But to Floyd Gottfredson, all of us, including Mal, owe the thanks of a lifetime for the wonder he wrought on those edge-yellowed comic pages of 20 and more years ago.

We will never be out of *his* debt.

Or his Mickey's.

Author's Afterword: Floyd Gottfredson, a "phantom artist" in the newspaper strips for 43 years, seems fated to remain one in this book also. The Walt Disney Studio, in its ineluctable wisdom, has refused permission to reprint any panels or strips by Gottfredson to illustrate this article. Their feeling was that Mr. Gottfredson had been unfairly singled out for praise among other Disney strip artists and authors, and that policies of King Features and Western Publishing Company, long contracted to utilize Disney characters and features, had been excessively criticized. To my arguments that this piece was written as a piece of criticism in historical perspective, that it dealt specifically with Gottfredson and established reader response to his work—not with the Disney strips as a group—and that no person bright enough to read a book like this would be likely to confuse anything I say with official Disney Studio opinion, there returned only silence. It seems that Disney-copyrighted art can only be used in conjunction with written material essentially praising the entire studio-factory in accordance with official Disney handouts, and that anything differing from such promotional data is to be denied use of such art. Fortunately, Western Publishing has recently (and unbelievably) republished an entire Gottfredson daily narrative—called "Mickey Mouse at the Bar None Ranch"—in *Walt Disney Comics Digest* No. 40. This issue should still be available from the publishers (North Road, Poughkeepsie, N.Y. 12602) at $.60, or, if not, from established second-hand magazine sources to anyone interested. (The same issue includes a redrawn Gottfredson story, "Monarch of Medioka," and the contrast is highly illustrative of the comments made in the foregoing chapter.)

In closing, I should like to add that nothing in this article necessarily reflects the views of anyone employed at the Disney Studio, and that no one there with whom I discussed strictly factual data in preparing it failed in any way to reflect official studio views with regard to any matter discussed herein.

INTRODUCTION TO

THE PROPWASH PATROL

THERE was a time, not all that long ago, when one of the great tragedies of being young was that you might not get a chance to fight in the Big War, preferably to fly into single combat—or better yet, to fight singlehandedly against a flock of foes and overwhelm them the way they did in the comics. Nowadays such heroics are handled in comics primarily by Snoopy in his bloodless battles with the Red Baron, but the World War II comics made aerial combat the dream of many a beardless boy.

Remember the total saturation of air-war you had in the World War II days? Virtually all the comic strips fought the war, the movies were filled with the roar of airplane engines and the chatter of machine guns and, even if you read nonviolent comics, someone was sure to paste in somewhere a picture of a fighting plane and the slogan "Keep 'em flying!" You were pressured in school to buy War Stamps (after the war they became Savings Stamps) and collect paper and scrap to keep 'em flying. Even your breakfast cereal propagandized at you by offering, either in the package or for a pittance and a boxtop by mail, model planes and airplane-spotter cards so you could recognize the German and Japanese bombers as they flew over Cleveland and avoid confusing them with British fighter planes on the same route.

Dick Lupoff takes you back to the days when airplanes were a vital part of every growing boy's dreams and reveals that those dreams are not that far beneath the surface in him.

Dick Lupoff, co-editor of *All in Color for a Dime* and *The Comic-Book Book*, is the author of *Edgar Rice Burroughs: Master of Adventure*, and *Barsoom: Edgar Rice Burroughs and the Martian Vision*. He has contributed articles and short stories to many national magazines, has written for television and radio, and is the author of a growing list of novels including *One Million Centuries*, *Sacred Locomotive Flies*, *Into the Aether* and *Fool's Hill*. He is an instructor of English at the College of Marin in California. He has never been in an airplane.

CHAPTER 3

THE PROPWASH PATROL

by DICK LUPOFF

WE were air-minded in those days. Those days were the days and years of World War II, the last war, I think, that ever got a "good press" in this country. Korea got a mixed press; at first it was a clear-cut and generous response to aggression but, as the fighting dragged on inconclusively, casualty reports poured in weekly, political wrangling arose over so-called no-win policies, Truman fired MacArthur, truce talks went on and on and on at Panmunjom ... we got tired of Korea. And Vietnam, of course, has been an unmitigated disaster from anyone's viewpoint.

But World War II ...

Maybe it was just because I was a small boy at the time, or maybe it was at least in part because we had something pretty close to a controlled press, with the OWI—the Office of War Information—feeding coverage to the media and military cameramen providing "official" footage to the newsreels.

But mainly I think it was because the American people really *believed* in the war effort, we believed that the world was divided into two great warring forces, one good and one evil, and of course our side was the side of good. The "gray areas" that make it so hard to tell the good guys from the bad guys any more were ... well, not quite *absent* 30 years ago, so much as conveniently brushed aside, overlooked.

The good guys were America, Britain, France, China, Russia. The bad guys were Germany, Japan, and their agents, dupes, and collaborators. About the only country to receive equivocal treatment was Italy—somehow we felt that the Italians had been led into war on the wrong side by a vain and foolish dictator, and would gladly have opted out of the Axis cause at the first opportunity (which of course they did).

This world-view was both reflected and reinforced by movies, press, radio, and—for us kids—the comics. We thrilled equally to the news and to fictionalized narrations. Our heads were filled with exhilarating visions of heroic marines storming ashore on lush, sandy, rocky islets in the Pacific, rooting out fanatical subhuman Japanese defenders with bomb, bullet, flamethrower, and bare fists.

We imagined ourselves, faces and hands darkened with lamp-black, dogtags taped together to avoid sound, parachuting silently into occupied France to make clandestine contact with daring *maquis* and assist them in sabotaging Nazi installations, preparing for the great day of liberation that lay ahead.

But above all we dreamed by day and by night of soaring high over the war zones in sleek sky-chariots, mighty engines roaring as they hauled us into single duel with the enemy: P-47 versus Messerschmitt 109, Lockheed Lightning versus Focke-Wulf 190, Grumman Wildcat versus infamous "Jap Zero." The only rivals for our affection that those zooming fighter planes encountered were the mighty bombing craft, the Boeing B-17 Flying Fortress, the Consolidated B-24 Liberator, the carrier-borne Grumman Avenger torpedo-bomber (skimming low over the warm Pacific swells to deliver a load of deadly steel fish against a Japanese destroyer flotilla ...), and finally the mighty B-29 Superfortress, rising from steel-mat runways on Saipan to make firebomb runs against paper-walled Japanese cities until finally the *Enola Gay* ...

We flew with Jimmy Doolittle in his B-25s and floated with him on his life-raft afterwards, we rose with Richard Bong and Pappy Boyington to dogfight and glory.

Of course I was a small boy.

On the home front there were things to do beside dream of combat. We saved our dimes to buy War Savings Stamps, carried ration coupons and tokens along with the dollars our mothers gave us when we went to the grocery store for food (grocery store,

64

right?—not yet supermarket). We did our bit in wartime scrap-metal campaigns, reminded Mom to save that bacon grease and turn it in, collected newspapers for paper drives.

Sometimes we even gave comic books—speak of childhood trauma!

But most of all we trained ourselves to be aircraft spotters. In my house, at least, we bought aviation magazines and books at every opportunity; pictures of warplanes were clipped and hung on bedroom walls as if they were pin-ups of Betty Grable or Marlene Dietrich.

I remember that my personal treasure chest was divided into sections: one for comic books; one for bubble gum cards, "send-away" premiums, and the like; and one for the paraphernalia that reflected my personal air-mindedness. In the last category were balsa-wood scale models, a wall-chart of aircraft silhouettes (courtesy the Aluminum Company of America), *The Aircraft Spotter's Handbook*—thumb-indexed, publisher I'm afraid long since forgotten—and *Know Your War Planes*, a beautifully printed 44-page booklet featuring "26 American fighting planes in action painted by William Heaslip and 96 authentic silhouettes of warplanes of the world—American, British, Russian, German, Italian, Japanese."

Know Your War Planes was published in 1943 and found its way into my hands while still hot off the press. A notice inside the back cover says that additional copies may be obtained for $.10 each (stamps or coin) from the Coca-Cola Company, Department WP, Box 1734, No. 1, Atlanta, Georgia, U.S.A. I still have that little book.

I think I'll send for a fresh copy this afternoon.

It was inevitable that "air-mindedness" find its way into the comics, and in fact it did so before the United States ever entered World War II; before, in fact, the war broke out in Europe.

There's substantial disagreement over the parentage of the comic book. Comic specialists like Bill Blackbeard and Maurice Horn maintain that the comic book is basically a mutation—and not a very desirable one—of the (newspaper) comic *strip*. Those who support this position point to the obvious similarity of format—panel-breakdown, graphic narrative techniques, dialog in speech ballons, and so on—and to the undeniable historical fact that most early comic books were mere compendiums of newspaper strips, which gave way to new material only as the supply of reprintable newspaper comics began to run out.

Others, though, such as Jim Steranko, suggest that the real parent of the comic book was the pulp fiction magazine wherein cavorted cowboys and athletes, aviators and detectives, seafaring men and soldiers of fortune, as well as war; and, yes, even superheroes, long before the comic book was so much as a gleam in the eye of the late Mr. M. C. Gaines.

Aviation adventure was one of the staple categories of pulp magazine, with titles ranging from *A* to *Z*. (Literally—from *Air Wonder*, a kind of hybrid aviation/science-fiction magazine founded by Hugo Gernsback, to *Zeppelin Stories*, the content of which should be obvious.)

In addition to these (relatively) conventional pulp magazines, which featured a melange of yarns grouped around the general theme indicated in their titles, there were the "single-character" pulps that appeared month after month featuring the same hero in an open-ended series of exploits. The best-known of these were *The Shadow*, *Doc Savage*, and (in the science-fiction realm) *Captain Future*. But in all there were scores.

In the aviation field they included *Bill Barnes*, *G-8* (recently resurrected as a paperback book series), *Dusty Ayres*, *Tailspin Tommy* (who made it also to screen and comic-book page), and *Terrence X. O'Leary* (the *X* stood for *Ex*-cellent).

Most of these magazines concentrated their attention on fictionalized exploits of imaginary heroes of the *First* World War. The skies over France and the earth-bound adventures of temporarily grounded aviators trapped behind German lines offered fertile territory for authors' imaginations but, by the time the War to Make the World Safe for Democracy had receded two decades into the past, the writers may well have wondered if they were not mining a played-out vein.

O'Leary turned for several issues into a space-action magazine; others cast about for new skies to conquer, and the gathering clouds of the approaching War to End Wars offered silver linings.

The Fiction House pulp line—*Jungle Stories*, *Fight Stories*, etc.—was far from unique in maintaining a series of comic books at the same time that the pulps were going along vigorously. Fawcett, Dell, and Standard (Pines) Publications all did the same, as did the giant Street & Smith firm with its hugely successful Shadow and other characters. But Fiction House maintained the closest correspondence between its parallel pulp and comic series, at times running not merely the same characters but even the same covers on *Planet Stories* and *Planet Comics*, and *Rangers* (of Freedom) magazine and *Rangers* (of Freedom) comics.

Fiction House also published a *Wings* magazine devoted to aerial adventures of World War II, and matched it with *Wings Comics*, to which I shall return shortly.

For the "air-mindedness" that swept the nation—and the comic books—was not limited to what we usually think of as aviation strips. It seemed that *everybody* was flying in the comics, and not just the outright superheroes either—Spy Smasher had his marvelous Gyro-sub, Batman the Batplane, Wonder Woman her odd transparent robot plane; while Hawkman flew with the aid of artifical wings and *n*th-metal belt, Bulletman with the assistance of his gravity helmet, Starman with that of his Star-rod, Ibis courtesy of his magical Ibistick, and so on.

But the three great aviation comics that flourished during the war (and for some years after) were Fiction House's *Wings Comics*, Hillman Publications' *Air Fighters Comics* (later *Airboy Comics*), and Quality Comics' *Military* (later *Modern*) *Comics*, whose bellwether feature, *Blackhawk*, survived in the comic books until (relatively speaking) just yesterday.

These were the great three, and of them the first, if not the greatest, was *Wings Comics*.

The publication began a year and a half before the United States entered World War II; its first issue was dated September, 1940, suggesting that the outbreak of war in Europe the previous September provided the inspiration for *Wings*. The Luftwaffe's deadly gull-winged Junkers 87 Stuka dive-bomber did a lot to make the world aware of the role aviation would play in the new war, and the waters of the English Channel already reflected the images of the Heinkel and Dornier bombers that, along with their fighter escorts, would face defending Spitfires and Hurricanes in the impending Battle of Britain.

With the United States strictly speaking at peace and theoretically neutral regarding the war, there was a small problem in getting *American* heroes into those flaming skies, but the staff of publisher T. T. Scott (and the Iger-Eisner studio, to which much of Fiction House's creative work was farmed out) found inspiration in several real-world practices of the period. There were Americans who had traveled to Canada, there to apply at British recruiting offices with the end result personified in the "Yankee

Flier in the R.A.F." phenomenon. Simultaneously, General Claire Chennault was leading the famous Flying Tigers, the American Volunteer Group of fliers who piloted Curtiss P-40 Warhawks against the Japanese invaders of China.

All of this information, I confess, is largely the product of latter-day research on my part. I didn't really get into *Wings Comics* until after the United States entered the war, and then I did so largely through the hand-me-down enthusiasm of my older brother.

But the jingoism and uncritical pro-war and pro-aviation attitudes of the time are clearly visible in surviving copies of the old comics that my brother handed down to me in later years.

Once the United States got into the war there was undisguised gloating on the part of publishers of war-flavored comics and pulps. Let me quote here an editorial from the oldest copy of *Wings* I've been able to dredge up, the September, 1942, edition:

Wings Salutes You!

Wings celebrates its second birthday . . . its second year of success.

For this we want to thank our vast audience . . . thank you particularly for your enthusiasm and your loyal support of *Wings* in its reckless infancy before the U.S. entered the war.

In those days loudmouths insisted that Hitler, Mussolini and the Japs were nice guys . . . merely misunderstood. We could get along with the Axis, do business with it, they were fond of claiming . . . on Axis terms of course!

They called *Wings* "warmonger" and "alarmist" because, long before Pearl Harbor, it chose to dramatize and glorify the Yank aces . . . those dauntless, unconquerable chips off the old block who had rushed to join the R.A.F. in high battle, or who volunteered with Canadian war-birds, or with Chiang Kai-shek's lean squadrons.

To those who stuck by *Wings* through thick and thin we offer our heart-felt thanks.

Once again *Wings* reminds the world that Yank love of adventure and freedom and Yank hatred of tyranny and brute aggression will live as long as there is an America. These qualities are part and parcel of America. This gallant spirit is what made our country great, and will make it greater.

Carping critics or not, *Wings Comics* will continue to glorify the freedom-loving, devil-may-care Yank spirit that sparks America's swift-growing air fleets across five oceans and as many continents.

Keep 'em flying!

The Editor

Skull Squad, the lead feature in that 30-year-old issue of *Wings Comics*, was about a kind of hero-team of the same name, a trio of R.A.F. fliers assembled before U.S. entry into the war: Jimmy Jones, American; Sandy MacGregor, Scotsman; and Kent Douglas, Englishman. Its structure was simple, and typical of the *Wings Comics* approach to air-war fiction.

There was little characterization, almost no motivation (hell, there was a *war* going on, it was just us against them, that's all!), very little background, and hardly even a plot. Just action! Kent arranges with a commando-forces captain to raid German shore batteries in France preparatory to a commando raid. (The purpose of the raid is to free commandos captured on an earlier raid.)

Shortly after, red-haired Sandy MacGregor gives the American Jimmy the good news about the impending action (all of these guys are just aching for a fight, there's nothing they love more than fighting, there's nothing they dig more than killing, but it's all right because they're good guys killing bad guys), and the only one let down is Lisbeth, the pretty canteen girl, who wants to come along but is told she has to stay in England.

Following this the Skull Squad take off in their blood-red attack bomber. (I think it's a Douglas A-20 Boston, but the details are not too clear in *Wings*.) They spot the commando boat in the Channel, about to be sunk by a German patrol boat, so the Skull Squad sink the Nazi boat with bombs—only to be signaled by the commandos to land on the French beach!

The Skull Squad do so, and the commandos come ashore with a stowaway "spy." "We don't know how he got on!" the commando leader says, "But he insists he knows you chaps! Here he is! Recognize him?"

"By Jove! It's Lisbeth!" Kent exclaims, only to be hushed by one of the other Skull Squadders ("Shh! Don't tell the captain!"); of course they take Lisbeth along with them; soon they get involved in a battle with a flight of Messerschmitts above the very area where the commandos are carrying out their successful raid on the prison in which their comrades are held.

Kent, Jimmy, and Sandy, with Lisbeth in tow, outfly and outshoot the Messerschmitts until finally one of the German planes collides with the Douglas. Kent and Sandy parachute safely; Jimmy gives his chute to Lisbeth, crawls onto the Messerschmitt, takes the chute from its dead pilot, and jumps. They all land safely, join the commandos, who have now freed their comrades, and everyone sails happily home to England.

Suicide Smith is the second feature in the book (he carried the sobriquet "Blitzkrieg Buster" at this point in his career) and is both better written and better drawn than *Skull Squad*. We meet Suicide just climbing out of his trim monoplane (we see only part of the plane—it might be either an AT-6 Texan trainer converted for personal transportation or a Douglas Dauntless torpedo-bomber similarly adapted) to report to Major Olsen, who quickly involves him in a spy plot centered around Frisco Flo, a gorgeous redhead.

As the airplanes that were featured on the excellently drawn covers of *Wings* and in the stories provided considerable appeal for us air-minded American lads in the forties, the likes of Frisco Flo and Lisbeth the canteen girl presumably appealed to our older brothers. Flo is a breath-taking siren. Her auburn-rich red hair flows to her shoulders in sensuous-looking waves; she wears a floor-length yellow dress cut all the way to the sternum at the top and slashed well up to the thigh at the bottom. The artist (anonymous, but with the style of the Eisner school—perhaps Lou Fine) lovingly shades every line and curve of Flo's generous bosom and graceful hips. She stands usually with one hand on her hip and her dress clings so that even her navel is clearly delineated!

Caught in a nest of Japanese agents, Flo talks her way out of hot water by claiming to have been their prisoner; she slugs a sergeant and puts on his flying suit, then steals his plane (it's a Douglas TBD Devastator), picks up Suicide Smith as passenger, gets entangled with a trio of Japanese fighters off the coast of Mexico, gets shot down, shares a parachute jump with Smith into the Pacific, gets picked up by a Japanese patrol boat and taken to a small island where she sells Smith to the Japanese for 1,000 yen. While the Nips show Smith their giant dirigible (that will "soar above stratosphere, dropping hundreds of bombs") we're treated to some lingerie-art shots of Flo putting on a different yellow dress.

Enter now a Nazi liaison officer, Count Von Muck. Puffing cigar smoke from one corner of his mouth, the fat, monocled Von Muck growls: "Fraulein Flo, you work for low stakes. To get Smith aboard mein U-boat, I vould pay ten time dot sum."

Flo's response is a single word, "So!" She promptly feeds the

Japanese guard captain drugged sake (we get some neat garter-art as she sits on his desk), stabs the Japanese turnkey, and takes Smith at gun-point to Von Muck's submarine. Von Muck repays Flo's treachery with treachery of his own: "Aha! Thank you, Fraulein Flo! I vill take Schmidt back to Bremen. Our gestapo vill make him reveal his anti-blitz tactics, but I haf no marks for you. Der Japs vill pay you for your treason."

"Why you double crossing pig!" Flo replies. Can't blame her for being peeved, I guess, but all these nasties are just waiting for a chance to sell each other out.

At this point the Japanese super-dirigible just happens to be passing overhead. Coincidence played a huge part in these stories, as you may already have begun to notice. Smith grabs a trailing rope and climbs from the submarine to the dirigible, taking Frisco Flo with him. They get into a fight with the Japanese crew, killing several, but "Suicide finally goes down before superior numbers." (Our heroes were *never* defeated in fair and equal combat—they were sometimes felled by treacherous blows from behind, drugged, hypnotized, etc., etc., and fairly often put down by superior numbers, but *never* whupped fair 'n' square, never-never-never.)

Suicide is lashed to a bomb but Flo plays her trump card when the Japs threaten her with similar treatment. "Under orders from Vice Admiral Tojura I discovered the secret West Coast arsenal and tattooed its location in special code. You cannot read it . . . and if you kill me it will be destroyed!"

Now where is this tattoo? On her thigh, of course, providing the artist an excuse for three more luscious garter shots.

Stalemate—until, "several miles off the Golden Gate" the Japanese prepare to launch a small airplane to "direct our aim by radio!" Flo flips a guard with a jiujitsu trick, grabs his gun, frees Smith, seizes the patrol plane, and the two of them take off! "Wriggle into one of the chutes, Flo," rasps the blond and stern-faced Smith in heroic low-angle close-up. "I'm going to ram that flying sausage!" Smith and Flo do the twin-chute thing again, the plane and the dirigible go down in flames, and we fade out on a scene back in Major Olsen's office with Olsen, Smith, the slugged sergeant, and Flo all making accusations of one another. Flo has her hand on her hip as usual, and I have a feeling that she talked her way out of it again. But I expect I'll never know for sure.

Actually it was a helluva good action story (credited to Capt.

71

A. E. Carruthers, who almost certainly never existed), very nicely drawn, with plenty of good shots of aircraft (if that was your thing; in 1942 it was mine), nicely delineated human figures (those of Smith, Count Von Muck, and even the bit-players and sword-carriers as well as the cheesecakey Frisco Flo), and all of those fights, captures, escapes, chases, and confrontations packed into just eight pages.

As a work of fiction, I think it would have been a whole lot better if "Captain Carruthers" had stretched out, devoted some space to characterization, and saved up his action for climax situations in the story, instead of running at full-speed from start to finish. But as a pure action yarn, this Suicide Smith adventure can't be faulted; *Wings* wasn't the kind of comic you'd curl up with on a rainy afternoon, I guess, but it *was* one that you could fold in half and shove in your pocket, and read for five minutes when you got a break. As such it was the kind of comic that a soldier might read—not a combat trooper, who lived daily with the violence and death that filled *Wings*, but a basic trainee or a desk-bound rear echelon type could really get off on *Wings*.

There were several other features in the comic that deserve attention, especially since the lineup of features didn't change a whole lot in the magazine's long career. (It lasted for 124 issues, all the way from 1940 to 1954, and the changes that it underwent in those latter years we'll get to in a little while, too.)

But back in 1942, *Suicide Smith* was followed by a flat-out combat feature called "Suicide Squeeze" by "Capt. Derek West"; there wasn't really much of interest in the story, which just dealt with a series of dogfights between Navy Wildcats and Japanese Zeros, ending with the destruction of a Japanese super-bomber. What is interesting is the format—a series of balloonless drawings with all dialog and narration set in separate, accompanying panels. To the eye accustomed to the usual comic-book format, the drawings look strangely stylized and formal, clean and grace-ful but somehow remote. Speech balloons seem to lure us right into the panel, while the separated narration draws the eye *away* from the picture.

That, for what it's worth, and with due respect to Prince Valiant, Flash Gordon, and their respective creators, is my view.

The closest thing to a title-feature in *Wings Comics* was, of course, the story about Captain Wings himself, who originated in *Wings'* sixteenth issue. (In smaller type he shared his billing with the "Hell-Diver Squadron.") Again the art was anonymous but admirable, with the viewpoint cutting between ground and air, between "camera-angles," and between long, medium, and close-up shots in fine cinematic style.

For once there was an attempt to characterize and motivate the leading player of a series—most of the *Wings* crew were just good guys fighting bad guys, but not so Captain Wings. His real name was Boggs, and he was a sort of desk-bound C.O. of a fighter squadron stationed in Australia. Day by day he would send his men off to fight the Japanese, and day by day they would return with word of casualties, ever more resentful of their "ground officer" who sat safely at base while they flew to their deaths one by one.

Boggs sends his men back into the sky again and again, until they are near open rebellion. "Link," Boggs says, "You're squadron leader. Keep in touch with me! I'll relay orders!"

As Link climbs into his Curtiss SB2C he bitterly retorts: "That's it! You'll sit here and order men to their death! I've heard that you once flew in the R.A.F. and were called Captain Wings! Bet you started the rumors yourself!"

A few hours later, a ground-based radio operator turns to the nattily uniformed Boggs and quotes a message just coming over his earphones: "Hell-Diver Squadron reporting . . . Jap beachhead established . . . three Hell-Drivers been knocked down . . . Is Captain Boggs cleaning his finger nails? Call you later . . . Link!"

Too much for Boggs! "Poor devils!" he exclaims, "I'm going!" He climbs into flying gear and climbs aboard the only plane left— a Curtiss JN-4 Jenny, a World War I trainer! He flies to the beach where his men are offering air-support to defenders against a Japanese landing column, finds a flight of Japanese Naka 97 fighters, and heads straight at its leader.

"The American flying that strange craft seems determined to crash me! I had best yield!" says the Japanese commander. (He must have been educated in the United States to speak English so well—most likely he attended Yale and/or Berkeley.)

As the Japanese pulls away, Captain Wings, in close-up, remarks: "That yellow devil's nerve cracked! Now the formation is broken, we'll have more of a chance!"

But, forced to fight such a rickety old plane, Wings blacks out in a power-dive, crashes at an enemy base, and after a fist fight with a German pilot (obviously on exchange duty with the

73

Japanese air arm) is knocked unconscious. Well, he was still groggy from that blackout or he couldn't have been beaten by a single Nazi.

Wings is carried into a Japanese aid station, where Jerry Austin, an American nurse, has been forced to work. A fiendish Japanese doctor injects a hypnotic drug in him (this sequence is interspersed with numerous leg-art shots of Nurse Austin), and Wings is sent up with a flight of Japanese planes to attack the American base!

Jerry stabs a Japanese doctor with a stolen scalpel (we saw her conceal it in the top of her stocking) and rides with Wings, whom she clouts with a fire extinguisher in the cabin of "his" Jap plane.

Stay with me, now, this story has plenty of plot—Jerry parachutes to safety, Wings recovers his will at the same time that he recovers consciousness from the blow with the fire extinguisher; he turns on the Japanese and shoots one down just as they encounter the Hell-Diver Squadron. Jerry Austin finds her way safely to the Hell-Drivers' base, the Americans win the air battle and defeat the Japanese invasion, and Wings, now back in his accustomed role of Captain Boggs, sneaks back to duty!

Then there was *Calhoun of the Air Cadets*, but he wasn't very interesting, and the feature was quickly discontinued.

Not so the long-running comedy relief feature of *Wings Comics, Greasemonkey Griffin* by "Kip Beales" (who may even have been a real person for all I know).

"G.G.," as he was known, ran along for years and years in *Wings*, despite getting the worst reader response of any feature in the magazine. The Fiction House comics took a leaf from the pages of their companion pulp magazines and ran letter pages, a nearly universal practice in the comics of the 1960s and 1970s, but a rare thing in the so-called Golden Age. In *Wings Comics* the letters page was called, naturally enough, "*Wings*' Air Mail," and readers were encouraged to send their comments on the stories and art to the editors.

The page was divided into two sections, one featuring "long" letters of as much as two paragraphs, the other with capsule remarks a line or two in length. This format hardly permitted the development of lengthy discussions like those in "The Vizigraph," the letter column of *Wings*' Fiction House companion, *Planet Comics*.

But it did allow for comments from as many as 40 or 50 readers each month—and there's nothing to keep a reader coming back for more like finding *his* letter and *his* byline on the letters page!

A common practice among "Air Mail" correspondents was giving a breakdown of the value of the magazine—I never saw this in any comic published by anyone other than the Fiction House group. Here's the way one Earl Nietsttew (hmm—backwards that is Wettstein, a more likely name) of Minneapolis rated *Wings* in the August, 1945, issue:

> 4 cents for Captain Wings. Best drawings and stories.
> 3 cents for Jane Martin.
> 1 cent for Clipper Kirk.
> 1 cent for Suicide Smith.
> Half cent for Air Mail.
> Quarter cent for Skull Squad.
> One-eighth cent for Greasemonkey. Kick him out.
> One-sixteenth cent for the story.
> One-sixteenth cent for Wing Tips.
> Total 10 cents for one of the best comics on the market.

Earl Nietsttew's opinion of Greasemonkey Griffin was not out of line with those of the majority of the "Air Mail" correspondents. G.G. was exactly what his name suggests—a ground-borne mechanic of the lowest grade, assigned to an air base somewhere in Great Britain. Typically, his adventures involved his getting caught up in the middle of spy-plots or other intrigue, getting carried away in high-powered warplanes and/or experimental craft, and blundering through to triumph only to close out with a final pratfall.

The artwork was superior to the writing in the yarns, but somehow, to me, there was very little empathy with Griffin himself. I did not feel that Greasemonkey Griffin was a *person*— he was just a figure going through plot situations. And in varying degrees this was true of all the folks in *Wings*—they weren't made of flesh, they were just shapes performing acts and, while I could sometimes get behind their adventures on a pure thrills-'n'-excitement level, and while I certainly dug those pictures of airplanes (if I'd been older I might instead have dug the pictures of ladies), they were no substitute, even to an eight-year-old reader, for the feeling of real *companionship* offered by some of the more character-oriented comics.

Well, I suppose that's true to this day, and it applies to novels and motion pictures as much as to comics.

There were a couple of other features in *Wings* that deserve mention. The "story" that reader Nietsttew thought worth one-sixteenth of a penny was of course the standard text short story that comics carried to meet postal regulations. I never read a single one in *Wings*, and seldom any at all; the only ones I found consistently worthwhile were the *Jon Jarl* series by Otto Binder, which ran in *Captain Marvel Adventures*; fully 99 percent of the text stories in comics were throwaways, printed only because the mailing-permit regulations called for text material. They weren't written to be read, they were written to satisfy the postal reg's, and that is what they did, and that is all that they usually did.

Wings ran a few nonfiction features—a series of illustrated biographies of military aviation heroes (Lieutenant Edward H. O'Hare, Wing Commander Douglas Bader, Lieutenant Commander "Butch" O'Hare—and, yep, he was the same Edward H. O'Hare; they really dug him at *Wings*—Sergeant "Shorty" Gordon, Lieutenant Harold "Swede" Larson, Major Marion Carl, Lieutenant Colonel Francis Gabreski, Sergeant Meyer Levin, and so on) was one such feature.

Another was "Wing Tips," a page of tips on flying and aircraft maintenance. I've never been able to figure out for sure whether the people who put out these features—and similar ones ran in a number of aviation-oriented comics—really believed that aviation cadets and actual Air Corps personnel were reading them and learning anything useful, or whether it was all a shuck to make kids think they were reading stuff aimed at real aviators. I've never been able to figure that out, and if you have, I think I'd prefer you not to tell me. Let us preserve at least a *few* bright illusions.

There was a captive fan club run through *Wings Comics*, similar to the Supermen of America, Junior Justice Society, Captain America's Sentinels of Liberty, Captain Marvel Club, and others. This one was called Wings of America, and when you joined you got a neat metallic membership pin to wear on your shirt, but wartime materials problems stopped that. The announcement was terse:

> Special Notice: Due to the metal shortage, *Wings Comics* is no longer able to obtain membership pins for *Wings of America*. Club emblems will not be available to our readers until after the war. We suggest that all our readers buy War Savings Stamps every month to speed Victory.

Ironically enough, that announcement appeared in *Wings Comics* for August, 1945—the month the war ended! Still, I have been unable to find any evidence that Wings of America was revived after the war. Too much trouble for too little return, I suppose— or maybe it was just that the sense of involvement was going out of the business.

There were a couple more continuing story features; I should mention *Clipper Kirk* (by "Cliff DuBois") but it was so much like all the others that I hardly know what to say except "more of the same." In this precious 1942 edition of *Wings*, the *Clipper* strip opens with a symbolic splash panel—a Grumman Wildcat fighter decked out in British markings dives at a Messerschmitt 109; the Grumman's machine guns are blazing away, the Messerschmitt is on fire and its pilot is apparently trying to climb out and parachute before he is killed. Ominous black clouds back up the scene, while a red-robed skeleton reaches one sinister, bony hand for Death's due.

The story itself opens with Clipper Kirk sitting in a cafe in Port Said getting his orders from his C.O. (That's a nice way to get your orders, I suppose—when I was in the Army we did things somewhat differently.) A few minutes later Kirk joins his girl friend Tonia at another table. Kirk himself is a typical sandy-haired, square-jawed, *Wings Comics* hero. Tonia—could you have guessed this?—is super-shapely, with long, wavy dark hair and a yellow dress that shows her amazing pectoral development at one end while it reveals her lovely legs nearly to the thighs.

"Clipper," Tonia says, "I'm worried. That waiter at your table ... he was eavesdropping."

"You mean Henri!" Kirk replies. "Nonsense, Tonia, he was only waiting for our order."

Of course Tonia was right, as anyone with half an eye could have told. Henri is swarthy, frowning—no, *scowling* is a better description—and watching Kirk and his C.O. out of the corner of his eyes while walking in the other direction. A dead giveaway for a spy, if he doesn't trip and half-kill himself with that stunt.

Yes, Tonia is right, Kirk gets ambushed and shot down, is bombed by his attacker, and barely escapes with his life. How's he going to get out of this? Well, dig it—

He just strips to his underwear ("I'd best get rid of these R.A.F. duds!"), flags down another German plane that just happens to fly overhead after dark, and passes himself off as a German. ("Heil Hitler, comrade!" Kirk says, "A dog of the R.A.F. shot me down and left me for dead." The reply: "Heil Hitler ... come aboard!"

The Nazi aviator flies Kirk to the secret German base and as they stand around drinking beer, who drives up but Henri the treacherous waiter with Tonia as his prisoner! "You see, Clipper," explains the luscious Tonia, "the waiter noticed that you were talking to me after I returned to Port Said that day."

Clear enough.

Okay, Kirk and Tonia overcome Henri and a Nazi sentinel; Kirk sends Tonia home with the waiter and sentinel as prisoners, and "At dawn Kirk is among the Luftwaffe airmen seated in a Stuka, ready for the flight." In midair Clipper shows his true colors by shooting down three Stukas, tricks two more into colliding with each other, flies back to the Nazi base and bombs it, then abandons his plane in the desert when it runs out of fuel.

Just at this point, who drives up on her way back to Port Said but—Tonia! Lovely, just lovely. Did I mention that coincidence often played a role in these stories?

The whole thing was really great fun if you could take it on the right level.

As the years went by the features in *Wings* evolved in several ways. Captain Wings, for instance, pretty well dropped his identity as Captain Boggs the ground officer and became just another hero-aviator. That is, what little interesting characterization there was to him faded away. Instead of flying whatever aerial flivver he could lay hands on while his men were using the modern aircraft assigned to the unit, he got himself a sleek North American P-51 Mustang with a custom paint-job—stark black-and-white, with stylized bird-wings painted on its wings, and eyes and mouth painted on its nose. The latter device was of course borrowed from the practice of Chennault's Flying Tigers, although their standard aircraft was the Curtiss P-40 rather than the Mustang.

At various times in his career Wings moved around the world, fading to a kind of background narrator rather than central character (at this point his adventures were drawn by Lee Elias in a style much reminiscent of that of Milton Caniff), but he stepped back onto center stage to engage in a series of old-style air adventures at the time of the Korean war.

The quality of the writing and drawing varied, of course. In one of the finest *Captain Wings* stories of the "narrator" period we find Captain Wings reading the diary of a dead Flying Tiger pilot. The diary tells how the pilot sold his services to a Chinese warlord only to discover that the warlord is collaborating with the Japanese.

The flier is making plenty of money, but he faces a crisis of conscience (Captain Wings and his sidekick Lieutenant Griper turn up in the story at this point, in secondary roles) and finally crashes his plane, deliberately, to avoid killing Wings and Griper.

Whereupon his *ghost* is summoned by the ghosts of an American buddy and a Chinese girl—the warlord's daughter—and shown scenes of Japanese aggression and atrocities, a Japanese soldier shooting a Caucasian priest and raping an American girl, and so on. "That might be your Martha, Tom—if we don't win," the second ghost says. "He lies. Don't forget that farm. It's yours for the asking. Come, come, we must hurry!" urges the ghost of Loto, the warlord's daughter.

Tom makes his decision: "Get out of my way, Loto. You're right, Jake, there are things more precious than money. Things money could never buy!"

He somehow makes it back into his own body and is revived by Wings and Griper. "Sure, I'll be all right . . . " Tom says. "I've got work to do—got to join you Army guys! I've got to fly again—fly for both Jake and Martha and the kids!" And we fade out on Tom receiving the Medal of Honor, having downed an even dozen Japanese aircraft.

Then there was Jane Martin, at first a flight nurse, then after the war a saleswoman for an airplane company, and later still an airborne reporter. Her adventures weren't substantially different from those of the male heroes, except for the even greater opportunities offered the artists to include cheesecake shots, which they did with alacrity.

Jane got tangled up with the expected array of bright-yellow, fiendish Japanese, gross and brutal Nazis, and (after the war) gangsters and thugs. In her latter years she did some cold-warrioring as well, smuggling anti-Communist refugees out of Eastern Europe and the like.

Wings only ran one costumed adventure hero in its decade and a half of life; he was the Phantom Falcon but, except possibly for the idea of the costume itself attracting readers, I can't think of why he was included. He had no particular superpowers *á la* Superman, nor any of the Batcave-Batmobile-etc. gimmickry of Batman. He was just a standard *Wings Comics* aviator-adventurer, only he wore this tight costume with a hood and a cape . . .

I think the Phantom Falcon was Clipper Kirk in disguise. Or maybe he was really a fellow named Chet Horne. It doesn't matter much.

What does matter is the one other major feature of *Wings Comics*, which I've been saving for last: *Ghost Squadron*!

It may be just my personal bias in favor of the fantastic at work, but I must state that of all the features in *Wings*, the one I enjoyed the most was neither the fast-paced adventuring of Captain Wings or Suicide Smith, nor the leggy, spunky Jane Martin, nor the perpetual comedy-of-errors of Greasemonkey Griffin, but the *Ghost Squadron*.

The Squadron had a run of a good many years; I don't know the exact issue number in which it first appeared, or that in which it last appeared either, but it was not in the earliest or the last issues of *Wings*. It was bylined by our old friend "Capt. Derek West" and among the artists who worked on the feature was Maurice Whitman, who was not technically on a par with such *Wings* artists as Bob Lubbers, George Evans, Lee Elias, and Bob Powell, but managed to instill a spirit of brooding menace into his stories that more than overcame his inadequacies of detail. His characters might be anatomically imperfect, but they had identifiable natures that brought them closer to the vividness required in proper fiction than most of the *Wings* crew ever had.

I think the peak period for the Ghost Squadron was the late 1940s and, in the moldering copies of *Wings* I've managed to dredge up, three tales in particular of the Ghost Squadron stand out. Perhaps not coincidentally they all were published within a relatively short span of time—December, 1947, April and June, '48. Captain West didn't give his individual stories titles, it was just *Ghost Squadron* issue after issue, but I have given these three stories titles just for my own satisfaction. I call them "The Society of the Flying Skulls," "The Adventure of the Polish Bride," and "The Room of a Million Windows."

"The Society of the Flying Skulls" opened with an English flying cadet—well, perhaps Irish—named Charlie Kelly being invited to join a sort of air-cadets' fraternity of just that name. He is told to report for his initiation at midnight, where he will be made to pass a flying exam in an ancient biplane. Of course he's a new cadet and doesn't know how to fly, but everyone knows that it's all a put-up job, the trainer is rigged to remain stationary.

Before going for his initiation Charlie takes his girl Gwen Morrison to a dance, where he proposes to her. She accepts and they plan to be married as soon as the war is over. (Well, the story was published in 1947; World War II went on and on and on in the comics.)

But Charlie's rival Joe, who had been after Gwen's prospective fortune, un-rigs the trainer; Charlie steps into it at midnight, it taxis down the field, rises into the air, dips into a dive—and Charlie is killed!

Flash forward a year. Gwen has recovered from her grief, Joe has now proposed and been accepted, and there's no waiting for him. We see a fancy full-dress wedding with Charlie's ghost (ghosts look greenish and shadowy in *Wings Comics*) hovering around, trying to warn Gwen against Joe. He fails, though; Joe and Gwen are married and Gwen's dad gives them a wedding present of 50,000 pounds—nearly a quarter million dollars in those days!

Joe goes on to combat duty—Spitfires versus Focke-Wulf 190s—and when a buddy needs help, Joe refuses to give it.

"He's ridin' me hard. For the love of heaven, help me, Joe!" crackles the radio.

But Joe thinks: "Not me—I'm goin' to play deaf. Why should I risk my neck for Larry. Maybe I am yellow but I'm goin' to live!"

Back on the ground Joe weeps crocodile tears over his dead pal, making the excuse that his radio was out of order so he never heard the cry for help. But a ground mechanic checks out Joe's radio and finds it in perfect order. "How would you like to read the headlines, 'Millionaire's son-in-law court martialled for cowardice?' And you will read 'em, Joe, unless you make me a little present—of ten thousand pounds," the mechanic threatens.

Joe heads for Morrison Castle to get the money. His father-in-law had converted the place into a convalescent hospital for wounded servicemen, and Gwen is working there as a nurse. Joe finds old Mr. Morrison leaning over a balcony late at night and shoves him off. The old man dies, a coroner rules the death accidental, Gwen inherits a fortune, and Joe pays off his blackmailer.

But—several weeks later, Joe again visits the castle. The little daughter of a hospitalized soldier shows Joe her toy flying model. "Why—it's the same model as that old training ship Charlie died in," Joe thinks.

The toy airplane gets caught in a tree; Joe tells the little girl he'll get it for her and climbs a ladder—and the moment he takes the toy in his hand he's fascinated. "An old PT-13. And it has the same number twelve."

Charlie's ghost hovers. "That's right Joe. It's just like the murder plane."

"Why—that doll pilot—it looks like me!"

"It is you, Joe. *That pilot is you!*"

"I am on a ladder," Joe frantically tells himself. "I'm getting the plane for a little girl. *No! I am in the plane!*"

Now little Julia calls, "Captain, are you sick?"

But Joe is lost: "The plane's taking off. It's taxiing down the runway!"

And now Joe seems to be sitting in the trainer, with Charlie's ghost behind him, and the controls won't work, and "I've gone into a spin! I'm going to crash!"

And Julia calls "Please come, somebody. The captain's going to fall!"

And we see the plane crash with Joe in it—while we also see him falling to the ground, landing on his head, breaking his neck.

And while Charlie's ghost summons that of Joe, saying "You're dead, Joe . . . and I've had my revenge," a passing soldier looks at the corpse and says "What a horrible death for a hero!"

All I can say is, Phew! That's heavy stuff for a shoot-'em-up and leg-art book!

Four issues later, while Captain Wings fought the mysterious Mr. Atlantis for the world's mineral resources and Suicide Smith met the Jivaro tribesmen of Vengeance Valley accompanied by some super John Celardo cheesecake, Captain West came back with "The Adventure of the Polish Bride."

This one came to him in the form of a letter from one of its leading actors, Lt. John Howland, whose sweetheart Hulda was being treated in West Germany for amnesia. Howland thinks the treatment is too rough on Hulda—every time she gets back a flash of memory she bursts into terrified screams.

He breaks in and removes Hulda at gunpoint, steals a Bell P-63 King Cobra fighter plane, and heads with Hulda for her home town in Poland. (At least the war was over in this story.) A ghostly voice comes over Howland's radio, and a ghost monoplane appears, both offering to guide Howland to Hulda's home town. They land and see a ghostly vision of Polish cavalry, then in an old and half-wrecked church they come upon—Hulda's mother! An ancient crone, looking a bit like the actress Maria Ouspenskaya, whom you may remember from the *Wolfman* films.

"I know you," says mama. "I knew you would come back for the wedding. I have waited a long time for you."

Hulda falls to her knees and begs, "Tell me what happened, Mama. I can't remember anything. Please tell me, Mama!"

But mama only says, "Don't touch me! Do you understand? Don't touch me!"

What's this? Hardly standard comic-book fare.

Howland addresses mama: "Listen—Hulda's been sick—she's got to know who she is—so speak up and tell her what you know!"

Mama points to a stained-glass window, where Howland looks and sees a scene from the past. He sees a Polish cavalry encampment in 1939, sees Hulda and a handsome Polish officer, Leopold, who was her fiancé.

Now Hulda, too, sees the vision of the past. She sees herself climbing a tower the night before her wedding. She sees herself sending military information to the German agent Kurt in return for jewels to wear at her wedding. "Such a little work for such a grand present," the ghostly Hulda whispers as she sends off a carrier pigeon to Kurt.

But in the morning there is no wedding. With Hulda and John Howland we see the German forces smashing into Poland, Leopold leading a futile, courageous cavalry charge against Panzer armor. We see Leopold crushed beneath Nazi tank-treads.

And now, back in the present we hear Hulda scream: "Forgive me, Leopold! I didn't understand they would butcher my people!" Hulda plunges from the church window and dies on the ground.

Her mother, in proper Ouspenskaya fashion, comments, "It is better so, for now she can make her peace with those she betrayed."

Heavy, heavy stuff for comics.

And then there was the story of "The Room of a Million Windows," one of the rare successful multilevel fantasies ever created. If you're wondering what I mean by a multilevel fantasy, you'll see in a minute.

The scene is set in a ghostly looking but luxurious drawing room where beautifully gowned figures of women and impeccable gentlemen in evening dress are gathered around a chess board. The players are two lovely women. One is blonde, and wears a peach-colored gown that demonstrates her attractions in standard *Wings Comics* fashion. Her opponent has black hair, wears harlequin eyeglasses, a low-cut red gown, and long, sophisticated red gloves; in one hand she holds a foot-long cigarette-holder.

Outside a window, amazingly, can be seen an American Navy plane and a Japanese fighter of World War II vintage engaged in a deadly dogfight. (Ah, World War II was back on, we see.)

A narration panel reads: "Nobody knows the whereabouts of the *room of a million windows* ... and there is no name for *the sisters* who wage their endless duel there ... nor can you tell when your number will flash across that mystic screen of fate, and a finger will point, and a voice speak ... "

Yes, as the two strange sisters pursue their game of chess, we realize that they are controlling destiny, that the participants in the aerial battle correspond to the pieces on the board, that the moves in the chess game are reflected in the war outside!

The dark sister takes the lead in the game. The American plane is shot down, its two-man crew find themselves in a Pacific jungle. One man is courageous, he wants to hide in the jungle, continue the war. His companion is weak, cowardly; when Japanese searchers invite their surrender over a loudspeaker he wants to give up. The Japanese now set out through the jungle after the Americans.

And in that celestial gaming room, the sisters discuss their game:

"See, sister, it is all over. You have no chance. Shall we start another game?"

"No! I don't concede. I still have another move on the board. There—that's it!"

Back in the jungle the two Americans quarrel. A Japanese scout overhears them, throws a grenade. Broken bodies are hauled away.

In the room of a million windows: "The game is over, sister. Your move was feeble. Now I have you checkmated."

"Not yet. You overlooked this piece. There's still a chance."

Back on earth, a Japanese surgeon speaks to a military man.

"That one is dead, honorable captain. But there is a chance this one might live."

And now we see the ghosts of the two Americans. The courageous one is eager to get back into his body and back into the war. The coward is a coward still: "It isn't fair," he complains, "I wanted to surrender."

The doctor works furiously, but there is a bright flash in the room as the electricity short-circuits, and in the celestial setting we hear the light sister complain to the dark: "You cheated! You upset a piece! And just as I was recovering, too!"

"Why, sister," her opponent answers, "everything is fair in this game. It's your move."

"But—but you've put the coward's spirit in my strong one's body. You've weakened my strategy. Still, I'll play on."

And on earth the ghost of the brave flier watches dismayed as his body recovers with the weakling's spirit in it! The Japanese get the coward to sell out, to broadcast for them, and finally to lead a flight of Mitsubishi 00s against an American carrier.

Tension builds amazingly as Captain West cuts between the pending battle on earth and the chess game in the room of a million windows, until the light sister (playing white) moves a piece.

"So, you finally moved, eh, sister?" gloats her foe, moving her own, red piece. "It was very stupid indeed. I have you nicely cornered now."

"Ah, sister," replies white, "you fell into my trap! Watch this."

"You ... you've broken my defense ... stolen the weak piece and put the strong in its place!"

And outside we see a Zero being hit by something bright. "The lightning ball—my chance to regain my body!" exclaims the brave flier's ghost. "And I did it ... I'm back in my own body again. Now I'll show those Nips something!"

And so, to the successful conclusion of the battle, while above the light sister gloats, "It's over, sister. I've won again!"

Wow!

Wings Comics struggled on until 1954, its aviators switching from old prop-driven craft to jets, switching as the times changed from the foes of World War II to criminals and spies, to Communist agents and Korean, Chinese, and Soviet enemies, but somehow the fun had gone out of war. There was no more glamour to it, no more excitement. It had become a dirty, ugly, and depressing business, and even the bright colors, the square-jawed heroes, the leggy and busty heroines of *Wings Comics* couldn't make it fun again.

So *Wings* died, the last of the old-fashioned, pure pulp-type air-war comics, in 1954. The last issue carried a brave slogan: *"All NEW! Jet Aces of Warbird Skies!"* But the genre was played out. Other aviation comics came to other fates—and of course, when I opened this chapter I mentioned *Wings, Military*, and *Air Fighters* as the great three, and then talked only about *Wings*. The others are a different story, and I'll tell it in another chapter.

But *Wings* could just never get over its infatuation with war, and when the American people fell out of love with war, *Wings* had nowhere to go, and so it ended, an idea whose time had come . . . and gone.

INTRODUCTION TO

FRANKENSTEIN MEETS THE COMICS

DON Glut, Chicagoan transplanted to Los Angeles and onetime publisher of a fan magazine portentously titled *Shazam*, combines several fascinating interests in his daily activities. A devotee of the fantastic in the cinema, a student and creator of comic books, and probably the world's leading authority on the famous Frankenstein monster in all of its incarnations, he presents here an examination of that famous creature's many encounters with the paneled page.

Himself a comic-book writer of no mean talent, Don has contributed stories to a number of publishers, the greatest portion of his work going to Gold Key. For that firm he has written many one-shot stories featured in the *Mystery Digest* series, as well as creating several continuing characters, including the rather nicely worked out barbarian-action-fantasy hero Dagar.

He has also written a series of novels featuring the Frankenstein monster. By an oddity of the publishing business, they have appeared, to date, only in Spanish translation. In case you read Spanish and would like to seek out copies, their titles are *Frankenstein resucitado, Frankenstein y el Robot, Los huesos de Frankenstein, Frankenstein y Dracula, Frankenstein y el Hombre Lobo, Frankenstein en el Mundo Perdido, Frankenstein y la Momia, Frankenstein y el Gorila, Frankenstein y el Dr. Jekyll, El horror de Frankenstein,* and *Frankenstein y el Vampiro*. You don't have to be much of a linguist to figure out the meanings of most of those titles!

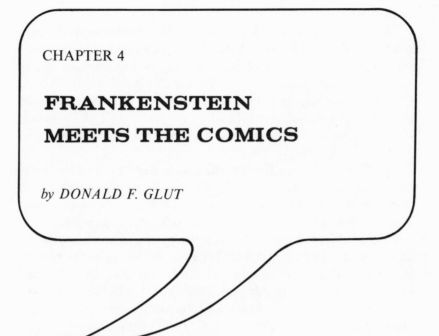

CHAPTER 4

FRANKENSTEIN
MEETS THE COMICS

by DONALD F. GLUT

DR. Victor Frankenstein stared at the giant form lying on a platform in his laboratory. The creature was at least 15 feet tall, assembled from parts of many corpses and covered with a white sheet.

In his enthusiasm Victor Frankenstein thought he had created a perfect man. A lightning storm raged in the bleak heavens as he eagerly manipulated the controls of his laboratory apparatus. When the giant humanoid received the life-giving jolts of electricity, it sat up on the platform. Victor stared into the face of his living creation, oblivious to the ghastly features he himself had stitched together. Perhaps he did plan to give the creature a new face. But with the absentmindedness of most unorthodox scientists, he had overlooked that single detail.

The face of the being was that of a hideous monster. The dead white flesh barely covered the misshapen skull. The blood-gashed forehead was high with stringy black hair hanging in uneven lengths almost to the shoulders. The two bulging orbs rarely looked in the same direction. A skeletal stub, which Victor assumed to be a nose, was set up between the eyes. The lips were torn to reveal a set of ugly teeth. Despite the proximity of the wretched face, the scientist failed to recognize the potential horror he had created.

The actual blame for the creation of this Frankenstein monster belongs to Richard Briefer. A previous appearance of the monster had been an adaptation of the film *Son of Frankenstein* in the premiere issue of *Movie Comics* (April, 1939), published by Picture Comics (now National Periodical Publications). But this was presented as a one-shot combination of movie stills and artwork. It was Briefer who took the Frankenstein concept and developed it into a series.

Apparently Richard Briefer had always been a fan of the novel *Frankenstein*, written by Mary Wollstonecraft Shelley in 1818, and of the series of *Frankenstein* movies then being made by Universal Pictures. Both seemed to have greatly influenced his work.

Before he actually utilized that concept of a scientist creating a monstrous living being, Briefer began to do his own experimenting. Briefer had been writing and illustrating *Rex Dexter, Interplanetary Adventurer* in *Mystery Men Comics*, published by Fox. Rex was a poor man's Flash Gordon who rocketed about the universe battling unearthly menaces. In the fifth issue of *Mystery Men Comics*, (December, 1939), Rex defeated a fiendish robot with a squarish head, sunken cheeks, black hair and bangs, and a pair of electrodes protruding from the head. The robot was obviously patterned after the Frankenstein monster of Universal Pictures and was virtually the face of Briefer's own future monster.

Taking the basic facial structure of Universal's Frankenstein monster (high forehead, straight black hair and bangs, and scars) and altering it enough to avoid any problems with copyright infringement, Briefer put his monster into a comic strip and tried selling it professionally. He was not one of the upper echelon of comic-book writers and artists and never would be. His style was simply too loose and unfinished looking to compete with the work of some of the fine draftsmen then seeing their work printed. Therefore he took his series to Feature Publications' *Prize Comics* (the title which gave that comic-book line the name of Prize Group), where he sold it under the title *New Adventures of Frankenstein*, supposedly written and drawn by "Frank N. Stein." (Naturally no one believed that the pseudonym was authentic. Fans of *Rex Dexter* could immediately recognize Briefer's style, which during the 1940s would be applied to a few more strips, including *Pirate Prince* in *Silver Streak* and *Daredevil Comics*,

Dick Briefer's Frankenstein monster series, *New Adventures of Frankenstein*, appeared in Feature Publications' *Prize Comics*. Briefer signed the work "Frank N. Stein."

published by Lev Gleason.)

Prize Comics, which made its debut in March, 1940, was one of the more successful magazines primarily featuring superheroes in the forties. National, Timely, and Fawcett led the field in the superhero business. *Prize Comics'* star characters included the Black Owl, who did his best to imitate the Batman; Doctor Frost, who controlled coldness as an opposite of the Human Torch; the Great Voodini, who seemed to have been a fan of Mandrake the Magician; and Power Nelson, a futuristic imitation of Superman who traveled to the twentieth century. None of the *Prize* heroes could compete with the original characters who inspired them. It would take an ugly antihero like the Frankenstein monster to give the magazine its special distinction.

When the monster came to life in Frankenstein's laboratory its movements were sporadic. Inadvertently the creature knocked his creator unconscious, then fled the castle to find his place in the world. As expected, the ugly beast was persecuted wherever he went. He experienced happiness for the first time in his short life when he came upon the cabin of a blind man who fed and befriended him. When the blind man's son returned to the cabin and found his father in the company of a 15-foot-tall horror, he blasted the creature with a shotgun. The monster was driven away by an angry mob who attacked him with clubs and stones. Briefer merely adapted these first four pages, which appeared in *Prize Comics* No. 7 (December, 1940), from the plotline of Mary Shelley's novel. The Frankenstein castle and fantastic laboratory reflected Briefer's own interest in the Universal movies and an attempt to present what was already familiar to filmgoers.

Readers had been led to believe that the Frankenstein story was set many years earlier in the wilds of Central Europe. But those who read the *Prize* version were surprised to learn that the hideous monster had been created not far from Manhattan ... in 1940!

After the Frankenstein monster committed the cardinal sin of throwing two children into a lion's cage, the fiend caused some more destruction, then climbed to the top of the Statue of Liberty. Obviously Briefer was drawing on the popular images created by the monster movies. Anyone who had seen the movies' King Kong ascend the Empire State Building could not help but make the association. Atop the Statue of Liberty, the monster snatched people from the crown and dashed them to their deaths. Luckily, with the coincidence typical of the comic books, Victor Frankenstein was in the vicinity with his fiancée, Elizabeth. Victor ascended the crown and leaped upon his murderous creation. He missed the fiend and landed in the Statue's left arm. Instead of crushing his maker, the monster gently placed him within the crown. As the police opened fire with their guns, the bullet-ridden giant plummeted—again like Kong—to an apparent death beneath the waters off Bedloe's Island.

Later, Victor wondered why the monster had saved his life. Suddenly there was a crash of glass and the fiend loomed through the broken window. "I *spared* you to *live*—to live in *misery* also—to *watch* and *see* the *suffering* and *grief* that *I, your creation*, will cause the *human race*. You will *chase* me, but *never get me! I go now*, always *haunting* and *tormenting* you!"

Victor was still brooding over the horror he had unleashed upon the world in *Prize* No. 8 (January, 1941). Realizing that such misery was the result of creating a soulless creature, Frankenstein resolved to destroy the monster in the only practical way. He would build another! And the second monster would be even less human than the original. This monster had the head and paws of a giant crocodile and the brain of a madman. Frankenstein should have known better.

The reptilian horror and the Frankenstein monster fought atop Radio City. Although the crocodile-man should have been the winner, the monster killed him and escaped via an elevator shaft to a subway excavation. Apparently Victor had not considered the consequences had the reptile-man won.

The Frankenstein monster had become the greatest supervillain in *Prize Comics*. As the *Prize* superheroes were occupied with their own lesser adversaries, someone was needed to battle the monster on more equal terms. Victor Frankenstein was becoming so neurotic over the monster's every new crime that disposing of the brute would obviously have to be someone else's responsibility. While not equaling the monster in size and raw strength, his new adversary would have enough courage and sheer goodness to combat even so terrible a fiend.

A young boy named Denny was the sole survivor of an automobile crash caused by the monster. Denny's parents were killed in the wreck and Frankenstein felt responsible. The boy's legs were injured and only the surgical skill of Frankenstein saved him. But Denny was forced to remain in a wheelchair. Frankenstein resolved to completely cure the boy, seemingly aging 20

93

years under the strain. While the monster commanded the criminal underworld and continued to war against humanity, Denny received periodic treatments. During the ten years following his cure Denny lived as the ward of the broken Dr. Frankenstein, training himself to physical perfection. Wearing a black riding outfit and a pin with a picture of his pet bulldog Spike, the young man became a superhero of sorts with the single purpose of destroying Frankenstein's monster.

Dick Briefer may have been a fan of the old *Bulldog Drummond* stories. Drummond was a detective aided in his adventures by a valet named Denny. Just as Briefer had applied the Frankenstein concept to *Rex Dexter* he seemingly applied Bulldog Drummond to *Frankenstein* (the *New Adventures* and "Frank N. Stein" had been dropped). The Frankenstein monster had threatened to demolish New York's subway system. But Denny intervened, defeated the monster's hired thugs, and finally captured the giant himself. When a reporter photographed Denny running from the scene and found the bulldog pin which had fallen from his black outfit, he ran the headline in the morning newspaper: " Bulldog' Captures Monster!" With the bulldog emblem on his chest, "Bulldog Denny" vowed to be the eternal enemy of the Frankenstein monster.

The ten years in which Denny grew into Bulldog Denny also affected the monster. In his original Briefer conception the monster was too large and powerful to be defeated by one even of Denny's prowess. During those years the monster had grown considerably smaller. And although he was still a hideous creature, his face lost most of the gruesome features that it had when first created.

When Victor Frankenstein was written out of the strip to be replaced by the more appealing Bulldog Denny, the monster assumed his name. Briefer had tried to remain accurate by not calling the monster "Frankenstein." But the public had already been confusing the monster with his maker for years and finally Briefer went along with the trend. Frankenstein, as he was now called, continued his battles against humanity, at one time even going to Hell to team up with the Black Owl's demonic adversary Doctor Devil (*Prize Comics* No. 22, July, 1942) until Denny proved his goodness by defeating both of them.

The United States had entered World War II. Bulldog Denny knew that in Germany there existed a monster far worse than

The second appearance of Dick Briefer's Frankenstein monster was in *Prize* No. 8, January 1941. The monster spares Victor Frankenstein's life so that he may live and suffer.

Frankenstein. The hero was called to Washington for defense work in *Prize Comics* No. 24 (October, 1942). But Frankenstein was still at large and a terrible threat. Before he left for Washington, Bulldog Denny called together a strange group whose combined efforts, he hoped, would demolish the creature called Frankenstein.

Seated around the table and addressed by Bulldog Denny were a number of heroes who had been respectively battling evil in their own strips in *Prize Comics*. There was the Black Owl, in reality wealthy idler and playboy Doug Danville, who put on a blue-and-red costume with cape and owl mask to battle injustice using only his developed skills and strength. Also seated at the table were Yank and Doodle, in reality Dick and Rick Walters, who donned star-spangled costumes to become "America's Fighting Twins," junior versions of Captain America, to fight for Uncle Sam. There was Doctor Frost, who had no secret identity, wore a blue-and-green outfit, and used his freezing abilities to put evildoers on ice. The Green Lama, a character adapted from the pulp magazines, wore a monk's green garb and used supernatural powers to combat evil. Finally among the group were the General and the Corporal, the bumbling stars of a humor strip then being run in *Prize Comics*.

All of these stalwarts had their own favorite villains in *Prize Comics*. But none of them had ever encountered so enduring a monster as Frankenstein.

The Black Owl, once the most popular *Prize* hero and usually featured on the covers (until the introduction of Yank and Doodle some issues earlier), was the first to tackle Frankenstein. The costumed hero used his greatest weapons—his fists—on the monster. But, unlike Bulldog Denny, he was not experienced in battling Frankenstein. The Black Owl would have been dashed off the side of a cliff if the General had not shot the Corporal from a cannon smack into the rear of the monster's head.

Using the powers that he had acquired in Tibet, the Green Lama spoke the mystic words, "Om! Mani padme hum!" Immediately the most loathsome of monstrosities seemed to appear before Frankenstein. Unable to overcome the horrors, Frankenstein fled from them and into the slamming fists of Yank and Doodle.

Being battered by two young boys in Halloween costumes was certainly the most degrading encounter of all for Frankenstein.

Captain America and Bucky battled the revived monster in "The Curse of Frankenstein,"
published in USA Comics No. 13 (Summer 1944). Copyright © 1944, Marvel Comics
Group, renewed 1972, and reprinted by its permission. Copyright © 1974 by Marvel
Comics Group. All Rights Reserved.

But even though they gave the brute a workout, they could not accomplish what even Bulldog Denny had failed to do. Leaping at the monster head first, Yank and Doodle fell to the ground with Frankenstein-sized headaches.

Exhausted, the monster fled from *Prize's* one-shot imitation of National's Justice Society of America. It took Doctor Frost a single panel to do what all the other heroes combined had failed to do. As Frankenstein dove from a cliff to the water below, Doctor Frost gestured. Frankenstein's head crashed hard into a sea of solid ice, knocking him cold.

Even after such a defeat, Frankenstein revived and continued his war on mankind. The real war was still going on and patriotic readers knew that there were heroes whose courage and fighting ability rivaled even that of the Black Owl, the Green Lama, and the rest of the *Prize* roster of superheroes. In the thirty-third issue of the magazine (August, 1943), Frankenstein was captured by the combined might of the armed forces.

Frankenstein was about to enter a new phase of his artificial life. He had already lost his stark white complexion and had acquired normally toned flesh. A scientist named Professor Carrol, feeling that Frankenstein had never been given a chance in life because people hated him for his appearance, defended him in court. Despite the horrendous crimes perpetrated by the monster for so many years, he was given over to the doctor for treatment.

Professor Carrol's transformation of Frankenstein into a decent citizen involved special injections, hypnosis and psychiatric treatments, and the services of a plastic surgeon, barber, and tailor. Carrol changed the beast into a mild-tempered "Mister Frankenstein." The world would soon forget that he was once a terrible demon. Perhaps there was good reason to overlook his crimes. After all, could Frankenstein's evil acts really compete with the atrocities performed by the Nazis?

Dick Briefer began to change his style. His artwork had always been slightly cartoony. There was nothing wrong in being cartoony, especially since it gave Briefer's work a particular individuality, a quality lacking in so much comic art. Briefer must have realized that a horrible monster out to destroy humanity was hardly frightening considering the real horrors of those wartime years. He began to further exaggerate his drawings until the tone became almost that of a humor strip.

"Mister Frankenstein" was more than a mere human being. He

Frankenstein (now the name of the monster) took up residence in a haunted-looking old mansion in Mippyville where he was at home with the bats, rats, and spiders.

was an American who felt the urge to do what virtually all American comic-book heroes were doing in 1943—fight the Nazis. With Frankenstein added to the list of *Prize* heroes, other comic-book companies' heroes, and John Wayne battling the Germans, it seemed like Hitler and his maniacs had little chance for survival.

In *Prize Comics* No. 34 (September, 1943) Briefer did one of his rare non-Frankenstein stints for that magazine, drawing the final installment of *The Green Lama* (replaced the next issue by *The Flying Fist and Bingo*, another superhero strip). The issue was also significant in that *The Black Owl* and *Yank and Doodle* were united into a single feature. Frankenstein began his new life by attending school, beginning with the first grade. The entire flavor of the magazine was changing. Emphasis was placed on youth (the Black Owl playing second banana to Yank and Doodle), especially with the introduction of *Buck Saunders and His Pals*, another "kid gang" strip by Joe Simon and Jack Kirby. There was hardly room for the gore and horror so prevalent in the early *Frankenstein* stories. Still there was a considerable helping of murder and violence interspersed with the humor of a bumbling giant in grammar school.

Frankenstein fought Nazi spies on the home front until *Prize Comics* No. 39 (February, 1944). The Gestapo captured the giant, drugged him, and entrusted him to a Nazi scientist who undid everything Professor Carrol had accomplished. For a while Europe was haunted by a hideous creature in a Gestapo uniform, who brutally killed anyone failing to raise his arm and exclaim "Heil Hitler!" Eventually Frankenstein escaped his special treatments and regained his red-white-and-blue memory and patriotism. For a while he worked as an undercover agent against the Nazis, sabotaging trains and wiping out German troops from the sidelines, until he was discovered and forced to flee for his unnatural life.

For a while Frankenstein came under the influence of a vampiress named Zora, who turned him into a kind of Jekyll and Hyde. By day he was "Mister Frankenstein" and by night he was the hideous beast set upon the world by Victor Frankenstein. Frankenstein eventually drove Zora away with garlic and was able to settle down to a peaceful existence.

More changes were taking place in the format of *Prize Comics*. Many of the once-popular superheroes were forced to surrender their places to a new plethora of humor strips. Within a few issues strips like *Ham and Eggs*, about a pig and a rooster, *Sir Prize*, knight of the Castle Booboo, *Peter Pelican and Grouper*, and *Caveman Frolics* dominated its pages. With the end of World War II the editors of *Prize Comics* apparently felt that their audience would prefer to breathe more easily and see gags instead of violence. People wanted to laugh.

With the new format of *Prize Comics* Frankenstein was given a stitched cut running down the middle of his forehead. His face had already changed to a travesty of its former appearance. The peg of a nose simply couldn't have been placed any higher above the eyes. The changes were gradual and there was no break in story continuity. And yet the creature now claiming to be Frankenstein was in fact the very same monstrosity that once terrorized New York and threw innocent children to the lions.

Frankenstein was no longer a mildly humorous strip but outright comedy using funny versions of the old horror characters. The creature with a transplanted heart of gold now lived in a ridiculous world of inane vampires, werewolves, mummies, ghouls, and related fiends. This horror-humor strip predated a similar television series, *The Munsters*, by about 20 years.

When *Frankenstein* became a humor strip, Dick Briefer went wild. His already loose style exploded to the point that he often did not pencil his work but inked right from scratch. He worked so fast that when he used up his supply of drawing board he scribbled his drawings on the back of wallpaper. To further economize, Briefer, when using drawing board, cut it in half in order to get two pages of finished artwork for every one page of board.

Frankenstein was so popular in his humorous incarnation that the publisher of *Prize Comics* awarded the brute his own 48-page comic book. *Frankenstein* No. 1 appeared in 1945 ("By Popular Demand!" as the cover boasted). With the new book Briefer was able to do something he should have done much earlier—give Frankenstein a new origin and attempt to sever his connection with the old gruesome monster. That was fine for new readers of the feature. But for those trying to reconcile the original *Frankenstein* strip with the new version running in *Frankenstein* and *Prize Comics* it provided only confusion.

An anonymous mad scientist tried to eliminate his boredom in "Frankenstein's Creation" in the first issue. His black cat acted the role of Fate by accidentally knocking a book from the shelf.

The mad scientist stared at the book through his thick spectacles. It was *Frankenstein* by Mary Wollstonecraft Shelley.

Inspired by the book, the mad scientist resolved to create "the most terrible beast man or animal has ever known!!" Taking his shopping list to a shady undertaker, he purchased such necessary ingredients as "two eyes, two ears, a forehead, half a nose, some lungs, a stomach, a half pound of hair, black preferably—quarter pound of cream cheese—" Even mad doctors can mix up their shopping lists.

After Frankenstein came to life in the scientist's laboratory, he was injected with a drug capable of giving a rabbit the ferocity of a lion. To the doctor's disappointment, Frankenstein loved flowers and animals and would no more think of attacking the human race than of harming an ant. After escaping an explosion, which destroyed the mad scientist in his castle, Frankenstein set out to resume the absurd existence he was already enjoying in *Prize Comics*.

Frankenstein took up residence in a haunted-looking old mansion in Mippyville (given to him by the mayor) where he was at home with the bats and spiders. He eventually married his dream woman, a hideous creature who proved to be a domineering social climber and a nag. After a quick divorce Frankenstein went back to a solitary life. Later he joined a type of commune of freaky characters such as the hag Awful Annie and other impossible creatures.

More changes were occurring within the pages of *Prize Comics*. Westerns were enjoying new popularity due to the influence of motion pictures, radio, and that new medium, television, which was beginning to run the old theatrical cowboy films. The publishers of *Prize Comics* agreed that sales might be increased if cowboys replaced the funny animals, *Yank and Doodle* ("starring" *The Black Owl*), and *Frankenstein*. *Prize Comics* No. 68 (February-March, 1948) opened with *Harry Tracy, Last of the Western Bad-Men*. It was the last issue to feature *Frankenstein, Yank and Doodle*, and others, including Briefer's one-shot *Max the Magician*, which was even sloppier than *Frankenstein*. In April of that year, the sixty-ninth issue of *Prize* became *Prize Western*. The following year *Frankenstein* No. 17 (January-February), the cover of which depicted "Franky" high above the city standing before a huge clock and about to be impaled by a madman using a clock hand as a spear, was the final issue of the humorous series.

Frankenstein and its association with Dick Briefer seemed defunct—at least for the next three years.

But comic-book trends run in cycles. During the early 1950s a new phenomenon emerged to replace the superheroes who had dominated the color pages since the late 1930s. The superheroes, with the exception of a few seemingly immortal characters like Superman and Batman, were hanging up their tights, capes, and masks and going into retirement. Readers no longer wanted stories of mystery men zooming through the air and thwarting crime. They craved stories of vampires, werewolves, and zombies told in realistic fashion. The more grisly the scenes depicted, the more blood and dismembered limbs, the better. The new heroes were crypt and vault keepers who chortled gleefully as a vampire sank his fangs into the throat of a young maiden or as a henpecked husband chopped his wife up into little pieces and used them in some ghastly method of revenge.

The time was ripe for the return of the Frankenstein monster, but not the blundering boob who preferred sniffing daisies to snapping spines. The Prize Group decided to continue *Frankenstein* with the eighteenth issue (March, 1952), again with Dick Briefer writing and drawing. But Briefer's drawing style had to be considerably revamped in order to meet the standards established by the other companies publishing horror comics. Despite the gore, the new readers of comic books would not have accepted the cartoony Frankenstein of the early *Prize Comics* issues. Briefer had to discipline himself.

Frankenstein No. 18 began an entirely new story-line with Briefer's individualistic art style in its most sophisticated form. Though still not up to the caliber of some of the better artists working for the competition, his drawings were never swiped from other sources and seemed extremely appropriate for *Frankenstein*.

Briefer's latest and final version of the Frankenstein monster was still based on the previous concepts. The beast had a high forehead, flat head, and a ridiculously small nose up between the eyes. Among the innovations were an open wound with torn stitches that revealed the skull underneath and a torn lipless mouth that showed the misshapen teeth even when the brute's mouth was closed. There were more ghastly features about the 1940 Frankenstein monster, but the 1952 version was even less pleasant to behold owing to the more realistic style in which it was rendered.

As always, Briefer took care not to bring down the wrath of Universal Pictures for using their copyrighted Frankenstein monster face. The basic features, including the distorted excuse for a face, suggested the Boris Karloff monster. The obvious trappings were changed. Karloff's stitchless scar was moved from the side of the forehead to the center, and all of the Universal monster's metal clips and electrodes were eliminated.

In "The Rebirth of the Monster" two villagers broke into the castle of the Frankensteins, which had not been opened in a century, to learn if the old legends about Henry Frankenstein creating a monster were true. (After 11 years of "Victor," Briefer now chose to use the name "Henry" in conformance with the character in Peggy Webling's stage play of 1927 and the 1931 movie starring Karloff.) Lying on a slab next to the skeleton of its creator was the giant monster. The sudden rush of cold air that accompanied the villagers' entrance also brought them death, for it revived the monster. Both were crushed by the creature's enormous hands.

Reborn, the Frankenstein monster ravaged the village. Bullets did not stop the monster, for Henry Frankenstein had given him a leathery flesh that sealed as soon as a bullet penetrated. In these small Central European towns (especially prevalent in Universal's *Frankenstein* movies, on which Briefer patterned his current locale), no one ever thought of calling the army to blast apart an eight-foot-tall giant. It was more fun to take up blazing torches and garden rakes and clubs and form a mob to pursue and destroy the monster.

The great-grandson of Henry Frankenstein flew to Europe from the United States to destroy his ancestor's creation. Believing the descendant to be his creator, the monster relaxed its guard and received a burning torch in the face. In agony, the monster jumped into the water. Frankenstein realized that he had been spared to experience the horror brought upon the world by his ancestor.

Briefer's earlier versions of the Frankenstein monster were hardly reticent. The new version, however, was designed more for the benefit of readers familiar with the Universal movies, wherein the monster was usually speechless. They could more readily identify with the new conception, which never uttered a word or received as much as a single thought balloon. The monster's thoughts were a mystery and the technique seemed to work.

Young Dr. Frankenstein pursued the monster, which had stowed away aboard his America-bound ship. In the United States the doctor last saw the monster destroying some foreign spies before the laboratory in which they were hiding blew up in *Frankenstein* No. 19 (Summer, 1952). He was written out of the series, leaving the monster to roam across the countryside encountering such creatures and fiends as Indian zombies, a scientist who devolved lizards into dinosaurs and evolved a wildcat into a beautiful girl, and a Mexican werewolf.

Seemingly Briefer assumed that his new audience had not read or at least would not remember his early stories in *Prize Comics* and the humorous *Frankenstein*. He never stole the poses for his drawings but he did reuse or at least adapt from his own past plots. The sources didn't really seem to matter. Briefer had already adapted stories from his first *Prize* series into the funny series. By the 1950s, Briefer had *two* past series to rewrite into "new" stories.

"The Monster's Mate" in *Frankenstein* No. 23 (February-March, 1953) was based on a story from *Prize Comics* No. 26 (December, 1942) in which a scientist created a female horror for the monster, only to have her destroyed by the usual mob of villagers. In the new story the monster, now mysteriously back in Central Europe, befriended an ugly giant woman from a circus. When she was killed by the townspeople, the monster, as had his predecessor in the forties, lashed out with a terrible vengeance. This story was only partially based on the *Prize* tale, since the original involved the creation of a female monster. *That* part of the story was eventually adapted to *Frankenstein* No. 28 (December-January, 1954), "The She-Monster," in which a mad doctor brought a murderess back to life as a companion for the monster.

In the thirtieth issue of the magazine (April-May, 1954), now with the cover title of *The Monster of Frankenstein,* Briefer had a sculptor pour molten bronze over the monster in order to form a perfect, life-sized statue. When the bronze hardened the monster ripped his way out, grabbed the whimpering sculptor, and poured liquid bronze down his throat. This time Briefer hit the jackpot. The plot had already been used in the original *Prize* series *and* in the humorous *Frankenstein* book.

Briefer's plots were now showing less imagination than in earlier years. It was becoming standard and expected to see the monster trusting some questionable character who only planned to use the giant for his own ends, probably eventually to eliminate him in some grisly fashion. The monster would learn of the treachery and inflict upon the puny human the same terrible death. The stories were gradually becoming caricatures of the stories that began with *Frankenstein* No. 18. The lack of care and originality didn't really matter anymore. A monster more powerful than the one created by Frankenstein, and with an even more distorted mind, had appeared to threaten the comic-book industry.

Comic books in general, but especially horror and crime comics, were being attacked by that most terrible of monsters—censorship. Primarily through the efforts of Dr. Fredric Wertham in a series of magazine articles and in his book *Seduction of the Innocent*, people were told that comic books were the greatest evil ever to infect humanity. Wertham cited case upon case wherein emotionally disturbed children from questionable environments had read comic books before embarking on lives as juvenile delinquents. Naturally it followed that every delinquent child in the country was made that way because he read comic books. It certainly seemed logical to parents trying to find a scapegoat for their own failure to raise their children correctly. (This was years before it was "proved" that television and movie violence was the real culprit.) A scapegoat was needed and comic books conveniently provided one. Some horror and crime comics published at the time were in offensively bad taste. But the whole industry was under attack and with the mass panic spreading, so that dealers would not place horror and crime comics on the display racks, the publishers tossed in their towels, coffins, and torture devices.

The Comics Code Authority was established, forbidding the necessary ingredients of the horror comics. By the beginning of 1955 there would be no more horror comics in the fifties tradition.

The publishers of the Prize Group of comics could see the hysteria coming and knew that the book had little future. Since the twentieth issue only one *Frankenstein* story was run per book, the others being nonseries horror and science-fiction fillers. With the thirtieth issue two *Frankenstein* stories appeared per book. These were tales originally scheduled for issues that would never be printed. The gruesome *Frankenstein* could never pass the restrictions of the Comics Code, and the publishers were using up the inventory while they could.

The cover of *Frankenstein* No. 33 (October-November, 1954)

Syd Shores's Frankenstein monster in "The Monster Returns," *Marvel Tales*, June 1950, was depicted as having pointed ears, fangs, and claws. Copyright © 1950, Marvel Comics Group, and reprinted by its permission. Copyright © 1974 by Marvel Comics Group. All Rights Reserved.

was historical and mildly nostalgic. The art was a serious version of the last issue of the funny series, with the monster about to be harpooned by the clock hand. The last story in the book, "Frankenstein and the Plant," was about a mad scientist who developed a carnivorous plant whose buds assumed the shape of its last meal. Naturally the story ended with the plant's buds looking exactly like the face of the scientist who provided its last dinner. The story had been done before, when Frankenstein was a friendly oaf. There was no longer any reason for Briefer to show much originality. *Frankenstein* No. 33 was the swansong issue.

Dick Briefer proved that a monster could survive in a world of superheroes (at least in the Prize Group lineup). He took an established character, adapted it to the tastes of contemporary comic-book readers, and eventually evolved that character from a hideous monstrosity to a patriotic citizen to a bumbling dumbbell, and finally to a misunderstood misanthrope in a world of prejudiced human beings. It was this final version of the Frankenstein monster with which I first came into contact in 1954. I had always been enthralled by the concept of Frankenstein and was delighted to see that the monster had his own comic book. Unfortunately the issue I bought from the newsstands for a dime was the second to last. And I somehow missed the last! But that single issue of *Frankenstein* had appeal, as did the Universal movies featuring the character. Years passed before I was able to acquire a complete run of *Frankenstein* (*not* for the original cover prices!) and learned that Briefer had been developing the strip since 1940.

Comic books numbering in the thousands have used the Frankenstein monster or theme, if we consider individual stories published all over the world. But Briefer's version, enduring from 1940 to 1954, was the only one with the necessary appeal to make it a success for such a long period. Perhaps the drawing and even the scripting were not up to par with some of the competition. But to those of us who had read Mary Shelley's *Frankenstein* or seen the Universal movies, Briefer's series (including the funny version) had all the right elements.

With the arrival of the Comics Code, the Prize Group ceased all publication of horror comics. Editorship of the line eventually changed over to Joe Simon and Jack Kirby, who continued doing romance stories, mystery stories, and a few other types of books before the Prize Group went completely out of business. Briefer freelanced, working for companies like Marvel Comics, until he

In the "Your Name Is Frankenstein" series, the monster spent years digging his way to the surface from a bog swamp.

too, unfortunately, vanished from the scene.

While Briefer's Frankenstein monster waited in limbo to be reborn in 1952, the American Comics Group (ACG) introduced its own series, *Spirit of Frankenstein*, in *Adventures into the Unknown* No. 5 (June-July, 1949). The ACG horror stories were always tame by comparison with those published by other companies. Dr. Lambert Pardway resented his young colleague Dr. Warren for the fame he had acquired in the scientific world. The latest acheivement of Dr. Warren was inventing a giant robot with a bald head and plastic "skin." The crafty Pardway talked Warren into placing his brain into the robot upon his death. Inadvertently Warren created another Frankenstein monster with the robot controlled by the evil mind of Pardway. For two years the series appeared randomly in *Adventures into the Unknown*. But to readers familiar with Briefer's work and the movies, this simply wasn't Frankenstein. In the sixteenth issue (February, 1951) the series was discontinued.

The most successful Frankenstein stories other than Briefer's were those that did not attempt to create a new or competing series.

In December, 1945, *Classic Comics* (now *Classics Illustrated*) devoted its twenty-sixth issue to an adaptation of Mary Shelley's *Frankenstein*. The script was faithfully written by Ruth A. Roche and interpreted by artists Robert Hayward Webb and Ann Brewster. Like Briefer, Webb and Brewster used some of the physical characteristics of the Universal movie monster, including placing bolts at the neck and joints. But the creature was given an almost black skin and was barefooted in order to make it different enough to avoid a lawsuit. Miss Roche was obviously extremely familiar with the original novel. Her breakdown as interpreted by the artists remains as a veritable storyboard for the definitive movie version of *Frankenstein*, if it is ever filmed.

Entertaining Comics (EC) published a number of Frankenstein-type stories, but only one of these, "The Monster in the Ice," in *The Vault of Horror* No. 22 (December-January, 1951–52), featured the original monster. The story was illustrated by "Ghastly" Graham Ingels and told of the discovery of the Frankenstein monster in a block of ice. Anyone who saw the monster's face went mad. That was understandable. In attempting to only suggest the Universal concept, Ingels created one of the most hideous versions ever to appear in a comic book. The eyes bulged

"Your Name Is Frankenstein," written by Stan Lee and drawn by Joe Maneely for *Menace* No. 7, September 1953. Copyright © 1953, Marvel Comics Group, and reprinted by its permission. Copyright © 1974 by Marvel Comics Group. All Rights Reserved.

from their sockets, enormous tusks protruded from the mouth, scraggy hair hung from the distorted head. Most other EC *Frankenstein* stories had relatively pleasant monsters. Jack Davis, with his ability to lend humor to an otherwise gruesome story, had a mad scientist create his own Frankenstein monster for a museum exhibit in "Mirror, Mirror, on the Wall" in *Tales from the Crypt* No. 34 (February-March, 1953) with his own adaptation from the Universal monster. Interestingly, most of the story was from the creature's point of view, from its first awakening in the laboratory to its final death in a hall of mirrors where it was frightened to death by its own multiple images. In the fortieth and final issue of *The Vault of Horror* (December–1954, January, 1955), in Ingels's "Ashes to Ashes," the Frankenstein line created a perfect baby girl after generations of developing what was originally a blob of earth. There was no longer any need to adapt the Universal monster for the Frankensteins had at last created a being of perfection.

The EC Frankenstein stories were always extremely literate and drawn by some of the best comic artists in the business. They usually ended with a shock ending after an emphasis on plot and characterization. The Atlas (now Marvel) horror comics of the period did their best to imitate the ECs, but stressed action and monsters over content. Atlas has the distinction of publishing more unrelated Frankenstein stories than any other company.

Captain America and Bucky battled the revived monster in "The Curse of Frankenstein," published in *USA Comics* No. 13 (Summer, 1944). The monster was eventually lured into a bog of quicksand. Although creatures purporting to be the original Frankenstein monster continued to appear in that company's comic books, it was obvious that they had not read this first story or did not remember any of their others. For instance, in *Blonde Phantom* No. 14 (Summer, 1947), in the story "Horror at Haunted Castle," the beautiful heroine fought a Baron Frankenstein who looked exactly like the monster. In the 1950s the Frankenstein monster appeared in *Marvel Tales* No. 96 (June, 1950) in "The Monster Returns" by Syd Shores, which depicted the beast with pointed ears, fangs, and claws. In "The Monster" by Paul Reinman, *Marvel Tales* No. 106, a very Universal-looking monster attacked a motion-picture crew in the Frankenstein castle. Jim Mooney created another Universal-type monster for his "Monster's Son" in *Strange Tales* No. 10 (September, 1952), which

BUT THE HORROR ON THE TRAVELER'S FACE IS NOT CAUSED BY ANYTHING SO HARMLESS OR INANIMATE AS A TREE -- EVEN A HAUNTED TREE. NO... THERE, LOOMING UP BEFORE HIM IS...

JUST BEFORE HIS LIFE IS SNUFFED OUT BY STEELY HANDS, THERE IS A LOUD EXPLOSION. THE DOOMED MAN NEVER KNEW IT WAS A ROAR OF THUNDER FROM A CLOUDBURST...

THERE IS A CRASH OF LIGHTNING... AND THE BOLTS HIT THE TREE...

...AND THE TREE, FIRST SPLIT, TOPPLES AND PULLS THE ROOTS FROM THE SOIL.

IT HAS BEEN A LONG TIME SINCE THE MONSTER HAS SEEN HIS LITTLE BIOLOGIST FRIEND, BUT ONCE MORE HE LOOKS DOWN UPON HIM...

DISINTERRED FROM THE GROUND IN WHICH HE HAS LAIN FOR SO LONG, THE BONES OF THE LITTLE MAN ARE STILL INTACT, AND BONES AND ROOTS OF THE TREE THAT SPRANG FROM HIS BODY ARE BOTH ENTWINED.

ONCE AGAIN THE TOWNSPEOPLE WILL FIND ANOTHER VICTIM OF THE "EVIL" TREE -- AND THEIR AMAZEMENT WILL BE COMPLETE WHEN THEY SEE WHAT IS ENTANGLED IN THE ROOTS. BUT NOW THE TREE IS DESTROYED, AND THE FRANKENSTEIN MONSTER NO LONGER NEED PROTECT IT. THE RAIN STILL FALLS AS HE GOES OFF...

THE END

Briefer's "The Tree of Death," *Frankenstein* No. 31, June-July 1954.

showed that the brute was a scientific genius capable of creating an offspring. Probably the best of these stories is "Your Name Is Frankenstein," written by Stan Lee and drawn by Joe Maneely, for *Menace* No. 7 (September, 1953). In this story the monster, after years of digging his way to the surface from a swamp bog, found the humans he tried to save as uncaring as always, and preferred to return to the earth. Perhaps the most unbelievable was "The Lonely Dungeon" in *Mystery Tales* No. 18 (March, 1954), which proved that it was the monster who created Dr. Frankenstein, and who was in turn built by the caretaker of his castle.

In March of 1963 Dell Comics published a version of *Frankenstein* adapted from the Universal movie of 1931. Three years later the second issue of *Frankenstein* (September, 1966) appeared on the newsstands. But this was not the Frankenstein that had appeared in the film. Frankenstein was now a superhero (to take part in the resurgence of such characters) who wore a red costume, sported a white crewcut, and fought criminals. Other characters that also began as one-shot movie adaptations (Dracula and the Werewolf) also became costumed crimefighters. Frankenstein adopted the secret identity of Frank Stone. But when a menace appeared on the scene Frank yanked off his rubber human mask and became Frankenstein to pit his superhuman strength and stamina against the forces of evil. The stories were poorly written and even more poorly drawn by Tony Tallarico. The series was a terrible idea to begin with. It died with *Frankenstein* No. 4 (March, 1967), with Frankenstein revealing that his familiar green countenance was also a mask. Someday his real face would be shown. But that someday never came. No one was sorry about it.

Frankenstein's monster has also been a series character in foreign countries. *Frankenstein*, published by Edicao la Selva from 1959 to 1960, was one of two series published in Rio de Janeiro. Some of the stories, mostly of the Briefer school, were swipes of both Briefer's plots and drawings. The monster, now called only Frankenstein, was a brutal killer who met up with a number of mad doctors and vampires. A second series from Rio de Janeiro, published in 1969 by Editora Penteado and running only two issues, featured some mild horror stories labeled "adults only." Perhaps this was due to the many South American horror comics featuring the sexy adventures of Dracula, the Mummy, the Wolf

A Brazilian version of *Frankenstein*.

Man, and the Phantom of the Opera also being published at the time.

During the 1960s, the old-style horror comic books provided the format of the black-and-white horror magazines pioneered by Warren Publishing Company's *Creepy* and later *Eerie* and *Vampirella*. As these were not officially comic books but comic magazines (standard magazine size) they did not have to subscribe to the Comics Code and could go all out with the horror. A suitable place for the Frankenstein monster had been created. Like the stories published by Atlas, the Warren Frankenstein tales had no continuity with each other. Each of them led to a final shocking effect.

The first such series, Skywald's *Frankenstein Book II*, premiered in the third issue (May, 1971) of *Psycho*, a magazine similar to *Creepy* in format. Written and illustrated by Sean Todd (actually Tom Sutton), the series began after the climax of the Mary Shelley novel. The monster, a more ugly version of the Universal creature, and given to long dissertations like the original conception in the novel, salvaged his creator's corpse from the icy waters of the Arctic and used its superintelligent transplanted brain to turn Frankenstein himself into a resuscitated horror. The monster was exhibited with a company of freaks in Paris in the next issue's "Freaks of Fear" (September, 1971). In Paris the monster met Quasimodo, the hunchback of Notre Dame. The third installment pitted the Frankenstein monster against an octopuslike horror in the sewers beneath Paris. The effort devoted to this series was appreciated but the long-winded dialog of the monster—who looked like the speechless brute of the movies but spoke endlessly, like the creature of the novel—became stultifying.

In 1972, Marvel Comics began publishing *Monster of Frankenstein*, a new comic book adapted by Gary Friedrich and drawn by Mike Ploog, to join Marvel's *Werewolf by Night* (also drawn by Ploog) and *Tomb of Dracula*, comics now permitted by a slight relaxation of the Comics Code, under a 1971 revision. Very shortly after, DC introduced a shorter *Frankenstein* series in *Phantom Stranger*. DC's series was written by Len Wein and illustrated by Michael Kaluta. Both the DC and Marvel monsters were the original and both series began with the monster being chipped out of the polar ice where the novel left him—however, the Marvel series was set in 1898 and the DC series in 1973.

Of all the Frankenstein comic-book stories published since

1939, Dick Briefer's efforts remain the most memorable even though they were far from the most literate or artistic. There was something compelling in that flat head, those sunken cheeks, that impossible nose set between the eyes. Briefer's Frankenstein monster, whether battling Bulldog Denny in the subway tunnels under New York City, or napping in the garden outside his haunted house, or working some horrible vengeance upon a little man who feigned friendship only to exploit misplaced trust, had power—a strange charm by which the series endured until the coming of the Comics Code.

Victor Frankenstein had created a being charged, as the movies told us, with eternal life. Dick Briefer's version was somewhat less immortal. Still, it survived for almost 15 years. When compared with other characters bearing the name of Frankenstein who lumbered through the comic books, that was quite an impressive feat.

INTRODUCTION TO

BLUE SUIT, BLUE MASK, BLUE GLOVES—AND NO SOCKS

THE most remembered comic-book heroes tend to be those who never took themselves seriously and whose adventures could be read simultaneously as adventure and as humor—Captain Marvel, Plastic Man, and the Spirit, for instance.

The Spirit bridged the gap between comic strips and comic books by appearing in a coverless 16-page (later eight-page) comic book that circulated with the Sunday funnies in newspapers. An incredible amount of action, adventure, whimsy, parody, satire, humor, and fantasy appeared in those Spirit stories, which ran only seven pages. Today's comic-book writers, who seem to feel that a minimum of 20 pages is needed to tell a story and who often write multi-issue serials of 20 or more pages an installment, would do well to examine the Spirit stories to see how to do more with less space.

Maggie Thompson has spent all her life in the proximity of writers and not surprisingly has become a writer herself. Her grandmother, Margaret McGee, is a poet who published her first novel when she was 70. Her mother is Betsy Curtis, who has had science-fiction stories published in all the leading SF magazines. Maggie is married to Don Thompson, co-editor of this book and the preceding *All in Color for a Dime.*

She is the mother of Valerie (born in 1967) and Stephen (born in 1972), who have not yet written anything for publication.

Maggie has illustrated articles by Don and has sold articles to magazines on her own. With Don, she is active in both SF and comics fandom and writes columns, articles and reviews for such unlikely magazines as *Monster Times, The Buyer's Guide to Comics Fandom*, and *Worlds Unknown*. She keeps threatening to write a Gothic.

CHAPTER 5

BLUE SUIT, BLUE MASK, BLUE GLOVES— AND NO SOCKS

by MAGGIE THOMPSON

JUNE 2, 1940, was a Sunday. That morning, families all over America settled down to read their newspapers, each person grabbing a favorite section. One read about Nazi bombers raiding the Marseilles and Lyon areas (Paris reporting 56 German planes downed in a day—including some in the Rhône Valley forays) and about the British evacuating Dunkerque under bomber and artillery blasts. One considered movie listings, trying to choose between the well-reviewed *Grapes of Wrath* and *Road to Singapore* and maybe Mickey Rooney's latest—*Young Tom Edison*. Another grabbed the radio page and decided (once again) that Jack Benny, Edgar Bergen, and *One Man's Family* would be his evening's home entertainment. It was old and favorite fare.

But the lucky kid who was first to grab the Sunday funnies found new pleasure there.

That day the world was an unsettled place. Within less than a year, Hitler had invaded Poland, Norway, Denmark, the Netherlands, Belgium, and Luxembourg—and much of the British Commonwealth was fighting him. A few Americans were leaving home to cross the border into Canada—to seek out the war. And the United States was a temporary refuge for Canadians who were trekking south, hunting sanctuary from Canadian draft quotas.

The second year of the New York World's Fair had begun. Lines were being drawn for the political fight that would end in November with Roosevelt's whomping Wendell Willkie by 5,000,000 votes.

The 35,000-ton U.S. battleship *Washington* was launched at the Philadelphia Naval Yard; it was the first capital ship to hit the water in America in 19 years. A fever was growing steadily, impelling us to war.

But we were entertained by other things. Over 45,200,000 radio sets were estimated to be in use. Jack Benny, Guy Lombardo, Bing Crosby, Frances Langford, and Lowell Thomas were more familiar than our relatives. A nation listened to *Information Please* and *Lux Radio Theater*. The kids listened to *Let's Pretend* once a week—and *Amos 'n' Andy* were known all over the country. The *New York Daily News* polled other papers and named Mickey Rooney and Bette Davis King and Queen of the Movies.

First class mail was $.03 an ounce and, if you mailed a letter for *local* delivery, it was $.02 an ounce. (Air mail was seldom the service of choice—because it cost $.06 an ounce and that was just too much to pay ...) And the penny postcard cost a penny.

Into this world of June 2, 1940, the Spirit was born. Chances are that most kids grabbing that Sunday section would care more about finding a new hero—one whose adventures would go on for more than a decade—than they cared about FDR. The once-a-week hero would wander through a violent world while the *real* world went through war, atom bomb, formation of the U.N., cold war, and well into the Korean "police action." And, too, through the first commercial television broadcast and the growth of that medium—which was among the most powerful forces in loosening the grip on children's entertainment that had been held by comic books.

There it was, held in many a small hand. The upper-left-hand corner proclaimed it a "WEEKLY COMIC BOOK," and the upper-right-hand corner pointed out that it contained "3 COMPLETE STORIES." Sure enough, it was a comic book—thrust in the midst of the traditional weekly comic strips. It was comic-book size and shape but without a cover. It had 16 pages and, yes, three complete stories.

The second story in the book was "Lady Luck" by "Ford

Davis"—and it took four pages to tell of an escapade by Lady Luck ("a name veiled in mystery, spelling adventure, action . . . "). She was a criminal-on-the-side-of-good, cracking safes to help right wrongs—who changed from the ballgown-wearing Brenda Banks to the green-cloaked "mysterious costume of Lady Luck." Her costume consisted of green dress, green gloves with a white shamrock design, green cloak, and wide-brimmed green hat pulled jauntily over her face. No mask. In fact, the mystery about the costume consisted of why no one recognized her and why on earth she would select such clumsy garb—especially the high-heeled shoes—for climbing about on window ledges. They were green high-heeled shoes. By the end of the first story, naturally, Police Chief Hardy Moore was already falling for Brenda.

The third story was about "Mr. Mystic"—supposedly by "W. Morgan Thomas." With nice artwork by Bob Powell, this five-pager introduced another magician to the comic-book world. "Ken," an American, gave up his place in a plane evacuating "a tiny country in the path of an invader"—apparently in Europe: the premier's name was Professor Padewski. To save the premier's memoirs, Ken took a single-engine plane and just escaped destruction—only to be caught in a storm which blew him far off course "to the south-east." *Very* far off, since the plane "flutters into a mysterious canyon somewhere in the Himalayas." (Quite a gas tank, even with the storm's boost.) Apparently, this fulfilled a prophecy of seven lamas who lived where the plane crashed. Unconscious, Ken was taken by the seven—"We shall brand him with our sign and make him all powerful!" "After we burn the symbol on his forehead, the mysteries of life shall be known to him." After tying his arms to a beam, one of the lamas cried, "Oh, holy branding iron, impact thy wisdom in our choice! With this brand, I name thee ruler of magic, disciple of the seven lamas and knight of righteousness." Awakened by the pain of the branding, Ken was informed that his every wish would come true, whereupon he promptly replied, "Yeah? Well I wish I was free to beat your ears off!" He was magically freed—but the lamas had left. Eventually, he found himself clothed, and a voice from the sky told him: "You will be known as Mr. Mystic, endowed with unlimited powers to combat the forces of evil plaguing the Earth. Go, and do your work!" Which he did. With humor and good art and scripting.

It was the first story in the booklet, however, that gave its name to the little comics, as far as the kids were concerned—for the pamphlets were untitled as a unit. The only name appearing at the top of the first page—which was all the "cover" the booklets possessed—was the name of the paper that circulated them. But they became known as "Spirit sections"—because the life of the weekly comic was, indeed, the Spirit.

"The SPIRIT by Will Eisner" was the heading on that first strip in the first booklet—and it was not by any means an earth-shaking story. Denny Colt ("criminologist and private detective") offered to help Police Commissioner Dolan get Dr. Cobra. Colt announced to his friend Dolan that he wanted the reward for Cobra and asked for an hour's head start towards capturing the villain. Colt found the evil scientist in Chinatown, tangled with him and his assistant Leeng, fired his gun accidentally into a vat of strange chemicals, and was drenched by the liquid. When the police found him, he seemed to be dead—with rigor mortis already set in—of heart failure. He was buried in Wildwood Cemetery. Later, a mysterious figure held Dolan at gunpoint, announcing his intention of claiming the reward for Cobra and calling himself the Spirit. (He later told some crooks, "I am the Spirit of good ... but I can also be the Spirit of evil.") Dolan confronted him to confirm that he was, indeed, Denny Colt—and Colt explained: "When I tried to capture Cobra, the vat with some chemicals in it, smashed! I was put in a state of suspended animation! Believing me dead, you fellows buried me ... I came to several hours later and broke out of my grave!"

Dolan and the Spirit tracked down Dr. Cobra and captured him together—with Dolan saving the Spirit by shooting the villain as he was about to stab the crimefighter. Denny announced that he intended to remain dead and take up the job of being the Spirit. "You know, Dolan, there are criminals and crimes beyond the reach of the police, but the SPIRIT can reach them!" "But how about food, money? Where'll you live?" "In the cemetery ... As for money, I'll collect the rewards ... Oh, we spirits get along fine!" He even had calling cards—miniature tombstones on which was printed (carved?)

"THE SPIRIT

Address: Wildwood Cemetery."

Dolan cautioned Denny that if he went outside the law, he would have to arrest him. "IF you catch me!" replied the newly hatched crimefighter.

Denny was Denny throughout. Blue snap-brim hat, blue suit, red tie. No gloves—and no mask. Just a good-humored detective type—out to join the ranks of outside-the-law crimefighters. (Consider the contradiction in terms in your idle moments . . .)

Thus began a strange New Wave in comics. There was little about this experiment in marketing besides its new concept of *existence*. It reversed an earlier trend in comics. Instead of reprinting comic strips in comic-book form (which is how comic books had begun, years before), Will Eisner, Everett M. Arnold (the copyright-holder), and the Register and Tribune Syndicate (the distributor) reversed the trend. They brought the comic book to the newspaper—and were to succeed quite well for more than 12 years.

But this is not why Eisner and the Spirit are so fondly remembered, more than 30 years after that initial appearance.

New marketing concepts may cause waves in the world of the dollar, but they don't do much for the memories of a generation of kids. What stuck in *their* minds were the *stories,* told by a master of the new art of the comic book.

The first story—the origin of the character—was routine. Not so were the tales that soon developed. The Spirit got a mask and gloves, both of which he wore constantly, and the plots grew strange. The story told on October 19, 1941, has remained fresh in minds that no longer remember grade-school classes attended the next day. "It is the year 2941 *A.D.* and humans still trod the earth—Why not—?? People as we know them change very little in 1,000 years—" Two archaeologists, digging in the western United States, uncovered a Spirit section (preserved by the sap of a tree nearby). It told the story "The Oldest Man in the World"—in which the Spirit tangled with an incredibly ancient codger who had been sabotaging a new Rocky Mountain airport. Police shot the robed old man, whom the Spirit then tried to comfort: "Here—Have a drink!! WHEW! Looks like that bullet entered your heart . . . Before you DIE, tell me, why did you—"

"I DIE? Thunderous blasphemy in empty chasms, NO! TEN MILLION TIMES NO!!! I am AGELESS! I SHALL LIVE FOREVER!! . . . LOOK! . . . Little ant of the earth—SEE—My wound has STOPPED BLEEDING! It is HEALED!"

In cackling frenzy, the bearded one decided to tell the Spirit the secret of his miraculous survival. "Eons ago—BEFORE THE BIRTH OF TIME—I was banished from the pale of men! I was SENTENCED to LIVE FOREVER—for a crime so great that the tiny fishes on the ocean floor recoiled with SHAME!" He had tried to kill the President at the airport "BECAUSE I WISH TO STOP THE GROWTH OF THE HUMAN RACE! *There are too many people on earth*!! They are crowding me off the surface— Soon cities will be all over and I will have no *wild country* to HIDE in! HAAAAAAA I will halt the growth of the human race for ONE generation!! Yes—I will destroy all the CHILDREN on earth! I will lead them to the sea—and DROWN them!!"

And off he went, playing his flute, as the Spirit stood open-mouthed. Sure enough, the next day he began his trek, gathering children as he went, leading them to the sea. The Spirit, circling over the sea cliff in his autoplane, decided to die when his death would serve a purpose—to jump into the sea, taking the old man with him. He leapt from the autoplane (piloted by his assistant, Ebony) onto the old man on the cliff—and they both fell towards the sea. Ebony swooped down and caught the Spirit in mid-fall, "while far below, the sea sucks a new victim, down, down into her cavernous depths."

The archaeologists finished the story. One scoffed: "The oldest man in the world—I cannot believe THAT! He was a charlatan— A FAKE—and the Spirit was a fool to risk his life . . . " Suddenly, he collapsed, a knife in his back. The other was felled by a shepherd's crook. And, over the bodies, there stood the old man— who broke into crazed laughter, shouted "CRASHING THUN-DER IN THE CAVES OF THE DEAF!" and danced off, playing his flute.

Now, *that* story was remembered—and remembered vividly— for many, many years.

As the world grew, so the stories of the Spirit grew. Eisner moved his creation into science fiction as well as fantasy, develop-ing story-telling in comics into an art form—and doing it with humor as well as power and freshness. In fact, the plots and concepts were so powerful that they overshadowed the character of the Spirit at times. (This was unusual in a medium in which the hero himself is usually the *raison d'être* for a heroic series.) It was the *spirit* of the Spirit that moved *The Spirit*. He viewed life with tongue in cheek, as well as with the determination that Right

Should Triumph.

And *Eisner* viewed life with a creative approach previously unseen in comics. The art was stunning and experimental—to such an extent that other comic-book artists studied his work. The influence of the strip was enormous in the world of cartoonists— and many fledgling artists studied the techniques that Eisner's work-force developed over the strip's dozen years. (In 1950, letters reached the point where Dolan and the Spirit's kid assistant Sammy, answered fan mail for one entire story. It was revealed that the Spirit was 73 inches tall. How much did he weigh? Sammy checked and then embarrassedly announced, "The day of the gaunt, thin, hawk-like crimefighter is OVER!" When a question from a prospective artist came in concerning production methods, Eisner phoned Dolan to say: "Original Spirit pages are drawn on two-ply kid-finish Bristol Board, 13 inches wide by 17 7/8 inches deep ... A B6 lettering pen is used for 'balloons' and a number two brush or a Chinese brush for inking!" While he had Eisner on the phone, Dolan asked with a fiendish grin, "WHY DOES THE SPIRIT WEAR HIS GLOVES DAY AND NIGHT ... EVEN WHEN HE GOES TO BED??" Eisner hung up. Dolan muttered, "Cartoonists are too @#***!! sensitive!")

The layouts and storytelling devices were unusual and stimulating, and the reader was led to breakneck reading paces by unusual combinations of script and panel. Harvey Kurtzman, years later, ran a display in *Help*! magazine of some of Eisner's artistic techniques, using sample panels as well as a sample story. Rain, running water, and the like (all problems of the comic-book artist) were imaginatively handled. Splash panels (the story introduction on the first page) were incredible—with imaginative methods of working in "The Spirit" as title. One story had it spelled out in paper washing down the street to a gutter. Several had the word spelled out in odd-shaped buildings. The name might be found on a "Wanted" poster—or printed on a storefront window, or written on a road sign, or traced on fogged glass, or half-buried in snow— or it might simply be done in elaborate lettering to set the mood. All this artistic virtuosity was not simply Will Eisner's alone, but his was the name signed to the strip.

Will Eisner was born during World War I. Prior to World War II, he had developed a career in the world of cartooning, doing strips for different comic books and finally joining forces with other creative hands to turn out an assortment of comic strips.

Jerry Iger and Eisner set up a group of people (one writing and doing character design, one penciling, one inking, one lettering) to turn out comics. "We made comic book features pretty much the way Ford turned out cars," Eisner commented to an interviewer years later. In 1940, he sold out the shop to Iger and formed a partnership with Arnold.

"I always thought of myself as a craftsman when doing The Spirit. The Spirit was really a culmination of all the talent, skill and imagination I could muster. Prior to that time I was just making a living. The Spirit was the first major effort in my life where I was able to do something I wanted to do, and was doing something I thought was meaningful, and at the same time making money on it." He discussed his work at length with an interviewer for the magazine *Witzend*, John Benson. Eisner told Benson, "Comics before that were pretty much pictures in sequence, and I was trying to create a *thing*, an art form."

Eisner was guiding force, creative hand, and supervisor on the strip from the beginning—and the strip suffered greatly when he left it in mid-1942 to serve in the U.S. armed forces during the war. Fans of his work all over the country rejoiced at the return of his hand at the very end of 1945. Many of the same people worked on the strip during the war who worked on it while he was there, but the switch was noticeable: the humor virtually disappeared, as did imaginative layout, outré stories, and technical pyrotechnics. Without Eisner, the stories were pedestrian, the art very staidly well-drawn, and the plots mostly limited to detective stories.

But those working for Eisner were a talented lot, whether working with or without his help. On the strip worked such men as Tex Blaisdell (artist on *Little Orphan Annie* since the death of Harold Gray), Robert Powell, Alex Kotzky (now doing *Apartment 3-G*), Lou Fine, Ruben King, Jerry Grandenetti, Jim Dixon, Marilyn Mercer, Wally Wood, and Jules Feiffer. Some penciled, some inked, some scripted (Feiffer was among these), but Eisner held things together. When he lost interest in being the mainstay of the strip, it fell on hard times, dwindled and died.

The first issue of the armed forces' *P.S. Magazine* came out in June, 1951; it was "published monthly in the interest of Preventive Maintenance for service-wide distribution to all organizations as part of the PREVENTIVE MAINTENANCE PROGRAM"— and was to take over where *Army Motors* left off when the United

States demobilized in 1945. Eisner's name appeared on the cover—a drawing of two privates carrying a "dead" jeep in the midst of an Army convoy. *P.S.* was free from your favorite motor pool, motor officer, or motor sergeant. The magazine passed issue 200 in 1969, having helped maintain matériel during the Korean Conflict and the Vietnam War. (Eisner told Benson: "I'm a teacher; I'm turning out instructional material. I don't feel the slightest feeling of guilt, or separation, or any relationship between that and what I might think about war as war, or war-mongering as war-mongering ... I have been devoting the last 20 years, really, to developing the comic strip media, which I have always experimented with, into a serious teaching tool. This is really the thing I'm proud of. And I'll teach anything with that tool.")

So Eisner turned to straight instruction—and *The Spirit* fell by the wayside. If your paper didn't carry the strip, you did have a few other chances to see it as its grip on life loosened. (Remember, this 16-pager probably had the largest circulation of any comic book ever. By mid-1942, papers carrying it included the *Philadelphia Record*, the *Detroit News*, the *Washington Star*, the *Chattanooga Evening Times*, the *Newark Star-Ledger*, the *Syracuse Herald American*, and the *Baltimore Sun*. Distributed by the Register and Tribune Syndicate, it reached an enormous audience.) Kids in towns like Cleveland, which *didn't* have a *Spirit* supplement on Sunday, could find reprints of the stories in comics from Vital and Quality (which existed in some sort of symbiosis) from September, 1942, through November 1950; Fiction House from Spring, 1952, through 1954; and Harvey in October, 1966, and March, 1967. His own comic ran a total of 22 issues with Quality, five with Fiction House, and the two with Harvey; he also ran as a feature in *Police, Modern*, and *Three Comics Magazine*. Only Harvey ran any new *Spirit* work (aside from an occasional cover) in comic books. The feature was brought totally up to date by a very odd feature in *New York* (then the *Herald Tribune*'s Sunday magazine) on January 9, 1966. But more on that later. In 1973, almost simultaneously, Eisner authorized limited circulation black-and-white reprints of *Spirit* stories from the first ones, and Denis Kitchen's Krupp Comic Works in Milwaukee began issuing a *Spirit* underground comic book with reprints and with new covers and some new *Spirit* comics by Eisner. Neither of these publications was widely distributed, however.

Those who saw it loved the strip for its *stories*. There were stories of far-out fantasy (time was condensed into an element and injected into a man contemplating murder); of overwhelmingly villainous men (the Squid, a master of disguise, worked for "the Fatherland" and was fought by the Spirit); of strange politics (Mr. Bowser, the dogcatcher, was unanimously elected mayor when Mayor Blast was injured in a criminal attempt to frame him for suicide); of seasonal tales (there were tales for spring, Thanksgiving, Halloween, and Christmas—"The Christmas Spirit" of course). There were glorious parodies—like the one for September 18, 1949: the splash page was the "cover" of *Lurid Love* (subtitled "Sickening stories, about other peoples' misery & heartache") and the story included a page-for-page takeoff on love pulps of the day (love problems answered by Wanda Lust; a blurb advising that the magazine was "Written for people in love—about people in love—by people in love"; even ad parodies).

It was possible to build up a chronology of the life of the Spirit from the series. Told in various issues, the story began as follows: Denny Colt was a kid in the "slums of Central City's lower East Side." He lived with his uncle, a has-been fighter, and met the young girl Sand Saref. His uncle became involved with crooks who shot Sand's policeman father—and Denny's uncle then "did the only thing his punch-battered brain could tell him. He killed himself on the spot." (Sand was totally embittered towards the law by this and had allied with the world of crime by the time she showed up as an adult in 1950.)

As Denny Colt grew up, he became an aide in the commissioner's office—and at some point gained an inheritance from his father, Denny Colt, Senior. (It can be assumed that it was in some sort of trust fund to be turned over when he became 21—thus explaining his poverty in youth.) The Spirit had to explain to tax men later, "I've been living on the principal of that inheritance and the LEGAL TAX was PAID YEARS AGO WHEN the estate was LIQUIDATED ... " He apparently struck out independently at some point, since he was a private detective by the time of the first story.

After Denny's "death," he set up housekeeping in Wildwood Cemetery (in a fancy, apparently underground apartment) and acquired an assistant and a girl friend. Ebony, the assistant, was a short Negro stereotype when introduced, and he appeared in the first story driving a cab. By the third week of the strip, the Spirit called a cab and noted: "Say, every time I call a cab, you turn up!

Are you the only cabby in town?" "No suh, Boss, but ah sho' is de fastest! Mah name is Ebony White!" "Swell, Ebony ... From now on, you'll be my exclusive cabby ... Now, step on it! We've a few stops to make!" "*Yassuh, Mr. Spirit Boss!*" From that moment, Ebony was the Total Sidekick, holding the gun on captives, rescuing protagonists when necessary, and living with the Spirit in that strange apartment in Wildwood. (If the apartment was a do-it-yourself project, as it must have been to remain secret, it was one of the fanciest. Windows were round, there was some sort of large picture window, and of course it had a fully equipped laboratory.)

In the earliest strips the locale was New York City (which was to the north of Wildwood), and a woman lawyer, the Black Queen, at one point decided to hold up New York City and rob it of $50 million—by cutting off Manhattan and cleaning out the Treasury Building. (That story introduced the autoplane—the Spirit's invention—which looked like an ordinary red car till a button was pressed which telescoped wings from just over the front fenders and revealed the propeller coming out of the engine. No, it was not a stunning gimmick, but it came in handy as a plot device for years—even when it occasionally got forgotten in the midst of a story, as when the Spirit traveled to Sumatra by autoplane and returned by boat.)

July 21, 1940—less than two months from the strip's beginning—the Spirit was framed for murder and began a career that ducked inside and outside the law for years. "I'll continue to fight crime, but from now on without the aid of the police!" This work plan occasionally threw his friend Dolan into embarrassing situations, since their friendship continued to be close and strong (especially since Dolan's daughter soon broke her engagement to Homer Creep and started a steady relationship as the Spirit's One True Love). At one point and another the outlaw would be sanctioned by this or that law enforcement body; he became a confidential agent-at-large for military espionage in October, 1940—and at one point (in the spring of 1949), the governor made him special deputy to Dolan.

The follow-up told of an attempt by the Spirit and Ebony to take up a legal life. They took a $60-a-month apartment and were besieged instantly by telephone man, reporter, telegrams, laundryman, electrician, salesmen, and the like. Suddenly, the carefree outlaw was confronted with piles of regulations and tons of paperwork. "I'M THROUGH! The only danger there is around here, is getting WRITER'S CRAMP!!" And later, "Dolan ... I can't stand by and see gangsters make a monkey out of justice because of a regulation!! I guess I can only fight crime in my own way ... no forms ... NO RULES!" The story ended with a "vast dragnet" to capture him ...)

The finances of freebooting were the subject of a few stories. In April, 1947, he had owed $25,000 back taxes—but a job he did paid off the debt. By April, 1950, Dolan worked out for him, "No matter how we FIGURE it, this crimefighting buisiness [*sic*] costs you $20,000 a year more than you REALIZE from your inherit-ance." They tried ads in a Situations Wanted column. (At the end of the story, he was still short $7,000 and decided to travel overseas to pick up more money—which resulted in stories alternating for a time between the Spirit in Africa and Sammy, Dolan, and the rest in Central City.)

There were two changes in the strip, you see, from the earliest days. Early on, it was decided that the city in which Dolan was commissioner was Central City ("80 minutes to Washington ... by air"—and in all respects but name and politicians it was still NYC). ("My whole background is a city boy ... all my culture is city culture ... Central City was New York City as far as I was concerned, and the city politics was obviously what I knew and understood," said Eisner.)

The other change was in assistant. Ebony served faithfully for nine years. He was a rich character, a humorous character, a varied character. He had heartbreaks and loves, likes and dislikes. He was brave and loyal and fierce. He was known to solve cases that the Spirit fouled up. He had his own circle of friends, chief among whom was Pierpont Q. Midas. He saved the Spirit's life, often.

But he became an embarrassment because—in character design and speech pattern—he was a Negro stereotype. From the first, he had blubber lips and pop eyes. He was a comedy-relief shrimp whose comedy often came from his deciding that he deserved more respect than he was given. It was never made absolutely clear what his age was; to begin with, he was a cab driver, but later on (in 1946) it was necessary to point out that he was privately tutored by the Spirit. His other friends were children. The year 1946, in fact, seemed to mark the first effort to Do Something about Ebony. In the strip for February 10, a Negro major criticized another character who mocked Ebony: "You're being very unfair! It's no disgrace to talk with a SOUTHERN drawl! What's more, my grandfather was a minstrel during the Civil War and I'm PROUD of him . . . "

As a sort of substitute, Blubber the Eskimo (same size as Ebony—and same general type of character) was introduced, and Ebony went off to Carver's School for Boys. (The title was changed shortly—and it was referred to as Mr. *Carter*'s school.) By mid-May, however, Blubber headed back to the North Pole and Ebony returned home.

It took till 1949 to drop Ebony conclusively—and the Christmas strip that year did not show him. The new sidekick was a kid (similar in design—but white) named Sammy.

"Ebony was done with a great deal of love and affection," Eisner told Benson. "To me, Ebony was a very human character, and he was very believable . . . at the time. With all the idealism I had then, I felt that he deserved to be treated as a human being, and have emotions. Remember, that was a breakaway in itself . . . no one ever showed Negroes in comics with any emotions other than weeping over the death of poor little Mandy, and the little white girl. Only Ham Fisher did anything like it and he stayed with the safe stereotype." (Which is all well and good unless you happen to be one of those who enjoyed the late Walt Kelly's work on *Our Gang* from 1942 to mid-1949. We watched him evolve the character of Buckwheat quite swiftly from the cowardly comic stereotype of the *Our Gang* movies to the completely rounded, nonstereotyped *individual*, Bucky. *That* was a character of great humor, *none* of which came from looks or accent or superstitions.)

Reportedly, though, Ebony never brought criticism at the time from black groups, and some even praised Eisner for the use of the character. Nevertheless, Ebony's disappearance was thorough, though one nostalgic scripter apparently forgot it in 1951 long enough to have the Spirit wonder whether Ebony would pop up out of the hideout as the Spirit took someone through Wildwood.

One thing did *not* change in the strip—and that was the bevy of women who became involved with the Spirit, many of them lusting after his fine, manly body.

The first *lasting* Other Woman in the Spirit's career was Sylvia Satin alias Silk Satin alias Black Satin. In the prewar years, she was the main rival of clean-cut, normal-American, pretty-blonde Ellen Dolan for the attentions of her Robin Hood friend. Satin was introduced in 1941 and hung on grimly, popping up every so often to match wits with the Spirit and to see whether she couldn't win him *this* time. Originally an international crook, she became a British agent (winning a total pardon for her crimes) and eventually settled in Scotland as an investigator for the insurance firm Croyd's of Glasgow. (She was the widow of a German count and had a daughter, Hildie, born in 1939.) While she had no success winning the Spirit (who *liked* her *but* ...), she *often* outwitted him.

Many women entered the Spirit's life after the war—but four stood out as favorites who returned again and again to complicate things for the crime fighter: P'gell (introduced October 10, 1946), Saree Raymond (January 12, 1947), Sand Saref (January 8, 1950), and Darling O'Shea (July 9, 1950). All of them loved the Spirit; all tried to win him away from Ellen Dolan—who managed to hold out against this assortment of devastating females. (On occasion, a sorely wounded Spirit would lapse into a coma or other unconsciousness murmuring "Ellen ... " He never paid this tribute to any of the others, much to their chagrin.)

The gorgeous siren looked out at the reader and said, "I am P'GELL ... and this is NOT a story for little boys!!" She began her life in the strip married to Hans Dammt (a Nazi) in Turkey but promptly had him killed for $500,000 and married Emil Petit (who had arranged the assassination and had another $500,000). Petit was more than 300 years old (thanks to a secret formula), but P'gell arranged to do him in and he died in front of her, turning to skeleton and dust. She married *his* murderer and continued her career. "Oh, brother, what a man!! If only you were a crook, what a team we'd make!" she exclaimed to the Spirit after saving his life. And she went through husband after husband, accumulating money as she progressed; by January, 1947, she'd had seven marriages and was about to marry a certain Mr. Raymond and become headmistress of an exclusive girls' school. ("C'n you think of a better background for advising young girls on the rough road of life?")

The daughter of the widower Raymond was Saree—a bobby-soxer who developed a crush on whatever eligible male happened by. She and P'gell made quite a team after Raymond joined the list of P'gell's dead former husbands. Eventually (after an episode involving her hiding crooks in the school), P'gell married Mr. Quinse (who owned the school, a treasure, and a big loan

P'Gell, one of the women in the Spirit's life lost a lot of husbands, not always as a direct result of her own machinations. P'Gell made a career out of marriage and, somehow, marriage seemed to be swiftly followed by widowhood. The layout of this 1947 page is typical of Eisner's approach to story breakdown. Copyright © 1947, Will Eisner, and reprinted by his permission.

company). She later tried teaching French in Riverbend University (60 miles south of Central City).

Sand Saref was "the big love" of Denny Colt's youth—and would occasionally return, like P'gell, to try to persuade him to go crooked. There was great mutual affection—but it was a sort of nostalgic thing.

In 1906, Tydeland O'Shea bought 25 acres of barren land; four years later, he owned 300 oil wells and 5,000 acres of rich country. At age 55 he married, but two years later he and his wife were killed in an oil well explosion, leaving their baby daughter, Darling. Darling O'Shea was the richest woman in the world and madly in love with the Spirit; in her introductory story, she hired him as her bodyguard and battled the passenger-cargo ship *Imperial* for possession of him (the ship was intensely jealous) and barely survived. For Darling was determined, gutsy, and powerful—and came up to just above the Spirit's belt buckle. She was a little girl—but *some* little girl! "I may be young in years . . . but I am old in knowledge . . . " At ten years old, she was a total match for a mentally unbalanced murderer and kidnaper unlucky enough to threaten her—and she even managed to unsettle the Spirit occasionally.

But Ellen was his True Love. (In 1942, Eisner briefly explored what would happen if they ever married. There were bows decorating the underground hideout, ruffles on the lab shelves, and even Ebony's room was straightened up.) Her love was true, and she'd lend a hand even at times when it seemed as though the Spirit was lost to her. While there were several strips in which she seemed the stereotype of Female Nitwit, Eisner would occasionally delve a bit deeper to make her a rounded and independent person, thoroughly suited to someone the stature of his hero. In November, 1950, she ran for mayor of Central City with such comments as, "Most men practice equality like a LITTLE boy practicing on the piano, one hour a day and then FORGET all about it!" The women loved her; the men adored her. (The Spirit was so infuriated that he backed Mike Poltax on the Prosperity Party ticket—a chap of such sterling quality that he kidnaped Ellen.) Ellen won the election by a landslide—and that was that. It made no difference to the couple's relationship, and Ellen did quite well at the job. (This sort of thing seldom happened in comics; Lois Lane was still turning in copy 30 years after meeting Superman.)

134

Villains appeared and reappeared in the series, with three major ones. The Squid was *the* major prewar menace. Introduced January 18, 1942—in the section with the first mention of the U.S. entry into the war—his aim was the destruction of American defense and he was fought by the team of the Spirit (working for Army Intelligence) and Satin (working for British Intelligence). The Squid was identifiable by green hood and goggles, blue gloves, hat, and trenchcoat. As happened now and again, everyone seemed to have masqueraded as everyone else by story's end—with the Squid donning a rubber mask over hood and goggles at one point. He soon came to regard the Spirit as his personal enemy—and the feud lasted till, in December, 1945 (just after Eisner returned to the strip after the war), an "atom bomb" blew up the villain once and for all.

He was soon (the following July) replaced by the Octopus, an important war criminal, who was initially fought by the Satin-Spirit duo (with Satin now working for the U.N.). "The OCTO-PUS is the head of a vast criminal ring that is forming again! Every criminal worth a lead bullet ANYWHERE on the earth operates with his consent . . . He is the king of crime!" And all you saw of the Octopus were his gloves and sleeves; he was even more secretive than the Squid. (Maybe they were brothers? Their methods and style seemed much the same . . .)

The other master villain was also a postwar threat—a *nasty* creature who made a living after the war by bilking relatives of people missing in action. Mister Carrion had as pet the vulture Julia—a bird as vicious as Carrion himself—who almost killed Blubber, the Eskimo kid sidekick.

It was not, however, any of these who made *The Spirit* the incredible memory it was. Other strips had gorgeous girls. Other strips had great villains. Other strips had developing characters. But *The Spirit* had concepts, plot-lines, story ideas like no other strip. "My big influence in stories . . . is the short stories—the O. Henry short stories, the Ambrose Bierce short stories, and so forth . . . *The Spirit*, actually, as I saw it (and as I saw comic books), was nothing but a series of short stories. They were the pulps in visual form," Eisner said.

Some of them involved the world of the Spirit as a cartoon character. One had Eisner complaining about the life of a cartoonist: "Here I am, a STOOGE to a CRIMEFIGHTER—HE has the adventures and I work my head off DRAWING 'em!!—

One of these days I'm going to have adventures of my own and I'll make the SPIRIT draw 'em! Gee—SIGH—WILL EISNER by the SPIRIT Hmm—Wouldn't look so bad at all!!" A crook came in, ransacked Eisner's files, found out the true story of the Spirit's origin. "Boy, the underworld would pay a fortune for dis!!" And the story went on from there.

Some had fantastic bases for stories: Ebony bought Aladdin's lamp, which gave three chances to call on the genie; the first two times, the genie would help you; the third, he would kill you. Mortimer J. Titmouse, a janitor in a nuclear plant, played at inventing an atomic bomb—until he developed one that worked. Everyone shoved Tooty Compote around until the day he told someone to drop dead—and the man did. The continuing story of Boot Camp, where crooks hid out in the Rocky Mountains—without aging. Santa Claus got amnesia and wound up with hoods—whom he finally got to deliver Christmas presents for him. Time ceased to exist for everyone in the world—except for one crook. Professor Tempus J. Fugit confessed to killing the Spirit—on January 21, 1970. (In that one, 20 years from the "now" of the story, the Spirit had married Ellen. There was a new super-thruway from Central City to Los Angeles. The Spirit had a son; the Spirit wore a mask and blue cape, hat, and gloves—while the son wore a blue cape. There was full employment, fine homes where there used to be slums, and not a gun in the city. Eustace Dolan was the state governor. And "a man with a GUN would be in a GREAT position of POWER.")

Some had inventive story-telling devices: The parallel stories of lookalikes convict Carboy T. Gretch and husband Cranfranz Qwayle, were told in opened comics pages which paralleled until the stories met. The "Song of Little Willum"—about Gitch the goonie—approximated Longfellow's trochaic meter and threw in some comments on comics:

> "Meanwhile" . . . ah yes, "meanwhile"
> What's a comic without "meanwhile"?
> Helpless are we minus "meanwhile" . . .
> So for us to use our "meanwhile"
> We must switch the scene to Dolan's.

And some of the story-telling devices were even bound up in parody: A "cover" of the Spirit for *Rife* magazine, with inside "photo articles" on the various members of *The Spirit*'s cast of

The Spirit was blinded for three weeks' worth of stories and was cured by Doctor Floss, who was secretly in love with him. His return to the world of the sighted gave Will Eisner a reason for drawing in several main members of the cast: Officer Klink, Ellen Dolan, Dr. Floss, Commissioner Dolan and Ebony. The last panel shows Carrion, a recurring villain, and his pet vulture, Julia. Copyright © 1947, Will Eisner, and reprinted by his permission.

characters. Some stories had advertising takeoffs for opening pages: "She's Ugly! She's Engaged! She Uses POOL'S TOAD-STOOL FACIAL CREAM. Plucked from the heath at the fleeting moment of a maddening midnight moon." "Distinguished Men prefer Borschtbelt's Buttermilk." Some were totally wild stories, such as the mystery involving Al Slapp (creator of stupid mountain boy *Li'l Adam*), Elmer Hay (creator of *Little Homeless Brenda*), and Hector Ghoul (creator of *Nick Stacy*): "No ... no ... Don't call the cops ... I didn't kill SLAPP ... Why, the only time people read HOMELESS BRENDA is when he deigns to mention her in his strip!" The Spirit defeated Hay's giant Oriental bodyguard by painting over his blank white eyeballs.

On the other hand, there were stories of power and suspense. There was an extended sequence in which the Octopus blinded the Spirit (in which much use was made of all-black panels). There was one in which the Spirit was wounded in the left leg—and weeks later faced the threat of amputation as the doctor's recommended treatment. There was almost always a lot of action in a Spirit story—and quite frequently a good dollop of violence. The Spirit was bashed and clouted and shot and submerged and kicked and clawed and starved and tortured and choked. That mess of chemicals, which put him in rigor mortis in the first place, must have had some life-preserving properties to bring him out of all that intact.

But maybe not so intact, after all. In 1952, the strip began a rapid decline. The art was perfunctory, the Spirit became a humorless clot—reacting to one villain by clenching his teeth and snarling, "YOU FAT SLIMY RAT!" Stories were often retellings of earlier stories. *Lady Luck* and *Mister Mystic* had been dropped long since and the booklet was only eight pages long. Even when there was humor, the art was unimaginative and far more crude than ever before. On July 27, 1952, the title was changed to *Outer Space*—and *featured* the Spirit. September 28, 1952, was the last Sunday on which people found him in their funnies—except for one last surprise.

The *New York Herald Tribune* ran a Sunday magazine called *New York*; the issue for January 9, 1966, which featured articles on "The Great Comics Revival," gave prominent attention to the Spirit. In addition to articles by Eisner's ex-staffers Jules Feiffer and Marilyn Mercer, the magazine contained a generous dollop of *Spirit*—a new strip done to fit the larger format and running five

The Spirit had some of the most punishing fights of any comic-book character, fights which usually ended with the Spirit looking about as beaten as his opponents. The cast in the last panel (left to right): Spirit, Lord Elby, Hildie, Dolan, Satin. Copyright © 1947, Will Eisner, and reprinted by his permission.

of those giant pages.

It dealt with the attempts of Hobart Naught (Assistant, Deputy Vice Commissioner for the Investigation of Indefinable Waste, appointed 1933) to wipe out John Lindsay before the election, so that Naught's bureaucratic stronghold wouldn't be eliminated. Naught's secretary, it turned out, was Ellen Dolan—who learned of the scheme and went to Wildwood to get help to thwart the plan. (Of the old characters, only Ellen and the Spirit hadn't aged. She hadn't seen the Spirit in years and commented that when she had given up hope that he'd marry her, she resigned herself to spinsterhood and took a city government job.) Ebony was fat, wore glasses, short haircut, and business suit, and said, "I'm an executive in Haryouact . . . I'm not anxious to get mixed up in city politics." Dolan wouldn't help because this was his last chance to be police commissioner of New York City. (He was 87 and not likely to get another chance.)

The Spirit wore a single-breasted suit, a narrow tie, and button-down collar. Otherwise, he was the same old Spirit—except for the socks. People have pointed out that the Spirit never wore socks; the leg that showed between cuff and shoe was almost invariably colored "flesh" in those old sections. The reason has been cloaked in as much mystery as why the Spirit always wore his gloves, even to bed. But in the *Herald Tribune* that Sunday, the Spirit wore baggy socks—and even appeared briefly without his gloves. It's as though Eisner decided to break the traditions with that "final" appearance.

(There were new stories in the Harvey comics—a retelling of the spirit's origin in No. 1 and the life story of Zitzbath Zark—who grew up to be the Octopus—in No. 2. But the attempt was abortive and succeeded mainly in increasing the demand for the few tattered old *Spirit* sections that survived into the mid-sixties, thus causing their prices to go up.)

But the influence remained and continues in comics to this day. It was felt in the EC comics of the early fifties—and it can be seen in cartoonists' styles now.

The parodies Eisner worked with were brought to full fruition in such later magazines as *Mad*. In 1946, the Greater Buffalo Press, Inc., noted that it had *Spirit* sections "together with translation into Spanish, available as an aid in learning Spanish." In 1972, English teacher Glen Johnson was using *Spirit* sections to teach American Indian children English.

The sound effects that made Eisner's work so atmospheric and reminiscent of radio drama are parodied in this 1950 episode written by Jules Feiffer. It features a caricatured Feiffer drawing a summary of the year's adventures. The style was that which he used for a little-kid humor strip, "Clifford," which provided a back cover to the Spirit booklets. Copyright © 1950, Will Eisner, and reprinted by his permission.

As noted, the Spirit is now in underground comix.

A comics fan wrote Marvel Comics a letter which ran in *Fantastic Four* No. 32 (November, 1964). He said that in No. 29, they had "printed probably the world's first photo-within-a-comic." More than once, the Eisner studio experimented with photos incorporated in standard comic-book stories—and did it more successfully than later hands, to boot. Twenty years before Marvel's "first."

Maybe someday there will be a hardcover collection of the best of those influential works. It should sell like the proverbial hotcakes—not only to those who remember the strip with fondness but also to art students, to lovers of well-told short stories, to fans of great comic art, to popular-culture historians, and to fantasy and action fans.

Meantime, those who were lucky enough to read the newspapers or comics starring the reincarnated Denny Colt will have to depend on memories.

They'll remember the imitators who sprang up after the birth of the Spirit—Midnight (in *Smash*) and the Mouthpiece (in *Police*) from Quality, to name a couple. Blue suit, mask, blue hat, etc ... But no humor of any high level at all—and not the spirit of the Spirit.

They'll remember Aunt Mathilda (sister of Diogenes Dolan's "poor dead wife"—yes, Dolan apparently had more than one first name over the dozen years of the strip). Mathilda went through more than five husbands (that varied, too). "Hinkey married me of his own free will!! He might have been unconscious and the Justice of the Peace tied up ... but IT WAS LEGAL!! I WANT MY MAN!!!"

They'll remember Hazel P. Macbeth—a genuine fourteenth-generation American witch. (She entered the competition for Miss Rhinemaiden of 1950—and was highly regarded by Central City's children.)

They'll remember the classic song that was a continuing gag for months—"Every Little Bug"—which grew to such proportions that words and music were run in April, 1947. In fact, the biggest guest star the sections ever had—the only real-life guest—was Robert Merrill, who (it was announced) would perform the song. (Whether or not he ever *really* did couldn't be turned up by research.)

They remember the stories of the Christmas Spirit, a year's-end tale of joy and hope, no matter what the year. Some were light, some were tear-jerkers, but you didn't forget them.

They remember the strip for December 31, 1950, when Eisner's assistant (looking just a bit like Jules Feiffer) shot Eisner and did a recap of the past year's adventures. Feiffer drew the little-kid strip that ran on the back page of later sections, about a boy named Clifford. So the recap showed Clifford as the Spirit, opening with the statement: "I must be the SPIRIT and I must NEVER carry a gun! But still I MUST fight crime BARE-HANDED! No OTHER crimefighter can make THAT stupid statement!" And the strip was a gorgeous parody of elements of Eisner's style—including his nifty love for sound effects. Feiffer put in shoe-heel-on-concrete sound effects in sandy desert scenes. (Eisner's style has been called "filmic"; it actually derived as much from radio, with its emphasis on sound.)

They remember King Hobo and Willum Waif. They remember the candy-sucking kid.

And they wonder.

They still wonder.

Why *did* the Spirit wear his gloves day and night, even when he went to bed?

INTRODUCTION TO

IT'S MAGIC

IN a broad sense, it's the magic of the comics that *The Comic-Book Book* is all about—but within the magic pages there is that somewhat narrower class of stories that are *literally* about magic and about magicians. These stories have a long history and a loyal following.

Dick O'Donnell is the oldest contributor to *The Comic-Book Book*. He declines to state his year of birth, but says that he is a native Hawaiian who has spent almost his entire life in the islands, and that he now lives in Honolulu, retired from a career in civil engineering to pursue his hobby of—magic.

The heroes of his boyhood were the stars of comic *strips* rather than comic books—this preference he shares with another contributor, his friend Bill Blackbeard—and as a result, the bulk of his chapter is devoted to the greatest of comic-strip magicians, the great Mandrake.

Your editors, with Dick O'Donnell's agreement before the work was done *and* his approval of the manuscript after it was written, have taken the liberty of extending his chapter to include a number of latter-day comic-*book* magicians, including most prominently Ibis, Zatara, Dr. Fate, and the Spectre. Perhaps it is going a bit too far to say that we obtained Dick O'Donnell's *approval* of the added material. After we sent him the manuscript extension we received back an airmail postcard, the text of which read as follows:

"All right, if that's your real opinion. But please make sure that you don't tell your readers that it's mine."

Very well; in the words of a friend of ours in the publishing business, *"Caveat Lector."* And while we're at it, a snappy *Abracadabra* too, and on with the sorcery!

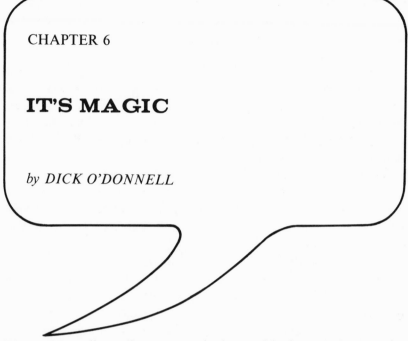

CHAPTER 6

IT'S MAGIC

by DICK O'DONNELL

WHEN your editors first approached me with the request to write a chapter for them dealing with magicians in the comics, I agreed at once. Although I must confess that I long ago stopped reading the strips in the *Honolulu Advertiser* except for one or two favorites, and although I had not picked up a comic magazine for 20 years or longer, I held a strong, lingering affection for those wild and colorful tales of adventure, and for those, in particular, dealing with the exploits of magicians.

For there were magicians galore in the newspaper comic sections and in the early comic magazines of the 1930s and 1940s. I set out to dredge what information I could from my memory, supplemented this with some treasures culled from a few bundles of flaking newspapers that have lain in my attic for untold years, and was aided immeasurably, on a recent visit to the mainland, by Mr. Bill Blackbeard of the National Newspaper Archive and Academy of Comic Art.

One of the first things I learned in my researches was that the first great comic-strip magician was not my old friend Mandrake, but a secondary character in a little-known daily feature by Mel Graff, called *The Adventures of Patsy*. Appearing in the early 1930s, Patsy was a little girl who got herself into endless hot water, much of it in mythical kingdoms of the Graustark or Zenda variety, where she would embroil herself in palace intrigue at the drop of a hat.

For several such adventures, which Mr. Blackbeard kindly showed me in tinted reprints in the *Famous Funnies* magazine, Patsy enlisted the aid of a mysterious *Phantom Magician,*, who was clad in the outfit of tights, cape, and domino mask favored by so many later adventure heroes including the Phantom (no relation despite the similar name) and Superman and Batman and their compatriots without number.

But while the Phantom Magician was an interesting precursor, the first truly important comic-strip magician, and by far the greatest of all time, was Mandrake, the creation of Lee Falk and Phil Davis, the same Falk and Davis who later created the nonmagical Phantom.

Telling the youth of today that Mandrake was a great feature, I have found, is an exercise in futility. They know of that master of mystical adventure only through the modern newspaper strip—drawn since Davis's death by Fred Fredericks—or through latter-day comic-book revivals. Both are weak, puerile things, with tame and simplified plots, no pace, crude and characterless drawing. Certainly a reading of this *Mandrake* leaves one with no impression of anything very worthwhile.

But, ah, when I think of the thrill of reading the *Mandrake* feature as it existed 35 years ago, when Falk and Davis were at the peak of their energies, I can come to only one of two conclusions. Either Mandrake was a truly great strip which has been laid low by the passage of time—or else my memory of it has acquired a luster with the years that utterly distorts and deceives me in my recollections of those pages.

In those days of the 1930s that seem so long ago, I used to go down to Diamond Head to watch for the Matson Liners headed in from the mainland with all manner of goods and supplies, including usually some three-week-old copies of the *San Francisco Examiner*, a Hearst paper that carried *Mandrake* in both its daily and its Saturday editions, for in those days Hearst used to put out two color sections each weekend, the full-sized Sunday section that carried *Prince Valiant* and *Blondie* and the other heavyweight strips in head-on competition with other Sunday papers ... and a tabloid-sized Saturday color section.

Because no one else carried a color section on Saturday, Hearst

146

could run secondary features in this section and still gain a competitive advantage over rival Saturday editions. *Mandrake* was included in the Saturday lineup, shining there all the brighter because of the relatively lackluster strips that accompanied it.

The Matson Liner would steam into Pearl Harbor and I would know that within hours my father would reach into his pocket and pull out a whole dollar, and send me to the big newsstand on Kamehameha Boulevard, where I would buy a run of *Examiners* and hurry home with them, and while Father read the political news and the sports sections, I would devour the comic strips from the daily papers and the color comic sections from the weekend editions.

One of the earliest *Mandrake* adventures that I read was "The Kingdom of Murderers." I believe that this was the first *Mandrake* color adventure—the daily strip had begun in 1934, and a few months later the weekend series commenced with this tale.

Already Mandrake's appearance was fairly well settled—he was a tall, well-built man with dark, neatly combed hair and a sharply trimmed moustache. He was dressed in full tails with a silk top hat and a crimson-lined black cape.

In short, he appeared as a stage-magician, a prestidigitator, a fast-finger man if you choose to take apart that word, but he was, in the comics, far more than that. He was an actual magician, possessed of supernatural capabilities. This is only one of the many ways in which the strip grew pallid in later years, for by the 1950s Mandrake typically would "gesture hypnotically," following which a mild trick, such as a disappearance or the substitution of a bunch of flowers for a tommy-gun, would be seen, leaving the reader uncertain as to whether this was mere illusion—or more.

In his early years Mandrake had unquestioned magical powers, and exercised them quite freely in the course of his adventures. Mandrake's servant and aide, Lothar, was present from the outset, at first portrayed with deep, blue-black skin and red lips, but within less than a year he had attained the rich brown pigmentation that he was shown with thereafter.

The omnipresent (and insipid) girl friends, Trina and Narda, did not join Mandrake for many years. In his earlier adventures he enjoyed the company of a series of female friends. In "The Kingdom of Murderers," early in 1935, Mandrake's female companion was one Rheeta, a lovely although taciturn blonde whom he had transformed to human form from a tawny-coated pantheress. No illusions here, no hypnotic gestures. He outright turned the pantheress into a human woman.

In that tale, Mandrake agrees to assist two agents of the International Police in penetrating the "secret and hidden kingdom of murderers," and after one of the police agents is himself assassinated, Mandrake, Lothar, Rheeta, and the second police agent, Pierce, get under way.

Mandrake has captured the assassin of Pierce's partner and, when the killer refuses to guide them to the hidden kingdom, Mandrake calls up the murderer's *shadow* and commands it to lead them. En route to the kingdom they are harassed by "ghosts," but make their way into the kingdom anyway, and discover that the "ghosts" are projections of an infernal machine operated by members of the kingdom of murderers.

Mandrake turns these killers into beasts—an ape, a seal, an ostrich, and a horse.

He encounters the king of this hidden retreat, the killer Bull Ganton, who plans to execute Rheeta (no women allowed) and enslave the others. Instead, a wrestling match is arranged between Lothar and the champion of the murderers, to take place on a trestle over a pit of flames.

While Mandrake and Bull Ganton look on, Lothar hurls his foe off the trestle—Mandrake rises, gestures, and raises the victim from the pit, safely back to the trestle. "A simple trick I learned in India," Mandrake explains.

There follow complex reversals of fortune as Ganton imprisons Mandrake and has him strapped into the "dynamite chair," an explosive device of execution; Pierce sets loose a flock of carrier pigeons summoning all of the murderers in the world to the hidden kingdom, Mandrake breaks free, and so on. In the end the kingdom of murderers is destroyed and Mandrake and his companions return to the outer world.

By the next year Mandrake's adventures were making the hidden kingdom of murderers look mundane. Take, for instance, "Mandrake in the X Dimension." A scientist has discovered that beings from the X dimension are kidnaping Earth people for unspecified purposes. His own daughter disappears into the X dimension, so he sends Mandrake and Lothar in a machine of his own devising to rescue the girl.

Here Mandrake and Lothar find a world worthy of Alex Raymond's Mongo—"wheelmen of living metal instead of flesh"

Mandrake's magic is handy for standing off an army by making him a hundred-foot giant—or making him look like one; it is often hard to tell where hypnotism leaves off and real magic begins with Mandrake—but the muscles of Lothar come in awfully handy when magic fails. Presumably magic is involved in Mandrake's fashion-plate appearance after such a narrow escape, though. Copyright © King Features Syndicate Inc. 1937.

use captive humans to work their mines for coal and metals and to curry to the needs of these heartless living robots.

For them, oil is food and rust is the only disease! Humans toil as miners, oilers, and polishers. Rebellion is met with instant repression. All metal things in this world live—when a miner sits down to rest for a moment, a scrap-metal band curls about his throat and chokes him until he yields or dies!

Mandrake and Lothar rescue the girl and the other prisoners of the X dimension, of course, and after their return to our own world, the master magician and his giant servant entered one of the finest of all Falk and Davis's fantasies, "The Land of Dementor."

Dementor is apparently more a Graustark than a truly alien land, but its ruler, the monstrously fat Prince Paulo, is himself a fascinating creation, alternately comical and horrifying in his manias. Mandrake encounters him first with the prince riding a horse facing backward; Mandrake remarks on this silly practice, and to Prince Paulo's demand he says that he was merely talking to himself.

"Well!" responds the Prince, "You're a man after my own heart! I always talk to myself because I like to converse with intelligent people!"

Paulo shows Mandrake his castle (which is built upside down) in which he keeps a young man imprisoned in an electrified cage, jolting him with current whenever he wishes him to sing. Paulo also keeps the beautiful Sybil, "loveliest flower in Dementor," imprisoned in a giant fishbowl.

When Mandrake tries to straighten things out, Paulo has him seized and thrown into a dungeon. Suddenly huge pointed metal girders begin to transfix the room, like a magician's swords in a sword-box; Mandrake dodges one after another, but he exclaims: "Whew! This *is* a tight spot! Magic's no help against machinery!"

But Mandrake does use magic to send an astral projection to summon Lothar, who pulls Paulo away from the machinery and frees Mandrake.

Now a great duel ensues:

Paulo calls out his army against Mandrake.

Mandrake transforms himself into a 100-foot tall giant towering over the troops!

Paulo calls out a huge cannon and fires it at Mandrake!

Mandrake shrinks to normal size and multiplies into a regiment of swordsmen!

And so it goes, until Mandrake triumphs over Paulo and the mad ruler is replaced on the throne by Marlock, a noble who also proves to be the mourning father of Sybil, who is reunited not only with her father but also with Dormus, her sweetheart, the singer.

I think that in this adventure Phil Davis's art was at its finest. The human figures are without exception beautifully rendered and gracefully appealing, even that of the gross Paulo. Sybil is lovely, Mandrake is noble, Lothar is powerful. The castle is beautifully rendered, the drafting of the "spike room" looks like a creation of imaginative artist M. C. Escher, and the scenes of the duel between Mandrake and Paulo are works of art, each panel.

But if Davis's greatest work was in the Dementor sequence, Lee Falk's writing may have been at its peak in the 1938 adventure, "Mandrake on the Moon." (Not that Davis's art is poor either— it is very fine, up to the strip's level.)

In this tale, Mandrake, Lothar, the scientist Professor Thursby, and his beautiful daughter, Laura, travel to the moon in Thursby's rocket ship, *Stardust*. The story is a combination of pure fantasy— for, after all, that is what magical stories are about—with science fiction and elements of myth.

The notion of traveling to the moon in a rocket ship, of course, was science-fictional; otherwise the travelers might have gone by flying carpet, astral projection, or other mystical means. Having reached the moon, they don breathing helmets (science fiction) but no vacuum-suits (fantasy). Laura and Lothar fall into a crater but, even though the fall is some 60 feet, they land unhurt and are able to jump back out (science fiction).

The surface of the moon proves to be uninhabited and essentially rather dull, so the four travelers climb back aboard their craft and fly to the far side of the moon. The near surface *had* shown an ancient wall of clearly artificial construction; perhaps the far side will reveal its makers' identities.

On the far side is revealed, "hanging between barren peaks . . . a great shining dome." The travelers land the *Stardust*, find an entranceway into the dome, pass through a series of airlocks, and confront a gorgeous, coral-tinted bird as tall as a man! Shades of Stanley Weinbaum's "A Martian Odyssey"!

But no, the bird is revealed the next week to be a pet. Its master—a handsome man, identical in form to Earthmen, dressed

151

in a flowing toga. Without a word he leads Mandrake and his party on a tour of a lovely city, Lunatopia, magnificently delineated in Grecian architecture with flowing fountains, music, luscious food and drink, no apparent labor. At bedtime the Earth-folk are shown how to use lunar "air-mattresses" which actually do float in the air.

Once spoken communication is established between Earthmen and Lunarian, the lunar being explains the history of his people. There had once been a magnificent civilization on the moon when that world was young and lush and Earth was still younger and uninhabited. As the moon grew old and lost its air and the waters of its seas, its people had migrated en masse to the ancient earthly continent of Atlantis, where they had reconstructed their great civilization.

A golden age passed and then Atlantis began to experience the cataclysms that led to its eventual disappearance. What to do? The Atlanteans returned to their spaceships and sped back to the moon, leaving behind only a few stragglers and diehards on Earth. Back on the moon they constructed a series of domed double-cities on the side of that world facing away from their lost Earth. Each city contained a surface community of beauty, culture, and comfort, and an underground city filled with automatic machinery which performed all the work.

The few Lunarians who remained on Earth became the ancestors of modern mankind—and the originators of the legend of Atlantis!

Now the visiting party's host takes them on a tour of the underground machine-city. "The machines generate their own power and lubrication," he explains. "For centuries they've worked without being touched by human hands! They're perfect!"

Mandrake says: "Amazing! But why do we have to see them from behind these bars? It looks like you keep your machines in jail!"

"We do! It sounds silly—but they were built so long ago, we know nothing about them! Some believe the master-machines *think* just like we do! Yes—we're a little *afraid* of them!"

Shades of E. M. Forster's "The Machine Stops"! The theme of decadence and domination by machinery is pursued to its logical revolt-of-the-robots conclusion, but rather than closing the lunar sequence for Mandrake, this leads to still another adventure—for the moon's flaming and molten core is inhabited by *fire people*.

Mandrake and his companions proceed to an encounter with these fantastic beings, and so the strip proceeded, and none except a few researchers and collectors have seen its like in a generation and a half.

The difficulty here is that *Mandrake the Magician* and other classic newspaper adventure strips, including the great *Flash Gordon, Prince Valiant, Tarzan,* and Falk and Davis's own *Phantom,* were designed, created, and published in a certain manner, intended to be read in a certain manner, and those who approach them in a different manner, albeit through no fault of their own, simply fail to comprehend the art form.

The problem is two-fold, one of graphic presentation and one of structure of continuity.

Mandrake and other newspaper comics were drawn in rather large size, intended to be presented on either full-size newspaper pages or (as with *Mandrake*) at least tabloid size. Each panel was fairly large, and the artists—Phil Davis, Alex Raymond, Hal Foster, Burne Hogarth—were able to lay out a scene and put into it a number of figures and an amount of graphic detail and technique appropriate to its size.

Even today I can look at a *Mandrake* page from a 1935 Saturday *Examiner* and see that each panel is a work of art.

When the Mandrake strips were collected by the King Features Syndicate and republished in *King Comics, Magic Comics,* and the David McKay Feature Books from 1936 onward, they were reduced in size by approximately 65 percent. The reader can follow the story-line well enough, but the beauty of the drawings is almost totally lost. There remains, perhaps, enough of a suggestion of Phil Davis's delicate brushwork and line to permit one to imagine what the page should look like, if one has seen full-size pages, but for the reader who knows *Mandrake* only through reductions such as these, there is simply no way of understanding the art and detail that went into the strip.

As for story structure, comic-book readers are accustomed to tales constructed in conventional short-story pattern: a problem is presented, it is further developed and complicated, and it is finally resolved. This is, of course, the classic beginning-middle-end structure.

Newspaper strips are simply not made this way. They are, in one sense, totally open-ended serials, but in fact they run in cycles, generally of 13 weeks' duration (a quarter of a year).

Within those 13 weeks it is necessary (in a weekly strip) to have 13 episodes, *each* with a beginning, middle, and ending. (Cliffhanger technique merely displaces the end of each week's episode to the opening of the following episode.)

Each episode is a semi–independent unit, yet over a period of 13 such episodes a full adventure develops.

A batch of half-a-dozen Saturday *Mandrake* pages in an issue of *King Comics* is simply not the way the strip should be read. And, in fact, the complete adventures collected in the McKay *Mandrake* Feature Books, while better than the King format, were still not ideal by any means.

I can only suggest that the reader find some way of getting access to a series of the old Hearst Saturday color sections, then turn to the *Mandrake* page in each and prepare himself for a remarkable treat. Of course, doing this may take magic . . .

Once the comic book began to come into its own, and specially created material began to displace reprinted newspaper strips as the dominating content of these magazines, it was not surprising that a number of magicians appeared, some of them rather closely based on Mandrake, others not nearly so much like him. Just for amusement I have made a list of some 30-odd of these sorcerers, the magazines in which they appeared, and the publishers of the magazines.

Perhaps some will ring a bell for you; if not, just speculate upon the endless variations on this theme represented herein. I follow the list with comments on just a few of the most interesting specimens as they seem to me.

There were: Balbo the Boy Magician (*Master, America's Greatest*, Fawcett); Blackstone (at least four different series published by Vital, Marvel, EC, and Street & Smith); Hale (*Dynamic, Punch, Harry "A" Chesler*); Houdini (*The Great Houdini*); Ibis the Invincible (*Whiz, Ibis,* Fawcett); Jupiter, Master Magician (*Prize Comics,* Prize); Kardak, the Mystic Magician (*Top Notch,* MLJ).

There were a great many magicians whose names began with *M*—alliteration as a device was favored long before Spiro Agnew came along—and left. These included: Magar the Mystic (*Red Raven,* Timely); Mantor the Magician (*Human Torch.* Timely); Marvo the Magician (*Lightning,* Ace); Marvelo, Monarch of Magicians (*Big Shot,* Columbia); the Master Mystic (*Green Giant,* Pelican Publications); Monako, Prince of Magic (*Daring Mystery,*

Top hat firmly stuck on her head, Zatanna, daughter of Zatara, tumbles into the "World of the Magic Atom" with The Atom, in quest of her missing father. Her costume was similar to her father's with a difference (vive la difference), mostly the substitution of fishnet stockings for morning trousers. Copyright © 1965 by National Periodical Publications, Inc., and reprinted by its permission.

Timely); Merlin (*National Comics,* Quality); Merzak the Mystic (*Mystic Comics,* Timely); Dr. Mystic, the Occult Doctor (*The Comics,* Dell); Mystic Moot and His Magic Snoot (*Ibis,* Fawcett); and Mystico, the Wonder Man (*Startling,* Better Publications).

After that they're scattered again: Nadir, Master of Magic (*Adventure,* DC); Norgil the Magician (*The Shadow, Doc Savage,* Street & Smith); Dr. Occult (*New Fun,* DC); Colonel Porterhouse (*Whiz,* Fawcett); Red Reeves, Boy Magician (*Silver Streak,* Comic House); Sargon the Sorcerer (*All-American, Comic Cavalcade, Green Lantern, Sensation,* DC); Solar, Master of Magic (*Captain Aero,* Holyoke); Stardust the Super Wizard (*Fantastic,* Fox); Tao-Anwar, Boy Magician (*Super-Magician Comics,* Street & Smith); the Wizard with Roy the Super Boy (*Shield-Wizard, Pep,* MLJ); Yarko the Great Master Magician (*Blue Beetle, Wonder World,* Fox).

And then in the *Z's* there's another cluster: The Great Zarro (*Great Comics,* Great Publications); Zatara the Master Magician (*Action, World's Fair, World's Finest,* DC); Zatanna (*Adventure, Justice League of America, Supergirl,* DC); Za-Za the Mystic (*Za-Za,* Charlton); Zambini the Miracle Man (*Zip,* MLJ); Zoro the Mystery Man (*Slam-Bang,* Fawcett).

The list is assuredly incomplete, but I think it captures the bulk of the magical fraternity among comics heroes of the past nearly 40 years. A few of those mentioned deserve some comment.

Blackstone and Houdini, of course, were both magicians in real life, of the prestidigitational sort. Houdini specialized in amazing escapes and was thus in a sense the prototype of Jack Kirby's modern Mister Miracle. Blackstone went in more for the white-tie-and-tails illusionist approach; in his various comic-book incarnations he turned his powers to the entrapment of criminals, and gave a few magic pointers to his readers.

Mystic Moot was a somewhat remote parody of Ibis the Invincible, alongside whose adventures Moot's appeared. Moot was the creation of Basil Wolverton, one of the all-time masters of the grotesque and the comical; as Ibis derived his power from the magical Ibistick, Moot got his from his nose. His adventures were very funny, and usually confined to half a page.

Colonel Porterhouse was a comic-relief feature that appeared in Fawcett's *Whiz Comics,* and would be of little concern here except for a series of adventures early in the 1940s in which the Colonel was depicted, in each *Whiz Comics,* reading that same issue of

Whiz to his little niece and nephew. In each issue, Porterhouse concentrated on a different story, and his pages were turned into a parody of that story—in one issue, Captain Marvel; in others, Spy Smasher, Lance O'Casey, Golden Arrow, and, of course, Ibis.

The Porterhouse parodies were very funny, possibly superior even to the Harvey Kurtzman–*Mad* parodies of a decade later. Perhaps with the thawing of the long-standing DC-Fawcett impasse, they could be revived and reprinted in collected form, or at least run as a reprint series in one of DC's magazines.

Dr. Occult and Dr. Mystic were very similar characters created by Jerry Siegel and Joe Shuster in the years before Superman finally emerged. Students of the history of comics heroes must regard the Occult-Mystic figure as a definite prototype of Superman, performing many of the feats Superman later performed, but doing so by supernatural rather than superscientific means.

Of all these magicians, by far the most significant two were Zatara the Master Magician and Ibis the Invincible.

Zatara appeared from the first issue of *Action Comics*, thereby setting the pattern of a magical feature in support of major superheroes. He was closely patterned on Mandrake, with traditional formal dress (he wore morning clothes and silk hat rather than tails), slicked-down hair, and crisp moustache.

For the giant Lothar, Zatara substituted an Asian giant, Tong. (Both Lothar and Tong also resemble Milton Caniff's Big Stoop and even Little Orphan Annie's companion Punjab, but that is of only passing concern.)

The early *Zatara* strips were drawn by Fred Guardineer, whose style was well suited to comic-book pages—he drew with a heavy, vigorous line and used large areas of solid color. The master of this principle, of course, was Clarence Beck, who drew *Captain Marvel*.

Zatara's power, according to the narration panels, lay in his eyes, and he was on occasion rendered *hors de combat* by being blindfolded. But when performing feats of magic, he spoke magic words—at first mere jumbled phrases, later the words of command with the sequence of their letters reversed. As—"SGUHT, PEEW YENOM!" Slow-witted readers, after a few issues, were advised by narration panels to read Zatara's words backwards for a surprise.

A few of Zatara's earlier adventures had some of the high-soaring imagination of Mandrake's. One example was "The

Terror from Saturn" in *Action* No. 14, in which a flaming triangle appears on Earth bearing word of a possible interplanetary war with Saturn. Zatara, aided by the scientist Djersinsky, travels to the ringed planet where he encounters a race of bald, green-skinned humans whose Prince Porra might have served as the prototype for DC's later John Jones—J'onn J'onzz, Manhunter from Mars.

Zatara undergoes a few Mandrake-like adventures among the Saturnians, convinces them that they can solve their own problems on Saturn and need not invade Earth, and returns home.

A more typical adventure, however, was that of Zatara at the New York World's Fair, in *World's Fair Comics* for 1940, the predecessor of DC's *World's Finest Comics*, which exists to this day. In this adventure (not signed, and clearly not by Guardineer) a group of thugs invades the fairgrounds and Zatara hunts them down and rounds them up with bits of magic.

Many artists worked on Zatara; Joseph Sulman was one of the most prolific, and was rather good; even Joe Kubert got his artistic hands on the master magician at least once. The main obstacle in the strip was not the art, which was no worse than the comic-book norm, but the writing, which was unfortunately no better than the comic-book norm.

In common with many DC heroes of the 1940s, Zatara used a basically exotic identity-gimmick and power in very mundane situations. He would, in one story, go after bank robbers and turn their guns to flowers; in another he used a city-wide television hookup to command thugs to give themselves up to the police.

In a fairly amusing yarn in *Action* No. 31 he turned the leaders of two warring nations into mannikins and forced them to a successful peace conference, having first used his powers to minimize casualties and aid escaping refugees; in another he used his magical powers to trick a potential rival into giving up a magic lantern, which Zatara then destroyed to preserve his own uniqueness.

In brief, where the greatest achievement of Falk and Davis in using Mandrake was not the conception of the character himself but the imagination with which he was carried into exotic adventures, the failure of Zatara lay in the lack of imagination applied to the plotting of *his* adventures.

Zatara disappeared along with so many others during the great character washout of the late 1950s and was presumed totally lost

Patsy, Thimble, and the Phantom Magician

The Phantom Magician wore tights, a cape, and a domino mask, an outfit later favored by many other adventure heros including the Phantom, Superman, and Batman. Copyright © 1938, Famous Funnies, Inc., renewed 1966 by Famous Funnies, Inc., and reprinted by its permission.

until his daughter (!) turned up in the late 1960s looking for her dad! The Zatara-Zatanna theme has been used several times in that series (*of which more later*) and, while Zatara has never been revived as an independent feature, it remains a possibility.

The second of the two significant comic-*book* magicians was Ibis the Invincible, who originated in the first issue of Fawcett's *Whiz Comics* in 1940 and was to Captain Marvel thereafter as Zatara was to Superman.

Ibis was not closely based on Mandrake or Zatara—the similarity was limited to the theme of utilizing magical powers as the basic characteristic of an adventure hero. The writing and drawing were the product of the usual anonymous Fawcett crew, generally farmed out to the Binder or Beck-Costanza studios; very likely the best single drawing of Ibis was the one by Mac Raboy for the first issue of the single-character *Ibis* comic launched in 1942. The cover, which is reproduced in *All in Color for a Dime*, shows Ibis using his magic wand, the Ibistick, to raise a figure of a woman or goddess clad in ancient dress from a cloud of green smoke that billows above a huge sorcerer's urn.

Ibis had a full-fledged origin story, a short version of which appeared in *Whiz*, a more complete version in that first issue of *Ibis*. In this tale Ibis, properly known as Amentep, had been a prince of Egypt some 4,000 years ago. An evil Pharaoh, misled by the false priest Mesu, abandoned Osiris and the benevolent gods of Egypt and made league with *Set, the Master of Inferno* and a legion of demons.

The evil Pharaoh lusted for power, glory—and the resplendent one, the Princess Taia, betrothed of Amentep.

As the people were ground under Pharaoh's heel, Amentep spoke out, leading protests against tyranny. He was thrown in jail, and there received from his uncle the fabled wand of mystical power, the Ibistick. In rebellion against the tyrant, Taia fell, an arrow in her breast. Enraged, Ibis beheaded the tyrant and, in grief, commanded the stick to slay himself. It refused—it would do no harm to its rightful master.

So Ibis instead commanded it to make him sleep some 4,000 years. Revived in modern times, dressed in a dark business suit with only a red turban to distinguish him, Ibis found the mummy of Taia, used the Ibistick to revive her—she had been in suspended animation, not dead—and proceeded to a series of modern adventures.

These adventures ran for some 15 years. Many of them dealt with mystical topics—Ibis in combat with demons and dark gods of various sorts; when this was the case, the stories, however limited their logic might be, generally offered something interesting to the reader. When, as occasionally happened, Ibis fought ordinary criminals or spies, the strip tended to descend to the poor level of the weaker Zatara yarns.

If there is a lesson to be drawn from all this, it would seem to be that an exotic hero must have an exotic challenge to hold him up; plunged into a mundane setting and plot, as was so often done, the exotic hero merely looks silly.

All of the magicians I have mentioned so far were essentially mortal men gifted with certain supernormal powers. There was yet another class of magicians in the comics, heroes whose might so far exceeded that of a mere Mandrake, Zatara, or Ibis, that they truly transcended the category of "mere" magicians and became—something more. These were the mind-bogglers, the farthest-fetched heroes in all the history of the comics:

Doctor Fate and the Spectre.

There are many comic-book heroes whom I remember more for their potential—alas, all too often never really tapped—than for the actual stories. Chief among these were Doctor Fate and the Spectre. Both had concepts that stretched the mind, but both had too many adventures that were, despite the supernatural elements shoveled into them, prosaic.

The Spectre could grow larger than the solar system or shrink smaller than an atom. He could fight a duel with comets as weapons (against a foe who could do the same!). He could ski on stars, raise the dead (with one exception), stop time, and talk with God.

The Spectre really was omnipotent. He could, quite literally, do *anything*.

It sounds like a good deal, I hear you cry. How does one qualify for this sort of superheroship?

Well, first you have to die. The Spectre really was a spectre—a ghost.

The Spectre was a creation of the fertile mind of Jerry Siegel—who had, with fellow Cleveland high schooler Joe Shuster, created Superman. Siegel's byline appeared on every story in the Spectre's entire run in *More Fun Comics*, where he appeared in issues No. 53 through No. 101 (February, 1940, through January-February,

1945). Artist Bernard Baily drew the strip; he did Siegel one better by signing it both at the beginning and at the end of each story. Baily also drew the early adventures of Hourman.

Siegel may have felt that if Superman did so well with his powers, Spectre would do even better with more. It's sort of like, if a little bit of salt is good, a cupful will be great; the result is about the same.

For a while, it is fun to follow the adventures of a hero who can do anything, but after that it gets kind of boring. Spectre could do anything except create suspense, it seemed. Besides, he was pretty frightening in appearance and attitude.

The Spectre was the ghost of Jim Corrigan, a "hard-fisted" police detective who was beaten by crooks who had kidnaped his fiancée, Clarice Winston. The crooks dumped him into a barrel and encased his still living form in concrete, then chucked the whole thing into the river. You can't get much deader than that and it is not a pleasant route to take to get to be a superhero, no matter how powerful.

Jim Corrigan's spirit rose from the barrel and headed for Heaven, with only a momentary pang at leaving Earth and his fiancée. He was looking forward to eternal rest but a voice— obviously God's, although never explicitly stated to be His—told him that he could not have his eternal rest until he had wiped out all crime on Earth. *All* crime, mind you. A tall order, but he was promised special abilities.

He returned to the river where his body lay and discovered that he did not need to breathe, that he could walk on water, levitate, or disappear at will, grow or shrink to whatever size he wished, and walk through walls. Armed with these powers and many more he didn't yet know he had, he went to rescue Clarice from the hoods who had killed him.

This turned out to be a two-part origin story (*More Fun* No. 52 and No. 53) and that was where the first part ended. Although the Spectre appeared in full costume on the cover of No. 52, Corrigan never got to wear a costume until part two.

With a mere 52-word synopsis, the second part began exactly one panel later. The last panel of the first installment showed Corrigan walking into the wall of a warehouse; the first panel of the second showed him emerging, halfway through the wall, in the room where "Gat" Benson's gangsters were menacing Clarice.

The hoods never had a chance. Their bullets either bounced off

Comic book fans lose sight of the literal meaning of the titles of comic books and see
nothing humorous in the contrast between the hugely emblazoned "FUN" and the grisly
form of the Spectre coming through the walls to protect his fiancée and avenge her kidnaping and his own murder. Can't be much "More FUN" than that, can there? Copyright © 1940, Detective Comics, Inc.; renewed 1967 by National Periodical Publications,
Inc., and reprinted by its permission.

Corrigan or passed through him harmlessly, depending on his whim. One by one, he called the thugs to him and had them look into his eyes, where they saw either Death incarnate or the very pits of Hell. They died or went mad at once. One wild shot had struck Clarice and he touched the wound; it closed and healed and vanished. She remembered none of this.

Corrigan figured that life as the wife of a ghost was no life for the woman he loved, so he broke his engagement with no explanation to her. Clarice refused to accept that and the series continued with the stock comic-book situation of the heroine chasing the reluctant hero with marriage as her object. But there were some differences from other strips using this device. For one thing, Corrigan was more than willing to marry her but felt that his lack of mortality (not necessarily *im*mortality; with his powers, it is conceivable that he *could* have wiped out crime and got what was always referred to as his "eternal rest") prevented this; I'm not sure why. Also, Clarice was in love with Jim Corrigan, not with his alter ego—nobody but the most ardent necrophile could have loved the Grim Ghost, as he was called with the traditional comic-book love of alliteration.

For some reason, Corrigan made a costume for Spectre the hard way, sewing it laboriously by hand (a strange talent for a hard-fisted police detective) when he could have created it from moonbeams, spider webs, or cool night air with a perfunctory thought.

His lack of skill as a tailor may have accounted for the bagginess of his green shorts, which he wore over a skin so deathly white that it looked almost as if he were wearing snowy tights. Green gloves, cloak, and a floppy hood completed the costume. The face of the Spectre was the same deathly white, with dark, shadowed eyes (close-ups often showed the pupils to be tiny skulls) and a grim, tight-lipped mouth. He was quite imposing, more than a little frightening.

To assume his identity as the Spectre, Corrigan needed no convenient phone booth—though just how convenient *is* it to change clothes in a phone booth?—or facile alibi to explain his absence while the Spectre was in action. He could go about his business, talking, eating, fighting crime, while the Spectre, like a supernatural amoeba, split invisibly off from his body and took on a corporeal form of his own. The two halves of Corrigan's personality could exist simultaneously and independently, so no secret-identity problems ever arose. Eventually, when Corrigan's concrete-encrusted corpse was about to be discovered on the river bottom, Corrigan was restored to life absolutely independent of the Spectre, who kept right on fighting crime and the supernatural entities that began appearing right after he made the scene. I said earlier that there was one exception to Spectre's dead-raising abilities: I meant Jim Corrigan—God (the Voice) did that at the Spectre's request.

In a more or less typical story (*More Fun* No. 61), newspaper headlines praising the Spectre enrage the police chief, who orders Corrigan to arrest the Spectre. One of Center City's biggest promoters is just then threatened by the Spectre—actually a bogus Spectre—and is turned to gold in front of the chief and Corrigan. A witness who is about to name the culprit also is turned to gold. Corrigan is given a free sample of chewing gum by a feeble social outcast and, seeing a car following him, plays a hunch and turns himself to gold. Two men jump from the car, pick him up with astonishing ease, considering how much a gold six-footer would weigh, and toss him in the river. The Spectre emerges from the water and follows them, foiling another assassination attempt by turning the gum to worms. When one of the hoods calls the boss to report the incident, the Spectre shrinks, enters the phone, and races through the wires—a trick revived in the sixties and given to the new version of the Atom—only to be frustrated when the boss breaks the connection. Corrigan visits Clarice and meets Gustave Gilroy, who knows a scientist who is trying to change the atomic structure of objects. Spectre bombards the scientist with L-rays, which cleanse his mind of evil—the L-rays were a bunch of letter *L*'s which came out of the Spectre's eyes. He then finds Clarice in the grip of the bogus Spectre, who has kidnaped her father. Just then, he is caught in the grip of an "occult occurrence"—this happened in several stories, with no explanation and with varying results—which flings him an hour back in time as Jim Corrigan. Using the extra time, Corrigan arrests the real Spectre, turns him over to the police chief, escapes, and then goes back as Spectre to nail Gustave (now, oddly, called Gustaf) Gilroy, the man masquerading as the Spectre. Gilroy confesses and commits suicide by turning himself to gold.

Whew. All that and more in just one short story.

God was presented as somewhat sneaky. In one instance, just as Clarice is about to be killed, the Spectre is called away by God.

Clarice has a bullet heading toward her skull and God has chosen that time to decide that the Spectre is getting a raw deal and to offer him a choice of taking his eternal rest *right then* or of going back to wipe out all crime. Of course, should he decide to take up the harp, that will be the end of Clarice. (Presumably, Clarice has not led a blameless life, else he would be assured that she would join him in Heaven.) He chooses to return to earth to finish off crime and save Clarice.

The strip was weakened later by the introduction of Percival Popp the Super Cop, a supposedly funny, big-nosed, buck-toothed bumbler who rose from supporting character to star, with Spectre taking second billing. It was one heck of a long fall from what the Spectre could have been.

Doctor Fate also appeared in *More Fun Comics* (No. 55 through No. 98; May, 1940, through January, 1944). For the first dozen issues, he had no secret identity and his origin was unknown. This was most effective. Doctor Fate was always in costume and dwelled in a doorless and windowless tower in "witch-haunted Salem," surrounded by musty tomes, weapons, and devices both of advanced science and advanced necromancy. He exited his tower by walking through the walls or by using some arcane machine. He was a wizard of incredibly ancient origin and virtually unlimited powers; he certainly was not a stage magician who happened to possess some real magic. He had been a wizard back when the Druids were altar boys.

Dr. Fate wore blue tights with yellow boots, shorts, gloves, and cape. On his chest was a large golden medallion of unspecified purpose, strung on a cord about his neck. His head and face were covered by a completely smooth bullet-shaped golden helmet with only two eye-holes.

A girl named Inza, whose presence in his life was not explained, wandered at will about the world and called on Dr. Fate whenever she was in difficulty. She got in trouble often, usually as a result of some slumbering wizard's awakening or some bush-league Merlin stumbling across the Book of Thoth and becoming a major-league Merlin. Things like that happened all the time.

Dr. Fate had achieved complete control of energy, and blows or bullets directed at him were turned into power for him. He could emit rays of energy which were capable of knocking over buildings or thoroughly disposing of unsavory characters. He had

Doctor Fate, the superhero most likely to have been liked by weird fantasist H. P. Lovecraft, lived in a doorless and windowless tower in Salem. Just getting in and out of his own living room required magic. His cape, gloves, boots, shorts, epaulets and helmet were yellow, the rest of his costume was blue—the effect was quite striking. Inza tended to get into supernatural difficulty in her wanderings, sort of scouting up work for Doctor Fate. Note the long center bar on the "E" in captions and balloons, giving a hyphenated look to the lettering. Copyright © 1940, Detective Comics, Inc.; renewed 1968 by National Periodical Publications, Inc., and reprinted by its permission.

a crystal ball and spells for all occasions at his command. He could fly, too.

Gardner Fox, who wrote the earliest stories, had obviously read a great deal of H. P. Lovecraft, although the strip was not directly derivative. The hints of elder gods and vanished civilizations, of wizardry that was actually a form of science far beyond what we have attained, and "witch-haunted Salem," which smacks unmistakably of Lovecraft's Arkham, all point to a familiarity with Lovecraft's writings. Most of the stories were illustrated by Howard Sherman. The unknown letterer made his mark on the strip, too; he made his *E*'s with the center bar longer than the other two, making the dialog look as if it were filled with hyphens. It was different—hard to read, but different.

Dr. Fate whips Wotan (apparently unrelated to Norse mythology, Wotan had a green skin, a Mephisthophelean face, and wore red tights with a high, stiff, flaring collar and a green floor-length cape) in his first appearance, in No. 55. In the next issue, he goes to the land of the dead to make sure Wotan is really there. He is not, so Dr. Fate returns to Earth and whips him again, leaving him in a magical trance, encased in an air bubble and hidden beneath the Earth. In a later story Wotan is freed, and this time Dr. Fate kills him.

Doctor Fate took the cover and lead spot in *More Fun* away from the Spectre and he deserved to. His stories had much more of an air of mystery, helped largely by the fact that no one really knew much about Dr. Fate.

Then, in issue No. 67, they went and spoiled it by giving him an origin story which threw out the ancient wizard bit entirely. In the origin, he is young Kent Nelson, exploring in the Valley of Ur "in the year 1920 or thereabouts" with his father, Egyptologist Sven Nelson. Sven thinks the pyramids had been built by people from another planet; he doesn't think the Egyptians knew enough to do the job. Kent finds a man standing in an open casket and, following telepathic directions, turns a lever and frees him from suspended animation. The man is Nabu the Wise, who is close to half a million years old and from the planet Cilia. His people built the pyramids; unfortunately, Sven never learns his theory was right because he dies of poison gas prepared by Nabu's people to prevent intrusions. Nabu attempts to make up for this by teaching Kent the secrets of the universe. He then gives young Kent the costume and name of Doctor Fate and disappears without a word of explanation. Since these stories appeared in the early 1940s, Doctor Fate had suddenly gone from being millennia old to being barely 20. The Lovecraftian aura was shed with the years.

The beautifully mysterious face-covering was sawed off just below the eyes, revealing the Doctor's nose and mouth and concealing only his hair, forehead, and the area around his eyes. His powers were sawed off, too; starting with the idea that he was only invulnerable from outside harm and that his lungs were vulnerable to lack of air, they developed the idea from simply making him susceptible to gassing or drowning to the point where he could be rendered unconscious by strangling him or by hitting him in the solar plexus to knock the air out of him.

Then they decided to make him a real doctor, an M.D.—he got through medical school and became an intern in just half a page—and he spent the bulk of the rest of his career chasing petty crooks.

Both the Spectre and Doctor Fate have been revived from time to time by DC. The Spectre had his own book briefly in the sixties and Doctor Fate has made several guest appearances in *Justice League of America* and *World's Finest Comics*. The revivals stick to the original powers and costumes but really don't offer much else.

Some magicians also made an appearance in the superhero revival of the 1960s. The best of these was Doctor Strange, who began in Marvel Comics' *Strange Tales* and has appeared in his own book and as a frequent guest in other Marvel comics. Originally drawn by Steve Ditko and written by Stan Lee, he has undergone many changes of writer and artist without losing any of his extravagant speech patterns or much of his flamboyant costume. Strange (who actually is a physician-type doctor, according to yet another of those belated origin stories that come along by afterthought) lives in Greenwich Village and has an Oriental servant named Wong and an Oriental teacher known as the Ancient One.

Strange has black hair, white at the temples, and the moustache that few who weren't magicians could wear in the comic books without being either a villain or the girl friend's father. He wears a loose blue suit and a voluminous cape with a stiff, flaring collar of red and yellow; he wears a magic yellow amulet on his chest, an amulet that occasionally opens as an eye (the all-seeing Eye of Agamoto) and blasts Dr. Strange's opponents. For a while, he wore an all-over skintight black suit which covered even his face, but that was dropped. He tended to be colorful, but it was hard to follow his stories and even harder to worry about him, since the magic was of such an anything-can-happen variety: Dr. Strange could be thoroughly beaten at the end of one book and remember another, winning, spell at the beginning of the next. The stories were good, though, and the artwork was often excellent, even after the enormously talented Ditko left Marvel.

The now-defunct American Comics Group (ACG) created a horrendous flop in the magician category with Magicman. He was a soldier in Vietnam who turned out to be a descendant of Cagliostro and had magical abilities. He outfitted himself out of a costume trunk and looked as if he was on the way to the Artists and Models Ball. He wore a vaguely Arabian Nights costume with a fruity little string mask and made his magical gestures with limp wrists. Worse, he had a dumb and sadistic sergeant for comic relief and they hung around together even after they got out of the service. Fortunately, the strip did not last long. He appeared in *Forbidden Worlds* No. 125 to No. 141.

As noted, DC revived the Spectre in the 1960s. He had some tryout appearances in *Showcase*, a comic book where new comics were tested, then ran briefly in his own book. He had a few good stories, but he didn't seem to have his old verve; maybe the fact that his stories were censored by the Comics Code Authority contributed to his early demise.

DC also brought back Sargon the Sorcerer, a minor magician who had the power of controlling anything he had ever touched— as with most superhero limitations, this was badly abused by lazy writers who decided that, since he had touched the air, he could make the air do anything he wanted and he could beat up crooks with hardened air. When DC brought him back, it was as a villain in *Flash Comics*. Eventually, however, he reformed and helped the Justice League of America and became a good guy again.

The best and longest-lasting of DC's new versions of old magicians was Zatanna, a hitherto-unmentioned daughter of Zatara. Zatara had last appeared in *World's Finest* in 1951; in 1964, his daughter appeared on the scene, looking for her widower father. As far as we comic-book readers knew, Zatara was wifeless and childless in 1951, but Zatanna was obviously mature, certainly more than 12 or 13 years old.

She sought her father through a series of comic books, seeking the help of different DC heroes. She first appeared in *Hawkman* No. 4 (October-November, 1964) as "The Girl Who Split in Two!" The story was written, as were the rest of the stories in the series, by Gardner F. Fox, who had created Doctor Fate. Editor of all the books in which Zatanna appeared was Julius Schwartz. While searching for the source of certain art objects that had mysteriously appeared in the museum, Hawkman found in China a gibberish-speaking statue of a girl. Hawkgirl found another statue of the same girl, also speaking gibberish, in Ireland. When the two statues were brought together and merged, the result was the living Zatanna and the gibberish was revealed as two halves of the same words. She had split herself in two to try to simultaneously look for her father in two different places, but the result was immobility and incoherence. She had magically placed the art objects in the museum with what remained of her powers in order to attract Hawkman and Hawkgirl. Freed now, she said the words "ANNATAZ RAEPPASID"—using the same magical method as her father—and continued her quest.

Her costume was reminiscent of her father's but with considerable difference. Both wore top hats and morning coats but, where Dad wore gray trousers, Zatanna wore gray hotpants and mesh stockings. She also wore high heels and had a definitely feminine appearance. She sought her father in *The Atom* No. 19 (June-July, 1965), where "the world's smallest super-hero" helped her track down a wizard called the Druid in an atom world; in *Green Lantern* No. 42 (January, 1966), where "the emerald gladiator" helped her battle the Warlock in another dimension; and in *Detective* No. 355 (September, 1966), where she bypassed Batman ("the caped crusader") to seek Elongated Man's help and "the stretchable sleuth" helped her recover a copy of the magic book of *I Ching*—don't ask me why she didn't just pick up one of the many paperback reprints of the book. Each time, she got a little closer to finding Zatara.

The series concluded in *Justice League of America* No. 51 (February, 1967), where all those heroes plus Batman helped Zatanna rescue her father from a magical world.

Zatara was kind of forgotten after that, but Zatanna has

171

appeared frequently in *Justice League of America* and in her own series in *Adventure* and *Supergirl*.

She appears to be more popular than her father and it really isn't surprising; he may be a more powerful magician, but she has really great looks and attracts adolescent males of all ages—with the most powerful magic of all.

INTRODUCTION TO

THE PROPWASH PATROL FLIES AGAIN

THE desire to fly has always been strong in humanity, and so comic books, being designed, after all, as wish-fulfillment for their youthful readers, have always emphasized flying. Most superheroes can fly or jump so far that it is the same thing as flying. Those who cannot fly frequently have fantastic aircraft, such as Batman's batplane or the bird-plane of Airboy.

In this chapter, Dick Lupoff returns to the pilots of the comic books but with a somewhat more varied assortment than were dealt with in *Wings*—the private air force of a Polish (later American aviator named Blackhawk; a boy who flew a plane that flapped its wings; and a shambling half-vegetable, half-human monster that had once been a German ace in the Red Baron's Flying Circus.

None of these dauntless airmen could fly without mechanical aids but they had adventures as fantastic and science-fictional as their self-propelled colleagues in the trick suits.

From time to time, there are minor debates, teapots tempests, concerning whether such characters as the denizens of this chapter qualify as costumed heroes. They didn't wear masks but they did wear the same clothes at the time. Blackhawk and his polyglot crew wore uniforms, okay. But Airboy wore the same flying outfit all the time, not as a disguise but certainly not as a uniform—you can't have a uniform if only one person wears it, can you? So is he a costumed hero? And, if he is, what do you say about the heroes of the defunct television series Bonanza? They never changed clothes either—when does an idiosyncrasy become a costume?

Fortunately, the question does not arise with the Heap, also discussed in this chapter—he never wore anything at all.

CHAPTER 7

THE PROPWASH PATROL
FLIES AGAIN

by DICK LUPOFF

I<small>T</small> was the nation's disenchantment with war at the time of the Korean conflict that laid *Wings Comics* by the heels; that's a statement I'll stand by pretty stubbornly if anyone feels like debating, but I will concede willingly that there were other factors involved. After all, it wasn't just the war-oriented comics that fell away in the 1950s.

Most of the superheroes disappeared and, while many of them had been involved in World War II and the Korean War, others had concentrated their efforts on combatting criminals, spies, monsters, and other assorted menaces, all of which continued to be available. And the crime comics and horror comics suffered catastrophic cutbacks, chiefly as the result of Dr. Fredric Wertham's pseudoscientific barrages.

Even television, first coming into its own as a major entertainment medium, may well have been a factor in the decline of the comic-book industry, as was the general effect of inflation, which drove the cost of publishing upward at a steady pace. (The final collapse of the $0.10 price barrier on standard-size comics was a blessing in disguise: it permitted the publishers to peg their prices to general economic conditions instead of an arbitrary level established years before by historical accident.)

So much for economics, but why did *Wings* fail aesthetically? The fact is that *Wings Comics* and all the rest of the Fiction House group failed aesthetically because of a gross imbalance in the ingredients of their stories. The category of the story hardly mattered. Fiction House's six major titles over the years were divided into three categories—*Wings, Rangers,* and *Fight Comics* featured war stories, with *Wings* of course further specializing on *air*-war stories; *Jungle* and *Jumbo* concentrated on jungle adventures; *Planet Comics* dealt in science fiction.

And yet all of the magazines utilized the same formula: uninterrupted and generally violent action spiced with ample cheesecake. The backgrounds that provide atmosphere and sense of involvement were minimal—there were nice drawings of airplanes and the other implements of war, jungle beasts, spaceships and bug-eyed monsters—but very little to give the reader a sense of the stories taking place in real locations.

And the characterization of the continuing heroes and heroines—characterization, the most important single factor in fiction—was next to nil. Was Captain Wings really anybody? How about Flint Baker or Hunt Bowman or Lyssa of *Planet*? What of Ka'anga or Sheena, Fiction House's entries in the Tarzan derby? Or Rip Carson, Hooks Devlin, Señorita Rio, all leading figures in Fiction House's war books?

Nobodies, blanks, nonentities, Leckishes.

Leckishes?

A little autobiography. When I was a boy we had an imaginary fellow named Leckish, who used to hang around our family. When the telephone rang and my father answered and spoke briefly, and my mother asked who had called, my father would sometimes grunt, "Leckish, it was Leckish."

That meant that it was a wrong number, or a particularly objectionable solicitor, or something of the sort. Junk mail came from Leckish. Door-to-door salesmen were Leckish. Dull and forgettable movies starred Leckish.

Leckish was a *nebbish*.

Almost everybody in the Fiction House comics, and certainly in *Wings Comics*, was Leckish.

But fortunately not all the aviation heroes of those days were Leckishes, not by a long shot. Let's take a look at a few who weren't.

Let's look, first of all, at the Blackhawks.

The Blackhawks were an international gang of crimefighters who operated their own air force. The four by the "B" are, top to bottom, Blackhawk, Olaf, Hendrickson and Andre. The three relegated to the end of the title are, again top to bottom, Chuck, Chop Chop and Stanislaus. They were as ethnically stereotyped as characters in a James Bond novel. Chop Chop, the comic relief, later came under fire as an undesirable racial carica- ture. He was changed into a hip-talking karate expert, a more acceptable racial stereo- type, a few years before the strip ended its long run. Copyright © 1950, Comic Maga- zines, and reprinted by its permission.

The Blackhawks (the name applies in plural to a fighting team, in singular to any member of the team but especially to its leader) were the creation of the Quality Comics Group owned by Everett M. Arnold. Quality never attained the massive growth of the huge DC and Fawcett operations, but it was nonetheless one of the real leaders of the industry. The name *Quality* was well chosen; Arnold and his staff assembled a group of characters that included Plastic Man, the Spirit, Dollman, and Kid Eternity, as well as Blackhawk—a lineup that could stand up to any in the field.

Blackhawk first appeared in *Military Comics*, where he was the lead character from the very first issue, August, 1941, through the entire history of that magazine (it changed titles to *Modern Comics* in 1945), which ended in 1950, and beyond in a *Blackhawk* comic for an eventual 235 issues. That last point can take a little clarification: one of the Quality titles was originally titled *Uncle Sam*; as such it lasted only eight issues, but with No. 9 it became *Blackhawk*. As *Blackhawk* it reached issue No. 107 under the Quality aegis. At that point the Quality group went out of business but *Blackhawk* was taken over by DC and continued to the ripe old age of *243* issues!

What was the secret of *Blackhawk*'s success? Why did this feature last so long, and why is *Blackhawk* so well and vividly remembered today when *Captain Wings* is only a vague and dusty recollection?

The answer does not lie in the plotting of the *Blackhawk* stories, which were, admittedly, a bit more complex and subtle than the rough shoot-em-ups of the *Wings* characters, nor does it lie in the drawing, although as a separate matter the drawing in *Blackhawk* was far superior to the average of the comics industry.

The answer lies in one word: *vividness*.

The characters in *Blackhawk* were individually delineated, about as "subtly" as Doc Savage's assistants Monk, Renny, Long Tom Roberts, Theodore Marley Brooks, and William Harper Littlejohn. Which is to say, they weren't characters so much as one-dimensional *caricatures*, single characteristics stretched to cover whole personalities, but they had their vivid and contrasting characteristics, which the *Wings* crew never did.

And there was a sense of camaraderie and, yes, hominess among the Blackhawks. They flew matching airplanes, followed the same leader, whom they regarded with loyalty and respect

A typical Wings cover—flaming action, lovingly delineated warplanes, story blurbs that blend patriotism and old-style pulp sensation.

approaching worship; they worked together, fought together, and even lived together on Blackhawk Island, a place a little like Wonder Woman's Paradise Island. And this base of operations offered the reader a kind of psychological home-base; if ever you settled back, an invisible third companion to the illustrious pair of Baker Street, relishing the very familiarity of each sound, each implement, each odor in Mrs. Hudson's famous rooming house, you are familiar with the phenomenon.

Well, from Doc Savage to Wonder Woman to Sherlock Holmes, the comparisons are oddly assorted and yet significantly unified in that all who have encountered these varied adventurers bear forever after a recollection of them; the key ingredient lies neither in the construction of plots nor the rendition of the stories, but in the *vividness* of the characters and their headquarters.

What about *Blackhawk*, then?

That first issue of *Military Comics* was a multicharacter but single-theme magazine. That is, the features introduced an assortment of continuing features: *Blackhawk, Death Patrol, Miss America, The Yankee Eagle*—but there was a common theme, action against the wartime enemy. Of course the United States was not yet participating officially, but the Quality folks followed the same approach that the people at Fiction House did—they used stories of foreign aces, and of Americans fighting under foreign flags. Plus, the device of Americans combating foreign operatives who threatened the nation even in "peacetime."

The international makeup of the Blackhawk team is illustrative. The leader, Blackhawk himself, was introduced as a Polish aviator; in later years this version was modified to explain that, no, he was really an American who had volunteered to fly for heroic little Poland in her resistance to the onslaught of 1939.

He never spoke with an accent; his language was always the standard English spotted with colorful epigrams and wisecracks that marked almost every comic-book hero.

In that opening story, an outnumbered and outgunned squadron of Polish resistance aviators are methodically slaughtered by the Nazi "Butcher Squadron" commanded by Captain Von Tepp. (Later on a Baron Von Tepp appeared in the series—he was the captain's brother.)

One by one the brave Polish aviators crash in flames until a single freedom-flier escapes—Blackhawk, swearing vengeance against Von Tepp and the Butcher Squadron, against all Nazis,

The other half of the Fiction House formula of relentless fierce action, and. . .plenty of pretty girls! You paid your dime and you didn't have to choose—you got both the battles and the babes!

and against the forces of oppression everywhere. (He was called "Jack" in the origin story by Will Eisner; in a different, later origin he was called "Bart Hawk"—but *all* the rest of the time he was called "Blackhawk.")

As an origin story it wasn't bad, except maybe a little lacking in the bizarre and the exotic that we have learned to expect from comic-book heroes, but it does have a slightly familiar ring to it. In fact, it sounds one hell of a lot like the story of the Lone Ranger; substitute the Polish air force for the Texas (or was it Arizona?—no matter) Rangers, substitute Nazi aviators for western thugs, and substitute for the lone surviving cowboy-lawman a lone surviving aviator-hero. It matches pretty well.

The Blackhawks wore no nation's uniform; being a sort of multinational volunteer force throughout their career, they donned a uniform of their own design in a dark blue shade. Each was equipped with a visored military cap with brass insigne, military tunic closed by a *horizontal* flap and metallic buttons high on the chest, leather belt with brass buckle, broad-topped trousers of the riding-jodhpur variety, and well-polished black leather boots.

Blackhawk himself was further distinguished by wearing his tunic open at the throat, displaying a yellow scarf, and by a stylized hawk's-head symbol blazoned against a yellow circle on the front of his uniform.

The other members of the Blackhawk team were added early in the series, and with one exception fit neatly into the mold of aviators loyally following the lead of their commander. The lineup varied somewhat over the years, but usually it consisted of six members: Andre, Stanislaus, Hendrickson, Olaf, Chuck, and Chop Chop.

Most prominently featured in the series was Andre, a dashing Frenchman with a turned-up pencil moustache and slicked-back hair. True to stereotypes, Andre was an insatiable ladies' man, forever disappearing in pursuit of a skirt, and "vividified" (to coin a term) by his French accent.

Flying over an island outpost, the Blackhawks spot a distress signal. Andre is detailed to land and investigate. On the ground he is met by a sexy brunette who says, "Thank heaven you saw my signal, sir!"

Andre's response: "Mort de ma vie! Had I known zere was so beautiful a ma'm'selle I would have landed sooner! Permettez-moi ... ze name is Andre ... "

An early (1941) Greasemonkey Griffin strip by "Jap Rider." The feature was later signed by one Kip Beales. Note Griffin's faithfully rendered Hawker Hurricane—a Wings trademark was the careful delineation of actual World War II fighting craft.

A confederate of the beautiful lady's steps from hiding. "Good work, Dorna!" he growls, "He came into your trap like a rabbit!"

Andre says "Ze trap? Have a care . . . I am of ze *Blackhawks!*"

Why, a fella could practically learn to speak the French language from a stack of Blackhawk adventures, if he concentrated on Andre's dialog.

Hendrickson was an interesting fellow. There was a sort of standardized young-mature look that most heroes showed, varied usually only for kids. But Hendrickson (or Henderson as it was occasionally rendered) was a fat, jolly old coot with pure white hair and a big, snowy moustache. But he kept himself in good shape despite his corpulence, and kept up with his comrades on earth and in the air.

The nationality of Hendrickson was somewhat dubious—at first he seemed to be Dutch, bearing out the theme of the Blackhawks all being refugees from Nazi-conquered nations in Europe. But that changed, of course, and one of the ways in which it changed was that Hendrickson became an anti-Nazi German.

This might seem to be a minor distinction, but in fact it set Hendrickson in particular and the Blackhawks in general onto a more sophisticated and in a sense more decent level than most other wartime comics. For those comics were widely guilty of rather vicious racism, the caricaturing of blacks as shiftless, cowardly, and unintelligent being only one aspect of the phenomenon.

Another was the characterization of the citizens of enemy nations as subhuman beasts—Japanese were portrayed as bucktoothed, sadistic fanatics; Germans, as brutal monsters.

It's odd that in *Blackhawk*, where national stereotyping was used as the chief characterizing device, an important distinction was made: that between a political system and a people. Hendrickson was graphic evidence that the enemy was not the German people but the Nazi political movement. And throughout the career of the Blackhawks, with only a few regrettable exceptions relatively late in the game, distinctions were drawn between tyrannical governments and the peoples they controlled.

And as for Hendrickson—how was he characterized beyond those physical items? Why, the same way Andre was, by his dialect. As the Blackhawks see an inventor off to his secret laboratory, Blackhawk himself comments, "There goes a great man, gang—vanishing into the unknown with perhaps the greatest secret on earth today!"

"Jawohl!" chips in Hendrickson, "Und if someding should happen to Dr. Vardan, der vorld might never know!"

The other Blackhawks included the Swede Olaf ("By gar! I ban going to—"), the Pole Stanislaus, and the American Chuck.

Plus Chop Chop, the Chinese cook and comic-relief man. Chop Chop must have stood all of four feet high, and had an almost round head to go with his almost round body. His ears were huge and stood straight out from the sides of his head, his hair was pulled straight *up* and tied in a red bow that flopped about, and he had buck teeth that, to scale, must have been easily three inches long and an inch wide—*each*!

He was oddly dressed, too—green shirt and trousers, red shoes, apparently a red sleeveless tunic over his shirt, and a short yellow vest over the tunic.

Chop Chop was usually pretty cowardly, endeavoring to hide behind Blackhawk or anyone else handy when danger threatened, although if sufficiently provoked he could turn on his tormentor with a meat-cleaver that he kept handy for use in his duties as official chef of the Blackhawks. How did he speak? Are you kidding?

"Well, stlange interlude! Tough clooks still aflaid of Chop Chop, even without goldy pencil boom! Is most stlange! Evelywhere Chop Chop go, evelybody scleam and lun away in gleat flight!"

Chop Chop was Blackhawk's Woozy Winks, his Doiby Dickles, his Alfred the butler, and his Uncle Marvel all in one. He flew with Blackhawk in his plane many times, accompanied the team on their missions, suffered privation and imprisonment with them with never a word of complaint except for an occasional "O woe!" and he attained his reward in the form of a series of solo adventures in the later years of *Blackhawk Comics*. These adventures generally carried Chop Chop into exotic settings (as the mainstream Blackhawk stories carried the team into many parts of the world) and in August, 1949, we learned that Chop Chop was the identical cousin of His Royal Highness Chop Chin, Emperor of Won Lung, a small Asian kingdom. In the course of the adventure Chop Chin offers Chop Chop his throne, but the loyal chef refuses—he'd rather fight and fly and cook for the Blackhawks. Okay.

The artwork in *Blackhawk* was almost always first-rate; it was produced by a number of artists, but is most often associated with Reed Crandall, a fine craftsman who passed through the comic-book factories in the forties, contributed much to the greatness of the EC group in the fifties, and in the 1960s turned to book illustration with fine results.

Crandall himself is hardly the man you would expect to turn out those crisply rendered, military-looking figures. He is himself a rotund, jolly farm-boy from Iowa; the first time I met him (to discuss some book illustrations) he even wore the archetypical farmer's straw hat. I think it was the only one on Manhattan Island outside of theatrical costumers' shops.

But Crandall had an education in fine arts, and his drawings of human figures above all else were marked with a kind of vigorous grace that fit perfectly the motif of the somewhat stern, serious Blackhawks.

Second only to the humans in the strip were the airplanes the Blackhawks flew. In the early years of the strip they flew Grumman F5F Skyrockets—one of the oddest looking airplanes of the World War II era, and hence one of the most distinctive that could have been chosen for the Blackhawks to use.

The F5F was an experimental naval fighter; I do not believe that any of them ever reached combat outside the pages of *Military Comics* and its successors *Modern* and *Blackhawk*. The standard U.S. Navy fighter at the outbreak of World War II was the stubby little Grumman F4F Wildcat, a single-engine monoplane with the blunt nose typical of radial-engine craft.

Looking for a hotter airplane to replace the Wildcat, the Navy got the gull-wing Corsair from Vought-Sikorsky while Grumman proposed the Skyrocket. This was a twin-engine plane, and the oddity of its appearance arose from the mounting position of the wing: instead of being set somewhere back along the body, the wing of the F5F was in front of the airplane. The nose of the fuselage extended only partway into the trailing edge of the wing. The result was an airplane that looked like none other before or since, and this was the "official" plane of the Blackhawks!

(As things worked out, the Navy passed up the F5F and Grumman came back with the F6F Hellcat, a sort of "stretched" Wildcat with a more powerful engine and heavier armament. It was quite successful. There was also an F7F Tiger Cat, a twin-engine model again, but few if any of these saw combat service either.)

Over the years the adventures of the Blackhawks were generally

Captain WINGS

AND THE
HELL-DIVER SQUADRON

By Major T. E. Bowen

AUSTRALIA—HIGH ABOVE THE HELL-DIVER BASE, THE YELLOW CUR AND THE THOROUGHBRED MEET IN MORTAL COMBAT.

THE LAST MUMBLED WORDS FROM THE BLOOD-FLECKED LIPS OF A DYING MAN LEAD CAPTAIN WINGS INTO A WEIRD WEB OF MYSTERY. FIGHTER AND FIGHTER, THE STRANDS ARE DRAWN AROUND HIM BY A HATE-FILLED GIRL AND A CRUEL JAP DOCTOR.

The symbolism may be confusing—a Curtis Helldiver trailing smoke and its pilot bailing out as the plane tumbles into a spider web spanning the opening of a golden ring. And who is the golden-skulled figure with the ruby eyes? And why is there a dagger in his back? And who is that nurse? Only Major T. E. Bowen knew for sure.

edited by Harry Stein; later, by Alfred Grenet. Stories were written by a goodly number of people, including several of the top comics scripters of the era: Ed Herron, Bill Finger, Joe Millard, and the sometime pulp-fantasy writer Manly Wade Wellman. There were several artists, too; before Crandall got hold of the feature it had been drawn by Will Eisner and Charles Cuidera.

But Crandall was the classic *Blackhawk* artist.

After the war ended the strip had to find new directions, but the changes were actually less extreme than you might expect. In place of Nazi or Japanese militarists, the villains tended to be the leaders of private armies or other paramilitary organizations bent on world conquest. The Blackhawks traded in their Grummans for modern aircraft, switching first to somewhat modified Republic F-84 Thunderjets, and then to Lockheed F-104 Starfighters.

They continued under the aegis of the Quality group until 1956, and survived the suspension of the Quality comics by shifting over to DC, but DC unfortunately didn't really know what to do with the Blackhawks. Their adventures, which had always stuck fairly close to realism, grew wilder and wilder. The traditional dark-blue Blackhawk uniforms were swapped for some sort of garish red-and-green concoctions, and the Blackhawks became just another nondescript bunch of adventurers. DC even revamped Chop Chop into a short, slim, tough, jazz-talking judo expert, trading one racial stereotype for another. The final death of the title in 1968 seemed more a release than a deprivation.

But for the classic years of the Blackhawks, with good, tight writing and fine Crandall art, the feature must be remembered as one of the all-time best aviation comics.

Air Fighters Comics was started with the issue of November, 1941, just three months after *Military*. The publisher was the Hillman group, a company that delved into a number of publishing areas including (some years later) science fiction. The Hillman comics were few; aside from *Air Fighters* I know only of *Clue Comics*, a general hero comic which featured the Boy King (he was a boy king, right, and his costume was superhero tights plus a crown and an ermine robe), Zippo (whose shtick was roller-skates), and Micro-Face (who, yes, had a small face).

The first *Air Fighters* bore a vague resemblance to *Wings*

AIRBOY COMICS (Trade Mark Reg. U.S. Pat. Office), published monthly by Hillman Periodicals, Inc., at 4600 Diversey Avenue, Chicago, Ill. Executive and Editorial Offices, 535 Fifth Ave., New York 17, N. Y. Edward Cronin, Editor. Vol. 8, No. 7, August, 1951. Printed in the United States of America. Price 10c a copy, subscription rate $1.20 a year in the United States and possessions. Copyright 1951 by Hillman Periodicals, Inc. Entered as second class matter October 26, 1945, at the Post Office at Chicago, Ill., under the Act of March 3, 1879.

The blond with the goggles is Airboy, one of the few comic-book characters who aged at a normal rate. He started in 1941 at the age of about 11 or 12 and finished his career in 1953, now just a shade too old to continue being called Air*boy* any longer. His birdplane had jets and flapping batwings, came when he called, and provided him with someone to talk to. Copyright © 1951, Hillman Periodicals, Inc., and reprinted by its permission.

Comics. There were a group of aviator-heroes who might have been expected to continue in the magazine, but they were all pretty nondescript. Leckishes, if you will.

The Black Commander was featured on the cover, which advertised ten gripping air-action features, but none of them amounted to anything: *Tex Trainor, Test Pilot; Crash Davis, Navy Ace*; and the like.

A month went by. Two months. Three months. Six months. No second issue of *Air Fighters*. A fella might think that the magazine had gone out of business. Well, it hadn't quite, but it had gone back to the drawing board for a reworking, and when it reemerged it had a new lineup of features, two of which interest us today. One of these was *Airboy*. The other was *Sky Wolf*.

Airboy was the joint creation of Ed Cronin, the editor of *Air Fighters*, and Charles Biro. Biro was one of the classic creative geniuses of the so-called Golden Age; his greatest success came with the Lev Gleason group, where, in collaboration with Bob Wood, Biro was responsible for *Crimebuster* (in *Boy Comics*), *Daredevil* (the fellow in the blue-and-red costume with the spiked belt, no relationship to the later Stan Lee character of the same name), and *Crime Does Not Pay*, which was the all-time classic crime comic.

For publisher Alex Hillman and editor Ed Cronin, Biro dreamed up an aviation-oriented hero with a full complement of personality-establishing gimmicks: Airboy was an instant success when he appeared in the second issue of *Air Fighters*, a full year after the first. By the twenty-third issue of the magazine it had been retitled *Airboy*, and as *Airboy* it was published for the remainder of its history, lasting until May, 1953, a total of 111 issues in all.

Other features in the revamped *Air Fighters* were pretty routine fare, not essentially different from the weak lineup of the first issue. The new *Air Fighters* crew included the Bald Eagle (yep, he was bald), the Black Angel (a lady pilot who wore black tights), and Iron Ace (a pilot who wore armor and whose plane also carried retractable armor shielding). A friend of mine accurately described these things as "routine slaughter-the-Japs-and-Huns stories."

But Airboy . . .

In common with Jack Cole's classic Plastic Man, Airboy started his career in a monastery, tended by the friendly and solicitous monks. The lad was named Davy Nelson, apparently an orphan (although we later learned otherwise on this score) left in the care of the monks, particularly kindly old Father Martier. He was also befriended by other friars—Father Alonzo, Father Aloysius, Father Justus, Father Gregory.

But Father Martier was Davy's particular friend and benefactor, Father Martier, who was a lover of nature, whose particular fascination was the bats who flew about the monastery in the California dusk. Father Martier, who studied those bats and their mode of flight, and who struggled to build a model plane that would duplicate the flight of those bats.

Eventually he succeeded, creating a full-scale ornithopter, an airplane that could fly by flapping its wings like a bat or a bird. (In fact, for a while it was called the bat-plane in the story but, perhaps to avoid confusion with Batman's batplane, the term was switched to bird-plane, and Airboy called the ornithopter Birdie for many years.)

The bat-plane or bird-plane sported a sleekly pointed nose, a smooth bubble cockpit, a single pair of wings halfway back on the fuselage, and a vertical rudder. Both the wings and the rudder had curving, swept-back leading edges and ribbed, batlike trailing edges.

At first the bird-plane flew entirely by flapping its wings, which were covered with a flexible rubberoid material that facilitated their movements. The plane could take off and land vertically, hover in one spot, or fly at great speeds. In later years rocket exhaust tubes were added at the tail to facilitate even higher speeds.

At about the same time that Father Martier was working on his ornithopter, a local gambling figure attempted to take over the monastery and convert it to a gambling casino. There was a crooked mortgage, taken mainly to provide funds for commercial development of the new aircraft, and to make sure that the mortgage would be foreclosed, the gambler sabotaged the ornithopter so that Father Martier crashed and was killed on a test flight.

Young Davy Nelson, a lad of 15, dismantled the wreckage, discovered the sabotage, rebuilt the bird-plane, and donned the costume that he was to wear ever after as Airboy. He wore a red jacket with a huge letter V (the wartime motif of "V-for-Victory" of course) slashing its front from shoulders to waist. He wore blue breeches and brown leather aviator's gloves and boots. A pair of aviator's goggles mounted on a brown leather strap circled his California-wavy blond hair, and were pulled down when he flew Birdie with its cockpit open.

During the war Airboy fought the usual run of German and Japanese menaces. His activities were delineated by a number of artists—copies in my possession are variously signed by Bernard Sachs, Fred Kida, "Zolne" (Dan Zolnerowich), John Giunta, Dan Barry—and Carmine Infantino, who went on to become the editorial director of the entire DC comics line a quarter-century later.

Like the characters in *Gasoline Alley*, Airboy aged at a normal rate, an unusual accomplishment for a comic-book hero, most of whom were frozen in at one age for their entire careers. (Even odder has been the experience of Superboy, whose aging takes place at a severely retarded rate, about one-third normal.)

Aside from standard Axis foes, Airboy periodically encountered villains of a distinctly exotic nature. One such was Misery, a weird, cadaverous being whose eternal mission seemed to be the overseeing of the Airtomb, a huge dead-white aircraft to which deceased aviators went. Another, of more equivocal nature, was Valkyrie, a gorgeous sort of *femme fatale* cast in the mold of Milton Caniff's Dragon Lady.

Still another was Keller, "the fantastic Eastern man of mystery." Keller, a famous stunt flier, had disappeared after being blamed for a fatal accident, and turned up years later as the dictator of a lush Pacific island, where he taught the natives to construct airplanes in the form of ancient war galleys, and commanded both natives and aviators abducted from the outer world (for example, Airboy) to take part in fantastic aerial gladiatorial games.

Among the captive gladiators Airboy encounters an old acquaintance, Jimmy Collins, and they plot successfully to escape. As the two aviators wing their way eastward over the Pacific they work out a few more details of the weird incident. Collins says: "That's it, Airboy! Keller was mad ... but he knew enough to build only short range planes, so nobody could escape ... and now that he's dead, I'm sure those people will throw out the air battles he sneaked into their life ... "

"I hope so, Jimmy," says Airboy, "but the U.S.A. will want to *know* ... there's still a bunch of captive pilots to free!"

Although Airboy was at first an apparent orphan, his father turned up alive and well, like Little Orphan Annie's periodically reappearing Daddy Warbucks, in November, 1946.

"Take a good look at your *Dad*!!" the story was blurbed. "He's pretty okay, eh? Maybe you'd like to have *him* around as your 'partner' if things got *tight* for you as they did for Airboy. But how would *you* stand up?? What if it was a bright sunny morning, the kind of morning that to dreaming fliers opens the door to the 'wide blue yonder'—and also opens a newsboy's mouth ... "

And thus we were off into an outstanding Airboy adventure, opening with Airboy, "young prince of the skies," judging a model airplane meet at a local airport.

In the midst of the competition a really superior jet-powered model lands. In its cabin is a note addressed to Airboy, telling him to go to a local movie palace. He obeys, sits down in the last row at the Pix, and in a few minutes a well-dressed, middle-aged businessman enters, sits down beside Airboy, and—"Why! It's ... *you*! *Dad*!"

Airboy's father, Professor Nelson, explains that he has been at work for all these years, with three associates, on a form of super jet engine that will eventually carry man to the moon! So great is the secret that the four scientists totally isolated themselves from the outer world for the duration of the war.

Professor Nelson explains: " ... so we vanished from the public eye! That's why someone else had to take care of you ... but the war is over! And I suspect a Professor Fitzner of our group of wanting our discoveries for evil purposes of his own!"

After the show, however, Professor Nelson is kidnaped back to the secret island where he, Fitzner, and the others had their laboratory. Airboy pursues; his father, misled by his treacherous partners, nearly kills Airboy in a dogfight—but both land safely, and Airboy kills Fitzner. (No qualms about killing in these comics!)

"Fitzner tricked me, told me you were dead," says Professor Nelson. "Then I saw you! He was going to use the results of our experiments to gain power and money. But he didn't get a chance! *You* saw to that, my son!"

Other menaces faced by Airboy were designed to send a shudder through the reader, and as often as not they succeeded at that task. One such tale was a two-parter that ran in the December, 1948, and January, 1949, issues of *Airboy*, a story called "Airboy and the Rats." This mini-epic ran a total of 30 pages, plus two covers, and those who read it two decades ago still speak of it with awe.

The theme, set in a flashback to the Egypt of 3,000 years ago, is that of man's fratricidal self-destructiveness—and the sinister, patient intelligence of the rats, who wait in the shadows to take over the world when man has relinquished his hold. And where once Pharaohs moved in splendor there is only debris. "For today," the narration runs, "the *rats rule*! And this jumble of ruins is but one ancient civilization inherited by the furry terrors! There are the jungle-covered towers of Asia, the great stone temples of the Aztecs, and many more! It's fantastic . . . and yet, true! And in the year 1948 . . . in the City of New York . . . "

Two men stand, discussing the state of the world. "It gives me the shivers!" says one, "Look at the headline in that paper in the gutter there!"

The headline reads: "ANOTHER WAR MAY END CIVILIZATION!"

The second man says: "Atom bombs . . . jet planes! They'll ruin the world yet!"

The paper is swept down a sewer. The artist follows it, revealing a minor headline: "Authorities Amused by Professor's Warning of Rat Menace."

But deeper in the sewer, rats are gathering. They are able to converse with one another, and their leader is addressing them: "The day so long awaited has arrived and we, the rats of the western world, have been chosen to make the first move!"

The narration proceeds on through a tale of worldwide catastrophe, as rats cut off entire cities, massacre populations, destroy crops and factories. Airboy leads the opposition.

At the end of the first installment New York City is saved by pouring millions of gallons of oil into the Hudson River, soaking and destroying an army of rats swarming to attack the city.

But the following month the rat hordes renew their assault on human civilization. This time they amass a single grand army in the great gorge below the Grand Culvert Dam. Rats—billions of rats! And their headquarters has been found by Airboy through the device of deliberately allowing himself to be captured.

Now, using a secret radio transmitter concealed in his clothing, Airboy calls in an air strike that will destroy the dam and the assembled army of rats. But Airboy as well will be killed unless . . .

He summons his airplane Birdie with the same radio transmitter. Operating on remote control the airplane swoops low over the towering wall of water, drops down, picks up its master, and carries him to safety just as the waters of the Grand Culvert Dam crash down, wiping out the army of rats.

But are the rats defeated for once and all? "I know a little about them now," Airboy says. "Enough to know their cunning and strength—and *they* know that *I'm* wise to them—so they'll be scouting *me* as long as I live!"

That response of Birdie to Airboy's desperate summons raises an interesting point in regard to this particular feature. As the essence of valid fiction is human interaction, most comics heroes had to have some continuing foil, whether boy-sidekick, other assistant, running foe, police contact, and so on, with whom to interact.

In Airboy's case, this foil was his ornithopter Birdie. Airboy used to speak to Birdie as you or I would speak to another human. He called the aircraft his "girl," praised it, sympathized with its wounds when it was damaged, thanked it for its aid when it saved him as in the rats story ...

It was a distinctly odd relationship, but it gave Airboy somebody to talk to, and he needed that. In his last adventures he was employed by one Tex Calhoun, a millionaire oilman interested in scientific experimentation. Calhoun provided a human figure for Airboy to relate to, and also answered any bothersome questions about the source of Airboy's money. And there was Professor Nelson, and there was Valkyrie. But mainly, Airboy talked to his airplane when he was lonesome.

He faced one more chilling foe in the immortal Zzed, whom he encountered twice in 1950, in January and then again in May.

Zzed was a sinister figure—he looked a lot like the motion-picture actor John Carradine, with a gaunt, bony face, long ragged hair, and battered ancient clothes. He lurked in a mysterious and gloomy swamp in Georgia, where he waylaid and murdered passing travelers.

Meanwhile, across the continent in California, Airboy and his employer Tex Calhoun are visiting Calhoun's laboratory, where a staff scientist, Dr. Jenkins, has devised the theory that the great bulk of "brain energy" generated on the earth is not used, but is drained off into space, where it is concentrating at the behest of— something! And this great cluster of "brain energy" is moving through space, back toward the earth.

Back in Georgia Zzed murmurs strange, ancient words, prayers and incantations, until a weird tentacular apparition descends from space. There is a brilliant explosion and Zzed exclaims "*It is done*! Now Zzed is master of mankind!"

Now there are alarming reports of riots and violence in great cities throughout the world—it is, of course, the invader from space, powered by its collected "brain energy" to spread anarchy and hatred throughout the world. Airboy and Tex Calhoun make their way to Georgia and confront Zzed, who gloats: "I have the collected intelligence of all the years—*the star brain*!" Using this power Zzed can control all men, for the star brain exploits evil and hatred, and there is evil and hatred in some amount in all men. The cause of humanity looks entirely hopeless until—Airboy gets a little child, innocent of evil and hatred, to destroy the apparatus with which Zzed controls the star brain.

Zzed is defeated, but escapes, shrieking mad laughter in the finest tradition of his kind.

Zzed reappeared in a two-parter, May and June, 1950, and his swansong was a wild melange of melodramatic impedimenta—storms wracking the world, Airboy personally summoned by President Truman to save the world, Zzed operating from a new headquarters at the North Pole, an infernal device slowly melting away the polar ice cap, frozen mammoths and dinosaurs emerging into the modern world, etc.

I won't even try to recreate the story, you can do the job in your own imagination. It was a beaut!

And then there was the story of the tiny sea-slug accidentally raised by Airboy in a diving bell—the slug that began to grow—and grow—and *grow*—until . . .

I guess that by 1953 Airboy had just plain grown up. He wasn't Airboy any more, he was a man, and he put aside his melodramatics and probably took a job as a test pilot for an aeronautical engineering firm, or became an airline pilot at $40,000 a year or . . .

Airboy—Davy Nelson—are you still up there somewhere in the wide blue yonder? I'd like to know about it if you are.

I said that when the revamped *Air Fighters* appeared in November, 1942, a year after the weak first issue had come out, the two noteworthy features in it were *Airboy* and *Sky Wolf*.

Airboy, okay; *Sky Wolf*, well, the statement was true but, I must confess, somewhat misleading.

Drawn by Mort Leav and written by Harry Stein, *Sky Wolf* was basically just another war-flier strip. There were four Sky Wolves, differentiated roughly as were the Blackhawks (or Doc Savage's helpers), and their gimmick was that they flew in a brace of double-airplanes, craft vaguely resembling the F-82 Twin Mustangs that served in Korea but capable of splitting into mirror-image pairs of asymmetrical single-engined craft for extra maneuverability in dogfights.

Sky Wolf himself was distinguished by a sort of helmet-hood that he wore, which was formed like the head of a wolf. It did give him a fierce and dashing appearance, and his epic struggles against the Nazi Colonel Von Tundra, a sort of half-man, half-machine rebuilt from the human wreckage of an air crash, were fairly exciting.

The Sky Wolf's three companions, the Turtle, "Cocky" Roach, and the Judge, were a pretty adequate crew of fliers, too.

But the turning point in the adventures of Sky Wolf and Colonel Von Tundra came in their second recorded encounter (that is, because of the unsuccessful trial issue of *Air Fighters*, the *third* issue of the magazine). There has been a terrific dogfight. Both Sky Wolf and Von Tundra crash-land, but both emerge safely from the wreckage of their respective fighter planes. And this is what they met:

> It walked in the woods.
> It was never born. It existed. Under the pine needles the fires burn, deep and smokeless in the mold. In heat and in darkness and decay there is growth. There is life and there is growth. It grew, but it was not alive. It walked unbreathing through the woods, and thought and saw and was hideous and strong, and it was not born and it did not live. It grew and moved about without living.
> It crawled out of the darkness and hot damp mold into the cool of a morning. It was huge. It was lumped and crusted with its own hateful substances, and pieces of it dropped off as it went its way, dropped off and lay writhing, and stilled, and sank putrescent into the forest loam.
> Standing there was . . . a massive caricature of a man: a huge thing like an irregular mud doll, clumsily made. It quivered and parts of it glistened and parts of it were dried and crumbly. Half of the lower part of its face was gone, giving it a lopsided look. It had no perceptible mouth or nose, and its eyes were crooked, one higher than the other, both a dingy brown with no whites at all. It stood quite still

... its only movement a steady unalive quivering.

Pretty unappetizing apparition, and of course if you ever had the creepy pleasure as a kid to read of the adventures of the Heap in *Air Fighters/Airboy Comics*, you know exactly who that is.

The—thing was probably the most bizarre creation in the entire history of the comic medium. Odd heroes and odder villains thronged the four-color page. There was Fawcett's Hunchback, DC's metallic Robotman, and surely a high (or low) of some sort in the person of a hero called the Bouncer. Yep, his power was that—he bounced.

On the villain side there was Dr. Weerd, there was the Snail, there was the Rat, there were endless others. There was Solomon Grundy, a foe of Green Lantern's, and of a somewhat more equivocal nature there was of course the Frankenstein monster himself in the long Dick Briefer series and in many other shorter-lived incarnations.

But there was never a match for the Heap.

His origin story—well, his origin story was told and retold and retold with amazing frequency over the years, frequently with little fillips added or variations in detail that were not always consistent with earlier versions. But in skeletal form, the origin of the Heap went something like this:

Back in the latter days of World War I—sometimes the narration said 1917, sometimes 1918—there was a savage dogfight over a Polish swamp. The German squadron involved was no less than the famous Flying Circus of Baron Manfred von Richtofen. One of the greatest of Richtofen's fliers was another young German nobleman, the Baron Emmelmann (sometimes rendered as von Emmelman). Emmelmann had left behind in Germany a beautiful young wife and a darling infant.

In the great sky battle the baron is shot down. Parachutes were not used in World War I; if you were shot down, you rode your plane down, hoping to survive a crash landing. Few did.

But Emmelmann was possessed of a fanatical will to live. His love for his wife, his need to see his child were such that he would not let go the spark of life that remained in his mangled body after the smoke of his crash had cleared.

Over the years he lay there in Poland, not dead nor alive either. The life of the swamp grew together with the broken flesh of his body. A mindless, unconscious *thing* lay there for a quarter of a

The Heap is the shaggy one, looking sort of like a cross between a gorilla and a haystack. The other one is a man who fell into a volcano and became a lava man. The Heap stories had a brooding atmosphere of tragedy; the Heap was a cross between the animal and the plant world who fought vicious creatures all over the world. Copyright © 1951, Hillman Periodicals, Inc., and reprinted by its permission.

century, until, in the early days of World War II, there was reenacted a scene above the swamp similar to that tragic incident of October 12, 1918. (Or '17.)

The Heap rises from the swamp. It feeds on a stray sheep. In time it becomes master of its domain.

And now, in the little Polish town of Rodz, the Nazi Colonel Von Tundra, accompanied by the beautiful double-agent Frisco, holds tyrannical sway over the hopeless Poles.

That dogfight takes place. The Heap comes upon Sky Wolf and the Nazi half-man, and seizes the Nazi. Half-unconscious, the Heap carries its prey into the town where it sees a Wehrmacht soldier. It takes one look, this great, shaggy mass, and—hearts fly through the panel as the Heap falls in love!

Yes, in those early days the Heap was portrayed as a partly humorous feature, and as the years went by, while the character and the strip itself evolved (after a while the Heap was separated from Sky Wolf, and later Sky Wolf was dropped from the magazine), the Heap was never treated wholly as a horror feature.

At the end of the first installment of his adventures, the Heap is apparently blown up in an aerial bombing. But he returned again and again, his repeated "deaths" about as convincing as those of the filmed versions of the Frankenstein monster. You remember how *he* was variously burned, exploded, drowned, frozen, or whatnot, always to return when his services were needed again. So it was with the Heap, and after a while they stopped even pretending to kill him off. We all knew he'd be back soon anyhow . . .

When the Heap returned after that Polish episode his origin was retold with variations. Now the dogfight had taken place in the air over Siberia (!), his first food after regaining his mobility was a dog rather than a sheep, and the soldiers into whose encampment he blundered were Japanese troops garrisoned in wartime China rather than Germans in Poland.

Further, who turns up but the Baroness von Emmelman, working as a nurse! The Heap has a predictable run-in with the Japanese soldiers, a soldier turns his gun upon the Heap, but at the last moment he shoots not the Heap but Baroness von Emmelman instead!

Thus the Heap, "that formless thing of the swamps," "this hulk of the living death," goes from tragedy to tragedy. He is "killed" but the remains are imported to the United States by one

Professor Herman Kringle, a henpecked little man who uses the revived Heap to murder his wife. The Heap is shown as immensely strong—he picks up a twin-engine plane in one scene and throws it through the air!

In still later appearances the Heap is charmed by a small boy playing with a model of a World War I fighter plane—somewhere in the murky mind of this thing there stirs a memory of its past.

By 1946 the Heap had his own series in *Airboy Comics*; he adventured for a while with the boy Rickie Wood, but then wandered on again, appearing here and there throughout the world, with ever and again a return to that Polish (or Siberian) swamp in 1918 (or 1917) and a new retelling of the origin story. After a while there began to be Olympian overtones. The comic showed us quarrels among the Greek gods and goddesses, Ceres in particular, the Earth goddess, crying out against the cruelty and violence of the war god Ares.

Now it was by personal intervention of Ceres that the plant life of the swamp united with the spark in von Emmelman to create the Heap, and the Heap is hence a creature of peace and justice, hulking about the world fighting against oppression and violence. (Can you fight against violence? Well, people claim today to "fight for peace" and in an era when we "save" Asian cities by totally obliterating them, why not fight violence?)

In later years the Heap travels to France, to South Africa, back to Poland (now the swamp was near Wasau), and to America again. Almost every story had eerie overtones to it, and almost always the Heap was portrayed as a melancholy figure, an outcast from all life, a creature of pathos as much as of terror, if not more of pathos than terror.

Whether the creators of the Heap were conscious of this characteristic, or if things just worked out that way, I do not know; but consciously or otherwise they hit upon the great secret of monster story-telling. For if the monster is just a bogeyman waved to frighten children, he never will amount to much.

But if the monster is *pathetic*, then he is Quasimodo, then he is Karloff's Frankenstein monster, then he is truly touching and memorable.

And so was the Heap, that great, shaggy, half-man, half-plant, that child of the goddess Ceres, that tragic ace of the Flying Circus.

We see the Heap carrying the broken body of a child to its

swampy home, there to tend her with the gentle tenderness of the huge and the mighty.

The Heap could bring tears of pity to our eyes as well as gasps of terror to our lips.

That was his greatness, and that was the strange appeal that brings back his image to this day, the appeal of a very powerful image that stirs something deep within the subconscious memories of us all. Perhaps deeply buried recollections of those days when we were ourselves tiny babies, carried about and handled by our parents, huge creatures of inconceivable power . . .

One might wonder why the adventures of the Heap have never been chronicled in straight prose, but the fact is that they have. There is a story by the fantastic-fiction writer Theodore Sturgeon, called simply "It," which first described a thing remarkably like the Heap.

"It" was published in the famous science-fantasy magazine *Unknown*, with several illustrations by Edd Cartier. "It" appeared in the issue of *Unknown* for August, 1940, over two years before the Heap made his first appearance in the *Sky Wolf* strip. And in case you're wondering how closely It resembled the Heap, turn back to that description that I quoted. You know, the one beginning "It walked in the woods . . . " and ending " . . . a steady unalive quivering."

That description was not lifted from any blurb or narration panel of a *Heap* story. Nope. That's Sturgeon's own description of his nameless monster "It."

Hi there, Heap!

One thing we can note concerning comic books: the publishers admire success, and they make known their admiration in the proverbial "sincerest form" of admiration: imitation. Over the years following the discontinuance of *Airboy* with its feature *The Heap*, the image of that huge, hulking, powerful, half-human creature recurred again and again in the comics. Probably the most significant example was the Thing, a member of Marvel Comics' Fantastic Four hero team.

But by the 1970s several publishers seemed to decide, almost simultaneously, that it was time to bring back the shambling monster in more nearly his original form. Thus in quick succession the Skywald Publishing Company actually revived the "original" Heap in *Psycho*, an oversized black-and-white comic of the type pioneered by the EC Picto-Fiction series in the 1950s and

Captain Derek West's Ghost Squadron was a consistent winner, adding a heavy dose of supernatural mystery to the usual warfare-and-womanizing in Wings. This page led into "The Room of a Million Windows," one of the best yarns in the generally excellent series.

developed to success by Jim Warren's *Eerie* and *Creepy* in the sixties . . . Marvel brought out its carbon-copy Man-Thing . . . DC joined the party with the Swamp-Thing.

But the crowning vindication of Sturgeon's original vision came when Marvel introduced a new comic called *Supernatural Thrillers* in December, 1972. The entire first issue was devoted to a faithful adaptation of "It," using much of Sturgeon's original text as running narration and dialog! It had taken 32 years for "It" to come full-circle, from the pulp pages of *Unknown* magazine to the full-color panels of *Supernatural Thrillers*, but the story that had started off the entire fantastic sequence had finally been recognized and received the attention of a comic-book audience that had seen only imitations for those three decades.

INTRODUCTION TO

THE DUCK MAN

MANY of the comic-book characters discussed in this book and in the preceding *All in Color for a Dime* are creatures of the past, available today only in yellowing and increasingly expensive old comic books or in costly hardcover samplings. Others are still continuing to appear, but in vastly different form than in those golden days of childhood we seek to recapture here.

Donald Duck, as described by Mike Barrier in our next chapter, continues to be available in current comic books in the original stories of which Mike writes. The *Donald Duck* and *Uncle Scrooge* stories written and drawn by Carl Barks (to whom this book is dedicated) have been reprinted in nearly every issue of *Walt Disney's Comics and Stories* and *Uncle Scrooge* since Barks retired on a pension in 1966. Apparently his publishers feel, as his readers do, that Barks is irreplaceable.

It is fortunate that you need go no farther than the nearest comic-book outlet to find samples of Barks's Ducks—the Walt Disney Studios have refused to give us permission to reprint samples of the strip, apparently because they envision hardcover reprints of their own.

Mike Barrier is a newspaper columnist for the *Arkansas Gazette*, writing on government and politics, and a former assistant to the Arkansas attorney general. He was born in Little Rock and still lives there. He also is the editor and publisher of *Funnyworld*, an excellent magazine dealing with cartoon animation and with what, for lack of a better term, might be called "funny animal comics"—*Bugs Bunny, Fritz the Cat*, and, of course, *Donald Duck*.

Mike has been called "Barks's Boswell" and he probably knows about as much about "the good artist" as anyone except Barks himself and Barks's artist wife Margaret, who paints under the name Garé. Mike is completing a full bibliography of Barks's work, which will be published in a volume that will also contain an interview, an essay on Barks's work, reproductions from Barks's published work, some previously unpublished drawings, and some other material.

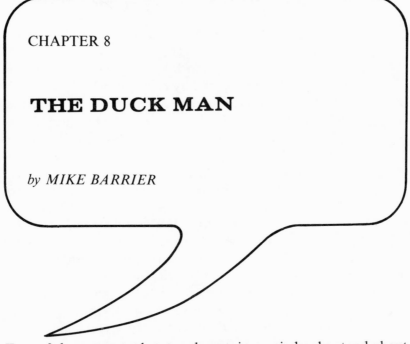

CHAPTER 8

THE DUCK MAN

by MIKE BARRIER

Two of the greatest adventure heroes in comic books stood about three feet tall, were covered with white feathers, and had bright orange bills and feet; one was dressed only in a middie blouse and a sailor cap, the other in a hoary broadcloth coat (bought in Scotland in 1902) and a silk topper.

I refer to Donald Duck and his Uncle Scrooge, of course. They were unlikely heroes, but their adventures in the Walt Disney comic books of the forties and fifties were much more exciting to me, and to millions of other children, than all the exploits of the costumed superdoers. They were more exciting because they were more real—and if it seems absurd to talk about reality and Donald Duck in the same paragraph, that reaction could occur only in readers who were not raised on the Disney duck stories written and drawn by Carl Barks.

One way Barks made his stories "real" was by sending the ducks to real places: Australia, the Peruvian Andes, Crete, the Arabian desert, the Himalayas, the jungles of South America, the depths of the Everglades ... the list could be extended indefinitely. But exotic locales alone do not explain the appeal of Barks's stories; other "funny animals" had such adventures, too. In any given issue, Bugs Bunny might be found in Tibet, Porky Pig in the

Canadian Northwest, Woody Woodpecker in Africa. What made Carl Barks's stories different?

One answer is that he gave his readers more. When most comics writers and artists sent their characters to foreign locales, they faked their props; there wasn't much to give you the feeling you were *there*, wherever it was. Barks, by contrast, never cheated. He filled file drawers with research material, so that his stories' locales would be authentic in detail. When, as in one 1950 story, Barks sent the ducks to ancient Persia, they were in ancient Persia—no question about it. The rich robes, the elaborate carvings, the murky, torch-lit hallways—all bespoke their Persian origins.

This goes a little beyond saying that Barks's stories had "atmosphere." They did, and sometimes it was like a rich perfume all through a story, as in the lovely "In Old California," in a 1951 issue of *Donald Duck*. That story, as a story, doesn't have as much going for it as a lot of Barks's adventures, but it is superb as an evocation of California before the Gold Rush.

Still, to say that Barks's stories had "atmosphere," and then stop, wouldn't do justice to them. It would be more accurate to say that they had size and weight—they were solid, firmly anchored in time and place. This was true even of stories that took place in the banal present.

I was always impressed by this aspect of Barks's stories, from the time I first became aware of him as an artist. That was in 1949, when I received the first issue on my subscription to *Walt Disney's Comics and Stories*, the monthly Disney comic book. In those days, every middle-class child in America had a subscription to *Walt Disney's* by the time he was in the first grade, and it was a source of considerable distress to me that I had to wait until I was in the fourth grade to get mine. I'm sure that the momentous nature of the occasion has made me remember the October, 1949, *Walt Disney's* better than I would have otherwise, but there were details of Barks's *Donald Duck* story in that issue that clung to my memory in an odd way. There was something strange about that story, and it fascinated me.

I think now that was because it was set recognizably in southern California, which was a very peculiar country when seen from the vantagepoint of a child in Arkansas. In the story, the nephews are convinced that a forked stick is a witching stick that can find water; Donald is skeptical, to say the least. In order to set his quarrel with the nephews to rest, Donald takes them to the desert to look for water. On the way, the ducks travel on a clogged California highway, and when Donald finally drills for water (in a desert that looks quite real, and like nothing ever seen in Arkansas), he bores into the Los Angeles aqueduct. The frightened ducks flee across the desert, until Donald's car overheats. Then, looking for water with the witching stick, the nephews find some foul-smelling hot springs supplying the El Rancho Swanko Super Desert Hot Springs Hotel and Health Resort—the sort of place that could exist only in southern California.

There was another detail in the story that didn't have much to do with California, but had much the same effect on me. At the end of the story, the nephews prove the worth of their witching stick by discovering that Donald's lameness is caused by "water on the knee." What, I wondered at the time, is "water on the knee"? The general meaning was clear enough, but I was still curious.

The important thing about such details—and the details in other Barks stories—is that they were *tantalizing*, not frustrating. Barks never let them get in the way of the stories he was telling. His stories built smoothly and surely, free of confusion; at every point, we knew what we must know. But there were always details, filling and expanding the world Barks had created, and suggesting that there was more to it than what we were seeing.

It was not just the real places that looked real in Barks's stories. When the ducks were at home in Duckburg, the strange furnishings of their homes—the little statues of men contorted into disconcerting positions, the goldfish bowl whose occupant almost filled it, the picture on the wall that was jammed full of scowling duck faces—looked surprisingly plausible too, as did the buildings, the cars, and the people on the street, many of them far removed from what we see in our own daily lives. Not that Barks added details helter-skelter; he actually used details of all kinds sparingly. His details stuck in the mind because they reinforced the mood of each story. Everything hung together; Barks's world was all of a piece.

Barks's stories were concrete in much more than their settings. His dialog was crisp and sassy, and Barks refused to limit his stories to a grade-school vocabulary. Consider, for example, Uncle Scrooge and Donald in a plush restaurant, when Donald is trying to help his tightwad uncle get rid of some cash that won't fit in his huge money bin:

"Five double orders of broiled bosoms of Caledonian chicka-
dees," Donald tells the haughty waiter, "including everything
from soup to nuts."

"Whipped cream on the nuts, sir?" the waiter asks.

"Yes! Topped off with a cherry."

"The cherry will be five dollars extra."

"Swell! Put on a handful."

Even the names in Barks's stories were vivid; they described his
characters succinctly. These are some of the cranks and eccentrics
who inhabited Barks's pages:

Blacksnake McQuirt, the glowering rustler.

Argus McFiendy, the monomaniacal butterfly collector.

Rockjaw Bumrisk, the pugnacious deadbeat.

Professor Artefact McArchives, leader of a scholarly expedition.

King Nevvawaza of Itsa Faka, an ancient Persian city.

Flinthide the banker and Groanbalm the doctor.

Foola Zoola, the vengeful witch doctor.

These characters moved through a geography that matches
them perfectly: the old Scottish castle of Dismal Downs; Waha-
go-gaga, the nephews' summer camp; Wambo Jambo, an African
city; and so on across the map.

But what mattered most were the ducks, and how Barks drew
them and put them through their paces. With them, too, Barks
was always specific. Their facial expressions, their movements,
their posture, their gestures—all told us what we wanted to know
about what the ducks were thinking and feeling. There was none
of the broad, crude shorthand that most cartoonists fall into when
they're drawing "funny animals." Barks was instead remarkably
precise, and he could accomplish small miracles just by focusing
on the changes in Donald Duck's expression.

For example, in a 1949 story called "Luck of the North,"
Donald has sent his obnoxiously lucky cousin, Gladstone Gander,
on a wild-goose chase to the far North. Donald's conscience is
bothering him and he can't sleep, but he doesn't realize what's
wrong until he gets up to prepare himself a snack—and then it
suddenly dawns on him that he may have sent Gladstone into
terrible danger. In the course of the next few panels, Barks depicts
some complex psychological shifts in Donald's face with unerring
precision, until finally Donald is literally weighted down (his head
squashed out of shape) by a thought balloon in which a grinning

polar bear is holding his bulging stomach after devouring Gladstone and leaving only his hat and spats behind.

In a 1952 story in *Walt Disney's Comics* (my own favorite of all of Barks's stories), Donald is reading a book while two of the nephews play with a toy gun, pretending to hypnotize one another. As we watch, Donald's expression changes subtly; he stops reading his book, begins listening to what the nephews are saying, and then becomes concerned, finishing with a frown just before taking the gun from the nephews and giving them a stern lecture on the dangers of hypnotism. It would be difficult to find a funnier example of stupid, self-conscious rectitude. (Naturally, Donald himself is really hypnotized by the nephews' harmless toy a little later.)

No actor could play such scenes better than Barks; no film comedian of the silent era knew more about comic timing. Barks had complete command of the comics form, and he used his skills to give his stories an emotional depth that is probably unique in the history of comic books. Unlike most of the people in the comic-book business, Barks was always honest with his readers and true to himself.

Carl Barks was born in Oregon in 1901. During the next 35 years or so, he said in an interview, "I was a fizzle as a cowboy, a logger, a printing press feeder, a steelworker, a carpenter, an animator . . . and a barfly." He failed as an animator at the Disney studio, where he spent six months as an "in-betweener" ("in-betweeners" draw the pictures that come in between the main action frames), the lowest rung on animation's ladder, after six years as a freelance cartoonist. Fortunately, the studio had the wisdom to put him in another spot, in the story department.

There, Barks says, "I was just a duck man—strictly a duck man," working on almost nothing except stories for *Donald Duck* animated cartoons. Donald had arrived at the studio not long before Barks, in a 1934 short cartoon called "The Wise Little Hen," and he quickly rose to stardom on the basis of his supporting roles in *Mickey Mouse* cartoons. Donald's trademark was his explosive temper; he was frustrated and defeated by life's little annoyances, and what made him funny was that he brought so many of his troubles upon himself. Donald was soon given his own series of cartoons, and his nephews were introduced shortly thereafter; they were expert at provoking Donald, and many

211

cartoons were devoted to their warfare with him.

Late in 1942, Barks left Disney's; he didn't like the work ("I didn't like the pressure and the fact there were so many straw-bosses looking over your shoulder to see how you were doing, criticizing your work all the time") and he wanted to avoid being locked into his job under wartime regulations. But his connection with the Disney studio—and especially with the ducks—was to continue for much longer than Barks could have envisioned.

Several weeks after Barks had left the studio, Western Publishing Company asked him to illustrate a ten-page *Donald Duck* story for the April, 1943, issue of *Walt Disney's Comics*. At that time, the Disney comic books were still getting off the ground, and the introduction of new *Donald Duck* stories in *Walt Disney's* was to be a turning point. Until 1940, the big Disney periodical was *Mickey Mouse Magazine*, a monthly that combined standard children's-magazine features with an increasing number of Disney comic strips. The comics were newspaper reprints: before 1943, very few comics were drawn especially for the Disney magazines. When *Mickey Mouse Magazine* was dropped in 1940 after 60 issues, its place was taken immediately by *Walt Disney's Comics and Stories*, which was made up almost entirely of reprinted newspaper comics. The same was true of the occasional *Donald Duck* and *Mickey Mouse* "one-shots" that also began appearing in 1940.

But original comic-book material, in the shape of superhero adventures, was selling well in those early days of World War II and, in any event, *Walt Disney's Comics* ate up the Disney newspaper strips so fast that some had already been reprinted twice by 1943. So the new *Donald Duck* stories were introduced in the April issue, and more original material followed. By the early fifties, most of the newspaper reprints had vanished, their place taken by new stories starring the likes of Bucky Bug, Grandma Duck, and Li'l Bad Wolf. Even the *Mickey Mouse* serials were new, staring in 1951, after a decade of stories based on Mickey's newspaper adventures.

When Barks illustrated that first original story, he asked permission to make some changes in the script; permission was granted, and Western then asked him to try writing the second *Donald Duck* story himself. For more than 20 years thereafter, Barks wrote and illustrated ten pages of *Donald Duck* almost every month for *Walt Disney's*. He also wrote and illustrated almost every issue of *Donald Duck* for nine years, and every issue of *Uncle Scrooge* for fifteen years after that. This close, continuous identification with the same characters for almost a quarter of a century has few if any parallels in comic-book history. The freedom Barks enjoyed may also have been unique. Barks has lived away from Los Angeles since leaving the Disney studio and, in his isolation, he was, in effect, his own editor. No one else saw his scripts or his drawings until he submitted them for publication, and only rarely did Western reject a story or order changes. Barks still had to work within tight restrictions—he was, after all, doing stories for comic books—and sometimes he chafed against them, but fortunately he was given enough breathing space to show what he could do as an individual artist. As it turned out, that was a great deal.

The real breakthrough came in the middle forties, in *Donald Duck*. Barks had been involved in the first issue of *Donald Duck* that contained original material, when he and his partner in the Disney studio's "duck unit," Jack Hannah, illustrated a comic-book version of an abortive *Donald Duck* feature cartoon, *Donald Duck Finds Pirate Gold*. The comic book was published in 1942, several months before Barks left the Disney studio, and it was probably because of that job that Barks was asked to illustrate the first *Donald Duck* story for *Walt Disney's*. As the duck artist for *Walt Disney's*, Barks was the natural choice to do another *Donald Duck* one-shot in 1943.

In that one-shot, *Donald Duck and the Mummy's Ring*, Barks stretched out more than he could in his stories in *Walt Disney's*. For me, the early stories in *Walt Disney's* are too tight and stiff; the timing is choppy, without that flow from panel to panel that Barks was to master in just a few years. His stories are like stripped-down *Donald Duck* cartoons. Donald and the nephews fight a lot, as they did in the cartoons, but the stories don't have the subtleties that good animation can provide. In the stories in *Donald Duck*, with 20 or more pages at his disposal, Barks got away from the cartoon format, and the results were better.

In "The Mummy's Ring," one of Donald's nephews is trapped inside a mummy case that is being returned to Egypt, and Donald and the other two nephews go to the rescue. The story doesn't hold up very well, especially when compared with the long stories that were to follow in a year or two, but its "rescue" theme is important. Barks was to enlarge upon that idea a number of times

213

within the next few years. The pattern of "The Mummy's Ring" was repeated in a 1947 story, when one of Donald's nephews was abducted by a clanking "ghost" in Spanish armor, but the rescues that really mattered were different; in them, the nephews rescued Donald.

Always, when they did this, the nephews were proving that they were entitled to Donald's respect. Sometimes, in the stories that were played mainly for laughs, they didn't get it, or else the rescues themselves were so ludicrous that any heartfelt expressions of gratitude would have seemed out of place. In "Maharajah Donald," a story that appeared in 1947 in a giveaway comic book, Donald is to be fed at dawn to some ravenous tigers. That night, the nephews stuff the tigers with cat food, and the contented beasts emerge in the morning bloated and completely uninterested in the quivering Donald. No matter how you look at it, that's a hell of a way to be rescued.

Some of these rescue stories had real emotional impact, however, and they shed light on what Barks was doing in most of his stories in *Donald Duck* in the forties. The best example is a story called "The Terror of the River" (1946). Donald is captured by a very convincing psychotic, who is operating a huge mechanical sea monster that is disrupting river traffic. The psychotic plans to bury his monster in a river bank and leave Donald to die, but the nephews come to the rescue in a tugboat, engaging the monster in a desperate tug-of-war. Finally, Donald emerges from the monster's throat and greets the nephews: "Howdy, MEN!"

This was the substance of all these stories. It was not just that the nephews were triumphing over adults; that happened repeatedly in the short stories in *Walt Disney's Comics*, where Donald and the nephews were in almost constant conflict up until the late forties. The nephews' defiance in those stories obviously had some connection with their cool independence in the longer stories in *Donald Duck*, but there was a big difference between the stories in the two magazines. In the long stories, the nephews weren't just getting the best of Donald, they were proving that they could handle adult responsibilities. They flew planes, they drove cars, they put their minds and hands to work more intelligently and skillfully than Donald did, and sometimes, they really did win his acknowledgment that they were "men."

It's hard to overstate the difference between this approach and those taken by most other comic-book artists and writers. Some of them sucked up to their young readers, patting them on the back and in effect condoning infantile behavior (that is, the sort of thing that became very familiar in the late sixties, in the days of the "youth culture"), but it seems clear that many artists and writers weren't pandering to their audience; they just felt that way, too. It's instructive to read a comic book like *Human Torch* No. 5. (1941), with its 60-page battle between the Torch and the Sub-Mariner; it's a child's fantasy, with all the casual destruction and ignorance of human affairs that is typical of such fantasies, and is illustrated with drawings just barely superior to what a talented child might produce. It's easy to see why a lot of kids found such junk very satisfying.

But crude wish-fulfillment—which is what the old superhero comics offered—is confining; it doesn't allow any room for the imagination to expand. By contrast, Barks's stories were liberating. Like good fairy tales, they touched and released our fantasies and deepest desires; they helped us to understand ourselves. When I was a child, I was in awe of Huey, Dewey, and Louie, and wanted to be like them—not because they warred with their "father" and got away with it, but because they were in fact more adult than the adults in their world. Adulthood wasn't something to be scorned or regretted, it was to be achieved, and the idea was to be better at it than the people around you.

This is why I loved Barks's stories so much—he didn't talk down to me. His stories had an integrity that was hard to find anywhere else in the comics. It showed in his meticulous drawings, in his sharp-edged dialog, in his carefully constructed plots, and above all, in the clear, strong emotions at the bottom of his stories. He retained this integrity in a field populated mostly by hacks who were ashamed to admit they had anything to do with it. He retained it despite working in a vacuum for years, with little or no knowledge of how well his stories were being received, or even how many copies were being sold. The self-respect that sustained Barks's high standards seems almost incredible in retrospect.

All of this makes Barks sound like a children's author of the highest rank, which he was, but he was more than that. His best stories of the forties, for all their fundamental appeal to children, are so sophisticated that adults may enjoy them more. As with Lewis Carroll and other children's authors of the past, Barks's greatest audience in the future will probably consist of adults.

This is especially true of his stories of the late forties and on through the early fifties, since it was then that Barks was probably at his best. His stories in these five or six years were free of any obvious patterns, such as the Donald-nephews conflict; the relationships between his characters were more complex than before, but no harder to understand. His stories were still funny, and still dramatic, but more of the comedy and drama were interior. Barks was still writing and drawing for children's comic books, of course, but he slipped out from under that net without anyone's noticing.

In some stories, Barks actually seemed to laugh at his earlier stories. The laughter wasn't harsh; it was just a signal that Barks had outgrown the framework of those stories, and was moving on.

There's "Lost in the Andes," for example, a 32-page story in a 1949 issue of *Donald Duck*. Barks has said that this is the story his readers seem to remember most fondly; it's not hard to see why.

As the story opens, Donald is a museum guard who accidentally drops a small square "stone" (actually a cube) from Peru—but when the "stone" breaks open, it turns out to be an egg. The museum sends an expedition to Peru by ship to track down more of these square eggs, and Donald and the nephews are brought along to do the menial chores. The nephews innocently cook an omelet, using some of the museum's square eggs, and the three museum men aboard all end up in the ship's infirmary suffering, the doctor says, from "acute ptomaine ptosis of the ptummy. An ailment in which the gastric ducts tie themselves into *square* knots." By the time the ship reaches Peru, only Donald and the nephews are in any condition to go after the square eggs.

The ducks press on into the Andes, where they find an aged vicuna hunter who remembers seeing the square eggs years before, when a dying American brought them out of the "region of the mists." The mists are forbidding, but the ducks start toward them cheerfully before the old hunter can tell them that no one who has entered the mists has ever returned alive.

The ducks soon become lost in the mists, finally emerging on the outskirts of a vaguely Incan city, which is hidden by the mists from the outside world. One of the inhabitants of the city approaches as the ducks watch from hiding. He's a grotesque little man, his face mostly straight lines and sharp angles, and he's singing: "Oh, Ah wish Ah was in Dixie! Hooray! Hooray! In Dixieland Ah'll take my stand To whoop it up in Dixie!" After a moment's hesitation, Donald comes out from hiding, slaps the little man on the back, and tells him that he's from the South, too—south Burbank.

In a 1946 story, the ducks had faced a menace that looked funny but really wasn't; the Gneezles, the goblins of the Everglades, talked like Southerners, too, but they wanted to feed the ducks to some alligators, and they never sang "Dixie." By having his little man sing "Dixie" (and then "Carry Me Back to Old Virginny") in a lost city in the heart of the Andes, Barks was letting his readers know that something new was afoot, and not to expect the heroics that had been standard in his long stories for four or five years.

But he wasn't simply rejecting his old stories; he was moving on to something new. This lost city in the Andes has a life of its own, and goofy as it is, Barks makes it all believable. It seems that the dying American who staggered out of the mists so many years before was "Professah Rhutt Betlah, frum the Bummin'ham School of English," who had stumbled onto the city much as the ducks did. He taught the people of the city to speak his own brand of English, and gave their home a name ("Plain Awful! That's what the professah frum Bummin'ham called it!"). The people of the city live on nothing but "aigs," and the ducks become national heroes of Plain Awful by finding the square chickens who lay the square eggs.

The ducks ultimately return to the outside world with the help of the Professah's compass, bringing along two chickens from Plain Awful. Back home, scientists jabber excitedly about the breeding possibilities—until *both* of the chickens begin to crow.

The changes in Barks's stories started becoming noticeable around 1948, when he was, in effect, parodying some of his earlier stories in *Walt Disney's*. In the May, 1948, issue, the warfare between Donald and the nephews was given new coloration by the addition of a psychologist, Professor Pulpheart Clabberhead, "the *friend* of all children." Donald is victimized by the professor's permissive theories but, at the end, it is not Donald who has abandoned those theories to pursue the nephews with a switch— it is the professor himself.

Supporting characters like the professor helped Barks's stories to loosen up, but the really important supporting characters had already been introduced by the time the professor took his brief turn on the stage. Donald's uncle, Scrooge McDuck—originally a crotchety, wizened old fellow—turned up in an issue of *Donald Duck* published late in 1947, and Gladstone Gander, Donald's slick, wavy-haired cousin, first appeared one month later, in the January, 1948, issue of *Walt Disney's*. Barks had no plans at first to keep using them, but they came in handy, and soon their rather hazy personalities came into sharp focus. By 1949, Scrooge had become much more lively, if no less elderly; he had also become immensely, visibly wealthy, with money cascading over his desk. Gladstone had progressed beyond being a mere chiseler, and was supernaturally, intolerably lucky.

Scrooge's pursuit of wealth quickly passed beyond mere greed; he loved money for its own sake, with a physical passion. In the early fifties, Scrooge's pile of money seemed to grow larger with each story, and his lust for it expanded at about the same rate of speed. When Donald asks Scrooge, in one 1951 story, what he is going to do with all of his money, Scrooge is obviously astounded by the stupidity of the question. "Why, I'm going to keep it right here, of course," he says angrily. "I just like to look at it! And I like to run around in it in my bare feet and feel thousand dollar bills crackling between my toes!" And he does, tossing his spats away in wild abandon. "People that spend money are saps," he says, as he grovels in the cash. "They don't know how to enjoy it!"

Scrooge's love for his money was expressed in a little ritual that was repeated for years; more than one child memorized it. It began in 1951, when Scrooge was standing at the edge of his ocean of coins and bills, contemplating it with evident detachment. "Now me, I know money isn't worth *anything*," he says to himself. "It's just a lot of paper and metal." But his mood shifts abruptly, to elation, and he plunges into the money. "But I *love* the stuff! I love to dive around in it like a porpoise! And burrow through it like a gopher! And toss it up and let it hit me on the head!" And he does all of those things. His enthusiasm is infectious and, in one story, the Beagle Boys, Scrooge's enduring adversaries, try to emulate him by diving into the money. Not too surprisingly, they smash into the coins, and their heads are left like soft tomatoes to the touch. How then, Donald and the nephews ask, can Scrooge play in his money as if it were water and he a champion swimmer? "Well," he says, "I'll admit—it's a *trick*."

Gladstone's luck dominated his personality as Scrooge's money-lust dominated his. Much of the time, Gladstone was arrogantly, even aggressively lucky. At the start of "Luck of the

North," for example, Gladstone insists on dragging Donald with him as he gives demonstrations of how fortune has blessed him. A creditor grabs Gladstone by the neck and threatens him with a punch in the beak if Gladstone doesn't produce five dollars; a ten-dollar bill floats into Gladstone's outstretched hand, and he pokes it in the creditor's face, demanding change. An old trunk Gladstone buys at an auction contains a secret money cache, Gladstone wins a watch at a raffle, and so it goes, as Donald seethes and rages.

Gladstone was so lucky that he didn't have to work, and not working soon became a point of honor with him. In a 1949 story called "Trail of the Unicorn," Gladstone tries to cheat Donald, rather than merely swamp him with good luck, and gets beaten up for his pains. A little later, his confidence restored, Gladstone reprimands himself: "I had a little bad luck on that deal I tried to rig on Donald—but that was because *cheating* is a form of *work!* Anyone as lucky as I should just sit around and let Dame Fortune dump a bale of mazuma in his lap."

Gladstone's sense of honor had become painfully acute by 1952. In a story published that year, the frustrated ducks break into Gladstone's safe in search of his good luck charm, but find only a dime. Gladstone weeps as he confesses that he once took a job, and *earned* the dime; he has been so ashamed of it ever since that "I hid it in the safe and never looked at it again."

Some people talk about Barks's stories—especially those with Scrooge and Gladstone—as if they were conscious satire, or social commentary. Another line of thought holds that Barks, because of his background, shared Scrooge's and Gladstone's preoccupation with money, and this was why so many of his stories were about it. Neither approach is very satisfying when tested against the stories themselves, but there's some truth in both of them.

Barks shakes off suggestions that his work contained social or political comments, but sometimes the message was unmistakable. A few of his stories were definitely satirical, but the satire was deep and black, more like Swift than any contemporary political satirist. Toward the end of Barks's active career in comics, his politics—which are conservative if not reactionary—came out from hiding occasionally, as when the Beagle Boys were sent to prison to be "rehabilitated" for the umpteenth time.

In fact, it's easy to see—without stretching the stories out of shape—that Scrooge and Gladstone really did embody two complementary beliefs, both of which have had wide currency in the United States. In Scrooge, we see the belief in hard work as the path to wealth; in Gladstone, the belief that perfect idleness is the most desirable state, so long as there is money to support it. Like Scrooge and Gladstone, people who hold such beliefs are united in the importance they attach to money, and in their hostility to useful work and creative play. But this sort of analysis can be carried too far; Scrooge and Gladstone were much more than ideas with feathers.

It was as natural for Carl Barks, in mid-twentieth-century America, to write and illustrate stories about money as it was for a Renaissance painter to depict the Madonna and Child. Good artists work with what is around them, but they are not limited by it. Barks *used* the American preoccupations with wealth and idleness and work; he wasn't imprisoned by them. It doesn't really matter if he worked with those ideas because he wanted to be a social critic, or because he remembered his own days of scrounging for a dollar. What matters is that he brought them to life in characters who were solid flesh and blood. His real subject matter was not money, but the ways in which human beings deceive and destroy themselves—and how funny they can be when they do it. Scrooge's wealth and Gladstone's luck were only stepping stones to that larger theme.

However, Scrooge and Gladstone were a liberating influence on Barks's stories. For one thing, Barks could play Donald against Scrooge and Gladstone, instead of just against the nephews. Gladstone's luck and Scrooge's money-lust were like two great natural forces that Donald had to survive. With relatives like Scrooge and Gladstone, it was hard for Donald not to be in the wrong place at the wrong time. For example, in "The Gilded Man" (1952), Donald and the nephews go to South America in search of an incredibly rare stamp, and after many hardships, they find it—on a letter addressed to a woman whose only heir is Gladstone.

In the late forties and early fifties, Donald was falling into other new situations in *Donald Duck*—he got mixed up with spies, charmed an enormous sea serpent with his flute, and sold steam calliopes to the Indians on the Kickmiquick River in northern Canada. Meanwhile, in the short stories in *Walt Disney's*, the intense rivalry between Donald and the nephews faded away, as they became more like a real parent and his children. All this means that Barks could flesh out Donald and the nephews to an extent that wasn't possible before. Donald's temper wasn't as explosive as it once was, but he was funnier than ever before, because his basic quality remained intact: he was still going through life wearing blinders.

In a wonderful 1953 story in *Walt Disney's*, Donald finds a beehive in his back yard, and after dressing to protect himself, he starts carrying the hive to the city dump—which is on the other side of town. Donald, oblivious to what is happening, passes through the center of the city, leaving chaos in his wake as the townspeople flee madly from the bees. Ultimately, Donald is the target for a barrage of water from the hoses of encircling Duckburg firemen. "I guess this is an example of just how *mad* some people can get," he says as the water pours in.

But it was Scrooge, more than Donald, who set the tone for Barks's stories in this period. Scrooge was fun; he was active, not like Gladstone, who was essentially a passive character. Barks liked Scrooge better than Gladstone, and his readers must have, too—Scrooge got his own book, Gladstone didn't. Scrooge enjoyed his money for its own sake but, for Barks, Scrooge's fortune was the peg on which he could hang some of his best stories.

Scrooge was even willing to spend money, when his ego was threatened. In one 1952 story, Scrooge butts heads with the Maharajah of Howduyustan, who also claims to be the richest man in the world. They compete to see who can build the biggest statue of Cornelius Coot, the founder of Duckburg, and the statues finally dwarf the Duckburg skyline. When it's all over, the Maharajah is wearing a barrel and Scrooge has done no more than empty his petty cash safe; his three cubic acres of money are untouched. As the story closes, Donald and Scrooge walk past the pitiful Maharajah, who sits begging on a park bench. "Uncle Scrooge," Donald asks, "why don't you be big hearted and give the Maharajah a dime for a cup of coffee?" Furious, Scrooge pursues Donald with his cane, crying, "A *dime?* What do you think I am—a doggoned *spendthrift?*" Scrooge always responded vigorously to attacks on his money, but he seemed to be especially cruel and unrelenting when the *status* of his fortune was attacked, as if he were a proud father defending his child's good name. His identification with his money was that complete.

Scrooge dispatched other pretenders to his throne just as

thoroughly as he had the Maharajah, but the Beagle Boys were a more serious threat, because they were more like Scrooge himself. The Beagles, a gang of burglars who went by prison numbers instead of names, were as devoted to the Protestant ethic as Scrooge, and this made them his perfect foils; the Beagles worked at least as hard at stealing Scrooge's money as Scrooge had worked at earning it. Scrooge's money bin—an enormous cube, many stories high and stuffed full of cash—made his fortune seem even more real than before, and gave the Beagle Boys a natural target. The Beagles and the money bin made their debut at almost the same time, and they soon became central to many adventures.

A change came over Barks's stories when *Uncle Scrooge* began publication in 1952, and Scrooge himself summed it up in the first issue. In between battles with the Beagle Boys, Scrooge tells the nephews how he got his money, reacting with a snort when they ask if he made it in banking. "I made it by being tougher than the toughies, and smarter than the smarties! And I made it *square!*" As he kisses a handful of coins tenderly, Scrooge tells the nephews, "You'd love your money, too, boys, if you got it the way I did—by thinking a little harder than the other guy—by jumping a little quicker—."

That story appeared the same month as the story in which Scrooge routed the Maharajah. Scrooge, who was so often nasty when he was still in supporting roles, changed when he was given center stage. He became a much more sympathetic character, without the broad streak of malice he had shown in earlier stories. That had to be, if Scrooge were going to be a star.

In 1953, Barks left *Donald Duck,* by then a bimonthly, and confined himself almost entirely to the new quarterly, *Uncle Scrooge,* and the *Donald Duck* stories in *Walt Disney's.* The stories in *Scrooge* were in much the same vein as the stories in *Donald Duck,* except that now everything turned on Scrooge and his money, and especially on his efforts to protect it from the Beagle Boys. The ducks continued to have great adventures, as Barks sent them to Hawaii, to Atlantis, to the Seven Cities of Cibola, and to Tra La La, a hidden Himalayan kingdom that was free of the curse of money—until Scrooge unwittingly introduced it, in the form of bottle caps.

What was missing from many of these stories was the emotional resonance of Barks's earlier stories. Scrooge was limited, as a character, in ways that Donald was not, and this meant that some

Carl Barks's own view of his retirement.

of the flexibility and great range that Barks had shown in the late forties and early fifties had to be sacrificed. To say this suggests that Barks's stories in the fifties were inferior to what he was doing earlier and, that may be true, but mainly, they were different. Simply as stories, and especially as masterful combinations of comedy and adventure, Barks's stories in *Uncle Scrooge* are hard to fault. The difference was that Barks wasn't extending himself as he had in his earlier stories. He couldn't; his format in *Uncle Scrooge* didn't allow for it. The publishers had given Scrooge his own magazine because Barks's stories with Scrooge had been so well received, so Barks had really constructed his own prison.

But there is nothing pinched or confined about Barks's stories throughout most of the fifties. He spun out a remarkable series of variations on his one basic theme of Scrooge and his money. Scrooge had to save his money from the Terries and the Fermies, round little creatures who lived in vast subterranean caverns and caused earthquakes; Scrooge competed with his most serious rival, Flintheart Glomgold, a South African tycoon, to decide who was the world's richest duck; Scrooge was carried by Harpies (called "Larkies" because some Dell editor found out "harpy" was sometimes applied to prostitutes) to the ancient city of Colchis from which he escaped with the legendary golden fleece—and so it went.

By the late fifties, weariness was beginning to show, and it dominates some stories of the sixties, before Barks's retirement in 1966 (his last stories actually appeared in 1967). There was just so much that anyone could do with Scrooge, and Barks had done it all.

Barks's retirement has not meant his total withdrawal from comics, much less the absence of any Barks stories from comic books. He still writes scripts for other artists to illustrate (in 1972, most of them were for a comic book about the Junior Wood-chucks, Barks's parody of the Boy Scouts), and Barks's earlier stories have been reprinted regularly in *Walt Disney's* and *Uncle Scrooge*. It's good that today's children still have the chance to get to know Carl Barks's stories, but the effect of reading them now—reprinted out of sequence, and sometimes chopped up—can't be the same as reading them when they were first published, 20 and more years ago. What was almost unique about Barks was his growth; other artists changed, but Barks grew—his stories got better and better—and some of us were lucky enough to be growing along with him. We never knew his name (like the other Disney artists, Barks never signed his name to any of his stories), so we referred to him simply as "the good artist." It's still hard to think of a better way to describe him.

INTRODUCTION TO

OF (SUPER)HUMAN BONDAGE

MOSTLY, comic books seem to be written for boys. As you soon will see, they also are read by girls, but they tend to be aimed at boys. This means, of course, that there are not so many major roles for women in comic books. Most females are "girl friends" of the hero and serve two functions—trying to learn the hero's secret identity and getting into trouble so the hero has someone to rescue. Or they wear few clothes.

Longest-lived of the comparatively few comic-book superheroines is Wonder Woman, who is one of only three costumed superdoers whose adventures have appeared without interruption since the very early forties. (The other two, whose births antedate Wonder Woman's, are Superman and Batman.) With the publication in 1972 of a hardcover collection of her stories, replete with essays by Gloria Steinem, Ms. Diana Prince, aka Wonder Woman, has become the symbol for liberated women. Actually, a better example would be Little Lulu, as depicted anonymously in Dell and Gold Key comic books by John Stanley—Lulu, after all, competed with her male peers on their own terms and on her terms as well, and nearly always emerged victorious. However, Wonder Woman is in the spotlight in this article, along with Mary Marvel, Supergirl, Black Cat, and others, and Little Lulu is saved for some future study.

Juanita Coulson is an Indiana writer of science fiction (*Crisis on Cheiron* and *The Singing Stones*, both from Ace Books) and gothic novels (*The Secret of Seven Oaks* and *Door Into Terror*, both from Berkley Books) and of several stories published in the science-fiction magazines. She is also the mother of a teenaged son and an accomplished cook, seamstress, canner, and domestic engineer (housewife, if you will). With her husband, Robert, she is the publisher/editor of *Yandro*, one of the longest-running science-fiction fan magazines and winner of the Hugo Award as best SF fanzine. She and her husband are also active in the Science Fiction Writers of America.

CHAPTER 9

OF (SUPER)HUMAN BONDAGE

by JUANITA COULSON

IN *The Great Comic Book Heroes* (Dial, 1965), Jules Feiffer, who up till then had been winning my nodding approval, blew it by saying: "Well, I can't comment on the image girls had of Wonder Woman. I never knew they read her—or any comic book. That *girls* had a preference for my brand of literature would have been more of a frightening image to me than any number of men beaten up by Wonder Woman."

Perhaps it was just as well for his delicate male ego that he didn't realize that girls did indeed read *Wonder Woman*, and tons of *other* comics; the poor boy might have been terrified. (But what kind of kid could Feiffer have been to have been shattered by the thought of mere girls reading his beloved comic books?) Since he went on to state that for him the Wonder Woman mythos paralleled every Jewish boy's idea of how to cope with reality, I suspect that Feiffer was seeing Wonder Woman strictly in terms familiar to his own upbringing. There were hundreds of thousands of comic-book fans in that era; surely *all* of them couldn't have been Jewish.

I'm not claiming that only girls bought *Wonder Woman*, but certainly some of them were clutching that comic book to their— if you will excuse the expression—bosoms (however much of that eight-and-nine-year-olds have). To give Feiffer his due, there were plenty of girls who avoided the adventure comic books; but our gang didn't consider those sissies "regular." They probably squealed and covered their eyes in the noisy, blood-and-guts war movies, too.

When Feiffer says he never knew girls read comic books, I believe him. They probably didn't, in his day. While my contemporaries were knee-deep in collecting comics, Feiffer was already one of the Enemy. Not the Axis, but one of those beyond-the-Pale beings—an almost-grownup. By the time Wonder Woman and her superheroine sisters burst—with the grace of deer and the speed of P-38s—onto the scene, Feiffer was much too old to be accepted by *my* generation. (Maybe he was too old, period. Many virile young men, by their own accounts, latched onto *Wonder Woman* with libidinous enthusiasm, but Feiffer expressed no such reaction; quite the opposite.)

My generation: a generation of Depression Babies and War Kids. We had been mere toddlers in the black years of the early thirties, and for us the universe was a slam-bang thrilling place dominated by World War II. It was an age of penny candy, cherry phosphates, "hey-wait-up-you-guys," horse-drawn ice-cream-vendors' wagons, hopscotch (the squares scratched onto the sidewalk with a chunk of gravel—nothing so sissified as chalk), scooters and soapbox derby racers built from scrap lumber and orange crates. (Remember orange crates?) It was also the Golden Age of comic books. Amid the rationing stamps, collecting of scrap metal, and making sure our loose lips didn't sink ships (an admonition we took seriously, though it's doubtful we kids knew anything of value to Hitler or Tojo), we were guiltily grateful that we didn't have to give up comic books "for the duration." After all, the comics were intensely patriotic, printing such slogans as: "Turn Out Lights Not in Use—War Production Needs the 'Juice,' " and "Tin Cans in the Garbage Pile Are Just a Way of Saying 'Heil!' "

In towns and cities throughout America, booming with war plants and rapidly shifting populations, our impressionable young minds were assaulted by none-too-subtle propaganda. Among other things, films and posters showed us Rosie the Riveter, WACs, WAVEs, SPARs, and WAAFs all "doing their part." The times they were a-changin'. At last, it was "in" to be a tomboy, a tough cookie—to fight back, just as our gallant women in uniform were rolling up their pretty sleeves to sock it to the Axis. Women were achieving a new status, and the comic-book superheroine appeared just in time to join the parade. And after the war, like many a real-life counterpart, the superheroine decided she liked being a career woman and stuck with her job.⌡

During the past three decades a host (hostess?) of fighting females have blazed a trail across those glorious, garish pages: Wonder Woman, naturally, was the first Empress. But there were also the pulchritudinous jungle (Playboy-type) bunnies, the super-sexy *Planet Comics* femmes, Mary Marvel . . . and literally scores of primary and secondary heroines and superheroines. Such as (in no particular rank or order or degree of completeness): Bat Girl, Supergirl, Sun Girl, Hawkgirl, Bulletgirl, Phantom Lady, Moon Girl, Black Canary, Black Angel, Black Cat, Zatanna, Maia, Invisible Scarlet O'Neil, Lady Luck, Marvel Girl, the Invisible Girl, etc. It would be quite impossible to mention them all, much less describe them. I can do no more than skip along the crest of the subject, sampling from a few of the important and/or interesting (not always the same thing).

I grew up on comic books, relishing those that headlined my own sex. As I matured, my youthful admiration tarnished with cynicism. In college I collected a minor in psychology and the scales fell from my eyes; *Wonder Woman*, and several other features, became morbidly fascinating, in retrospect. But while I was *young*—I adored the superheroines almost without question. Their lives brimmed with thrills and adventure, while most of the adult women I knew in real life were trapped in dull, drab existences. (Remember: At that stage of the game Women's Lib hadn't come a long way, baby—it hadn't really got off the ground.)

Like all my friends I cut my first permanent teeth on comic heroes like Batman and Superman (though the latter was so all-powerful he was dull), and when Captain America and the Atlas-Timely-Marvel superheroes exploded onto the stage I thought comics had reached a pinnacle of excitement. But then, while America was riding a historical roller coaster toward Pearl Harbor, to my delight a costumed marvel appeared just for us girls. (Or so I naively thought at the time.)

Wonder Woman! Diana Prince! Beautiful emigrée of Paradise Island!

Until that time women in comic books had either been spear-carriers for the superheroes, or that abomination, "girl friends." These were fragile creatures whose *raisons d'êtres* were screaming, fainting, being captured, and being rescued. All very embarrassing to read, if one were a girl. Being a kid was tough enough; at least one expected some solace from one's dream world. The costumed wonder (*you*, in clever plastic disguise) could bend metal, outrace a pursuit plane, and toss enemies around like paper dolls. Imagining oneself in her place was a pleasant respite from the tedium of spelling exams, cleaning up one's room, and taking a skinned knee without bawling. But even in my most wishful thinking, I couldn't envision myself as Batman or Captain America: I'd had the misfortune to be born a girl. But *Wonder Woman*! Didn't I just *dream* of growing up to be an Amazon! *Yeah!*

In 1941 a chap named William Moulton Marston, who signed his comic-book writing as "Charles Moulton," came up with the idea of Wonder Woman. For good or ill he opened the door for a long succession of comic-book heroines, and the end is not in sight. A psychologist—Phi Beta Kappa, Ph.D., LL.B., developer of the basis for the polygraph—Moulton, by creating Wonder Woman, provided the critics of the comic book with some of their deadliest ammunition, of which more later.

In a how-it-all-started article in *The American Scholar* Winter, 1943–44, Moulton, naturally, didn't say that his purpose was to unleash perverted sex and sick feminism on the unsuspecting world of comic books. Rather he claimed that his plan was to revolutionize comics and produce a superwoman. To be frank, that article has a hindsightish quality, yet there was a strong element of truth in it. For example:

> It's smart to be strong . . . But it's sissified, according to exclusively masculine rules, to be tender, loving, affectionate, and alluring. "Aw, that's girl's stuff!" snorts our young comics reader. "Who wants to be a *girl?*" And that's the point; not even girls want to be girls so long as our feminine archetype lacks force, strength, and power. Not wanting to be girls, they don't want to be tender, submissive, peace-loving as good women are. Women's strong qualities have become despised because of their weakness. The obvious remedy is to create a feminine character with all the strength of a Superman plus all the allure of a good and beautiful woman . . .

Right on, sister!

Er . . . I *mean*, brother.

I doubt if the National Organization for Women would ap-

The first page of the Wonder Woman origin story, complete with *different* art and some hints of the female supremacy theory on which the feature was based. It was usual with comic books for changes to be wrought in the mythology over the years; it later became a tenet of the Wonder Woman myth that no man ever could be on Paradise Island, as Steve Trevor is on this page, without ending the Amazons' paradise. Copyright © 1971, National Periodical Publication, Inc., and reprinted by its permission.

plaud his analysis of women's strong and weak qualities, but taken in the context of the milieu of the 1940s, Moulton was right. Girls *didn't* want to be girls. We wanted to be where the action was. Our real-life ideals were marching off to war and taking men's places on assembly lines. What red-blooded American girl could admire a *kinder, küche, kirche* philosophy under those circumstances?

The critics of the comics have castigated the superheroines for their violence, aggressiveness, and lack of femininity. But they've forgotten: the superheroine was born in that time just before and during World War II. The young comic-book reader was steeped in that war and its *Zeitgeist*. It wasn't very feminine to die in a bombing raid or a sinking hospital ship, either; but in every newsreel (between that week's serial chapter and the trailers) kids saw or heard about women dying in just such ways. Violence and aggressiveness were facts of our young lives. It seemed logical to us that they'd appear in comics, too.

Moulton's Wonder Woman insisted that Love was Good, that Peace was better than War—and that both preferables were intimately associated with the gentle and motherly sex. But this preachifying was always interwoven with scene after scene of Wonder Woman walloping the bejeesus out of evildoers. The kids got the message, just as our parents read between the lines of the politicians' speeches. The *leitmotiv* of the era was, We Are Fighting for Peace, and We'll Kill You If We Must. It didn't strike any of us as a contradiction. None of us heard the word "pacifism" during World War II.

Wonder Woman made her debut almost simultaneously in *All-Star* No. 8 and *Sensation* No. 1 (both Superman-DC Publications). Both magazines hit the newsstands very near Pearl Harbor and martial themes were prevalent, as they were in many adventure comics of the time. This despite the fact that, allowing for the month-or-several lead-time needed by comic-book distributors, the writers and artists were composing these stories *prior* to the U.S. entry into the war.

Throughout much of her career, *Wonder Woman* was inked by Harry G. Peter, one of the more frequently maligned artists of the field. Jules Feiffer called his work "dully drawn," and Jim Harmon, in *All in Color for a Dime*, described him as "an artist with an awkward but highly distinctive style." I never thought him awkward, but he was indeed distinctive; you'd never confuse his style with anyone else's. While Peter's bold-outline, minimal-detail, broad pen stroke work was not always satisfactory on human figures, his animal drawings were anatomically superior to those of his contemporaries.

On the cover of that first *Sensation Comics*, Wonder Woman is shown leaping gracefully toward a trio of baddies clustered in the foreground. These blackguards are shooting at our heroine, but she adroitly counters their attack by ricocheting the bullets off her heavy, black Amazon bracelets. In the background, Washington's Capitol Dome looms (providing a bit of free advertising for DC Comics). The costume she wore didn't change much (until a complete overhaul in the sixties). Like many a superhero, she adopted patriotic colors (her outfit was a gift from her mother, not an Ally but someone who knew a Right Cause when she heard about it), a red strapless longline bra with a yellow eagle emblazoned on the frontage, flared mid-thigh-length culottes (white stars on a blue field), curvaceously feminine red boots, and a golden headband decorated with a red star. (This last item doubled as a mental radio receiver.) In later issues the culottes were abandoned for blue-and-white walking shorts, eminently more practical for Wonder Woman's active life. (I never understood how skirted superheroines managed to wrestle with crooks without displaying a lot more of their then-unmentionables than the artists dared draw. Positive thinking and antigravity, most likely.) A shapely brunette, Wonder Woman wore her hair in a loose, shoulder-length style, scorning Andrews Sisters–style pompadours and overdone pageboy (for which thank God).

Not shown in these first issues was one of Wonder Woman's major weapons, and one that produced a large share of the coals of criticism later heaped on the series. This was the unbreakable magic lasso. In subsequent issues Wonder Woman carried it coiled at her belt. The lasso compelled anyone bound with it (including Wonder Woman, if she fell into the clutches of villains) to obey the orders of his or her captor. Usually said captor was interested in the formulae for nerve gasses or the blueprint for a Liberty Ship. (Shame on you for what you were thinking!)

Inside the front cover of *Sensation Comics* No. 1 the reader found a then-familiar burbling editorial from M. C. Gaines and a letter from Gene Tunney. You may well ask what *that* was doing in there; it's obvious from the thank-you-very-much-I-think tone of the note that Tunney was asking himself that same question. Gaines was fond of these puzzled little congratulatory notes from celebrities. *Sensation Comics* No. 2 featured an even more abrupt good luck message from Jack Dempsey; perhaps Gaines thought he'd better give the Manassa Mauler equal time.

While her origin story (which we'll get to in a minute) was appearing in *All-Star* No. 8, *Sensation Comics* plunged Wonder Woman into action and introduced her gimmicks and sidekicks. The gimmicks included her robot plane, her ability to outrun a flat-out auto, the previously mentioned bullets-and-bracelets skill of stopping a .38 slug with her bare jewelry (after all, she had superwrists), and if she couldn't fly she *could* jump out of second and third story windows and land unharmed. Later we would be told that the only way to render an Amazon unconscious was to clobber her at the base of the skull; it was Wonder Woman's version of kryptonite. Her sidekicks were a perpetual boy friend, Steve Trevor (who led a hard life—for example, beginning the first episode with a concussion and ending it with a broken leg), and Etta Candy and the Beeta Lambda Holliday College girls. Except for Etta, who was comedy relief, these sorority types were as interchangeable as a set of kewpie dolls and as far as I was concerned unnecessarily cluttered up the landscape.

In Wonder Woman's origin story it became obvious that Moulton had gone off on a tangent from Greek mythology, making a left turn at Krafft-Ebing and picking up Elizabeth Cady Stanton along the way. In Moulton's mythology, Hippolyte (later vulgarized as "Hippolyta"), Queen of the Amazons, is the compleat mother figure, sans father figure. After a series of *Iliad*-ish adventures never annotated by Robert Graves, Hippolyte and her subjects establish themselves on Paradise Island, a sanctuary verboten to men. Aphrodite, their patron goddess—with an assist from Athene—warns the Amazons to eschew the "Man's World" and all masculine society. Then she passes out "Venus girdles," belts which "remove all desire to do evil and compel complete obedience to *loving* authority." Emphasis is Moulton's. The goddess also demanded the Amazons wear "bracelets of submission," to pledge their dedication to Aphrodite's policy of love. (Aphrodite seems a strange choice for the patron goddess of a manless society, but perhaps Artemis was busy.)

Over the years, Hippolyte becomes lonely for a child, so she creates a statue of a perfect little girl and Aphrodite endows it with life. This Pygmalion gimmick avoided all the problems of depicting pregnancy for the artist, and it allowed Moulton to dip

Tin Cans in the Garbage Pile Are Just a Way of Saying "Heil!"

Perfect happiness as seen by Wonder Woman involves an era of always perfect weather (apparently thunderstorms are not needed in this "perfect" era). The short, dumpy girl on the left of that line of girls in gym suits is Etta Candy. The young man in the last three panels is the easily dominated Steve Trevor, who followed Wonder Woman about like a lapdog for years, blundering into trouble in typical clumsy male fashion. Copyright © 1944, Wonder Woman Publishing Co., Inc.; renewed 1971 by National Periodicals Publications, Inc., and reprinted by its permission.

into his psychological background. It was an unhealthy fantasy for the girl reader, too: here is motherhood without submission to intercourse or male domination, and with none of the real or imagined pain and degradation of childbirth. The young girl who accepted this philosophy might have that much more trouble adjusting to an adult role which included both marriage and childbirth. But it *was* a thesis geared precisely to the thinking of the girl-child of the 1940s, and I do admire Moulton's genius in concocting it.

Hippolyte's daughter Diana grows up to be Number-One Amazon, absolute champion at everything and loved by all her peers. Paradise enow. And then Steve Trevor, nearly dead, washed up on the shore of Paradise Island.

Trevor was a U.S. Army Intelligence officer, wounded while thwarting the bombing of an Army camp. (I knew Amazons had something to do with Greece, and I childishly wondered what a U.S. Army base was doing in that area in 1941.) Steve couldn't stay on Paradise Island, so he recuperated in Paula's lab. (Paula was an Amazonian combination of Edison, Einstein, and Dr. Schweitzer.) As Steve recovered, Diana discovered that she loved the big lug. Meanwhile Hippolyte decreed that someone had to take Trevor back to the Man's World; so she staged an athletic contest among the Amazons, forbidding her daughter to enter. However, Diana did enter, masked, and won, naturally. Resigned to seeing her fledgling leave the nest, Queen Hippolyte delivered herself of some motherly advice:

"Let no man chain [your bracelets of submission] . . . together or you will be forced to obey him—until you can get him or another man to break your chains." This echoed a warning from Aphrodite: the bracelets " . . . are to *teach* you the folly of submitting to man's *domination!*" As a budding feminist, I bought that. Wear those keen bracelets and you'd never have to grow up and play housewife. Peter Pan for little girls.

Hippolyte gave Diana several mental radio sets—birdcage-sized picture-phone sets (with tiny Greek-column trim). And instead of a car, Wonder Woman's graduation present was a transparent robot plane which she could summon with thought waves. It was a pretty stupid looking plane, shaped like a pregnant penguin, and it could defy every law of aerodynamics ever written.

Once in America, Diana swapped identities with a nurse named Diana Prince, so that she could stay close to Steve Trevor while he was in Walter Reed. (The real Diana skipped forever to South America with her boy friend.) Later she conveniently switched from nursing to being General Darnell's secretary; Darnell was Trevor's boss in Intelligence, so that hanging around the office not only let Diana be near her light o' love, but gave Wonder Woman a hotline to where the action was. In her Diana Prince guise our heroine was a female Clark Kent, wearing glasses, baggy uniforms, and a mousy hairdo. Like Lois Lane, Steve never—or almost never—suspected the truth; he was big-brotherish to Diana Prince the dowdy secretary, but it was Wonder Woman who really rang his chimes.

If the Wonder Woman thesis had stopped there, complaints might have been minimal. But Moulton continued extrapolating.

Like other comic-book stars, Wonder Woman did her bit for the war effort. But many of her adventures were pure fantasy or science fiction, set on alien planets, in other dimensions, or inside a leprechaun's tree. Moulton's "science" in these stories was comic-book average—meaning it was gibberish; further, his scripts were marked by peculiar stylisms: for example, while other writers referred to alien beings as "Jovians" or "Saturnians," Moulton used the terms "Jupiterians" and "Saturnites."

The 48 pages of *Wonder Woman* were broken up by the usual ads and the obligatory few pages of written text. The rest were generally turned into three chapters of rambling adventure— adventure studded with subtle and not-so-subtle feminism and psychosexual elements.

Wonder Woman No. 9 (Summer, 1944), for example, featured a three-parter called "Wonder Woman and the Reversal of Evolution." At the zoo, Steve Trevor's little niece is kidnaped by a female gorilla (bereaved by the loss of her baby). Wonder Woman and Steve track the beast to Holliday College, where Professor Zool is demonstrating his "electronic evolutionizer" to Etta Candy and the Holliday Girls. All hell breaks loose, and after a tussle Giganta, the gorilla, is tied up and placed in the evolutionizer. The professor throws the switch and Darwin revolves in his grave; the gorilla is transformed into a gorgeous queen-sized redhead, encased in ropes that barely conceal her charms. Despite having been "evolutionized" forward from gorilla to human, she's still savage and, during another brawl the professor's machine is accidentally set in operation.

Wonder Woman, Steve, the professor, the girls, and Giganta

are all thrown into a past populated (simultaneously) with cave-men, mastodons, and dinosaurs. While the others try to adapt to their new surroundings, Giganta is captured—and tied up—by cavemen and strikes a bargain with them. She helps the cavemen trap the others and tie them up. But when the cavemen start to sacrifice Steve to a dinosaur, Wonder Woman bursts her bonds, tears up the tree to which Steve is tied, and compels the beast to obey her by binding it with her magic lasso.

Professor Zool searches for his evolutionizer machine and is captured—again?!—by Giganta. When Wonder Woman comes to the rescue, Giganta, having watched and learned, ties the Amazon with her own magic lasso. Then the ex-gorilla throws Wonder Woman, still bound, into a cave which contains the evolutionizer and a sabertoothed tiger. Naturally, our girl triumphs, wrapping a stray loop of "her magic bond of Aphrodite" around the tiger's neck and subduing it.

The professor looks over the evolutionizer and discovers there are problems. Wonder Woman interprets: " . . . tune the hyper-atomic neutron tubes to the interruptive frequency of the kathodic rays." Yes. Still no luck. The gadget's battery is dead. Wonder Woman plays Ben Franklin, flies a kite and lets a thunderstorm recharge the machine's cells, somehow without blowing every circuit.

Thunderstorms are notoriously difficult to control. "Great Aphrodite! The evolution machine brought us to the Golden Age when everything was *perfect*!" Steve and Diana investigate their surroundings and encounter Queen Darla and King Aros, the humble and generous monarchs of this golden land. The queen is disturbed because Wonder Woman keeps Giganta tied up with the magic lasso. "She's dangerous," our heroine warns. "If freed, she'd try to kill us! Binding with the lasso of Aphrodite doesn't hurt the girl—it's good training for her." The queen insists, and Wonder Woman releases the ex-gorilla. Giganta's reaction is precisely what might be expected of one who is not governed by Aphrodite's maxim that loving submission and bondage are Good for You: "Wonder Woman's bonds were subduing me but now that I'm free, I'm *savage* again! With this human brain, I'll destroy the Golden Age of Love and establish a new order—A RULE BY FORCE!"

In other words—Man's World thinking—indistinguishable from that of a savage beast.

Giganta persuades some of the locals to rebel and leads the way to the palace, where Steve Trevor and King Aros are busy "doing homework." "Men and women take turns working at home and in the fields—you'll soon learn to like it, Steve." "I like it already—cooking's my hobby!" (This pair had been to some Women's Lib sessions, obviously.) The rebels nab everyone, but fail to notice Wonder Woman concealing her magic lasso. Queen Darla and Wonder Woman are bound back-to-back and placed on a funeral pyre. Behind the concealing smoke Wonder Woman snaps her bonds—she wasn't tied with Aphrodite's lasso, remember?—and quells the rebellion. Queen Darla laments that the Golden Age is over, now that her people know they can be wicked if they choose. Wonder Woman reassures her that "a greater Golden Age will come when humans learn it's more fun to be *good*!"

The men, having had a taste of superiority, decide to junk equality. After all, they're stronger. The chief rebel says he offered the women a chance to fight over who should be master, "but they said they'd rather submit. Women are afraid to fight."

Not *one* woman! Wonder Woman challenges this bonehead and wipes up the palace with him. But then the bully's wife berates Wonder Woman for picking on her poor husband. The Amazon chortles, "Ha ha! So you girls like to think your men are stronger than you are!" (Let's Pretend was the name of the game.)

Queen Darla decides to leave the kingdom to those who prefer a cruel Man's World rule and found a new colony. Giganta, given a choice, elects to go with the Queen and her party. "I'd rather be a woman's captive—you'll treat me more kindly." Things go pretty well in the new colony until Giganta—heretofore kept in loving submission by Wonder Woman's magic lasso—plays Pandora and curiously fiddles with the dials on the evolutionizer. And suddenly our original party is now in Amazonian Greece, before the time when Wonder Woman had been born.

Steve Trevor has a merry time escaping from a couple of husband-hunting Amazons, only to fall prey to Giganta. She compels him to release her by wrapping the magic lasso around him, so the ex-gorilla is loose once more.

Meanwhile, Diana meets her mother Hippolyte (who naturally doesn't recognize her); the Amazon queen explains that the Greeks, fresh from defeating the Trojans, are marching on her city. The Greek army is led by Achilles; no matter that Achilles died in the Trojan War—more of Moulton's mythology. Wonder

Woman acts as the Amazons' champion, flinging down the gauntlet to Achilles, and the outcome is a foregone conclusion. Giganta is recaptured, the Greeks are defeated. Total victory.

But an exhausting one. Steve Trevor's too tired to offer his usual proposal of marriage to Diana. Instead, she suggests she ought to propose to *him*, since she's an Amazon and it's husband-hunting season. Steve's willing, but Wonder Woman reconsiders: "I think I'll stay a career girl for a while yet—there's too much to be done without my trying to keep house in a man's world!" Whew! Thank Hera for *that*!

Wonder Woman discovers her magic lasso has become charged (who knows how) with enough electricity to operate the evolution-izer, so it's back to the twentieth century for our happy party and all's well that . . .

I think you get the general idea. Several disquieting threads ran through each *Wonder Woman* episode: Bondage is Good for You. Submission to a Loving Female Overlord is Good for You. But submitting to a *man* is Bad for You—because men are Bad.

When I was young, it didn't seem to me that there was any more "bondage" in *Wonder Woman* than there was in, say, Batman's adventures. Superheroes got tied up a lot, and escaped a lot. But the recurring "bondage" scenes in *Wonder Woman* attracted a pubescent male readership that ordinarily wouldn't have bothered with a comic book devoted to a superheroine. These fellows really dug panels showing females tied and kneeling in front of other females and saying, "I must obey your will." There was even a scene for paddling fetishists in *Sensation* No. 2, with Etta Candy flailing away at a villainess' fanny with a board.

(Etta Candy started as a six-foot lady wrestler. But perhaps that scene and others bothered Moulton, because Etta rapidly lost a foot of height and turned into an unmenacing pudgy little blend of Wimpy and Hugh Herbert—forever eating [candy] and screeching "Woo! Woo!")

There was a lot that was unwholesome in *Wonder Woman*, but not as much as some critics claim. Despite their suggestions that Etta Candy and the Holliday Girls would entice childish female readers into lesbianism, I'm afraid the Beeta Lambda gang gave me no queer little sexual thrill. They were comedy relief—exactly like General Jinjur's army of women soldiers in L. Frank Baum's *Land of Oz* (Baum wasn't glamorizing feminists but ridiculing them—and the innocence of his stories has rarely been questioned).

There were, occasionally (though not so frequently as some lecherous souls have pantingly insisted), scenes showing women kissing women. These too were supposed to be lesbian in character, leading the young girl down the lavender-strewn path to butchism. I beg to differ. To males—*some* males—the sight of two women kissing is . . . well . . . intriguing. But to the young girl—especially the adventure-comic-oriented tomboy—it was all pretty disgusting. Like those awful sessions at family reunions: "Give your Aunt Judy a kiss, dear." *Blech!!!* But plainly to the beady-eyed and sweaty-palmed men reading *Wonder Woman* these rare kissing scenes were all sorts of Significant.

Bondage and submission, the Holliday Girls, the paddling and kissing scenes—all called down the wrath of critics. And for the impressionable pubescent boy reading this stuff, it must have been rather weird and perverty material, I agree. But not necessarily for *girls.*

However . . .

There were two prominent facets of *Wonder Woman* that did indeed lay the seeds of discontent in the minds of impressionable girls, encouraging them in a man-hating philosophy that made later adjustment to a life role more painful than it need have been.

One element was the constant theme that corruption is exclusively a male province, that evil (and by implication, World War II with all its suffering and horror) was caused by men and by weak women obeying those men. That if women could be totally and absolutely isolated from male society and domination, and *submit themselves in loving bondage to queenly, motherly figures,* the new millennium would arrive. It was a twisted female chauvinism at its most extreme.

The second string to that bow was the relationship between Wonder Woman and Steve Trevor. To say the least, it was abnormal. Wonder Woman was superior to Steve in every way—brains, brawn, intuitive insight—and *he loved her for it!* Sometimes he positively wallowed in the fact. On rare occasions when he succumbed to the masculine urge to assert himself (foolish boy!) he usually ended up to his handsome blond locks in trouble and had to be rescued by Wonder Woman. (Who always forgave him for being stupid or momentarily fickle.)

Some of the Moulton-Peter stories were apparently too strong even for the Superman-DC Comics of the 1940s. Only now are they being printed. In one, "The Cheetah's Thought Prisoners" (*DC Special* No. 3, June, 1969), all the stops are pulled out. The

Cheetah, a villainess who'd been safe on the Amazons' Reform Island (where she was submitting to loving bondage), is dragged back kicking and screaming to the Man's World. She has an inheritance coming, but the male-chauvinist judge arbitrarily declares she must sign over her $3,000,000 to a man—the Cheetah's father. Quite naturally, this irks the Cheetah and she seeks revenge by employing a horde of costumed female minions to raid a millionaires' bash and the Beeta Lambda sorority house. While the millionaires' only survivor is a coward who hid under a bed, one Holliday Girl is left behind solely because she put up such a fight she was slugged and left for dead. *Men are cowardly, as well as cruel and greedy. Women are self-sacrificing and noble.*

Eventually the Cheetah is subdued by Wonder Woman's magic bond of Aphrodite, and the poor prisoner pleads, "Please take me back to Reform Island!" "Right—you need more Amazon reconstruction training before you are fit to be free." More loving bondage, in other words.

The reader was encouraged to sympathize completely with the Cheetah in her just cause. The poor girl was misguided, but *right*.

Moulton's *Wonder Woman* was so successful that it spawned a blatant imitator in *Moon Girl*, a 1947 series from IC Publishing (EC between the demise of *Picture Stories from the Bible* and the birth of the New Trend comics). Though imitative, it avoided the sicker themes of its older sister.

Moon Girl was based on the Atalanta legend (more mythology), but Moon Girl scorned to pick up the apple, and *won* the race—in this case against her suitor, Prince Menou. Afterwards, she's sorry and goes to America, where she and the prince team up to fight crime, taking as their aliases "Clare Lune" and "Lionel Manning." Clare had a "moonstone" which gave her some special powers, among them the assurance that no man could be her master if she didn't want him to be. And she had a "moonship" which she could summon telepathically (at least it wasn't transparent, too). And she didn't need Amazon bracelets to ricochet bullets; she simply caught them and threw them back. Like Wonder Woman, Moon Girl invoked pagan deities, but hers were male.

The writing was erratic and often downright bad—" ... a man and woman, whose characteristics are so outstanding, so virile ... "—and the artwork, by the derivative Sheldon Moldoff, was shabby most of the time. Despite this, *Moon Girl* was a healthier comic than *Wonder Woman*. There were no troops of nubile females, a minimum of female chauvinism, and Clare Lune never dabbled in bondage and submission. Moon Girl accepted the reality that a woman may be unhappy if she consistently bests her man—that the male ego is too fragile for that. No sense rubbing his nose in her superiority. Moon Girl lived with a problem confronting most highly intelligent women in the U.S.A. of the forties; compromise or loneliness.

Imitation—healthy or not—apparently wasn't sufficient. In *Moon Girl* No. 7 the prince was dumped and a girl assistant, Star, was substituted. Imitating Batman and Robin wasn't a smash either, and after an issue in which stories alternated between Clare-Prince and Clare-Star, the next publication in the series was a romance comic, and that was the end of that.

Wonder Woman was far from being the only superheroine in comic books, and the stories about her were equally far from being the only ones with sexual content—latent or blatant. One such category was the jungle comic. Some of these, like *Sheena*, were obviously designed to appeal to prurient interest. Others, like *Nyoka*, were sexually innocuous. But all of them were written to formula: a jungle setting and a heroine with a faithful male companion who *never* played the male chauvinist. *Sheena* (*Jumbo Comics*), *Princess Pantha* (*Thrilling Comics*), *Jann of the Jungle* (from the Atlas stable), the Edgar Rice Burroughs spin-off, *Nyoka* (from Fawcett) . . . all followed the formula in varying degrees. Sometimes, as a novelty, the heroine's companion was a chimp or a big cat, usually more useful than the men in these comics.

For example, Sheena's "companion," Bob, was a limp grade of cardboard. In almost every episode he was captured by evil witch doctors, diamond smugglers, Dschungel Korps Nazis, or someone else who had no business in the middle of Africa. Sheena always rescued him, though I'm not sure why.

A lot of the jungle comics went in for bondage-submission, but always on a heterosexual level. And most of them sported fur or leather garments, thereby sewing up a second segment of the sweaty-palm audience. It was obvious, even to children, that these comics were aimed at teenage—and older—boys. Sheena would swing through the pages Tarzan-style, her long blonde hair flying and her fur bikini plastered to her 42–22–34 figure. I'm sure it brought the drooling male reader back for more; plainly these fellows weren't buying the jungle comics for their *literary* quality.

A minor branch of the jungle comic was the exotica comic, frequently a one-shot. These were set in an unspecified Arabian Nights or pseudo-Oriental locale and specialized in male wish-fulfillment plots. Such as in *Malu the Slave Girl*, a sword-and-sorcery tale of the vague, distant past, involving a smidgeon of mysticism; the heroine was given to such unfortunate phrases as: "For what you have done I am ever your slave." I'll bet the boys at Fort Bragg loved it. I have no idea who published it.

In *Planet Comics* from Fiction House there was even less pretense of marketing for a kiddie audience. *Planet* was a comic-book version of a pulp mag, *Planet Stories*, and the covers were often identical—Guy, Gal, and Bug-Eyed Monster. The heroines in *Planet* were beautiful and scantily clad, and the violence-rife scripts were strictly pre-Code. As I recall, I was not only the only girl in my gang who read *Planet Comics*—I was the only *kid* in my gang who read it. But then I was a science-fiction nut. It was some time before I learned why my pals' big brothers also pored over those pages so feverishly.

There were heroines in *Planet* for all tastes. Hunt Bowman's li'l ole arrow-sharpener, Lyssa (blonde), defied death in an after-the-alien-invasion U.S.A. of the undated future. Gale Allen (golden redhead who switched to honey blonde) and her Girl Squadron of Venus were souped-up Holliday Girls, rambling around the solar system. Futura (raven-wing brunette) fought the Cymrad over-lords, while clad in no more than a gentian rag and her wits, through many an impressively drawn and overly talky story. Mysta of the Moon (platinum blonde) worked her way up from a mere robot assistant to an assortment of human male second-leads. Something for everyone—but mostly something for the sexually awakening young man.

I read *Planet Comics*, but I could never really identify with those supersexy male-fantasy women—no way. If *Wonder Woman* was the prototype of a comic that would appeal simultaneously to the kids and to prurience, the jungle comic inclined toward the latter, and *Planet Comics* opted whole hog for the hubba-hubba trade.

But at the same time there were dozens of other heroines and superheroines. Their fortes ranged from saintly wholesomeness to aberrations that made *Wonder Woman* look like apple pie. Some heroines were endowed with superpowers—flight, great strength, invisibility; others got by, like Batman, on intelligence, superb physical condition, and a few catchy tools and gimmicks. A lot of them were like the second feature at those Saturday afternoon matinees, entertaining, but not memorable—except to the devoted comic-book fan. They were sandwiched in between the first feature and the serial, as it were.

In the wholesome department, no one even came close to Mary Marvel, in my opinion. For the younger reader, she was the only serious contender besides Wonder Woman for the title of Queen of the Comics. I may have thought Mary a bit of a Goody Two-Shoes, but I enjoyed her adventures tremendously, and I was never nervous when an adult looked over my shoulder while I was reading her feature in *Wow Comics*. She also had her own book, which ran 28 issues, and she appeared in all 89 *Marvel Family* issues.

Fawcett's Captain Marvel was such a smash that an entire Marvel family was introduced. Mary Marvel was presented as Billy Batson's long-lost twin sister, carrying as proof of her kinship the ever-popular half of a broken locket, a mate to one Billy owned. When the two discovered their relationship and Mary learned of Billy's secret identity, it was only natural that she'd speculate on the interesting possibilities. In a very realistic exchange, Mary wistfully says, "I'm your twin sister—so maybe if I said the magic word, I'd change into something too."

Billy's response is all boy. "Naw ... old ... Shaz ... you know who ... wouldn't give his powers to a girl!" Certainly not! Superpowers were for boys. C. C. Beck usually wrote with tongue firmly in cheek and a solid knowledge of human psychology. When Billy said that to Mary, I—and thousands of other girls reading the same comic book—gritted my teeth; it was so damned true to life!

Undeterred, Mary pronounced the magic word and *voilà!*— Mary Marvel. Her "Shazam" represented a pantheon of goddesses from Olympus and points west: Selena, Hippolyta, Ariadne (!), Zephyrus (not even female), Aurora, and Minerva. Well, it was no more garbled than Moulton's pseudomythology. Mary had all the powers Captain Marvel had, and was prone to the same problems of being bound and gagged and unable to say her magic word. Her costume was a modest red dress with a golden thunderbolt emblem, backed by a white cape. I always caviled at that skirt—

every tomboy knew skirts were a nuisance in any sort of important activity, like climbing trees or smashing crooks.

Unlike Billy Batson's transformation into Captain Marvel, Mary's left her a young girl. And she thereby avoided any narrow-eyed criticism in the hidden sex field. Mary was innocent—good, sunny natured, occupied (when not chasing crooks) with school-girlish things. She was a sort of comic-book Girl Scout, and despite her superpowers I can't imagine that even the most delicate-egoed young male would have found her either frightening or sexually fascinating. If Fawcett hadn't been forced to give up the Marvel line, Mary Marvel would have received an instant seal of approval at the time of the Comics Code.

I was sorry to see Mary Marvel fly into limbo. She was a fine champion and a sterling representative of all that was entertaining and fun in the superheroine—from a child's point of view. Later on, she would have proved a handy club to beat critics with. It's a shame she was forced into all too early retirement. She's back now, from DC, and may do better this time.

A number of other comics featured heroines who were name-sakes of the superheroes. Some of them, like Mary Marvel, possessed more or less the same abilities as their male counter-parts—Supergirl, Bat Girl, Hawkgirl, and Bulletgirl, as a small example. Unfortunately, most of them were rather colorless—tagalongs or echoes of the men in their lives. None of them had Mary Marvel's verve. Supergirl has survived into the seventies, as part of a plethora of subsidiary supercreatures, shadows of the continuingly successful Superman. Like Mary Marvel, Supergirl remains a girl, albeit a teenage one, often concerned with dating and teenybopper interests. She's a pale and uninteresting creature compared to the heroines of the swinging Golden Age. For example . . .

One early heroine with a special power didn't parrot anybody, but strictly speaking she wasn't a comic-book heroine, even though she had her very own magazine. Invisible Scarlet O'Neil came from a newspaper strip, and later her adventures were put in comic-book form. Among other things, this meant better and longer plots than those in the average comic. In spite of her name, Scarlet didn't use her invisibility talent much. She didn't follow the Wonder Woman–Sheena formula, either. Her boy friend, Sandy, occasionally needed rescuing, but generally he stood on his own feet pretty well. In Harvey Comics' *Invisible Scarlet O'Neil*

Many years after Superman arrived on Earth as the sole survivor of the planet Krypton, a cousin appeared to play Supergirl. (Most of Krypton must have survived, with all the supercriminals, superdogs, supercats, supermonkeys and just plain superfolks who later turns up.) Supergirl tends to be more interested in clothing and dates than in fighting evil, but that may be because she is written, drawn and edited by men, not women. Copyright © 1970, National Periodical Publications, Inc., and reprinted by its permission.

No. 2, "The Fight For Survival," the entire cast is thrown back to caveman days. Unlike Wonder Woman's bout with the evolution machine, Scarlet's was that cheat on the reader, "it was all a dream." However, there were some nice touches.

In a conversation with a Cro-Magnon type, Scarlet is asked, "Tell me more of this land where the women are so impudent." (He means Chicago.) When Scarlet describes life in the Windy City the caveman rebuts, "And does not a woman marry the man who can best hunt her food and clothing in this land of yours?" Wryly, Scarlet concedes, "More often than I'd like to admit."

At almost the opposite end of the scale in quality and taste was a blessedly obscure "sickie," Iron Lady, appearing once in Hillman's *Real Clue Crime Comics* and once in *Airboy*. Like numerous other not-too-bright heroines, she wore an evening gown as a "disguise." (Since comics were written and drawn by men—and often *for* men—it's obvious they couldn't care less how much time it took to cantilever a female torso into one of those strapless creations, or the utter impracticality of fighting crime in such a number.) Iron Lady's red Pucci was set off by a white fur muff, and hidden in the muff were iron gloves, with which she crushed people. Not even Superman used his superstrength *that* way. In the April '47 issue of *Real Clue* Iron Lady corners a teenage murderer, and in the struggle the kid goes out a skyscraper window. Our heroine, *not* overflowing with that milk of motherly kindess that Moulton peddled in *Wonder Woman*, remarks, "It's just as well—when a rat goes young, there isn't the danger of what he might do if he had reached full growth."

A lot—perhaps the majority—of comic-book heroines had no special powers. A costume, athletic skill, fast wits, and a hell of a lot of luck, yes. But no superstrength or ability to fly or any of that jazz. A surprising number got their start as villainesses, more or less with hearts of gold. Sometimes they converted to the Good Guy's side because they were dazzled by the Pepsodent whiteness of the hero's smile. Sometimes they simply proved more popular characters than the heroes and eventually the publishers gave them a starring role.

Harlequin had a foot in both camps. She was originally a criminal, the bane of Green Lantern. By the time she was through she was on the side of Justice and had supplanted, or nearly, Green Lantern's comic sidekick, Doiby Dickles. Harlequin wore one of the more imaginative costumes around: wide clown ruffs at throat and hips, striped tights, a sleeveless blouse, a conical jester's cap, and a mandolin which seemed to be made out of Krupp steel, because she was forever swatting nasties with it without breaking even a string. (I was also half-convinced that she'd lent her name to a certain style of eyeglasses, since she wore harlequin frames instead of a mask.)

Another example of the heroine who moved in and took over was the Black Canary. She started as a female Robin Hood, donning a black bolero-jacketed, fishnet-stockinged costume whenever she wanted to relieve a Mafioso type of an ill-gotten diamond or other loot. She first appeared in *Flash Comics* No. 86 in the *Johnny Thunder* feature. Johnny was the comic relief in the Justice Society of America, and I always liked his bumbling misadventures. Then the Black Canary wormed her way into his affections and finally presided over his demise, a couple of times. Probably stole his Thunderbolt, too.

In the opening segment of *All-Star* No. 38 a bogus bunch of historically famous villains dispatched all the regular JSA members. Black Canary found Johnny Thunder before he died and hastily contacted the JSA's secretary, Wonder Woman. The two women bundled the bodies into Diana's robot plane and flew to Paula's lab where, after suitable nailchewing, our heroes were restored. One assumes they voted thanks to Black Canary after they'd crushed the baddies. But she was greedy; she wanted Johnny Thunder's whole gig. In another couple of months he'd disappeared completely. (His *name* was briefly resurrected in a cowboy comic, but it wasn't the same.) I always felt Black Canary stabbed Johnny in the back, the Jezebel. Now she's back and running around with Green Arrow.

Black Cat, a Lee Elias heroine from Home Comics, later Harvey Comics, came in for a chunk of criticism from Dr. Fredric Wertham, comics' noisiest enemy, because she dispensed karate and judo lessons in the pages of *Black Cat Comics*. Linda Turner was a movie actress, action-film type, with no special powers but those available to any woman in good condition. For a 100-pound female, karate and judo are useful skills; but if the kid readers followed the reasonably detailed instructions in *Black Cat Comics*, they could indeed have done each other some damage. I think Wertham's criticism was in this case justified. But in these days of militant Women's Lib groups chanting, "Rape is not a party— learn karate," Black Cat would seem a bit tame. She never taught the reader how to *really* cream a male assailant.

Police Comics' Phantom Lady not only had dumb boy friends but not even her father knew her secret identity—which is a trifle strange, since she didn't wear a mask. This meant she spent a lot of time worrying that people would recognize her. In other respects, she wasn't too bad. She didn't regard the men in her life as dunces—it's just that the poor dears were so preoccupied with affairs of state that they were unobservant, just like all men. Like all specimens of that era, the comic's view of life was excessively simplistic. At one point the heroine's senator father remarks anent an evildoer: "The law has proven that she did it. It'll be a fast trial and the electric chair, I suppose." None of this nonsense about appeals, no sir! At another point Sandra Knight–Phantom Lady exclaims, "America comes first—even before Dad." Patriotism conquers Electra. It smacked unnervingly of the later McCarthy era jibe, "If Mommy is a Commie then you gotta turn her in."

With the arrival of the Comics Code, what remained of raw violence and blatant sex in the superheroine comics died. A massive upheaval took place in the industry. If a super*hero* had been approved, then it was okay to have a super*heroine* with the same general bias. As a result Supergirl came into her own during the sixties, as did all her imitators. The best thing I can say for Supergirl is that she was Mary Marvel without spunk. Like Mary she was virtually sexless (except to a pervert), and since she had all of Superman's powers, she was also quite dull. I suspect her sucessful career is the result of habit-buying; some comic-book purchasers will continue to plunk down $.10 . . . $.12 . . . $.15 . . . $.20 . . . $.25 . . . $.35 . . . $.50 . . . !? . . . for anything with "Super" in the title.

One of the beneficiaries of the Comics Code has been *Lois Lane Comics*. She's still Superman's dumb brunette girl friend, but now she has her own comic, ostensibly to appeal to the female trade. Lord help America if she does. Lois Lane has become the repository for some of the worst and most irritating faults of the post-Code comics heroine.

The editors at DC couldn't decide where to aim Lois. At adventure-conscious boys? At teenybopper girls mooning over their silly ideas of "romance"? Or was *Lois Lane Comics* a place to dump all the writers' misogynist hangups? Lois Lane became a youngish Mary Worth, flitting into the lives of her friends, trying to find them husbands, trying to snare Superman, and now and

Actually, that bespectacled man behind the screen is not Clark Kent but a lookalike who is suave, charming, rich, brave, kind, gentle—practically perfect in every way. He has one shortcoming which dooms his relationship with the unbelievably fickle and flighty Lois Lane, however. Copyright © 1961, National Periodical Publications, Inc., and reprinted by its permission.

then actually doing a bit of honest thwarting-crime superheroine-ing. The end-product is a mishmash of inconsistency.

Now and then Superman appears in these stories, lending his masculine superiority to the affairs of Lois and Lana and their girl friends. Usually he's helping them snare dates—which activity the writers seem to consider the be-all of any woman's existence. Since Lois is an established career woman pushing (at least) 30, such plots make her seem like a case of arrested development.

Lois and Lana, most of the time, are Venus flytraps. It is nauseatingly apparent that the writers picture women as shallow, petty, idiotic creatures out to trap the happy bachelor. Superman included. This sort of thinking, echoing a male attitude in the "real world," was precisely the sort of nonsense that made the female gorge rise and produced that groundswell which was to lead to the Women's Liberation movement.

In *Lois Lane* No. 35, "Lois Lane's Other Life," Lois was an amnesiac, wearing glasses and schoolmarm braids. (I waited for some ass to ask her to remove the glasses so he could remark that she was beautiful without them.) In this guise, Lois emerged as a sensible sort who thought Clark Kent was more mature, emotion-ally, than Superman. She still couldn't see the resemblance between Clark and Superman, but then she was sick. Conse-quently, every male in the story became absolutely frantic to shock, force, or stampede Lois back to her normal fluffhead personality. And one wonders why. Were the writers unmanned by the thought that they had for a moment created a plain but intelligent heroine instead of a pretty and stupid one?

Occasionally Lois is allowed to function rationally, as in "The Fantastic Wigs of Mr. Dupre," where she and Supergirl team up to defeat a phony charities racket. But such sanity never lasts. The very next story might depict Lois as an idiot, or worse. For example, a story where she is smitten by an admirable, intelligent man and seriously considers marrying him (to Superman's con-sternation—dog in the manger that he is), until it's revealed the fellow is bald. At which point Lois immediately jilts the poor man. Women are shallow, you know.

Frankly, I wouldn't let a daughter of mine have anything to do with Lois Lane. For all its weird and perverty hangups, the original Wonder Woman was a better bet.

A bright spot in the new comics scene has been Marvel Comics. Stan Lee and Jack Kirby created a stable that, despite faults, was exploding with personality. The women weren't as well developed as characters as the men but, compared to the competition, they were great. Wanda the Scarlet Witch, Marvel Girl, the various Peppers and Bettys and other girl friends of the heroes—each was an individual. Most notable was—is—Sue Richards née Storm. Now and then the editors succumb to male-slant prejudice in writing for her, but in general she does well. She is not only the model of a modern superheroine, but doubles as an emancipated woman who refutes one of Dr. Wertham's pet objections to women in comic books.

In *Seduction of the Innocent* Dr. Wertham quoted an unspecified "comic-book expert" (Moulton, one assumes): "Women . . . are placed on equal footing with men and indulge in the same type of activities. They are generally aggressive and have positions which carry responsibility." In his rejoinder the doctor sneers: "What are the activities in comic books which 'women indulge in on an equal footing with men'? They do no work. They are not homemakers. They do not bring up a family. Mother love is entirely absent."*

Really! Doesn't saving the universe rank as "work"? I don't see any superheroes out running a drill press on the line. Making the world safe for all creatures is what superheroing is all about, isn't it?

Quite aside from that, Dr. Wertham's argument sounds mouldy in these days of Women's Lib. It's far from unusual for a woman to have both a career and a family, and Sue Richards, the Invisible Girl, handles both nicely, thank you. Sue gained her superpowers in a space trip with her brother Johnny, her future husband Reed Richards, and a family friend, Ben Grimm, back in *Fantastic Four* No. 1, in 1961. After a long engagement, Sue and Reed were married and, after a decorous lapse to forestall any nasty-minded gossips, Sue took a maternity leave to give birth to little Franklin. A capable sitter was located and Sue returned to her career—a perfectly normal life pattern today. Sue probably does a lot of baking and casseroling on her rare days off, storing them in the freezer for handy use during those really rushed days when she's saving the universe.

Homemaker, mother, and engaging in meaningful work on

*Wertham, Frederic, *Seduction of the Innocent*. New York: Holt, Rinehart and Winston, Inc., 1954.

equal terms with her men, *and* handling a whale of a lot of responsibility. What more could Dr. Wertham ask?

Sue is the exception, admittedly, but her development gives one hope that the comic books can adapt to the times. Unfortunately, Sue Richards and Marvel Comics are nearly unique. A sadder example of an attempt to adjust is what has happened to Wonder Woman. The Amazon fell on hard times in the sixties, with sales lagging. The Loving Submission is Good for You philosophy was abandoned and for a while Wonder Woman became a shadow of Lois Lane, motivated by dating and romance. By late '68, DC decided to dump everything and start fresh.

Paradise Island was relocated to the Pacific—or, in some accounts, another "dimensional plane"—and Diana Prince opted to stay put, thereby forfeiting her Amazon powers and "immortality." (I'd thought of Diana as a member of royalty, she *was* a princess, but I always assumed she could be killed. What's this "immortality" jazz?) Steve Trevor was killed off, leaving Diana Prince as a swinging single. To compensate for the loss of her super abilities, a wizened blind Oriental gentleman named—yes— I Ching coached her in karate. (It's never explained why someone named "The Book of Changes"—a Chinese occult art—should be a particular expert in a Japanese fighting technique. Of course it's possible, but I suspect that to the comic-book writers all them slant-eyes look alike.)

The new and unimproved Wonder Woman went to work in a boutique, and abandoned her red-white-and-blue costume for a wardrobe of Emma Peel jumpsuits. Some attempt was made to loosen up the hair style and rearrange her curves, so that the karate-chopping Diana Prince might be mistaken for Diana Rigg. (Not bloody likely.)

Another thing the new Wonder Woman lost besides her "immortality" was her old attitude toward men. A lot of those the "new" WW was attracted to turned out to be villains or male-chauvinist pigs. They all grudgingly acknowledged that Diana had some small talent as a crimefighter, but when push comes to shove they knew she was going to be nothing but a poor weak woman, and a man would have to make the difference one way or another. The disgusting part is, they were right. Diana got to show off her stances and chops in the early pages, but by the end of each episode she was usually batting her eyelashes and all but squealing, "Ooh, you big strong wonderful man!"

This is Wonder Woman? Where was the superheroine of yesteryear?

Gone were the psychosexual quirks that drew the ire of the Dr. Werthams. No Holliday Girls. No Bondage and Submission—except Diana to man's domination, whether I Ching's or her new plug-ugly boy friend. The pendulum had swung to the other extreme. This new *Wonder Woman* had been concocted for would-be Hugh Hefners. It was a *slightly* healthier fantasy than the original but this time it was aimed toward the cultural majority.

Now and then, by convoluted plot machinations, the editors flung Diana headlong into Amazonian adventures. But the thrill was gone. Hippolyte—now Hippolyt*a*—had dipped into the Miss Clairol and become a blonde that never was. Mars and the Aesir and who knows how many other *gods*, not goddesses, cluttered up the episodes.

Apparently, even with a belated awareness of Women's Lib, this nonpowered, noncostumed version didn't sell either, so DC returned to the old Wonder Woman in 1972. But the thrill did not return.

Now, even granting a kudo or two to the Marvel heroines, only in dreams—or comic-book collections—can one capture the flavor of that Golden Age of superheroines. Those superwomen who were superior and damned glad of it, and who entertained no doubts that Mother Eve, having been the second model, was a vast improvement over Adam's heroic prototype.

INTRODUCTION TO

LORDS OF THE JUNGLE

THERE may be some dispute to the claim, but many scholars believe that *Tarzan of the Apes*, among the other distinctions of that glorious rip-roaring saga, provided the basis for the very first serious adventure strip, with a continuing central character, in the history of the comics. Certainly from its initiation by the great Hal Foster, and through its ups and downs over the years under the pens of Foster's many successors, the *Tarzan* feature in comic strip and comic book has established uncounted records for longevity and cumulative readership.

The creator of the character Tarzan, upon which Foster and the others based the strip, was of course Edgar Rice Burroughs, the master of adventure fiction, whose jungle tales, science-fiction escapades, and other books have made him the center of an authentic literary cult, with an international organization (the Burroughs Bibliophiles), periodicals (the *Burroughs Bulletin, ERB-dom*, and others), and in recent years a number of critical, bibliographic, and biographical volumes devoted to himself and his works.

Camille Cazedessus, Jr.—"Caz" to all who know him—is a dedicated Burroughs cultist, owner of one of the world's leading collections of Burroughsiana, and editor-publisher of *ERB-dom*, a leader among the several journals devoted to analyses of Burroughs and his works. A longtime Louisianan, Caz spent a sojourn of several years on the ski-slopes and amidst the evergreens of mountainous Colorado, but has recently returned to his beloved bayou-country. From both locations he has operated a rare-book business, with the expected emphasis on Burroughsiana and associated fantastic materials.

In "Lords of the Jungle" Caz treats not only of the Ape Man's long panelistic career, but of other Burroughs creations that have reached the comic page—and, with a slight editorial assist, with a smattering of the scores of pseudo-Burroughsian features that have followed in their wake.

CHAPTER 10

LORDS OF THE JUNGLE

by CAMILLE E. CAZEDESSUS, JR.

THE most popular of latter-day heroes are still overshadowed by one sun-bronzed figure clad only in a rudely trimmed animal hide, swinging through the upper terraces of a distant jungle and voicing the victory cry of the bull ape. Tarzan of the apes simply doesn't need an introduction—or at least he shouldn't.

But then again, there are millions of people who think Tarzan has a son called Boy, lives in a tree house, and speaks in short, broken phrases. Such was the image given to Edgar Rice Burroughs's magnificent creation by the movie-makers of America for nearly a quarter of a century. And even with these drastic alterations in the character and personality of Tarzan, he continues to be a great hero to kids and adults from Baton Rouge to Berlin. Such is the power of motion pictures. One *Tarzan* book, in fact, though signed with Burroughs's name, reads so much like a Weissmuller movie that some bibliographers insist he didn't really write it. (It's *Tarzan and the Forbidden City*.)

Created in 1911 by a 35-year-old pauper, the first *Tarzan* story is an incredible 95,000-word saga written in longhand on the back of somebody else's stationery. Full of remarkable coincidences, some zoological errors, and impossible happenings, it was rejected by every major book publisher in America. When it finally appeared in Frank A. Munsey's *All-Story* magazine in 1912 it became the smash hit of the year, and it has continued to outshine every piece of imaginative fiction written since. So far, *Tarzan of the Apes* is the classic novel of the twentieth century, transcending all ideology, nationality, and geography—truly a story for all mankind, not just for the readers of *All-Story*. It is taking some time for the critics to accept this fact, as it took time for the book publishers who refused the manuscript to rectify their error in judgment. People make classics, not editors, publishers, or critics. And people have made *Tarzan of the Apes* a classic.

Tarzan of the Apes is an incredible story, and its immediate sequel, *The Return of Tarzan*, is even more so. But of the action portrayed in these two novels, only about two-thirds takes place in the primitive setting of the African jungle. The rest is set in Baltimore, in Wisconsin, on board ocean liners, in Paris, and in the Sahara. Little did anyone know that almost never again would Tarzan venture away from his "beloved jungle." Burroughs was off to a sensational beginning, but the real Tarzan was still emerging. A spark of fantasy was lighted in the second book, and fantasy was Burroughs's strong suit.

In that second book, Tarzan visited Opar, the fabulous city of gold, outpost of lost Atlantis, city of beast men ruled by La the high priestess of the Temple of the Sun and Queen of Opar.

With few exceptions, for the remaining books of the series (over two dozen before Burroughs was through) Tarzan sought adventure in lost lands of forgotten peoples. Kidnapers, runaways, thieves, German militarists, Communists, motion-picture crews, and prize fighters filled some of Tarzan's world, but Burroughs did best when Tarzan went to the lost cities of Opar, Xuja, A-lur, Trohanadalmakus, Castrum Mare, Kavuru, Ashair, Thobos, Cathne, Athne, Zuli, Almetejo, and the forgotten lands of Pal-ul-don and Pellucidar. The names themselves conjure up visions of mystery and adventure.

Hidden cities, lost lands, forgotten peoples. Here is fantasy-adventure, and here is where fans go to find the real Tarzan. Contemporary settings may have been good enough when they were written, but the classic Tarzan transcends spies, Russian agents, and Dutch guerillas. The classic Tarzan confronts lonely queens, tailed pithecanthropoids, mad kings, and primitive alien worlds. Opar, Pal-ul-don, Pellucidar: good, better, best.

There are exceptions, as in *Jungle Tales of Tarzan*. Here

"A gryf," replied Tarzan to Jane's terrified question, "and there is not a large tree near us. We shall have to go back. I cannot risk it with you along." "And if he discovers us?" she asked. "Then I shall have to chance the method I told you I had learned from the beast-man, called a Tor-o-don." "I never believed so huge a creature existed!" whispered Jane fearfully. They moved slowly so as not to attract its attention, and Tarzan almost believed they would succeed.

Then a low rumble rolled like distant thunder from the woods. "No use!" said Tarzan. "We must face the consequences." He caught the woman suddenly to his breast and kissed her. "One can never tell, Jane," he whispered. "We will do our best. Give me your spear, and—don't run. Our only hope lies in its stupid brain. If I can control it—well, we shall soon see." The beast had emerged from the forest. Tarzan raisd his voice in the wird notes of the Tor-odon's cry: "Whee-oo! Whee-oo!!"

For a moment the great beast stood motionless, its attention riveted by the call. The ape-man advanced straight toward it, Jane close at his elbow. "Whee-oo!" he cried again, per-emptorily. A low rumble rolled from the gryf's cavernous chest, and the beast moved slowly toward them. "Fine! The odds are now in our favor. Keep your nerve, Jane!" exclaimed Tarzan. "I have no fear," she replied softly. Thus the two approached the giant monster until they stood in the shadow of its mightly shoulder.

"Whee-oo!" shouted Tarzan, and struck the hideous snout with the shaft of the spear. The vicious side snap that did not reach its mark—that evidently was not intended to—was the hoped-for answer. "Come," said Tarzan, and taking Jane by the hand he led her around behind the monster and up the broad tail to the great horned back, "Now we shall ride in state," he said, as he guided the gryf in the direction they wished. The ponderous creature forged along until suddenly they came to a small clearing in the jungle.

Daily *Tarzan* strips drawn by Rex Maxon appeared in 1933 and continued throughout the remainder of the 1930s retelling stories of Burroughs novels and films. TARZAN daily strip from January 10, 1933. © 1933 by United Feature Syndicate, Inc.

Burroughs tells sensational short stories set in the period between the death of Tarzan's ape foster-mother and his first meeting with Jane. But the soul of Tarzan is fantasy. As Burne Hogarth has said, Tarzan is "the primal Adam, not the unreasoning titanic savage; the man-not-god, an elemental creature of primary fantasy ... a shimmering figment of myth and dream." Not just a hero: *the* hero. Other heroes are Tarzanic, Tarzan simply *is*.

When the Metropolitan Newspaper Syndicate hired Harold R. Foster to illustrate *Tarzan of the Apes* in 1928, they very likely had no idea of what would come of the project. To them it was an experiment, a gamble. Would a serious, adult adventure story, even one so famous as *Tarzan*, be accepted by the newspaper-reading public? Up till then such illustrated stories were comical and lighthearted japes aimed at readers who wanted stories of kids, cats, and commonplace families. They were "comics" that were really comical.

Realism was necessary to introduce a serious adventure feature, so a well-known advertising artist was hired to do the illustrations: Hal Foster. Preceded by a few small ads that simply said, "The Apes are Coming," *Tarzan* appeared in a number of newspapers on January 7, 1929. No single *Tarzan* strip is more highly regarded than this first Hal Foster classic. Foster's graphic interpretation of the first *Tarzan* story was remarkable; to this day it remains a completely acceptable adaptation of Burroughs's classic. It is the most reprinted, most imitated and most important *Tarzan* strip of all. In fact, it became the first "comic book" to feature *Tarzan*— and possibly the first serious adventure "comic book" ever—when it was reprinted in hard covers by Grosset & Dunlap late in 1929.

Reaction to the *Tarzan* newspaper strip was good, but Foster was busy with other work, so a veteran newspaper illustrator, Rex Maxon, was hired for the next story. Twelve weeks after the last installment of *Apes* a second such picture serial based on *The Return of Tarzan* commenced. The date was June 10, 1929, and from that day onward there has been a *Tarzan* strip running without interruption!

Apes and *Return* ran for ten weeks each, six days a week, with a single row of panels each day, running narration and dialog separate from and beneath the pictures. A one-week condensation of *Apes* was also made available to newspapers that chose to pick up the feature with the second story.

260

By 1935, Hal Foster's *Tarzan* had become a classic adventure page featuring fascinating pictorial sagas of Egyptians, Vikings, and jungle beasts. TARZAN Sunday page (2 panels) from 1935. © 1935 by Edgar Rice Burroughs, Inc.

After *Return* a series of longer adaptations—14 to 21 weeks in length—appeared, based on nine more *Tarzan* novels. Each serial strip was fairly true to the Burroughs book from which it was adapted, but by the end of *Tarzan and the Ant Men* in June of 1932 there wasn't much left in the backlog of books to keep up the pace much longer. A crisis loomed—the *Tarzan* adaptations were in demand, and Burroughs material to adapt was nearly exhausted. What to do?

In 1966 Rex Maxon told me that he had worked with "breakdown men" in preparing his *Tarzan* adaptations—at first George Carlin did the job, later Don Garden. In mid-1932 Maxon and his breakdown man began the longest serial strip ever published—a 40-week adaptation of *Tarzan the Untamed*. And for the first time, the strip deviated seriously from the Burroughs novel: instead of the Kaiser-vintage German villains Burroughs had used, the comic strip featured Communist agents.

The First World War had receded by now, Germany was in turmoil and not regarded as a menace, but the Great Depression was in full sway and "Reds" were the order of the day!

In terms of the *Tarzan* strip, something else had happened. The success of the daily strip had prompted the inauguration of a Sunday page, and *Tarzan* became one of the first serious adventure features to run in color, beginning in March of 1931. Rex Maxon, the daily artist, handled the Sunday page as well for the first six months, but it lacked something in flair.

The first sequence of the Sunday series, as an example, used none of the adult themes introduced by Burroughs, but concerned itself with two children, Bob and Mary, whom Tarzan rescued from some apes, and then again from pirates.

While Maxon continued on the daily strip, Hal Foster was called back to take over the Sunday page, and moved in with a bang! His first Sunday page was a 12-panel classic in which Tarzan battled a horde of apes against impossible odds, only to be rescued by none other than Lt. Paul D'Arnot, Tarzan's first human friend from Burroughs's first book. Foster obviously knew what to do with Tarzan: get back to Burroughs! It's a lesson that many adaptors have still not learned.

From the latter months of 1931 onward, the Sunday page, although not based on any single Burroughs story, soared to heights at first undreamed. Foster's early style was full of movement and clarity, but not really outstanding. Yet within a few

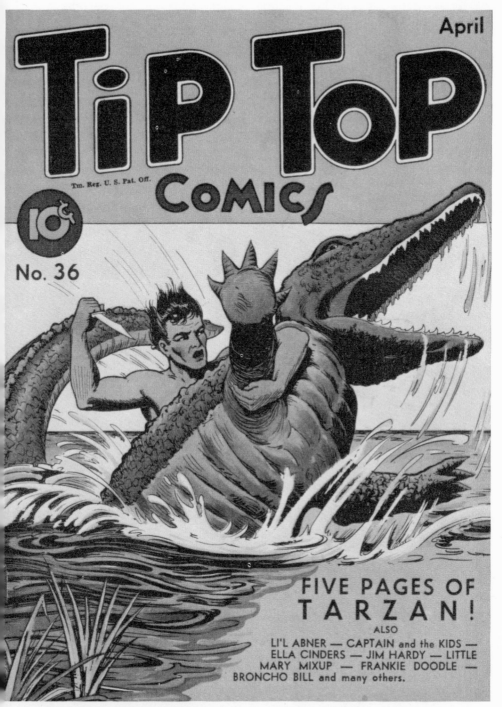

Hal Foster's Sunday *Tarzan* pages were featured in *Tip Top Comics*. Tip Top Comics magazine. April 1939 cover. © 1939 by United Feature Syndicate, Inc.

years Foster's genius became evident. *Tarzan* had become a classic adventure page featuring fascinating pictorial sagas of Egyptians, Vikings, and jungle beasts. The art became so pleasing in its movement, characterization, and detail that Maxon's daily strip was thoroughly overshadowed and all but forgotten.

Hal Foster was more than the best illustrator in the business: he was a real artist, a *creator* of heroes. And while *Tarzan* was fun to draw—and had provided an opportunity for the development of Foster's art and reputation—Foster wanted to create his own feature. So in 1936 he began researching English history of the legendary Arthurian age, determined to write and illustrate his own Sunday adventure page.

Foster's new creation, *Prince Valiant*, was introduced in February, 1937, and 11 weeks later, on May 2, the last Foster *Tarzan* page appeared. For nearly 300 weeks Burroughs's most famous creation had been illustrated by one of the finest newspaper artists of all time. Hal Foster would not easily be replaced!

During the years that the *Tarzan* comic strip had been running under the tutelage of Foster and Maxon, the modern comic book had evolved to something very like its present form. The issues were fatter and cheaper, and the emphasis was on material reprinted from newspapers rather than specially drawn features, and even before Hal Foster's second (and final) departure from *Tarzan*, the ape man had begun the first of a long series of appearances in regular comic books. The United Features Syndicate, which had taken over *Tarzan* from Metropolitan, began issuance of a monthly comic book of its own, *Tip-Top Comics*, in May, 1936.

Hal Foster Sunday *Tarzan* pages were featured in *Tip Top Comics* from the beginning, at first four or five pages in each issue then, as the public's response was felt, seven or eight. Tarzan often appeared on the cover of *Tip Top* in new drawings by Paul F. Berdanier.

In the summer of 1932, four years before *Tip Top Comics'* first issue, still another manifestation of the ape man's popularity was seen. Millions were flocking to movie houses to see the new talking *Tarzan* film, *Tarzan the Ape Man*, with Johnny Weissmuller, the Olympic swimming champion, in the title role. Maxon began adapting the film (thus moving two levels away from Burroughs) for the daily strip in March of 1933. This particular upswing in "Tarzan-consciousness," one of many in the past 60 years, led to the appearance of the first *Tarzan* Big Little Book, *Tarzan of the Apes*, with illustrations by Juanita Bennett.

Throughout the remainder of the 1930s the daily *Tarzan* strip retold the stories of ten more Burroughs novels and two more films, *The New Adventures of Tarzan* and *Tarzan the Fearless*. Maxon had done all the art except for a brief break resulting from a wage dispute, when William Juhré took over temporarily. Maxon's daily strip artwork continued to be used in Big Little Books and Better Little Books until 1948, frequently readapted (still another level!) to fit a new story.

By the end of the 1930s comic books were pouring from the presses in an ever-increasing flood, and the requirements for stories to fill their pages grew in proportion. With Tarzan already committed, other Burroughs creations were sought out for adaptation. After all, if *Tarzan* was so successful, why not other Burroughs features?

John Carter of Mars was introduced in *The Funnies* for April, 1939. The first four installments were drawn anonymously and I have not succeeded in determining the identity of the artist, but with the fifth installment the feature was taken over by John Coleman Burroughs, Edgar Rice Burroughs's son. The story, adapted from the senior Burroughs's Barsoomian series—of which the first, *A Princess of Mars*, actually antedated *Tarzan of the Apes* in both creation and first publication—ran for 27 issues of *The Funnies*, No. 30 through No. 56.

Its disappearance from the comic book was not the end by any means: John Carter was to turn up shortly with a Sunday page of his own. I shall return to that shortly.

But meanwhile another Burroughs comic feature made a unique appearance. *David Innes of Pellucidar* was to have run as a similar serial in Hawley Publications' *Hi-Spot Comics*. The first issue of *Hi-Spot* had already appeared, featuring *Red Ryder* western comic-page reprints but, in the second issue, dated November, 1940, the first installment of John Coleman Burroughs's adaptation of his father's Pellucidarian cycle appeared.

Red Ryder had more zap than *David Innes*, however—or at least the publishers felt this to be the case—and with the third issue *Hi-Spot* metamorphosed into *Red Ryder*. *David Innes of Pellucidar* was dropped, and the comic went on to a long history under the aegis of the Dell publishing organization.

Pellucidar—a lost, primitive world located *inside* the earth—

was not seen again in the comics for over 30 years, but consider the prices in the 1973 edition of *The Comic Book Price Guide* for the earliest issues of the old comic I've been talking about: *Hi-Spot* No. 1 (mint condition), $40; *Hi-Spot* No. 2, $135; *Red Ryder* No. 3, $35. That's some indication of the appeal of Burroughs!

The success of the reprinted Sunday *Tarzan* pages in *Tip Top* prompted United Features Syndicate to parlay their winnings in *Comics on Parade*, where the daily strip, with color added, was reprinted from the first issue (April, 1938) up through No. 29.

Dell, with which firm the *Tarzan* feature was to be associated for some 30 years, introduced a new *Tarzan* format in *Popular Comics* No. 38 (April, 1939). This was a three-page version, mainly text, with incidental color illustrations; the story was loosely adapted from Burroughs's *Tarzan, Lord of the Jungle*, and ran through issue No. 43.

At that point Dell moved Tarzan to *Crackajack Funnies*, where the next story was *Tarzan and the City of Gold*. *Tarzan* ran in *Crackajack* from issue No. 15 through No. 29 (August, 1940).

It was obvious that Tarzan was an immensely powerful draw in the comics (as he had been in every other medium where he appeared, including pulp magazines, films, books, and radio). Three more instances of the ape man's drawing power occurred about this time.

One was Dell's *Famous Feature Stories* No. 1 (1938), with a six-page *Tarzan* in the text-plus-drawings format, the drawings by Juanita Bennett. Far more impressive was Dell's *Feature Book*, the fifth of which was devoted to one more rerun of Foster's *Tarzan of the Apes* daily strips, further extended by additional drawings—some of them lavish, full-page scenes—by Bennett. This *Tarzan* ran a full 72 pages, and again the price of a copy on the collector's market is indicative.

Feature Book No. 4 (featuring *Dick Tracy*) lists today for $45; *Feature Book* No. 5 (featuring *Tarzan*) lists for $160; *Feature Book* No. 6 (featuring *Terry and the Pirates*) lists for $40!

But even the Dell *Feature Book* version of *Apes*—which was, after all, a reprint of daily black-and-white strips—couldn't come near equaling United Features Syndicate's *Single Series* No. 20 (1940). Titled simply *Tarzan*, this collection contained 64 pages of Foster's Sunday *Tarzan*s from 1932 and 1933—in full color! This was the best of the *Tarzan* comics from the thirties: Foster art in full color, stories of lost peoples in forgotten places—and the price

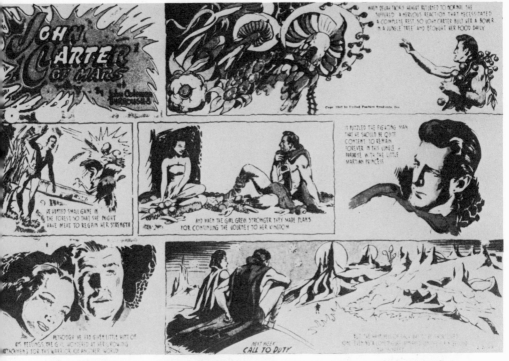

With Hogarth, Tarzan took on an electric, vibrant character that made the reader feel that the ape man was actually alive on the page. TARZAN daily strip (2 panels) from 1938. © 1938 by Edgar Rice Burroughs, Inc.

of a mint copy today is $180!

But while all this reprinting activity was going on in comic books, the *new Tarzan* feature continued to appear in the nation's newspapers, and in 1940 the Sunday page, already one of the most popular color features, seemed to surge to new heights under the guidance of Burne Hogarth. Hogarth was not new to the strip— he had taken it over from Foster in May of 1937, at the age of 26. A former student of J. Allen St. John, *the* classic Burroughs pulp illustrator, at the Chicago Art Institute, Hogarth came to *Tarzan* with both skill and dedication.

With Hogarth the figure of Tarzan took on an electric, vibrant, three-dimensional character that made the reader feel that the ape man was actually alive on the page. Bright colors, large panels, exotic settings, flashy villains, giant animals and dynamic figures saturated each Sunday page with such excellent layout that you didn't have to *read* Tarzan—you could seemingly watch him perform before your eyes!

By the early months of 1941, Hogarth had reached the climactic sequence of a lost-city story. He drew panels of exploding volcanoes, earthquakes, crumbling temples, waves of seething lava and bubbling water that are dazzling to behold! What Burne Hogarth did with *Tarzan* in the early 1940s was astounding, and he surpassed even the immortal Hal Foster in the context of *Tarzan*, for Foster had established his greatness with *Prince Valiant* more than with his earlier *Tarzan*.

And in 1972, long years after leaving *Tarzan* to a series of other hands, Hogarth returned to the ape man to illustrate a new edition of *Tarzan of the Apes* for the Watson-Guptill Publishing Company. This hardcover edition runs to 160 pages of text and drawings with 122 full-color Hogarth pages—an instant collector's item the day it came off the press!

The character of Tarzan has had international appeal from the beginning and during the 1930s the daily serial strip and Sunday page had been published in several European countries, where both versions were well accepted. Hogarth's Sunday version in particular was highly popular.

When the German army occupied Paris in the early days of World War II, severing most French connections with America, there was no way for French newspapers to obtain the *Tarzan* feature. Even in occupied France the demand for *Tarzan* was great—so much so that the French illustrator Andre Lignois

Hogarth's 1950 Tarzan was a ferocious superhero with demonic eyes and bulging mus-les. TARZAN Sunday page (2 panels) from 1950. © 1950 by Edgar Rice Burroughs, Inc.

produced a Sunday page that was carried in France during the war!

Not only did the war affect the distribution of *Tarzan*—it also influenced the content of the strip. There were plots involving mercenary armies and militaristic villains clearly inspired by anti-Nazi, anti-Fascist, and later anti-Japanese feelings; these of course appeared in the film *Tarzan* as well, and in Burroughs's novel *Tarzan and "The Foreign Legion"* laid against the background of a Japanese-occupied island in the South Pacific.

Oddly, many of these contemporary touches were omitted from the Sunday-page reprints in *Sparkler Comics*, where the feature had been continued from *Tip Top* in July of 1941.

And most inauspicious was the debut of the long-awaited *John Carter of Mars* Sunday page by John Coleman Burroughs. This color feature, drawn in a horizontal format for half-page presentation in large-size Sunday comic sections, seemed doomed from the start. It appeared first on December 7, 1941!

John Coleman Burroughs's style was at its best in *John Carter of Mars*, honed on the comic-book version and the short-lived *David Innes* as well as Big Little Book and some standard book illustration. The story moved nicely through the little-known world of Edgar Rice Burroughs's Mars (he called it Barsoom), but with the war on John Coleman Burroughs entered defense work. The senior Burroughs, despite his advanced years, went on duty as a war correspondent in the Pacific. *John Carter* appeared in a relatively few newspapers, and after a run of 69 weeks (three more installments were drawn but not used) it died on Sunday, March 28, 1943.

Meanwhile the daily *Tarzan* had undergone another change of format. From its inception under Hal Foster the daily strip had comprised a series of "close-ended" adventures, but in August of 1939 Rex Maxon converted it to a new approach. No longer were there separate segments of illustration and text, and no longer did each story begin and end with neat boundaries.

Now drawing and text were integrated more in the fashion of standard comic strips and, with what would have been the twenty-eighth separate *Tarzan* story, the story-line switched to the "open-ended" format, with one adventure blending smoothly into the next.

A sort of female Tarzan named Tarzeela was introduced in 1940. Her name was quickly shortened to Zeela. Mazon continued

John Coleman Burroughs's *John Carter of Mars* made its debut on December 7, 1941. Although Burroughs's style was as good as it ever was, the strip appeared in relatively few newspapers. Copyright © 1942, United Feature Syndicate, Inc., renewed 1970, and reprinted by its permission.

to produce the daily strip for seven more more years, leaving the feature at the end of August, 1947. He had been the *Tarzan* strip artist for nearly 18 years, and he hadn't had a single vacation in that time!

Hogarth, meanwhile, had fallen out with United Features Syndicate and had quit *Tarzan* late in 1945 to start his own Sunday feature, an adventure saga titled *Drago*.

Reuben Moreira took over the Sunday page. (Examples of his work are signed with the contraction "Rubimor.") Moreira's work began to appear in December, 1945, and to say that it was undistinguished is to be charitable. His major contribution to *Tarzan* was the design of a new logotype, replacing one that had been designed by Maxon in 1931 and used ever since.

Under Moreira, the Sunday *Tarzan* slipped into postwar relaxation and mediocre drawing. Moreira lasted only until August of 1947.

Hogarth was a hard man to follow—but then, so was Tarzan, and *Drago* wasn't exactly setting the Sunday audience on its ear either, so *Drago* was dropped. Hogarth resolved his differences with United (the problem was largely one of artistic freedom) and took over both the daily and Sunday *Tarzan*. The departure of Maxon from the daily strip and Moreira from the Sunday coincided nicely.

Hogarth returned to *Tarzan* with new energy and enthusiasm, but the double load of both continuities was too much for one man to carry. Under Hogarth the daily strip improved hugely in both conception and execution. He borrowed David Innes and "crossed" the *Pellucidar* and *Tarzan* story-lines by having the ape man accompany Innes to the inner world. (This device had been used by Burroughs himself in the novel *Tarzan at the Earth's Core*.)

To help him "carry double," Hogarth hired assistants to ink his own penciled drawings, and he chose well: Al Williamson and Dan Barry! Even so, Hogarth felt that he had to concentrate his efforts more on the Sunday page, so in January of 1948 he withdrew from the daily feature, which was taken over by a series of short-termers: Dan Barry, John Lehti, Paul Reinman, Nick Viscardy. Their terms ranged from a mere few weeks to a little under two years.

But Hogarth's brief stint on the daily strip was more than balanced by the sensational three years he put in on the Sunday

FANG SCREAMED. TARZAN DASHED FORWARD TO THROTTLE HIM.

NEXT WEEK: TRAPPED!

FANG CHUCKLED. "ONLY ONE PROBLEM REMAINS---- TO DECIDE THE MANNER OF YOUR DEATH!"

John Carter of Mars drawn in a horizontal format for half-page presentation in large-size Sunday comic sections. Copyright © 1943, United Feature Syndicate, Inc., renewed 1971, and reprinted by its permission.

strip from 1947 to 1950. Although the full-page format of the 1930s and early 1940s had been cut to tabloid size in 1947 and then to half-size in 1949, Hogarth made the most of the available space, and many feel that this period marked the all-time high for the Sunday page.

Nowhere in any previous *Tarzan* was there the same dynamic movement, eerie foliage, and use of fantasy themes as in this period of Hogarth's work. No longer was Tarzan the aristocratic Lord Greystoke of Hal Foster; now he had become a ferocious superhero with demonic eyes and bulging muscles. Surrounded by pointed leaves, sharp rocks, grotesque roots, and brightly colored silhouettes, Tarzan leaps, swings, and poses heroically in panel after panel. New perspectives, large panels, and contorted figures are common.

The pages are all signed "Hogarth," but there's something strange about them. The figure of Tarzan is not always the same. It wasn't always drawn by Hogarth, but by his advanced students at the School of Visual Arts in New York, a school of which Hogarth was co-founder! Again, these anonymous assistants were well chosen; their names, later discovered, were Wallace Wood, Al Williamson (again), and Gil Kane!

In 1950 Hogarth's squabble with the syndicate again broke out, and he departed from *Tarzan*—for the last time until the 1972 book version—on August 20, 1950. Bob Lubbers, a sometime assistant of Al Capp's, took over *Tarzan* with the Sunday page of August 27 and, although he managed a style suggestive of Hogarth's and some reasonably interesting adventures, there seemed little spark left in the page.

Tarzan Sunday-strip reprints were still appearing in the comic books, but this era was also drawing to a close. A government-published comic, issued for soldier-morale purposes during the war, had run *Tarzan* pages in 1945—this was *Jeep Comics*, almost unknown today except to the most fanatical of collectors. *Sparkler Comics* continued to reprint Sunday pages until its ninety-second issue (March-April, 1950).

And with Lubbers also doing the daily strip now, *Tip-Top Comics* ran his version, with color added, for 18 issues between 1950 and 1954.

But the future of Burroughs in the comic books was now with the Dell Publishing Company. Unlike many other characters and features, *Tarzan* had remained the property of its creator, Edgar

Tarzan the jungle man was by now (1954) so well and widely known that little attention was paid to Burroughs's original concept. Dell TARZAN Comics magazine. Four panels from 1954. © 1954 by Edgar Rice Burroughs, Inc.

Rice Burroughs, and after his death in 1950, of Edgar Rice Burroughs, Inc. Thus, rather than being owned by any publisher, the *Tarzan* feature was *licensed* to a number of publishers in turn, as contracts expired and new terms were negotiated.

Dell had issued two numbers of a *Tarzan Comics* in 1947, and in January, 1948, began publishing comics featuring a totally new and original *Tarzan* continuity, loosely based on the newspaper stories and movies of earlier years. Tarzan the jungle man was by now so well and widely known that little attention was paid to Burroughs's original concept.

The Dell *Tarzan* scripts were written by Gaylord DuBois, an experienced comic-book writer, and illustrated by Jesse Marsh, a veteran illustrator from southern California.

The first Dell *Tarzan* reintroduced Paul D'Arnot; the second, a lost city on the pattern of those created decades before by H. Rider Haggard ... and the third showed similarities to Burroughs's novel *Tarzan the Magnificent*.

But in Dell's fifth issue (marked No. 3 because the second series had started out with a new No. 1), a new and permanent "Jungle World" was created by DuBois, in contrast to the continually evolving world of the newspaper stories. In this world Jesse Marsh drew Tarzan as a pleasant-looking fellow living in a tree house with a brunette Jane and Boy. The movies had done their job: in the Jungle World, the film Tarzan had finally displaced Burroughs's creation, bringing with him the companions and conventions of Hollywood. The comic had Edgar Rice Burroughs's name on the cover, but that wasn't *his* Tarzan inside. *His* ape man was a cultured and articulate nobleman, *his* Jane was blonde; they lived in a fine house and their son—named Korak—was himself a grown man with a wife and child.

Well, at least the DuBois-Marsh Tarzan didn't speak the broken English of the MGM film version.

Even with the regrettable changes in Burroughs's conception, the Dell Jungle World was a fascinating and often exciting place, and the graphic style used *illustrations only* to tell the story, something accomplished only rarely in the newspaper versions of Foster and Hogarth.

DuBois and Marsh peopled Tarzan's world with beasts and men reminiscent of those found in Pellucidar. They included a great thorn desert, a swamp belt, the "Mountains of the Clouds," and beyond these Pal-ul-don, the lost land of the Ho-dons, Opar,

A-lur, and a slew of prehistoric creatures. Marsh even mapped the entire Jungle World, and Dell included his map in *Tarzan* No. 20.

Other DuBois-Marsh innovations may have proved surprising to Burroughs fans who knew Tarzan's world only from the master's books until they happened to pick up a Dell comic. There were Bara the giant eland, Alexander McWhirtle the famous paleontologist, Goliath the giant lion, Argus the great eagle, and so on. It was often very good, or at least fun, but it still wasn't Burroughs.

As the success of *Tarzan* in the comics had led to the adaptation of *John Carter* a decade earlier, Dell's good results with their version of *Tarzan* led to a new *John Carter of Mars* in 1952. Whether Jesse Marsh's somewhat flat and unappealing interpretation was at fault, or some other factor intervened, the Martian adventures failed to excite much public interest, and the new series lasted for only three issues.

Nor was all well with the newspaper *Tarzan* features. Lubbers continued through the end of 1953, but early the following year he gave up both the daily and Sunday strips. His *Tarzan* had been a reasonable continuation of Hogarth's efforts, lacking in fire and inventiveness but still fairly well done. His successor, John Celardo, failed even to maintain this level, and the strips began a serious slide in popularity that led, in later years, very nearly to their discontinuance.

Meanwhile, in postwar Europe the pent-up demand for all sorts of cultural and physical goodies was felt, and one small aspect of this renascence was a Tarzan boom. In France, large comic books were issued utilizing translations of a mix of current newspaper strips and those missed during the war. These were so successful that they were retranslated back into English for reprinting in Great Britain. Soon this cumbersome system was simplified when the British edition began to use photostats provided directly by United Features Syndicate.

Tarzan had appeared in British comics since the 1930s, in several series utilizing various daily and Sunday sequences, sometimes in color and sometimes in black-and-white. British *Tarzan* titles included the *Tarzan Comic, Tarzan—the Grand Adventure Comic,* and *Tarzan Adventures.* The last–named series was edited by Michael Moorcock, in later years a well-known fantasy author, editor, and publisher, but in the late 1950s a teenaged Burroughs enthusiast who delighted in writing his friends' names into stories when charged with the task of translating Continental *Tarzans* back into English.

Another notable Burroughs comic from England was a 31-part serialization of *A Princess of Mars* in the *Sun Weekly* (October, 1958–May, 1959). Retitled "The Martian," this serial ran at a pace of two pages per issue. The anonymous artwork was very nice, and the length of the adaptation—62 pages in all—would fit very nicely into one (thick) or two (thin) comic books, should any enterprising publisher ever undertake its reissuance.

In November of 1958 the *Tarzan* newspaper features struck bottom. The art was totally lacking in movement, speech balloons were introduced, and the daily and Sunday stories were integrated into one continuous childish, boring, monotonous nonadventure. Things couldn't get any worse, and for a long time they didn't get any better.

About this time, Burroughs fans throughout the English-speaking world were beginning to organize—an effort that led to the formation of the Burroughs Bibliophiles, an international organization which reached an eventual membership of several thousand. Fans began to deluge the Burroughs offices in Tarzana, California, with letters of complaint and requests for information. The essence of their pleas was twofold: to get some life back into the comic *Tarzan*, and to get many of Edgar Rice Burroughs's books, most of which were out of print, back into print, into bookstores, and onto newsstands.

Unfortunately, following the death of Burroughs himself in 1950, control of the corporation had passed to the master's longtime secretary and administrative assistant, a gentleman who was now elderly and apparently not very interested in the Burroughs literary properties.

The failure to tend to business at Tarzana led to a number of monumental problems, including the issuance of a number of unauthorized Burroughs books by no fewer than four American publishers, and the placing in jeopardy of many of Burroughs's copyrights. So great was the mess that it even became subject matter for a Congressional committee hearing!

In the field of comic books, the Charlton company seized upon the situation to issue an unauthorized *Jungle Tales of Tarzan*, the first issue dated December, 1964. Credit lines went to Joseph Gill as adapter—that is, scripter—and to Sam Glanzman as illustrator. The editor, Pat Masulli, issued his manifesto in the first issue:

278

In the 1960s John Celardo revived his *Tarzan* series by vividly retelling original Burroughs stories. Celardo worked on the strip until 1967. TARZAN daily strip from April 1-3, 1963. © 1963 by United Feature Syndicate, Inc.

The true flavor of Tarzan as created by Mr. Burroughs has rarely been tasted in comic books. We intend to change that. We intend to be as true to the original as possible. We pledge ourselves to a series of comics that will thrill and inspire, delight and entrance as did the original masterworks.

Jungle Tales of Tarzan lasted only four issues—its demise was the result of legal and commercial maneuvers, not lack of sales—but in those four issues it proved out Masulli's pledge, faithfully adapting stories from Burroughs's book of the same title. The Hogarth-Foster influence on Glanzman's artwork was obvious, and the four *Tales* comics are a welcome (if minor) part of any Burroughs comic-art collecttion.

Charlton's *Tarzan* may have been illegal—or at least unofficial—and the subsequent lawsuit painful, but it had been proved to Burroughs, Inc. that the problems arising from neglect of the literary properties would have to be faced, decisively and at once.

The president of the Burroughs Bibliophiles, C. B. Hyde, decided to take direct action to improve the newspaper strip. He contacted Celardo, who was doing his own scripting by now, and pressed some old Hogarth strips on him. Whether it was the influence of the classic *Tarzan* or simply the interest shown by Hyde, Celardo seemed to get some new energy and drive from the encounter.

In the winter of 1962 Celardo retold the original *Tarzan of the Apes* yet again in the daily strip, and three years later, in the summer of 1965, he gave Burroughs fans a treat by adapting for the Sunday pages "Tarzan and the Champion," a scarce Burroughs short story. But Celardo was growing tired of *Tarzan*—he'd been drawing the strip for 11 years—and he indicated that he wished to retire from the job. The problem was not critical, he was willing to stay on for a while (and in fact did continue until the end of 1967), but a new man would have to be brought in before too much longer.

Who could do the job?

The answer to that question lay in the comic-book version, in the person of Russ Manning, whose association with editor Chase Craig dated all the way back to 1952 when Manning, a young artist just out of the Navy, was introduced to Craig by Jesse Marsh. Manning had grown up on Foster's and Hogarth's *Tarzans*. He had initiated a secondary feature in the *Tarzan* comic

Russ Manning replaced John Celardo in 1967. Manning illustrated a series of 24-page adaptations of the original Burroughs *Tarzan* novels; some of the longer adaptations were extended to two or even three 24-page segments. TARZAN daily strip for December 23, 1967. © 1967 by United Feature Syndicate, Inc.

(*Brothers of the Spear*) late in 1952, moved up to a *Boy* story in '53, and illustrated his first *Tarzan* adventure in '54.

For another decade he continued doing work on various features, most notably the futuristic *Magnus, Robot Fighter*. Then, in January of 1964, Gold Key Comics (which had by now fissioned from Dell) introduced a new title: *Korak, Son of Tarzan*. The objectionable Boy had finally been eliminated and Tarzan's authentic son had come into his own! The new *Korak* stories were written by DuBois and illustrated by Russ Manning.

The following year Marsh retired and Manning took over the duties of lead artist for what was now Gold Key's *Tarzan of the Apes* with issue No. 155. To inaugurate the new phase in the comic's history, the Gold Key team went all the way back to the policy originally followed in Hal Foster's daily newspaper strip almost 40 years earlier: Manning illustrated a series of 24-page adaptations of the original Burroughs *Tarzan* novels; some of the longer adaptations were extended to two or even three 24-page segments.

Manning's natural talent and enthusiasm, coupled with the extensive experience he gained doing comic-book work, brought him to a peak of readiness for the newspaper strips. He took over the daily in December, 1967, and the Sunday page in January, 1968. His approach to the newspaper strips was a combination of traditionalism—for Manning had steeped himself in classic *Tarzan* art—and his own, original talent.

Once again the daily and Sunday features began an upswing. Once again it was proved that the creation of Burroughs's mind, even after half a century, retained its power and appeal, if only the adaptation was done with skill and with respect for the original.

The Gold Key era for *Tarzan* comic books was drawing toward its end, but it wasn't over yet. Gold Key continued both *Tarzan* and *Korak* as regularly published comics, with artwork by Giolitti, Mike Royer, Doug Wildey, Paul Norris, and (especially in *Korak*) Dan Spiegle.

In addition, with the two-season run of a *Tarzan* series on television, Gold Key issued four special *Tarzan of the Apes TV Adventures* comic books, alternating with the regular *Tarzan* book and in the same numbering sequence, and when the series was picked up by British television the ape man made a fresh reappearance in the British *TV Tornado*, *TV 21*, and *TV Comic* series.

Tarzan in 1971, spectacularly illustrated and written by Russ Manning, was well on the Burroughsian lost-civilization fantasy trail. TARZAN daily strips Nos. 9891 & 9892 from 1971. © 1971 by United Feature Syndicate, Inc.

None of the television-inspired comics were exactly outstanding. (For that matter the TV version of Tarzan left a lot of knowledgeable Burroughs enthusiasts less than overjoyed. Perhaps the height of silliness was reached in one story from *TV 21*. In this tale Tarzan is told blandly by Dana the lioness that "a monster eagle has carried off my youngest cub to its lair." When Tarzan pursues the eagle to try and rescue the cub, the eagle starts an avalanche to smash Tarzan, and when Tarzan escapes the falling rocks the eagle cries out in a speech balloon, "You shall not escape me now!"

These TV-inspired adaptations bumbled along as late as 1971, years after the television series itself had ended and, when the comics finally disappeared, I could only say, *Good riddance!*

But if the British *Tarzan* comics of the period were downright ridiculous, the American *Tarzan* strip was absolutely outstanding! Not only did Manning do a spectacular job on the illustrations, he was writing the stories as well, and as early as the summer of 1968 he had got Tarzan back on the old Burroughsian lost-civilization fantasy trail.

Tarzan discovered a lost Egyptian temple; Manning reintroduced the old Hogarth villain Dagga Ramba; Korak, Tantor, Opar, La, beast men, Paul D'Arnot, and Jane were gracefully reintroduced. Manning had Jane recount the story of her first meeting with Tarzan, then had D'Arnot do the same—both sequences based on the original Burroughs version, the perennial classic, the first source, *Tarzan of the Apes*!

In later sequences Manning showed Tarzan searching for Jane in Pal-ul-don; Korak (whom Manning features prominently), advancing toward Xuja in the Valley of Luna. Both themes feature the old Burroughs-Foster-Hogarth touch, and both are based on authentic Burroughs material.

In the daily strip there have been long episodic adventures in Opar, Pal-ul-don, and even—once more—in Pellucidar. Manning's version of *Tarzan* has become a legend in its own time, worthy of standing with the two earlier versions by Foster and Hogarth. May it have a long run in the newspapers of the world!

Back on the comic-book front, when the Gold Key license expired, Burroughs, Inc. was free to negotiate a new contract, and the complete set of Burroughs materials went to National Periodical Publications (DC). This meant that the new publisher might not only take over the *Tarzan* and *Korak* series from Gold Key,

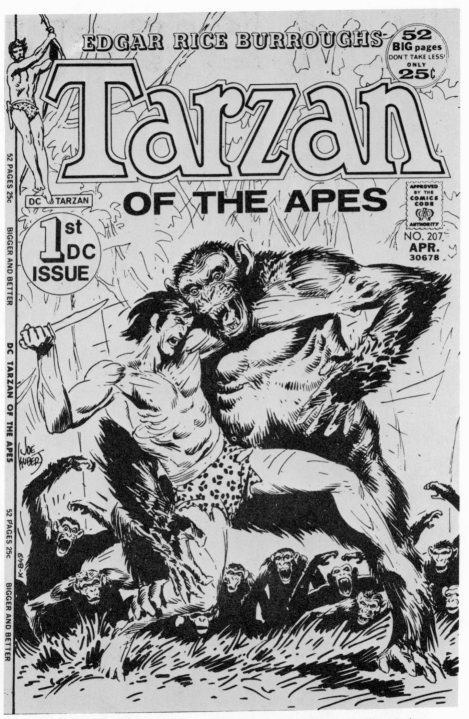

Joe Kubert's first issue of *Tarzan of the Apes* appeared in April 1972. His early issues showed a strong Foster influence but Kubert soon asserted his own vigorous style. TARZAN comic magazine cover, April 1972. © 1972 by Edgar Rice Burroughs, Inc.

but was able to examine the whole range of Burroughs's nearly 80 books in search of suitable material for comic-book adaptations.

Taking up where Gold Key left off, DC's first move was to continue the already well-established *Tarzan* and *Korak* series. But in doing so they threw away everything except the titles and the numbering, creating for all practical purposes brand-new series of adaptations.

Joe Kubert, one of the all-time great names in comic-book illustration, was named editor, writer, and chief artist for DC's *Tarzan of the Apes*, and he was the best choice one could have hoped for. His first issues, starting in April of 1972, showed a strong Foster influence dating as far back as some 1929 sequences. But quickly Kubert's own strongly vigorous style asserted itself. The first four issues comprised a masterful retelling of the classic *Tarzan of the Apes*. This was followed by adaptations of other Burroughs texts and of earlier classic comic-strip sequences. Kubert's *Tarzan* stands out not only on grounds of general excellence, but on the basis of Kubert's own distinctively innovative approach.

Korak, Son of Tarzan began with Joe Orlando, another comic-book veteran with credits stretching back to the EC period of 20 years ago, named as editor. Len Wein was assigned as writer and Frank Thorne as illustrator. The first new *Koraks* were well styled but tended to be somewhat static and talky, but the professionalism evident in the work overcame this drawback. Later, Robert Kanigher took over the writing and the book lost its Burroughs "flavor."

Perhaps more exciting for dyed-in-the-wool Burroughs fans were DC's explorations of less commonly adapted elements of the canon—including some stories and characters *never before* seen on the comic page. *John Carter of Mars* was reintroduced in the first DC *Tarzan*, with script by Kubert and Marv Wolfman and art by old-timer Murphy Anderson. *Pellucidar* and *Carson of Venus* (the latter a comic first) appeared in the first DC *Korak*. Both were written by Len Wein; *Pellucidar* was illustrated by Alan Weiss and *Carson* by Mike Kaluta.

These new features caught on with varying degrees of speed and enthusiasm, but the whole idea of using the broad range of Burroughs's material was so appealing that a new Burroughs comic was started, called *Weird Worlds*, and open to all of

Burroughs. The first issues took over the *John Carter* and *Pellucidar* series, with *Carson* scheduled to remain, at least for the time being, in *Korak*.

And yet to follow was a new series based on one of Burroughs's last and most intriguing creations, the uncompleted novel of a world *Beyond the Farthest Star*!

Unfortunately, DC soon dropped all but *Tarzan*.

Meanwhile, reprint albums of Russ Manning *Tarzan* sequences are being published in both England and the United States—the latter in an experimental digest-sized format.

Things continue to change rapidly in the Burroughs field, so rapidly in fact that almost any statement of the situation at any time is bound to become obsolete within a matter of weeks or months. But this much is certain: Burroughs's imaginative creations retain their timeless appeal, both in their original forms and in adaptations—provided that the adaptations are made with talent and dedication, and in particular provided that the adaptors remain faithful to the spirit if not the letter of Burroughs's original stories.

In the long sequence of Burroughs's appearances in the comics, there of course have been innumerable attempts by others to capitalize on his popularity by creating more-or-less thinly disguised imitations of his characters and stories. This of course is true in many media, whether in books and magazines, films, television, or the comics.

For instance, over the years there have been innumerable pseudo-Tarzans of both sexes. Two of the longest-running imitations were Fiction House's *Jungle Comics* and *Jumbo Comics*, the former featuring *Ka'anga, Lord of the Jungle* and *Wambi, the Jungle Boy*; the latter, *Sheena, Queen of the Jungle. Jungle* ran for 163 issues, from 1940 to 1954. *Jumbo* lasted 167 issues, from 1938 to 1953. In parallel there were *Ka'anga* and *Sheena* pulp-magazine stories and even a *Sheena* TV series starring the spectacularly formed Irish McCalla in the title role.

Other jungle-type comics have abounded, perhaps the most interesting being Stan Lee's *Ka-Zar*, with a brief run around 1940 and a revival in the 1960s. *Ka-Zar* combines features of Tarzan, Pellucidar, and a general lost-world theme, with the heaviest emphasis on Tarzan.

Nyoka, the Jungle Girl had a long run in Fawcett's *Master Comics*, plus a separate comic of her own that ran for 77 issues under Fawcett's auspices, then another 14 as a Charlton comic. The oddity of Nyoka is that she was a Hollywood creation, stuck into a movie serial based on Burroughs's novel *Jungle Girl* . . . but Nyoka herself never appeared in the novel!

Male and female pseudo-Tarzans continue to pop up—an example is Marvel Comics' *Shanna the She-Devil* (born in 1972 and canceled in 1973), but even odder is Marvel's adaptation of a Barsoomian-style adventure called *Warrior of Mars*.

Details behind Marvel's decision to do the *Warrior* feature are somewhat obscure, but there are rumors that when the Gold Key Burroughs license was about to expire, Marvel bid for the new contract, but lost out to DC. Looking around for similar material (this is unconfirmed, understand!) Marvel next bid for rights to the creations of Otis Adelbert Kline, a contemporary pulp writer of Burroughs's time, whose Martian, Venusian, and jungle-adventure series closely paralleled those of Burroughs. But these rights, too, eluded Marvel.

But Roy Thomas, a prolific scripter for Marvel (and later their editor, succeeding Stan Lee), was enough of a Burroughs fan to be aware of the controversy that has raged for some years over the possible sources of Burroughs's inspiration—and the theory, quite unproved, that Burroughs's Martian series was inspired by an earlier novel, *Lieut. Gullivar Jones: His Vacation*, by one Edwin Lester Arnold. This book was originally published in 1905, several years before *A Princess of Mars*, so a comic adaptation of its contents, even though resembling *John Carter of Mars*, could hardly bring a successful charge of plagiarism!

Result: *Warrior of Mars*, a rather interesting pseudo-Burroughsian feature. It only lasted a short time, however.

That's the way it goes in the comics. One good feature leads to another, and very often to many others, all of them drawing their inspiration from the original creative idea.

There have been many "pseudo-Burroughses," and there will in all likelihood continue to be many more in the years to come. But there is only one *original* Tarzan as there was only one original Edgar Rice Burroughs. His creations have thrilled millions— perhaps by now, even *billions*—in audiences of every sort over the years: magazines, books, newspapers, radio, television, motion pictures, even bubble gum cards. And of course the comics.

As long as the pressures of everyday life cause people to seek escape to exotic worlds of heroic fantasy in their reading—just that long will Edgar Rice Burroughs's creations continue to attract their huge following!

INTRODUCTION TO

THE SPAWN OF
THE SON OF M. C. GAINES

IN a field as huge and as varied as the comics, everybody has his
own favorites—his own favorite character, story, type of feature,
etc. And a good many comic-book enthusiasts have their favorite
writers and artists, whose works they admire and collect—Simon
and Kirby, Siegel and Shuster, Beck and Binder, Will Eisner, and
others. The same applies to various publishers' "lines" and their
peculiar characteristics—DC's and Fawcett's colorful superheroes, Fiction House's shapely babes and action-filled tales, Dell's
wholesome cartoon animals, and so on.

But although we all have our particular favorites on a personal,
subjective level, based most often on the circumstances of our
respective childhoods, it is also possible to take a step back from
those nostalgic recollections and examine the comics with a
certain degree of detachment. When we do that there is an
amazing degree of agreement—not to say unanimity—regarding
the publishing series that produced the best comic books in
history, and that series was the EC "New Trend" comics of the
1950s.

"Best," in this case, not only on the visceral level of personal
enjoyment, but on the basis of identifiable characteristics. The
ECs combined the best writing with the best art in the comic-book
field; they were thought out with intelligence and commitment,
executed with great skill and with equally great dedication. The
result was a unique corpus of comic art treasured in memory by
those fortunate enough to have read the ECs when they were
being published, and in fact by those foresighted enough to save
their copies when they had finished their first amazed examination
of each new issue.

Don Thompson here refreshes those evergreen memories of Bill
Gaines, Al Feldstein, and the crew of talented artists, writers, and
editors they assembled, and introduces us all to his Uncle Alonzo
Stroup, who . . .

Uncle Alonzo Stroup? Read on, good friend, read on!

CHAPTER 11

THE SPAWN OF
THE SON OF M. C. GAINES

by DON THOMPSON

In its issue of March 24, 1951, the
New Yorker published in the
"Talk of the Town" department
the following filler item:

> INCIDENTAL INTELLIGENCE:
> Educational Comics, Inc., 225 La-
> fayette Street, issues the following
> publications: *Vault of Horror, Tales
> from the Crypt, Weird Fantasy,
> Weird Science, Haunt of Fear* and
> *Crime SuspenStories.*

In its issue of April 7, 1951,
nearly two full magazine columns
were devoted to two letters, headlined "Department of Correction
(Jekyll and Hyde Division)":

EDUCATIONAL COMICS, INC.

PUBLISHERS AND LICENSORS OF

PICTURE STORIES FROM THE BIBLE

"COMPLETE OLD AND

NEW TESTAMENT" EDITIONS

PICTURE STORIES FROM

AMERICAN HISTORY

SCIENCE AND WORLD HISTORY

225 LAFAYETTE ST.

TELEPHONE CANAL 6-1994-5

NEW YORK 12, N.Y.

March 28, 1951

The Editors, *The New Yorker*
SIRS:

On page 20 of the March 24th, 1951, issue of your publication, you stated that this organization, Educational Comics, Inc. of 225 Lafayette St., publishes the following magazines: *The Vault of Horror, Tales from the Crypt, Weird Fantasy, Weird Science, The Haunt of Fear* and *Crime SuspenStories*.

This information is erroneous, and I, as vice-president of Educational Comics, Inc., demand an immediate retraction. Educational Comics, Inc. does not publish any of the six magazines which you listed in your defamatory item. We are engaged in publishing the highly educational material listed on this letterhead. I consider your comments a personal insult, since I, as vice-president of Educational Comics, Inc., would have absolutely nothing to do with magazines dealing with such shocking and distasteful subject matter as those which you list.

I am awaiting your immediate action and response in this matter.

Very sincerely yours,

WILLIAM M. GAINES
Vice-President

WMG/af

****

292

THE E-C COMICS GROUP

"THE BETTER-SELLING COMICS"

225 LAFAYETTE ST.

NEW YORK 12, N.Y.

TELEPHONE CANAL 6-1994-5

March 28, 1951

The Editors, *The New Yorker*
SIRS:
    On page 20 of the March 24th, 1951, issue of your publication, you stated that Educational Comics, Inc., of 225 Lafayette Street, publishes the following magazines: *The Vault of Horror, Tales from the Crypt, Weird Fantasy, Weird Science, The Haunt of Fear*, and *Crime SuspenStories*.
    Educational Comics does not publish these magazines. This information is erroneous, and I, as vice-president of the E-C (Entertaining Comics) Group, of 225 Lafayette Street, demand and insist upon an immediate retraction and correction.
    Having worked very hard to build up a reputation for the very finest entertaining comic magazines in the field, I note with chagrin that our years of labor and achievement are credited to a company which is not in any way responsible for this fine work. I am proud of our publications, and our sales attest to their popular acceptance.
    As vice-president of the E-C Group, I would have absolutely nothing to do with magazines dealing with such dry, unentertaining and obviously educational material as Educational Comics, Inc., publishes.
    I am awaiting your immediate action and response in this matter.

Very sincerely yours,

WILLIAM M. GAINES
Vice-President

WMG/af

Behind this dichotomy lies a tale, a sequel of sorts to Ted White's account of the origins of comic books, "The Spawn of M. C. Gaines," in *All in Color for a Dime*.

My Uncle Alonzo Stroup (honest) was not exactly the type of uncle popularized in boys' adventure books—clean-cut and daring, unattached and always ready to go to some remote area of the globe for adventure, and always willing to take along his favorite nephew for derring-do among the headhunters. But Uncle Lon had one big redeeming characteristic: he bought more comic books than anybody. All kinds of comic books, virtually every one published. Every Friday, Uncle Lon, who lived with his parents (my maternal grandparents), would blow his paycheck on beer and comic books.

I loved to accompany my mother on her frequent visits to her parents, not for companionship, since there was no one my own age to be seen on these visits, but to read Uncle Lon's comics. If he had held on to these comics—he must have bought every comic book ever published between the late thirties and the late fifties—he would be a rich man today. But I was fated not to have any rich uncles—he or my grandmother threw out every one of them within a couple of weeks after they were purchased. They weren't even given to me; they were to remain there for Uncle Lon to reread and for the benefit of my countless cousins (many of whom were semiliterate and couldn't care less). I don't think I ever was given a single one of Uncle Lon's comics.

But I got to read them and, since comic books were coming out in great numbers and always would be (we all fondly believed), what difference did it make if the old ones were thrown out to make room for the new?

By late 1951, when I was 16, my interest in comic books was only casual anyway. The superheroes were waning badly and I was developing other interests. A casual perusal of Uncle Lon's comics was enough; I needed no collection of my own.

One day, as I sat on the musty couch hastily reading comics so I wouldn't be only partway through some story when my mother was ready to leave—nothing is more frustrating than being unable to finish even a mediocre story—I came across a very different comic book. A horror comic book.

As was so often the case with my uncle's comics, it was coverless when it passed into my hands. The first page was a magnificent splash panel of a man in an orange suit being attacked in a swamp by a huge bat. The story title was "Vampire!" There was a lot more to read in this story than most, a number of mood-setting captions, lengthy speech balloons, and a clear yet detailed drawing style. A doctor in some swampy southern state was called on to treat a young lady with two holes in her neck, similar to those on some recent murder victims. The doctor had diagnosed that it was the work of a vampire and everyone was ridiculing him. The police chief had the audacity to say that someone was obviously draining the blood with a hypodermic needle and that it was a "routine police case."

The doctor was met at the girl's door by her father, who always wore a tuxedo and was never seen during the day. Eventually, the doctor concluded that the tuxedo-wearer was the vampire and that he had even been draining his own daughter's blood. He laid for the father in the swamp, drove a stake through his heart, and went to claim the daughter as his bride. But it seems *she* was the vampire and had appeared weak only because she had not fed lately. She broke her fast on the young doctor.

Man! I had never encountered anything like this.

The next story was forgettable and I forgot it, but it was followed by a compelling tale about a man who faked his death in a plague, arranged for his girl friend to dig him up, then rose from his coffin the night before burial and killed his wife. He then took another dose of the death-simulating drug and was buried, waiting for his girl to dig him up. Unfortunately, she contracted the plague and wasn't able to be there, so ... The art on this one was really unusual, a murky, moody drawing style with many lines and slightly slanted faces. The colorist seemed to use a lot of grays and blues.

The fourth story was a fairly interesting mummy story in a very uninteresting style. But still, there were two fairly good stories and two certified rousers. I wanted more.

But where would I get more? The comic book had no cover, so I didn't even know its name. The indicia (that little block of small, closely set type at the beginning of a comic that tells you who published it and where and how often) was missing, apparently having been printed on the cover. And I didn't have the book available to search for clues. I hadn't seen Uncle Lon's collection for more than a year previously and wasn't able to find any other comics like it.

I searched newsstands. I bought some godawful horror comics, the kind that blazoned on the cover: "We *dare* you to read these stories!" They were nauseating—dealing in things like giant crabs stripping bodies until they looked like the diagrams of human musculature you see in the encyclopedia, and mummies that sucked the guts out of people through their mouths (sorry to share that latter memory with you but I've been stuck with it for 20 years and maybe this will unload it)—nauseating but not frightening. I must have bought a couple dozen of these things, all of them dreadful.

When I finally found what I was looking for, I knew it at first sight. The cover was drawn by the man who had done the "Vampire!" story, the man with the clean, clear-cut, but beautifully detailed style. His name, I now noticed, was Johnny Craig. The comic-book line was EC, which stood for Entertaining Comics, according to the little trademark circle on the cover.

The first EC comic I found was *The Vault of Horror* No. 24, dated April-May, 1952. On the inside front cover (along with the indicia) was a photograph and biography of artist Craig and a listing of the nine titles published by EC at that time: *The Haunt of Fear, Weird Science, Crime SuspenStories, Frontline Combat, Tales from the Crypt, Weird Fantasy, The Vault of Horror, Shock SuspenStories,* and *Two-Fisted Tales.*

I was soon immersed in another story by Johnny Craig, again about vampires, dealing with an undertaker who found that someone was draining the blood from bodies laid out for embalming before he got to them. It was called "A Bloody Undertaking"—it didn't take long to learn that the gang at EC loved puns, particularly grisly ones. Sometimes they went to extremes, as in the story about a vampire cabdriver, which they called "Fare Tonight, Followed by Increasing Clottyness!"

The next story, signed "Ghastly," was by the other artist who had impressed me so favorably. From the letter column, "The Vault-Keeper's Corner," I learned that his name was Graham Ingels. He told the story of an old trapper whose wife died one winter; the old man was so afraid of the rotting that follows burial in the ground that he kept her frozen in the shed until he could accumulate enough furs to afford to have her interred in a metal vault so her body would be undisturbed. In the spring, he discovered that a lynx maimed in his trap had got into the shed and devoured most of his wife's body. At the time, I had not yet read Ambrose Bierce's "The Boarded Window" and I found the story very effective. Today, having read Bierce and having read the stories that served as the inspiration for many other EC stories, I still find it impressive. The EC writers might lift from the work of other writers, but they usually added a great deal to it. More on that later.

From that time on, I bought every EC and saved every one. But, despite all the love and care I lavished upon them, those copies today are frayed and worn—from frequent rereadings. The pitiful handful of earlier ECs I managed to obtain (often at scandalously high prices) usually are equally worn. People who

Johnny Craig's Vault-Keeper was the definitive version of that host of horror stories. Craig's people were usually handsome, clean-featured and impeccably dressed. In order to draw horrible people, such as the Vault-Keeper and the faces in the splash panel above, he resorted to warts, staring eyes, missing teeth and mouths festooned with slime. This page is from *Vault of Horror* #19, June-July, 1951. © 1973 by William M. Gaines.

read ECs tended to reread ECs. (One of the issues I found was the one with the "Vampire!" story; it was the second issue of *Haunt of Fear*.)

The EC line included three horror titles: *The Haunt of Fear, The Vault of Horror*, and *Tales from the Crypt* (*Tales* had originally been called *The Crypt of Terror* but the title was changed after three issues). Each one featured an eight-page lead story, which was told by the Old Witch and illustrated by Graham Ingels if it was *Haunt of Fear*, by the Vault-Keeper and illustrated by Johnny Craig if it was *Vault of Horror*, or by the Crypt-Keeper and illustrated by Jack Davis if it was *Tales from the Crypt*.

The other two GhouLunatics, as the three ghastlies were called, each had a seven-page story in the host's or hostess' magazine and there also was a six-page encore for the book's star illustrated by a lesser artist, usually Jack Kamen. Kamen drew very cartoony, stiff, artificial characters of the type usually seen in love-story comics. From various things said about him in the EC magazines, I gather he was and presumably is one heck of a nice guy, but I never liked his drawings. I preferred the more realistic artists.

Jack Davis, who drew the Crypt-Keeper stories, is today a very successful commercial artist, doing movie posters and magazine ads in great profusion. His horror stories tended to deal with persons getting their comeuppance from inanimate objects in which they had disposed of a murder victim (the man who pushed another into a vat of molten steel died in an iron maiden made from that steel; a man who rendered his victim into soap slipped on a cake of it, broke a leg, and drowned in a hot shower as the soap clogged the drain), or else with persons who were turned into something connected with their viciousness (crooked auto-dealers were used as car parts—their blood in the gas tank, their skulls as headlights—by the dead victims of their shoddy cars; a ballplayer was cut apart and used as sports equipment—his scalp dusted home plate, which was his heart, his hands were used as gloves, and so on, very literally *ad nauseam*).

The horror hosts, the Old Witch, the Vault-Keeper, and the Crypt-Keeper, were patterned after the radio horror-show hosts like Raymond, who opened the creaking *Inner Sanctum* door and told spooky stories, and like the Mysterious Traveler, who rode around telling spooky stories on a train back when trains sounded mysterious, before diesel horns replaced the exotic and mournful whistle with a raucous bleat. They rarely participated in stories—

His name is Graham Ingels, but he signed himself "Ghastly" and the name certainly fit his art. He drew the Old Witch who operated "The Witch's Cauldron" in *Haunt of Fear* and EC's other horror comics. His drawings conveyed an H. P. Lovecraft mood to the stories he illustrated, an air of moss and decay and fresh-turned graves. This is from *Haunt of Fear* #7, May-June 1951. © 1973 by William M. Gaines.

there were two gimmick stories which turned out to be origin stories on the Old Witch and the Crypt-Keeper—but introduced them, commented from time to time throughout, and closed off with a barrage of puns. They are widely imitated in today's pallid "horror" comics: National Periodical Publications has several hosts and hostesses, including Cain, Abel, and Eve (despite the biblical names, they are pretty standard and uninspired horror hosts) and a trio of witches. Creepy, Eerie, and Vampirella are hosts and hostess of three black-and-white comic magazines put out by Warren Publications, *Creepy*, *Eerie*, and *Vampirella*. Of those, only Vampirella actually participates in stories.

The Old Witch was a wrinkled old hag—Ghastly Graham Ingels drew the *oldest* looking old people—with one eye considerably larger than the other and with a downcurving nose that nearly met an upcurving chin over an almost toothless mouth. She wore a red hood and gown. The Vault-Keeper had warts, staring eyes, a long chin, and there were long gummy strands visible in his open mouth. He had about four teeth, three above and one below, and wore a mouldy green hood and gown. The Crypt-Keeper was tougher and meaner looking, wore a blue gown and no head-covering. All had straight and unkempt white hair.

Each of the other books—two war, two suspense, two science fiction—followed the same format of an eight-page lead story followed by a seven-page story, which in turn was followed by a two-page spread of house ads for other comics (including *Picture Stories from the Bible*) and an all-text short story; then came a one-page letter column and a six-page story and a seven-page story and one final page of advertising. For most of its existence, EC ran paid ads only on that last inside page and the two back-cover pages. The inside front cover was reserved for house ads or for biographies of the artists.

The two war books, *Two-Fisted Tales* and *Frontline Combat*, were edited by Harvey Kurtzman. All the other titles were edited by Albert B. Feldstein. Feldstein was the "af" who typed those Gaines letters to *The New Yorker*.

EC was always careful to credit the artists and made them big drawing cards. Since EC had virtually no continuing characters— there was a Sergeant Patrick Tubridy, serving with Her Majesty's army in Injah, who appeared in a number of war stories, there had once been a Moon Girl, and there would later be a number of recurring characters in *Two-Fisted Tales* when it switched from war stories to adventure stories, but that was about it—it was the artists who became the reason for picking up ECs every time they hit the stands. The artists and the stories.

Oddly, EC rarely credited the writers. This was because most of the stories were by the editors—not all, by any means, but most. Otto Binder, who wrote *Captain Marvel* and wrote for just about everybody, wrote for EC. Later on, they did some superb adaptations of stories by Ray Bradbury. Jerry De Fuccio, now an assistant editor of *Mad*, wrote a number of excellent text pieces and some fine stories, mostly for Kurtzman's war books, under the semi-pseudonym of Jerry Dee.

But, by and large, the stories in Kurtzman's books were written by Kurtzman and the stories in Feldstein's books were written by Feldstein. Feldstein and Gaines would hash out story ideas and Feldstein would write them—a story a day, every day, five days a week, in addition to all the artist conferences and other duties of an editor and publisher. Feldstein also found time to draw; at first he drew stories, later only a few covers. His covers were better— his figures tended to be stiff and not too exciting, but he did several memorable and beautiful covers, particularly on the science-fiction titles.

Later in that magic year of 1952, Harvey Kurtzman was to create another title for EC, the only title still surviving. It was called *Mad*.

Mad parodied everything. Comic strips and comic books and movies and Senate investigations and beauty contests and horror stories and war stories and everything. There were 23 comic-book issues of *Mad*. Then, since comics were being censored and EC was being driven out of business, *Mad* became a magazine. Later, Bill Gaines and Harvey Kurtzman had a serious falling-out and Kurtzman left. Gaines called Al Feldstein back to edit *Mad*, which looks as though it may last forever.

It took me several years to piece out the EC story. This is it.

M. C. Gaines, as noted in Ted White's article in *All in Color for a Dime*, holds a strong claim to being one of the persons primarily responsible for the very existence of comic books. He left the Superman-DC, All-American comics line, today variously known as DC (for *Detective Comics*, its oldest title) and National Periodical Publications Inc. Max Gaines wanted to found his own comics company.

He founded two in one—Educational Comics, Inc., and Entertaining Comics, Inc.—both under the EC symbol.

The Educational Comics line consisted of *Picture Stories from the Bible* (begun when Gaines was still with DC-AA-National), *Picture Stories from Science, Picture Stories from World History*, and *Picture Stories from American History*. There were four DC *Bible* issues from the Old Testament, a *Complete Old Testament Edition* (first published in 1943 and often reprinted), and two EC *Old Testament* issues containing selections from the earlier editions. There were two *Bible* issues from the New Testament (one from DC and one from AA), then a *Life of Christ Edition*, then a third *New Testament* edition (from EC), then a *Complete New Testament Edition* which reprinted all three. Then came another EC edition, reprinting the first issue. There were four *American History* issues and two each of *World History* and *Science*. All were dreadfully dull, the sort of thing teachers use, figuring if kids are going to read comics they might as well learn something worthwhile, so you get censored Bible stories and simplistic science lessons where children shrink and tour the digestive system, where germ soldiers are pursued by phagocytes, where ignorant natives laboriously polish rice so they can contract beriberi.

(That tour of the digestive system, incidentally, began in the mouth and ended in the—fortunately empty—lower intestine, then quickly doubled back to the small intestine for details on how the food gets into the rest of the body. One shudders to think of the tragic fate of our young explorers had they continued to the bitter end.)

These laudable but unsuccessful attempts to educate the comic-book reader were offered in ads in EC comics for years. Presumably the entire stock—including several reprintings—eventually sold and today they are sought after by completist collectors of EC comics.

The early Entertaining Comics line is a tangled web of short-lived titles that were turned into new titles without changing the numbering—the Post Office charges a large fee for new titles granted second-class mailing rights. One example should be sufficient: *Moon Girl and the Prince* became *Moon Girl* with the second issue, *Moon Girl Fights Crime* with the seventh, *A Moon . . . A Girl . . . Romance* with the ninth issue, and *Weird Fantasy* with the thirteenth—and then *Weird Fantasy* followed that numbering through No. 18, and followed that with No. 7 because the Post Office complained (understandably) that, despite the numbering, it was a new title. And that's not quite all. With issue No. 23, *Weird Fantasy* combined with *Weird Science*, which had had a similar spate of title-switching and had also achieved 22 issues under that title. The combined book was called *Weird Science-Fantasy* (which also was the title of an annual reprint collection from *WS* and *WF*) through issue No. 29, then the title was changed to *Incredible Science-Fiction*. The book died with issue No. 33 without again changing title.

Now, aren't you glad I let one example suffice? I didn't even go into how *Fat and Slat* turned into *Gunfighter*, which turned into *Haunt of Fear*, which continued that numbering for three issues before switching back to No. 4 and turning its old numbering (derived from the careers of *Fat and Slat* and *Gunfighter*) over to *Two-Fisted Tales*.

Be glad I didn't go into that.

The early Educational Comics line was not the stuff of which legends are made. *Moon Girl* was an insipid imitation of *Wonder Woman; Fat and Slat* was slapstick by Ed Wheelan, using characters from his pioneering *Minute Movies* comic strip; *Gunfighter* was a routine western with art by not-yet-Ghastly Graham Ingels. Other titles included love comics (*Modern Love* and *A Moon . . . A Girl . . . Romance*), kiddie comics (*Dandy Comics, The Happy Houlihans, Animated Comics, Land of the Lost, Tiny Tot Comics, Animal Fables*), crime comics (*War Against Crime, International Comics* later *International Crime Patrol* later *Crime Patrol,* and *Blackstone the Magician Detective Fights Crime*), and western comics (*Saddle Justice,* later to be even more ridiculously titled *Saddle Romances*).

The most distinguished of this lot was the one-issue *Blackstone* title and that only because it bears one of the longest titles of any comic book ever. Much later, with *M.D.*, EC had to at least tie for shortest comic-book title ever.

While EC floundered, Max Gaines died.

He died a hero's death.

A speedboat smashed into his boat on Lake Placid. He probably could have escaped, but he stayed to thrust a child out of the boat's path and to safety at the cost of his own life.

He left his son, William M. Gaines, $1,000,000 and a string of faltering comic books.

For a while, Bill Gaines continued to flounder along with his father's magazines, then he introduced some horror stories into his crime-fiction books. The horror comics caught on and EC introduced a whole line of "New Trend" comics—horror, science fiction, war, and crime-suspense.

The war books were like no war comics seen before or, sadly, since. They were packed like eggs with facts and drawn with extremely correct detail. Kurtzman's regular artists were Wallace Allen Wood (better known for his science fiction, but equally adept at turning out historical stories such as "Custer's Last Stand" and accounts of the careers of Caesar and Hannibal); Jack Davis (who had a feel for the reality of a soldier's life; his characters were like Bill Mauldin's Willie and Joe in a serious mood, but they had also the real soldier's chances of getting killed); and John Severin, both alone and with the collaborative talents of Bill Elder. Severin did incredibly detailed drawings that were the result of hours of painstaking research. When he drew a gun, it was accurate to the tiniest screw; when he drew a uniform, it was the kind that would have been worn by the man he was depicting, whether a Civil War soldier in one of the polychrome uniforms of the period early in the war before blue and gray became the standardized colors, or a soldier in the Afghan Border conflict.

When Kurtzman started *Mad*, he utilized his regular artists. It was the making of Elder, who today—as Will Elder—is the artist with Kurtzman on the *Little Annie Fanny* feature in *Playboy*. It gave a huge boost to the career of Jack Davis, whose humorous drawings are frequently featured in magazine ads, in network promotions for television programs, and in movie posters, such as the ones for *It's a Mad, Mad, Mad, Mad World*. He still does work for *Mad*. Wood appeared in more issues of *Mad* than any of the others but he remains best known for his science-fictional drawings. John Severin never seemed really suited to *Mad*, but he has done vast quantities of work for such *Mad* imitators as *Cracked* and continues to turn out adventure and war comics for Marvel and DC, the two largest comic-book companies of the sixties and seventies.

A typical issue of a Kurtzman war comic would resemble *Frontline Combat* No. 8 (September-October, 1952). Contents of that issue were "Thunderjet," a Korean War air-battle story drawn by the extremely talented Alexander Toth, an artist who did only two stories for EC, both masterpieces; "Caesar," an ironic story built around a capsule biography of Julius Caesar, beautifully drawn by Wood; "Chickamauga," a Civil War story expertly drawn by professional Southerner Davis; and "Night Patrol," a moody and again ironic story about a Korean War infantry patrol, drawn with realistic rain and fear by Severin and Elder and expertly colored by Marie Severin, John's sister and EC's colorist.

This variety appeared at a time when other comic-book companies were apparently unaware that there had ever been any conflict other than the Korean War.

I took that issue to my high school Latin teacher, Miss Henry, who doubled as librarian, and asked her to check "Caesar" for accuracy. She returned it saying it was accurate but it made the Romans out to be cruel, particularly the account of Caesar's treatment of the people of Uxellodonum—he had their hands chopped off. She admitted it was true but said that it was an isolated instance. I am sure the handless men of Uxellodonum would agree with my contention that once was enough.

The stories in *Crime SuspenStories* were very like the stories in the horror books except that the dead stayed dead and did not rise, rotting, from the grave to revenge themselves. The majority seemed to involve unfaithful husbands (wives) ridding themselves of their wives (husbands), only to be tripped up by some ironic happening. In a moody story drawn—and apparently written—by Johnny Craig, "The Execution," in *Crime SuspenStories* No. 12 (August-September, 1952), a condemned man was to be executed. He pleaded his innocence, he reviewed his alibi in flashbacks and saw again the witness who could prove he was elsewhere at the time of the murder but who never appeared to testify. His head was shaved—the barber paused for a panel while the lights dimmed, then resumed clipping the hair of the sweating man. At the end, the innocent was electrocuted and the man who threw the switch was revealed as the missing witness; his job had got to him to such an extent that he avoided reading any newspaper and was never aware that the executed man had been seeking him. He commented at the end that he always wished he could somehow help the condemned men.

I must mention briefly one other story in *Crime SuspenStories*, one with my favorite EC title. It concerned a murderer who disguised himself as a woman and was given away when he went to the men's room. The title: "Standing Room Only."

Shock SuspenStories was quite different from *Crime SuspenStories*. It was conceived as an EC sampler, to contain a crime story, a science-fiction story, a horror story, and a war story. The war story was dropped after one issue and replaced with a "shock" story. They were indeed shocking. A man was beaten to death by a crowd of overzealous "patriots" because he did not take off his hat to the American flag—he turned out to be a blind veteran. A girl was raped and the sheriff got a confession from a stranger and then let him be lynched—at the end the sheriff was revealed to the readers as the real rapist. An innocent Negro was "shot while escaping." A reporter was murdered by the Ku Klux Klan. A drug addict killed his father for a fix.

Strong stuff. It was not universally popular, but *Shock* managed to last 18 issues and died only when comic-book censorship came along to put an end to the entire EC line.

These stories had a lot to do with the shaping of my life. I have no idea how I might have turned out without them, but I know that they made me more understanding of differences between people and less quick to judge and far less quick to condemn. But the Comics Code Authority says they were bad and the Comics Code Authority is made up of honorable men. So are they all, all honorable men.

There also was an EC-published imitation of *Mad* called *Panic*; it used the same artists, largely, but the stories were written by Feldstein instead of Kurtzman. It lasted only 12 issues and never approached *Mad*'s success, artistically or commercially. Oddly, the magazine *Mad* under Feldstein achieved a tremendous commercial success few publications obtain, particularly few publications that do not accept advertisements.

The finest magazines in EC's "New Trend" line were the science-fiction comics, *Weird Science* and *Weird Fantasy*.

"We at EC are proudest of our science fiction magazines," they boasted in ads. But when a reader asked why they didn't publish more of them, they responded with a quotation from another letter-writer: "Please don't go out of business." To those who equate quality with commercial success, EC's science-fiction magazines couldn't have been very good.

Well, they were. They had lapses, many of them, both of taste and idea. They had their cliché stories, their stolen plots, and their absurdities. One of their commonest clichés was to have someone be mean to an animal or an insect and wind up in a comparable situation with some gigantic alien equivalent of the creature he had been mistreating—and with the roles reversed. A man with a tapeworm in his stomach found himself a parasite living in the gut of a gigantic alien monster. They did too many of these, with humans winding up in the salad of a gigantic cockroach or having their limbs pulled off by a giant daisy saying, "She loves me, she loves me not ... "

But they also did stories wherein a spaceship left Earth on a two-century journey to find living space in another solar system only to find, upon arriving, that the hopelessly overcrowded residents of that system had sent a ship to colonize Earth 200 years before; where the only hope for a womanless future was to bring females from the twentieth century but the immovable time machine was focused on the men's room at Grand Central Station; where an Earthman reached Mars and was thrown in the asylum with all the other nuts who claim to come from Earth; where a lost alien child landed on Earth and was slain by St. George.

Not all of the EC science fiction was good but enough of quality was printed to make them unforgettable. Not all were original, either. In their quest for adult stories, they frequently "borrowed" from stories by authors of magazine and book science fiction—Richard Matheson, John Collier, Anthony Boucher, Fredric Brown, and Ray Bradbury, among others.

In *Weird Fantasy* No. 13 (May-June, 1952, as opposed to No. 13, May-June, 1950, which was the first issue, as mentioned earlier), there appeared a six-page story illustrated by Wally Wood and titled "Home to Stay." In it, a boy and his mother awaited the return of the star-faring man of the family, often expressing the wish that he would come home to Earth and stay home instead of traveling in space. The spaceship exploded in mid-flight and the occupants drifted to their dooms in spacesuits. The husband-father drifted toward Earth and burned up in the atmosphere as a meteor. Below, his wife and son watched the falling star and the boy wished on it: "I wish ... I wish my daddy would come home tonight ... home to stay!"

Several readers pointed out that the story was a combination of two Ray Bradbury stories from *The Illustrated Man*: "The Rocket Man" and "Kaleidoscope."

Among those who pointed this out was Ray Bradbury, who

asked for payment and got it. He then agreed to let them adapt his stories and use his name on the covers. His stories began appearing in every issue of the SF magazines and frequently in the crime and horror publications. Some of those comic-book adaptations were collected in paperbound books by Ballantine Books in the late sixties: *The Autumn People* (horror) and *Tomorrow Midnight* (science fiction). Both books are now out of print and are sought-after collectors' items.

EC created in me a hunger for science fiction which has, quite literally, shaped my life. I went questing for stories by Ray Bradbury and discovered science-fiction magazines, starting with the November, 1952, issue of *The Magazine of Fantasy and Science Fiction*. I became a rabid science-fiction fan and entered that strange microcosm called science-fiction fandom, where I met all of those I consider my best friends (including my co-editor, Dick Lupoff) and where, in fact, I met my wife, Maggie. I do not live and breathe science fiction, but I sure do read it and I occasionally write it. Through EC I met science fiction, through science fiction I met my wife, and through my wife I became what I am today. I owe all that to EC and I am eternally grateful. I doubt very much that any other EC fan, no matter how dedicated, can claim such an indebtedness to that comic-book-world Camelot.

Ray Bradbury has profited slightly, as well. I have bought every book of his ever published. He must have realized enough on royalties from me alone to at least buy a reasonably good meal in a reasonably good restaurant.

Like all dream worlds, though, EC was not to last. In the early fifties it became fashionable to blame comic books for the shortcomings of youth. It is difficult to remember today, when everyone is completely happy with the things young people do, but there was a time when some were disrespectful to elders, dressed strangely, and occasionally did violence to themselves and others. Some parents thought they might be responsible but a psychiatrist named Fredric Wertham set their minds at rest in a book called *Seduction of the Innocent* (Holt, Rinehart and Winston, Inc., 1954), which places the blame squarely upon comic books and concludes by taking the parent off the hook:

> "It must be my fault," she said. "I heard that in the lectures. And the judge said it, too. It's the parents' fault that the children do something wrong. Maybe when he was very young—"
> "Not at all," I interrupted her. "You have done all that you could.

I have the whole chart here and we know it from the boy himself. But the influence of a good home is frustrated if it is not supported by the other influences children are exposed to—the comic books, the crime programs and all that. Adult influences work against them. We have studied that, and we know good parents when we see them. So don't worry about yourself. It's not your fault."

She seemed to come out from under a cloud. She thanked me and got up to go. When she was halfway through the doorway she turned slowly. "Doctor," she said in a low voice. "I'm sorry to take your time. But please—tell me again."

I looked at her questioningly.

"Tell me again," she said slowly and hesitantly. "Tell me again that it isn't my fault."

And I did.

Not surprisingly, a lot of parents liked hearing this and a spate of magazine articles by Dr. Wertham and others appeared, blaming all the shortcomings of young Americans on comic books.

The method of establishing a cause-and-effect relationship was backward from what I was taught in school about scientific method. The essence of the scientific method is to take a theory and try to disprove it. Dr. Wertham tackled it from another angle.

Instead of setting up control groups of children who read comics and children who did not and comparing how they turned out, Dr. Wertham found juvenile delinquents and asked them if they read comic books. Since nearly every kid read comics in those days before television conquered the country, the answer was almost always affirmative.

There you are. Juvenile delinquents read comic books, therefore comic books cause juvenile delinquency. What could be plainer?

In 1972, Dr. Wertham, stung by repeated criticism from comics fans and blamed for helping to kill EC, wrote a letter to the *Monster Times*, a New York tabloid devoted to horror movies, comics, fantasy, and something they call "sci-fi" (a term used by people who know nothing about science fiction to refer to science fiction). In his letter, dated April 1, Dr. Wertham states:

I have never mentioned EC comics in any of my writings or talks. This is part of the myth about me, which should be buried by this time. I looked up the bibliographical note at the end of SEDUCTION OF THE INNOCENT, the part that was cut out of the finished book by the publisher, under the pressure of comic book publishers, he told me after it had been done without my knowledge. It was pp. 399 and 400, which are missing from all the copies of SEDUCTION OF THE INNO-CENT sold, except for a few—very few—copies that slipped out before it was done. In that list, in which I gave the names of all the publishers referred to in the text of the book, the name of EC comics does not appear.

Well, well. Seldom do you see a man admit so frankly that he doesn't know what he has been talking about and writing about. Because Dr. Wertham most certainly did discuss EC in his book and, in his illustration section in *Seduction*, he reprints a cover by Johnny Craig for *Crime SuspenStories* (the title was cut off and Craig's signature was whited out, but the circle in which his name appeared remains) and two panels by Jack Davis (from the story referred to earlier, the one where a ball-player was chopped up and parts of his body were used as sports equipment), and three panels from a science-fiction story drawn by Bill Elder (in which a Martian woman murdered her husband because he had a navel, indicating he was a mammal and not an egg-layer like the Martians). All are from EC. The Davis is from *The Haunt of Fear*, the Elder from *Weird Science*.

There were frequent mentions of other EC titles in the text of the book.

Now, as to that "bibliographical note." It is true that—for reasons at which I cannot even guess—the publisher sent men out to bookstores with razor blades to excise the sheet on which pages 399 and 400 appeared. Thanks to comics fan Dwight Decker, who found an unmutilated copy, I have a photostat of the missing pages.

It consists of an alphabetical listing of "the names given as publishers on the comic books quoted or referred to in the text." Dr. Wertham's research into comics had not uncovered the fact that many publishers, including EC, used several publishing firm names, sometimes a different one for each title. Publishing is a chancy business and magazines do go out of business. Should a title prove unsuccessful, the creditors may seize the assets of the publishing firm—if those assets included a successful publication, the creditors could seize all or part of that publication. The use of different firm names keeps a loser from pulling down the rest of the line.

Had Dr. Wertham listed addresses instead of just names, he might have noticed that Educational Comics, Inc.; Fables Pub-lishing Co., Inc.; I.C. Publishing Co., Inc., and Tiny Tot Comics,

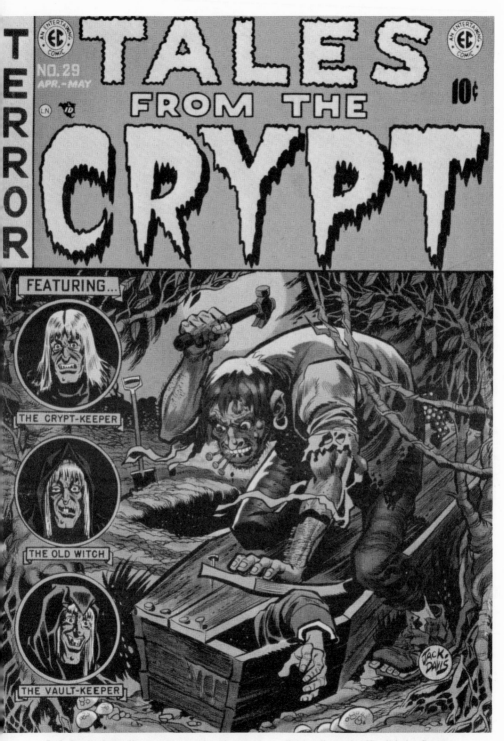

Jack Davis drew dirty, ugly people who came to dirty, ugly ends. He did the Crypt-Keeper's stories, stories which were mean and tough, like C-K himself. A professional Southerner, Davis also drew for EC's war comics, specializing in Civil War Stories. Since the demise of EC, his work has appeared on the covers of *TV Guide, Newsweek* and other periodicals and on movie posters. This page is from *Tales from the Crypt #29*, April-May 1952. © 1973 by William M. Gaines.

Inc., were all located at 225 Lafayette St. All those firms are in his bibliographical note, all are therefore quoted or referred to in the text, and all of them are EC.

The anticomics movement spread. Nearly every slick magazine ran lurid articles on the menace of the comics, nearly every issue of nearly every newspaper ran stories of gigantic comic-book burnings with mothers twisting their children's arms to "volunteer" to have their comic books publicly burned. Mothers' groups picketed newsstands; some used a highly effective tactic against supermarkets that sold comic books (yes, kiddies, comic books used to be sold in supermarkets—and in drug stores and in department stores and just about everywhere): they would fill their shopping carts with groceries and when they got to the checkout counter they would demand to speak to the manager; they would ask the manager to remove all those terrible comic books from the stands; and if the manager did not comply, they walked out, leaving a cart full of groceries for the store personnel to put back before the frozen fish thawed.

It worked.

Retailers and even distributors started returning comic books to the publishers without even opening the bundles. Many comic-book firms went out of business.

EC didn't. Not yet.

EC killed off the horror titles. The war titles had died of lack of interest shortly after the Korean War ended; *Two-Fisted Tales* continued for a while as a robust adventure book edited by John Severin and entirely illustrated by him. *Crime* and *Shock* were canceled. The science-fiction books had been combined into *Weird Science-Fantasy* and the title had changed to *Incredible Science Fiction*. These things all happened in late 1954 and early 1955.

There was a Comics Code Authority. There still is. It survives by requiring comics publishers to pay it a fee for "approving" (censoring) the comics and letting the publisher put an ugly little white trading stamp in the upper corner that says "Approved by the Comics Code Authority."

In a move specifically aimed at EC, which used all these words in the titles of its books, the Code prohibited the use of "Weird," "Fear," "Horror," and "Terror" in titles. (In the early seventies, the Code relaxed and allowed "Weird" and "Fear" to be used; they also relented and allowed vampires, werewolves, and ghouls to be used, provided they were used in the classic manner, whatever that means.)

EC tried to conform to the Code. The "New Trend" gave way to the "New Direction." *Mad* and *Panic* and *Incredible* survived and were joined by *Piracy* (rousing good sea stories); *Valor* (stories of courage, usually minus violence and very well done); *Impact* (punch-ending stories, usually with a heavy emotional wallop); *M.D.* (stories of doctors and patients; quite good and with an incredible amount of research); *Extra!* (newspapermen on the newsfronts of the world—good adventure stories with continuing characters, edited and written and about half of them drawn by Johnny Craig, who had also edited the last six issues of *Vault of Horror*); *Aces High* (World War I airplanes, including some fantastically good art work by George Evans, who loved to draw old airplanes and whose work reflected his love); and, so help me, *Psychoanalysis* (which was about persons undergoing psychoanalysis and was entirely drawn by Jack Kamen). Except for *Extra!*, all were edited by Feldstein.

At about this time, EC started experimenting with black-and-white comics magazines, coming out in 1955 with *Mad* as a magazine (not subject to censorship by the Comics Code Authority) and following with *Shock Illustrated, Crime Illustrated,* and *Terror Illustrated* (which carried on as their similarly titled comic-book predecessors had done) and *Confessions Illustrated,* a love book.

These "Picto-Fiction" books were done without balloons but with about six illustrations to a page and a block of type with each picture. They were unsuccessful—of course, I am not speaking of *Mad* now—and lasted two issues each, except for *Shock Illustrated. Shock,* the first of the nonfunny magazines to appear, was just rolling its third issue off the presses when the order came through to kill it. The sheets already printed were brought to the EC office and hand-stapled by Feldstein. There were 200 copies, which were given to staff and friends. A few went on sale on newsstands within easy walking distance of the EC office. Naturally, *Shock Illustrated* No. 3 is a collector's item of considerable rarity.

EC was even reduced to following trends instead of starting them. EC jumped on the big 3-D bandwagon of 1953–54, when everyone was publishing three-dimensional comic books which you could read with the aid of cardboard glasses with cellophane lenses, one blue or green and one red. EC published redrawn versions of old comic-book stories, much as they did with a large portion of the Picto-Fiction magazines later. There were two issues, numbered 3-D No. 1 and 3-D No. 2: *Three-Dimensional EC Classics* and *Three-Dimensional Tales from the Crypt of Terror* a title even longer than *Blackstone the Magician Detective Fights Crime*; with either one, EC probably holds the length-of-title record).

Despite the cleanliness and lack of violence in the "New Direction" line, the Comics Code Authority kept finding fault. There are two classic examples of Code censorship.

In the early days, the Code was a Catholic-controlled authority headed by a Father Murphy. (In the sixties, it was taken over by an attorney named Leonard Darvin.) The Code people objected to a beautifully drawn story (the artists were Al Williamson and Roy Krenkel and the splash panel—the large picture that intro-duces the story—was so beautifully detailed that colorist Marie Severin refused to risk obscuring it with color and instead used a pale yellow wash) called "Food for Thought," which appeared in *Incredible Science Fiction* No. 32. The Code enforcers said that flying lizards in the splash panel were satires on angels. Then they objected to the ending, where Earthmen are defeated by an intelligent plant. The Code forced EC to add an eighth page to the story so the Earthmen would win. That wrecked the budget on the issue—a page of paid advertising had to be dropped to make room for the eighth page.

With the next issue of *Incredible*, the Code found one story totally unacceptable. Gaines, caught seven pages short for the issue, decided to rerun one of EC's most popular stories, "Judg-ment Day" (originally in *Weird Fantasy* No. 18). In that story, which was praised by Ray Bradbury and other readers, an Earthman visited a planet of robots to see if they were ready to join the Galactic Republic. He found that the orange robots considered the blue robots inferior and discriminated against them. He declared the planet unready for the Galactic Republic and left. In the last panel, he removed the helmet which he had worn throughout the story and was seen to be a Negro. Joe Orlando illustrated from a script by Al Feldstein and it is a true comic-book classic, sensitively done and very effective, using the analogy to demonstrate the stupidity of prejudice.

Well, the Code Authority said EC couldn't print that story

unless the spaceman was made a Caucasian so they wouldn't offend anyone. Gaines blew up, told the CCA that they were bigots, and said he would print it anyway and, if they objected, make sure the reason for their objections got national coverage. He printed the story and canceled his entire line of comic books, concentrating on *Mad* and thereby making a fortune.

In 1972, he was named publisher of DC's comics line. DC is now the owner of *Mad*, though Gaines retains control.

So here it is 20 years later and respectability has caught up with EC. A movie based on some of the horror stories is out—it's even called *Tales from the Crypt*—and is getting good audiences and even several very good reviews. One of those good reviews, in *New York* magazine, was by Judith Crist, who 20 years earlier was one of the persons writing magazine articles about "horror in the nursery," that is, comic books. More movies are to follow. *Vault of Horror* is already in theaters.

Nostalgia Press has published a handsome huge volume in full color called *Horror Comics of the 1950's* (or, if you read the spine, *The EC Horror Library of the 1950's*). The book contains many of the best horror stories EC published with nearly all of the best artists represented. It is edited by Bhob Stewart and Ron Barlow and sells for $19.95. It even contains that story the Comics Code Authority wouldn't allow them to publish—a story that wouldn't harm anyone.

Ballantine Books published three paperback collections of EC stories (in addition to the two Bradbury collections already mentioned): *Tales from the Crypt, The Vault of Horror*, and *Tales of the Incredible.*

Gaines became richer on *Mad* than he ever would have on comic books and Feldstein has prospered as its editor. *Mad's* first editor, Harvey Kurtzman, who had several lean years and three unsuccessful satire magazines—*Trump, Humbug*, and *Help!*—after leaving EC, is writer and artist, with Will Elder and the help of other artists, including several EC alumni, on *Playboy's Little Annie Fanny* feature.

Many of EC's artists are still in comic books and their appearance in a comic is often considered noteworthy enough to mention on the covers. Several have made good livings by doing advertisements and commercial art.

Others have simply dropped from sight.

Ghastly Graham Ingels, for instance. Despite recurring rumors that he is teaching portrait painting in some remote area or that he is returning to comics, he disappeared into Florida so thoroughly that Gaines is able to communicate with him only through Ingels's agent.

I hope he prospers, wherever he is. Most of the EC staffers are prospering. If they hadn't had the talent to make something of themselves, they wouldn't have been EC staffers—the standards were high.

The ones who lost out when EC died were the readers.

But I can't complain too much about the stories that never were. The stories that were changed my life, molded my life, and made me what I am today. I'm relatively happy.

If only I had a complete collection of mint condition ECs, I would be completely happy.

"KILL!" HISSED THE VILLAIN
AS I SHUDDERED AND LISTENED

WE just couldn't get enough, could we? As kids we built our lives around the heroes of the comics, and seeing them on the newspaper or comic–book page wasn't enough. We devoured them in Big Little Books, movie serials, "real" books, on phonograph records, bubble gum cards—and on the radio!

There was just nothing quite the same as settling down beside an old cathedral-topped Stromberg-Carlson or a gigantic Atwater-Kent console superheterodyne for that marvelous children's hour of fifteen–minute thrillers that came on each evening just before dinner time. Sparked only by a few stirring organ chords, the magic of the human voice and the ingenuity of a sound effects man, those old radio performers created *worlds* before our very, ah, ears—worlds as real and stirring and thrilling as any produced on a Hollywood sound stage, if not more so, for these worlds existed not on a sparkling silver screen but *inside our own heads*.

Chris Steinbrunner, who here recreates a few of those wondrous worlds, is himself a veteran of radio and television, currently producer of the syndicated "Journey to Adventure" show. He is also the author of *Cinema of the Fantastic* (Saturday Review Press), *The Detectionary* (privately published by the Hammermill Bond paper company and a superscarce collector's item), *The Cliffhangers* (Curtis Books), and editor of *The Encyclopedia of Mystery and Detection* (McGraw Hill).

He was also—in a long-ago era—the author of a segment of the "Shadow" radio show. In this chapter he reveals the details of that and many other secret worlds.

CHAPTER 12

"KILL!" HISSED THE VILLAIN
AS I SHUDDERED
AND LISTENED

by CHRIS STEINBRUNNER

"KILL," the villains hissed, and though the decibels are dimming
I can hear them yet. They were the radio villains, battling the
radio heroes, full of murderous intent, and when the anxious
cautionary letters from parents made the radio stations avoid that
single dreadful word, why the villains just managed to say it in
other ways. "He'll be a dead man before morning." "We won't
have to worry about *him* anymore." "He'll never leave that room
[or plane or valley or strange town or haunted castle or what have
you] alive." "Shoot—and *don't miss.*" And as we hung in there,
shuddering and listening, we knew these were only circumlocu-
tions for the declarations of challenge and death, the battle
between good guy and bad, the confrontations—direct, boldly
drawn, and often inspired by the heroes of the comics—which the
voices, organ-swirls, and effects of melodramatic radio ushered to
life in the richly blood-and-thunder years of our growing up.

Growing up in the golden years of the comics was growing up
in the golden years of radio as well, for the latter casually
borrowed much of the stuff from which the comic stories were
made. It was a natural transition, almost: the newspaper strips

and later the comic books, with their swift, terse dialog and their sense of excitement, provided useful tools for the radio medium in its effort to capture the comics' own audience. And somehow the tapestry of the comics—the jungles and oceans and metropolises and lost lands and all the incredible settings ... the motor cars and airplanes and rocketships and chugging trains and all the engines of adventure ... the explosions and avalanches and gun battles and screams and all the climaxes of adventure—were easily reconstructed into radio dramatics, thanks in part to the listener's stimulated imagination and to the skills of the sound-effects engineers. And so, as youngsters in the thirties and forties and even fifties, we huddled in front of the massive-furniture radios of yore, ignoring homework and dinner and all the tribal duties expected of us; or clutched the box radio to our head with the blankets over our ears, blotting out the tiny light of the radio's dial and muffling its *agitato* sounds as we eavesdropped on a late-night murder show past our bedtime; or bent low over the car radio while transported on the obligatory Sunday drive, oblivious to parents and passing scenery while engrossed in the exploits of the Shadow.

What were we listening to, in all those weekday, postschool afternoons, those twilight thrillers, Saturday morning adventure epics, and Sunday afternoon mysteries? Radio's very own band of heroes, to be sure, created by the medium, but very often with the same nobilities and exploring the same terrain as the heroes of the comics. (And why not? The comics had a pacing and level of excitement that a child could appreciate. Radio was quick to borrow the continuity device of the newspaper comics for its continuing serial stories.) Very often the radio hero and the comic hero were one. And not always was this a case of radio borrowing from the printed page; quite a few comic-book adventurers in that four-color Golden Age were born as a voice alone.

Early radio reached into home and family as had no other medium before it; early radio drama experimented with borrowing comic-strip characters who celebrated and made comic the family virtues: such Americana as *The Gumps* and the social climbing Jiggs and Maggie of *Bringing Up Father*. The young Agnes Moorhead, carving a career for herself in the new dramatic medium, was both the abrasive, rolling-pin-wielding Maggie and, less violently, the wise Min Gump. Eventually, nearly all the domesticated comic-strip families would make an appearance on radio, from *The Timid Soul* and *Mr. and Mrs.* to *The Nebbs,*

Gasoline Alley, and the blustering *Major Hoople*, whom the introductory narrative would humorously call "that overstuffed philosopher."

Family-oriented comedy strips concentrating on offspring also made swift transitions to radio, from the very early *Skippy* (1931), to the older *Tillie the Toiler*, already making a life of her own while still maintaining strong family ties, and teenagers *Archie Andrews* and *Harold Teen*. Archie, who began his misadventures on radio in 1943—along with pals Jughead, Betty, and Veronica, and his exasperated elders and teachers—was a perfect mirror of his comic-book source, and had a healthy run of many years. But the most successful of all the family strips to come to radio was *Blondie* and her brood, a show which began in 1939 and was top-rated throughout the forties. *"Don't touch that dial,"* was the command that started each program, and most listeners obeyed. Husband Dagwood, around whom the show really turned, the home-life with its Middle America triumphs and concerns, the office and stern boss—whose raspy screech, *"Bumstead!"*, still vibrates in the corridors of memory—were elements that touched home—as did the strip in which they originated, in millions of homes across the nation.

At the same time that radio was experimenting with adopting the family strip, it gave birth to another comic-strip category: the child adventurer.

> *Who's that little chatterbox?*
> *The one with pretty auburn locks?*
> *Who can it be? It's Little Orphan Annie . . .*

This song, with many additional verses, in 1931 introduced to radio the spunky orphan who, for well over a decade, had already been a newspaper comics-page staple. With all her political attitudes intact, the Annie of radio at least had a perky little-girl voice, which helped you imagine her as that, and not as the midget woman you sometimes suspected the determined creature in the strip might be. (The radio version also helped you avoid staring at author Harold Gray's drawing device: his characters' dreadful, pupil-less white eyes.) Just as in the newspaper pages, though, Annie shared many scrapes with the munitions king she called Daddy Warbucks (listening attentively to his ultra-Fascist philosophy and giving him prodding little pep talks when his fortunes were momentarily wiped away) in such diverse settings as palatial manor houses set deep in woods, metropolitan office buildings, and even a deserted cannibal island, on which a mutineering crew had abandoned them, and where Warbucks had good cause to be grateful to his ward . . . for she kept him going when he was near death for a while. And when Oliver Warbucks was elsewhere making his empire grow, Annie enjoyed friendly chats with his two most trusted servants: Asp, the quiet Oriental killer, and the giant, scimitar-wielding, djinnlike Punjab. Punjab's devotion to the girl was obvious to all listeners; he was frequently to be found hovering close to her, rescuing her when danger approached with a deep-throated: "We must come away, Little Princess."

But those were Annie's salad days, those times with her rich guardian, one of the wealthiest men in the world. However, after Oliver Warbucks's frequent disappearances and simulated deaths, with Asp and Punjab also vanished for a time, Annie was left to fend for herself, generally without even pocket money. It was in these hard times that the plucky orphan often gravitated to the small towns and farming communities of mid-America. She was even given a set of foster parents, a rural couple appropiately named Silo, who loved Annie as much as "Daddy" did, though they were quite without his resources. But even the rustic towns to which Annie retreated were not without their dangers: crooked aldermen, grasping orphanage wardens, wicked landowners, proliferating arsonists, thieves of all descriptions, and even, as the program reached the war years, fifth columnists and foreign types whose names smacked of the Black Hand!

Although the Annie of the newspaper pages lit out of most locations too quickly to establish any permanent relationships with her peers, the radio Annie soon picked up a boy companion, a somewhat backward farm youth named Joe Corntassel, to exploit and commandeer. (Joe was created because of dramatic radio's axiom that lead characters had to have pals with whom to achieve dialog, and also to keep Annie from talking to herself in the alarming fashion she did in the newspapers. Communication with Sandy was also limiting, as all the dog could respond was "Arf.") It was easy to spot the driving force behind the Annie-Joe team, as the poor guy constantly gave way to her aggressive leadership. (He was played, with soft-voiced docility, mostly by Mel Tormé.) The following exchange will illustrate the differing zeals that motivated Annie and Joe. The pair have followed some suspicious persons on foot to a sinister part of town—the locale is called Sunfield, and how that name conjures up visions of the long-ago small-town Midwest—and, while crouched behind a parked car, observe the building their quarry has entered. Minutes later, their suspects leave the building, and the following whispered exchange takes place:

Annie: Great Gulliver! ... They're going to get into that car ... the one parked right in front of this one!
Joe: Whew! That's a break for us!
Annie: What do you *mean*, it's a break for *us*??!
Joe: It's a break they're not gettin' into the car *we're hiding behind*!
Annie (*Angry*): It's a *bad* break they're getting into *any* car! I hadn't counted on that ... How are we going to follow them *now?*

Clearly Annie was the aggressor. Joe was just a tagalong.

In one other way was Annie the clear aggressor: she virtually pioneered and dominated the field of children's radio premiums during the thirties. Premiums were devices that linked sponsors irrevocably with the heroism and spoils of their radio creations. Some treasure was offered in exchange for product boxtop or seal and generally a dime, "to cover mailing," which often made the prize self-liquidating in cost. The best and most fondly remembered premium was the famed Orphan Annie's Cold Ovaltine Shake-Up Mug. Ovaltine, the milk fortifier, was Annie's long-time sponsor, and the red-topped blue mug was heavy identification for the firm. On its plastic side a surprisingly fat-legged Annie, with her dog arfing in attendance, can be seen energetically skipping rope. "For extra pep 'n' flavor keen, drink CHOC'LATE FLA-VORED *OVALTINE!*" One needed all that pep and energy to shake the gray curds of the powdered fortifier into a blended chocolate-milk drink.

Not only did the immense popularity of the mugs insure a succession of them, there were other Annie premiums as well. One was a life-sized Annie face-mask, "just like" the ones used by the brave orphan on that cannibal isle to make advancing natives think a whole mass of girls were holding them at bay. Another was a decoder, for at one time Annie fell in with a cipher expert named Clay Collier. But the most outrageous of all her premiums was a sort of *dog-tag* offered during the years just before the war, eerily prophetic of a time when most young men would be wearing a similar ID. The Little Orphan Annie Identification Tag and Chain, "keen-looking," was oval-shaped, and bore the picture of an American flag plus "best of all, right above the flag, your initial, to show it's *your property*." And on the other side, your *official identification number*, stamped right into the metal. "Everybody gets a different number, that's going to be registered with your name and address at the headquarters of Annie's Identification Bureau, in Chicago! Then, if there's an emergency, or any boy or girl gets lost, people can send in to the headquarters, and find out the name and address which matches up with the number on any tag! And so it's *useful*, as well as being so wonderful looking . . . !" All it took was your initial, a dime, an Ovaltine seal, "and Annie will send you your Identification Tag just as quick as she can!"

It was a curious offering, and one wonders how many emergencies Chicago was called upon to resolve. It was, anyhow, a bad year for Annie and her Identification Bureau; the last year in which she was to travel solo. Ovaltine had decided the listening audience of children warmed more to heroic figures than to tales of their peers, and parted company with the little orphan. Drastic changes in program format seemed a necessity, so the radio Annie went out of Daddy Warbucks's life forever and became a child acolyte to an aviator named Captain Sparks, inspired not—as one might surmise from his name—from a comic-book title but from the program's new sponsor, Quaker Puffed Wheat Sparkies. (Breakfast foods, dependent upon the favor of youngsters, were the heaviest underwriters of children's radio drama.) It was a difficult adjustment for Annie and, even with her orphan's outlook which forced her to make the best of whatever life offered, her natural pesky aggressiveness would not allow her to be nudged from center stage for long . . . especially by a man. The program did not last, and Annie disappeared from radio, never to be heard again. No doubt the radio Orphan Annie can still be found, though, continuing her surveillances behind parked autos somewhere in the twilight of mid-America.

The hero Ovaltine chose to replace Annie was not only well out of his teens, he was certainly past 40. From the very first sound of the midnight bell followed by roaring airplane engine, which heralded each show, *Captain Midnight* promised "strange and exciting dangerous adventures—adventures that will lead us to all parts of the world." And to help us "understand" the captain's origins (he was an original creation of the Ovaltine ad agency, but later also appeared in a successful series of comic books), the first program provided an elaborate prologue, which took listeners

324

back to a battered Allied position during World War I, where an entrenched battalion, "at the moment of greatest peril," was saved from surrender by "the courage of one man." In the flickering darkness of a dugout, an Allied general addresses a young captain whose name he does not know—and makes a point of not asking. The aviator's mission is grave: "If you succeed tonight, you will have started a long and dangerous task—which, if you live, may require you a lifetime to complete." The general has deliberately kept the dugout dark, so he cannot even see the young man's face. "Your ultimate Purpose is the extermination of the most rascally and dangerous criminal in the world—a traitor to the United States—a fiend who has caused the fall of a thousand of your countrymen. I am speaking of the one known as Ivan Shark."

That first clash between Midnight and Shark—a villain so gigantic in melodramatic evil that he ranks with Fu Manchu and Mabuse, and certainly one of the greatest villains created expressly for radio—was played off-mike. We only hear the young captain's vow: "If I've not returned by twelve o'clock ... you'll know I've failed." Flash forward to the witching hour. We hear a bell-tower strike 12 times—and the motor of a returning plane. The Allied armies are saved! The general bursts into an emotional tribute to his airborne warrior, inspired by the striking clock: "To me—he shall always be—Captain *Midnight*!"

End of episode one ("Goodbye ... and *happy landing!*"). By the second show, the time has advanced 20 years. The captain is about to retire, but the nation is in trouble. Ivan Shark has been downed but not finished. He is out to destroy America. The only way to fight him is set up a series of secret squadrons in counterattack, each squadron strategically placed across the country, each knowing the identity only of its own commander, and the location and identity of all squadrons known only to a single unnamed leader. Would the captain take on the task of being this overall commander? He does not hesitate: "I have only one desire—to serve my country." He is immediately sworn in:

> With full realization that death may be my lot, and while life in me lasts, I pledge allegiance to the cause I have espoused. I solemnly swear to save my country from the dire peril it faces, or die in the attempt, and this oath I swear in the name of my country and *the Secret Squadron*!

The oath was taken in 1940. The captain would then have been well into his forties.

To compensate for the fact that he was already his middle years, no doubt, Midnight chose as his closest Secret Squadron lieutenants a "Betty-and-Bob" team of young associates in their teens, the kind with which many radio adventure heroes seemed to be most comfortable in sharing danger—in this case they were named Chuck Ramsey and Joyce Ryan. (Not that Midnight was portrayed as at all doddering—his voice was vigorous and muscular, seemingly equal to anything, and the challenges he took on might have fazed an Olympic athlete. But one noted occasionally that he appreciated the keenness of youth: "Thank Heaven for your sharp eyes," he remarked to Joyce more than once.) Also high in the Squadron ranks, perhaps mainly for laughs, was a coarse mechanic named Ichabod "Icky" Mudd. This quartet, carrying the numbers *one*-to-*four* in an ultrasecret paramilitary flying force whose members and groupings were unknown to one another, faced an incredible array of wartime enemies in every part of Occupied Europe as well as, every once and so often, that most diabolical of all villains, the hissing and sneering (and quite indestructible) Ivan Shark.

Midnight's adventures were extremely well written, but it was more than narrative that hooked the show's large youth audience: Ovaltine used the captain to hawk a brilliant series of superpremiums. The most unforgettable was the Code-O-Graph, "a complete code-building machine," made indispensable because each show finished with a coded sentence giving either a clue to the next day's happenings or cheerful advice on what made Midnight strong (double-chocolaty Ovaltine, of course). Not only did the decoder look sturdy and official, its cryptology was really quite complex—especially in a day when the Captain Marvel Club code, for example, was merely the alphabet reversed. Any enemy agent could break *that*! Every year a new code badge was issued, either to make room for an additional feature, such as a mirror for signaling, or because the old cipher had fallen into Ivan Shark's hands; whatever the reason, sending Ovaltine seals to Chicago became an annual mailing. There were other premiums as well: a plane-identifier, a very military-issue-looking Captain Midnight Shake-Up Mug, telescopic spy-scopes, maps to follow special adventures—such as when the captain fought Ivan on a "lost" island filled with prehistoric beasts. With Midnight, one somehow felt a part of a dedicated and noble cause.

The *Captain Midnight* program lasted for more than a decade (far longer than the Fawcett comic book based on him), with the determined captain pursuing Shark from war to peace. Rugged as he was, though, the aviator ultimately came up against some kind of Secret Squadron mandatory retirement rule, and the radio series came to an end. Some years later Ovaltine revived the captain and Icky for a brief series of TV half-hours. When, afterward, the show was placed into syndication without the milk fortifier's sponsorship, Midnight's name was changed (through dubbing) and the show was retitled *Jet Jackson*. Still later, a surprisingly youthful, crash-helmet-wearing Captain Midnight, perched in the cockpit of a fighter jet and pushing his favorite milk drink, was spliced to the head of a television revival of Republic serial chapters. But it was an end for the captain. The midnight bell tolled no more for him.

Even though flying was romantic in the thirties and forties, few aviators of the comic pages mapped new terrain on radio. To be sure, heroes who were not professional pilots—such as the radio Clark Kent and Dick Tracy—could, when circumstances warranted it, take over the controls of a plane with ease, and young Terry practically learned how to fly over pirate waters while on the air.

Hop Harrigan, "America's Ace of the Airways" (*crackle of filter: "CX-4 calling control tower. CX-4 calling control tower. Standing by. Okay, this is Hop Harrigan, coming in!"*), after some wartime flying adventures, settled down with his buddy Tank Tinker to the routine excitements of small American airports: mail heists, spies, flying serum, etc. Hop's greatest single achievement was dangling from the wing of his plane in one episode (a situation in which he also found himself in the Columbia movie serial fashioned from his adventures), but planes soon became faster and Hop couldn't do that any more. Indeed, despite his appearances as a secondary character in the Superman-DC comics lineup, Hop declined after the war years . . . just as small-plane pilots and mom-and-pop landing fields seemed to vanish in the face of giant jetliners and monster airports.

Don Winslow, although a Navy man (he made the transition from newspaper strip to radio in the late thirties), logged as much flying time as, say, Captain Midnight. Don was similarly a jingoistic military hero—although with a grown-up girl pal, Mercedes Colby, the daughter of the admiral, reflecting an interest in the opposite sex which Captain Midnight *never* indulged—and he defended his nation against a series of equally colorful villains, especially the particularly menacing international spy called the Scorpion.

One of the most popular of all newspaper-comics pilots crashed badly in his radio landing. Zack Mosley's *Smilin' Jack* was given a faithful rendering on the air in the late thirties (*crackle of filter: "Smilin' Jack . . . coming in on runway number one!"*), but even though he engaged in such commendable tasks as tracking down a mystery criminal known as the Voice (bent on stealing plans for "a new Army gun") the program was not popular. Many of the strip's familiar illustrative ploys simply could not translate to the other medium: one thing no radio actor could portray was a *smile*; no sound department, however skilled, could mimic in audio terms the buttons popping from Fat Stuff's bulging shirts, and the pursuing chickens which caught the buttons open-mouthed (although, to give the show the credit due, its sound-effects men *did try*); on radio, you never got to see Downwind Jackson's always-turned-away, always-hidden face *anyway*. The one thing the radio show carried over successfully from the comic strip was, unfortunately, Jack's love life—romantic entanglements with Dixie and with Mary, etc., about which most youngsters could not care less. This tender hangar encounter occurs after Jack has finished a long, grueling flight from "Michigan City"—such locations gave a sense of geography to the aviation shows:

> *Mary:* Jack, darling! . . . Oh, Jack, you're hurting me . . .
> *Jack:* Did you miss me, honey?
> *Mary:* You *know* I did! But you're going to stay here now, aren't you, dear?
> *Jack:* Sure! . . . Except for—
> *Mary:* Yes?
> *Jack:* Well, it's been arranged for me to give some flying lessons to someone . . .
> *Mary:* Flying lessons? To a *girl?*

Of course the girl is a secret operative; Jack has fallen in with the government in his efforts to stop the Voice. And when the girl, a stunner, arrives and gives Jack the code line by which he is to identify her—"Remember last night in St. Louis?"—Mary, overhearing her, gets entirely the wrong idea. It was this sort of love mush that turned off kids and prevented the radio Smilin' Jack from getting off the ground.

(When Smilin' Jack finally appeared in a movie serial—well played by Tom Brown—he changed, and hardly paid attention to women at all: he never suspected that the girl reporter who tagged along on his flights to Hong Kong and Pearl Harbor was actually *Fraulein Von Teufel*—"of the Devil" in translation—the Nazis' leading lady spy.)

Jack Armstrong was not a pilot by profession, but he flew light planes fairly well, and wanted you to fly as well! One of his best premiums was the control panel to a small aircraft, with a throttle stick for you to manipulate and a viewing screen above the controls where a miniature plane dangled—using it you could bank and climb and even nosedive just as though you were piloting your own craft. The entire kit, with the exception of the thread on which your robot airplane was suspended—that you had to take from your mother's sewing kit—was yours for a Wheaties' boxtop ("*Have you TRIED Wheaties, they're whole wheat with all of the bran . . .* "), and was, along with such other serious, no-nonsense premiums as pedometers and bombsights, typical of earnest Jack's educational zeal. He hardly *ever* smiled. Jack was monotonously superior . . . even Lenny Bruce once gasped in awe, "People were always laying great things on him, like expensive skis, and he puts on the damn skis and goes down the hill like a champion!"

Jack and his adoring pals Billy and Betty Fairfield, and their Uncle Jim, who adored him equally, traveled to all of the faraway places on the globe—like a *National Geographic* subscription come to audio life. Impressively educational, they could spend a whole episode floating down a jungle river, describing all the flora and fauna they passed, without a melodramatic thing happening, and yet you were still intrigued with their conversation and life-style. Jack, for some of his radio span, competed with—on another network—Chick Carter, the boy detective and adopted offspring of the famed and enduring Nick Carter. Chick was bang-bang all the way and beat up mystery villain after mystery villain. Jack Armstrong outlived him.

True, Jack in his later radio years underwent a subtle change in writers and policy. Uncle Jim went into retirement, and Jack took up with a onetime but very much reformed criminal named Vic Hardy, now heading (FBI, take note!) that secret governmental agency, the Scientific Bureau of Investigation. At once the program, which had been exploration-oriented, turned to crime. One of the first of the new dramas had Jack and friends looking for a missing man *whom the government wanted* at a snowbound ski lodge. Each show's opening narrative took pains to point out the slowly melting snowman standing in front of the lodge. Naturally, by the last episode, it came as no surprise that the missing man was dead, his body buried inside the snowman. The older Jack Armstrong program would have substituted for the corpse a lecture on the physical phenomenon of freezing.

(Jack, who was billed as "the All-American Boy" and had a healthy radio span of some 14 years, became, rather late in life, a comic-book hero as well, with most of the educational virtues of his show intact, no doubt at the behest of his publishers, the anemic Parents' Magazine group. Precisely these virtues—which had stood him so well for so long—did him in, and the comic book lasted only a dozen or so issues.)

Actually, radioland heroes, by and large, were a pretty straight bunch of guys, with Jack Armstrong not at all too far over the line. As a matter of fact, the very last comic-strip adventurer to clear a path to radio, Mark Trail (*cried the opening: Guardian of the forests! Protector of wildlife! Champion of man and nature!*), was very similar to Jack in that both endorsed the healthy outdoor life; Jack, though slightly younger than Mark, would certainly have agreed with the latter's conservationist outlook. However, although Mark's moral fiber was every bit as strong as any radio hero's, his spine was not quite so stiff as Jack's. Which was understandable, because in Mark Trail's day it was already the twilight of the gods for radio.

Because of the nature of his job, Mark stayed fairly close to the American wilderness, but earlier, during the Golden Age of radio adventure, the direction its heroes traveled was often eastward. Few bothered with the jaded capitals of Europe, although, among others, Captain Midnight spent some time during the war aiding the European underground and freeing himself from Axis prisons. Still, the lure was to Asia, with Africa in second place. (Of course, Tarzan—"*the bronzed, light son of the jungle*" who was the subject of two radio series and was played in the first by Edgar Rice Burroughs's son-in-law—grew up in Africa, "*land of enchantment, mystery and violence*" . . . and ominous drumbeats. Jack Armstrong made at least two lengthy treks to various parts of the Dark Continent.)

Don Winslow and his Navy buddy Red Pennington—*each show*

started with the hearty strains of "Columbia, the Gem of the Ocean"—dropped anchor at many an Asian port.

Captain Silver on his schooner, *The Sea Hound* (which lent its name not only to the radio show but was the title of a movie serial and comic book as well), sailed to the same Pacific areas, but as a civilian.

Terry encountered his first pirates on the Yangtze River (*each show started with a reverberating gong bleeding into excited chatter in "Chinese"*) while a footloose kid journeying through China with older adventurer Pat Ryan. (It is interesting to note that the same actors who first portrayed Pat and Terry Lee later became Clark Kent and Jimmy Olsen on *Superman*—Clayton "Bud" Collyer and Jackie Kelk.) As the years went on—following the lead of the newspaper strip—the radio Terry grew some, parted company with Pat, and earned his wings. Becoming pals with such Air Force types as Hotshot Charlie and Flip Corkin, he did quite a bit of his flying over the Burma Road. The lure of the Orient—from high Tibetan fastnesses to South Pacific coastlines and atolls—was compelling to the radio adventurers of the thirties and forties. And Eastern mysticism was a heavy influence, as well, on the radio magicians.

Foremost among these wizards was Chandu the Magician, actually Frank Chandler to the Occidental world, who became the first white yogi after taking study courses at one of those secret monastaries that surely influenced the later *Lost Horizon*. Chandu spent most of his radio hours, surprisingly, in the company of his sister and her teenaged children, a Betty-and-Bob twosome, and did a lot of traveling in the East, but the settings the shows presented were so vividly authentic one was almost *transported* to the crowded bazaars, the cold nights out on the desert.

In one especially memorable program, Chandu's sister and her offspring are in an occult temple looking at a painting of ancient Atlantis. They are hypnotically swept back into the streets of the city in the last moments before catastrophe strikes. The show's excellent narrative power makes the horror mount before our friends are pulled out of the trance; it was a weird feeling that radio—as we shuddered and listened—was superbly equipped to convey. Alas, Chandu—although he had two successful radio series, and starred in both a fantastic feature film and a campy movie serial—never crossed over to the comics.

Other radio magicians were more vaudeville- than yoga-trained.

Both Blackstone and Thurston had early shows (as well as their own comic-book appearances), solving spook mysteries and exposing an unending supply of fake mediums while effortlessly performing their tricks—for on radio the hand need *not* be quicker than the eye. The best of the stage magicians to move from the comic strips into the radio line of work was Lee Falk's dashing Mandrake . . . no mere sleight-of-hand artist (though he accepted theatrical engagements at times, mainly charitable) but a master of occult powers.

"*Invoco legem magiciarum,*" Mandrake would shout at the start of each program, invoking in Latin "the law of magic" as a sort of audio substitution for his well-known hypnotic gestures. In his first show (some five years after his newspaper debut) Mandrake was to be found in his "house of mystery and many secrets," staring dreamily at the dancing flames in the fireplace, the giant Lothar by his side. Naturally the magician is working himself into a semitrance: he sees in the fire the most beautiful face in all the world, a crown of jewels on her head—his beloved, the Princess Narda. (It is an interesting historical footnote that Chandu the Magician, who predated Mandrake by a few years, often pined for a Princess *Nadji*, who was a member of the Royal House of Egypt—though he mostly passed the time with Sis.) Mandrake stirs from his reverie to announce that someone is at the door. Lothar thinks otherwise, and in the following exchange demonstrates the incredulity of all servants, especially those who were giant and black, in the radio thirties:

> *Lothar:* How Master see all this? Many times have seen Master do great tricks of magic—suspend lady in air—cut lady in two and stick together again good as new—make fire come from mouth— but never before Master see through solid wall! Black magic?
> *Mandrake:* No, white magic. Only the forces of evil deal in black magic. Come, look over my shoulder at this tabletop and tell me what you see.

While Lothar seems remarkably easy to mystify, Mandrake does have a good trick to show: a small television-receiver set in the table, one of his home's many "secrets." Together they screen their caller, who is standing outside and nervously tugging at a concealed gun. *"Quick, in the mummy case, Lothar! Use the chute to the crypt beneath the trapdoor in the center hall! I shall talk to our friend inside this armored knight!"*

Events happen with sickening swiftness to the gunman outside.

The door opens and locks behind him, an invisible Mandrake taunts him, he teeters at the brink of a trap where below—a chilling sight—a murderous African giant awaits him with wide-open arms. Mandrake's voice provides introductions: another step and he would have fallen "into the waiting arms of Lothar— Lothar, whom I've seen rip a crocodile's jaws apart, break the back of an anthropoid ape!" Don't mess with Mandrake!

Terrified and now quite docile, the gunman is directed into the library, where Mandrake shows himself. All charm, the magician offers the gunman a drink, but the glass he gives him is empty.

> *Mandrake:* Watch the glass in your hand. Watch it carefully.
> *Gunman:* Blast my eyes if this glass ain't gone and filled itself to the brim with *ginger ale*!
> *Mandrake:* So it has. Try it. You'll find it quite refreshing.

The affable Mandrake next tells his visitor to find "an excellent Perfecto in your vest pocket," but the man, whose name is Borg, pulls out a revolver instead. *"When did you last see the Princess Narda?!"* Mandrake is perplexed; he thought Narda to be across the ocean. But no, the telephone rings, and we hear the princess herself: *"I've come from the other side of the world to ask your help! I need you so desperately!"* Mandrake rings off quickly before the girl can reveal her whereabouts; then, gesturing hypnotically, he forces Borg to drop his gun—the intruder groans, completely paralyzed. Suddenly, something is hurled through the window— an explosive device! *"Invoco legem magiciarum . . . !"*

Those who lived during the Depression thirties, having experienced their fill of hard times, had a leaning towards the irrational and the mystical, so the radio magicians had their day. But, because their occult trickery was too often visual in a medium without sight, they soon vanished. (Magicians did not dominate the comics either, but were a subtheme of some endurance.) Far more interesting a literary area which the comics explored, followed by radio, was science fiction.

As early as 1931 Buck Rogers—whose newspaper adventures were then two years old—tried his luck on radio, and the futuristic series, closely copying the incidents and characters of the parent strip, was popular, enduring nearly the full decade. Particularly effective was cackling, genial old Doctor Huer and his incredible inventions. The very first episode has Buck acting as guinea pig to instruments that picture his memory images on a screen which

Doc and Wilma are watching, thus both demonstrating the thirties' prophetic preoccupation with television devices and providing a handy sum-up of how Buck first got to the twenty-fifth century. (Escaping gas from a mine shaft had put him into suspended animation for 500 years, and he awakens in a world plundered by futuristic criminal gangs.) These tele-reminiscences are interrupted by an attack by Killer Kane, and the radio series is off and running ... from dangers at Niagara City to interplanetary adventures on Mars and the moons of Saturn, and even a quick visit down to Atlantis.

It is now a legendary story that parents' groups protested the many times Buck and Wilma Deering were isolated in situations alone, completely without the supervision then thought necessary under such circumstances ... especially since Buck, a fellow not without feelings, often had a kind word or two for his lovely lady pilot. Naturally the show's producers were quick to stifle even the possibility of impropriety, but it is interesting to reflect that this was the only radio adventure program so attacked. Buck's audience was paying *attention*—despite the fantastic settings, the show's hero and heroine were believable and human.

In contrast, countless Betty-and-Bob teams spent hours and even nights in shacks and caves without parental guidance on radio and without subsequent parental complaint from the audience. Captain Midnight logged quite a few solo adventures with adolescent Joyce—in canoes, planes, behind enemy lines—exploiting no more than her vigor and keen young eyes, but without a chaperone. Lamont Cranston and Margot Lane went away on long weekends together for *years* (generally to haunted houses and such), with no one saying a word; Margot's knowledge that Cranston was also the Shadow appeared to be not the only secret they shared. Batman and Robin's close, worshipful friendship went completely unquestioned until the accusation by psychiatrist Fredric Wertham made them more cautious.

Of all the radio adventurers, only Buck Rogers ran against public outcry. It was not that the others were less real, it was perhaps only that this show braked the excitement occasionally to try and build meaningful dialog (and relationships) between people, between Rogers and his friends. It's nice to think that Buck, who was, after all, from a small Pennsylvania mining town, was a vital, likeable, aggressive guy around whom a good-looking, interesting girl—even one of the liberated ladies of A.D. 2400—

might find herself in danger. Killer *Buck*.

Flash Gordon tried being romantic, too, but on radio he was a bust. Flash, "internationally famous American athlete and his beautiful American sweetheart, Dale Arden," made it to the airways soon after their newspaper strip debut in late 1934. But much of Alex Raymond's illustrative majesty was just untranslatable. An attempt to imitate the great artist's no-balloons narrative paragraphs by giving an announcer long descriptive sentences to read, often about major action highlights, was a poor substitution for drama. The lead characters (a young Gale Gordon played Flash) were curiously lifeless and some were badly chosen: Dr Zarkov is portrayed as having a hideously thick, harsh accent, not at all the friendlier fellow of the movie serial a year later.

The people of Mongo (understandably) speak English with an accent as well. Princess Aura (the thirties were *big* on royal females) commands Flash to "marry me and the empire is yours, and your friends go free" in a voice, alternately snarling and purring, that sounds very Chinese. Naturally, Aura being of the daughter-of-the-dragon school, much of her conversation with the American athlete bordered either on open lust or on sexually motivated vengeance:

> *Aura:* You shall *never* marry the Earth girl, Dale Arden!
> *Flash:* My dear Princess, if I must make a choice, I choose Dale and death!
> *Dale:* You've signed our death warrant, Flash, but I don't care—as long as we are together.
> *Flash:* I'm glad, Dale. That's just how I feel, too!

The radio program honed very closely to the early newspaper continuity, following Flash as he rockets to Mongo and clashes with Emperor Ming. (*"The Amazing Interplanetary Adventures of Flash Gordon," each show began to sweeping Wagnerian music, with plenty of urging to find Flash as well in the Hearst papers' "36-page" Sunday comics section.*)

Alas, it did not do justice to Alex Raymond's space epic. For instance, Flash's heroic sabotage of the radium furnaces of the Hawkmen's Sky City, suspended by rays high in the air—one of the highpoints of the strip's first year—is reduced on the radio to a sequence lasting only a moment or two, most of it announcer's narration. In the next moment Flash interrupts King Vultan's hasty marriage plans with Dale, striking him a blow that "would have killed an ordinary man" but merely knocks the Hawkmen's winged ruler unconscious.

> *Dale:* Oh, my darling ... I feel so safe in your arms. They are so strong and yet so tender.
> *Flash:* These arms were *meant* to hold you and protect you and by Heaven they *will*, as long as I have life!
> *Dale:* My dear ...

Flash Gordon's radio adventures didn't last long.

By far the most towering science-fictional radio-adventure hero to originate from the comics was Superman, as powerful in his radio format as he was in magazines. By 1940 the Golden Age of air drama was in full swing, and the exploits of the being from Krypton were given loving, expert care ... treatment which paid off. No doubt also because Clark Kent's amazing abilities were such rich food for the imagination, the series lasted and was popular.

Clayton "Bud" Collyer was superb as the mild-mannered *Daily Planet* reporter, actually an orphan from another world. When muttering to himself a phrase like, "This looks like a job *for Superman*," dipping his voice from its normal tenor to a muscular basso, he gave us a perfect audio substitute for the phonebooth costume-changes of the comics pages. Nothing else was needed to telegraph this transformation, and when followed, as was usual, by the cry, "Up, up, and away!" and a rush of wind, audiences across the country conjured mental images of a red-and-blue-costumed Superman hurtling through the heavens.

Woman reporter Lois Lane, openly derisive of her timid co-worker Clark but a good girl to have around when there was trouble, was portrayed clear-voiced and spirited by the marvelous Joan Alexander, who earlier each afternoon impersonated another feminist heroine, Della Street of the *Perry Mason* radio serial. (Perry also served duty for a brief time as a newspaper strip.)

One can judge the level of quality of the *Superman* show when one realizes it had the absolute *luxury* of two announcers: one (generally Dan McCullough) giving a bright, hearty pitch for the sponsoring Kellogg's cereal and its many right-on premiums (such as aircraft-spotters and ready-to-assemble walkie-talkies which, if your friends sent away too and hooked them all together, would provide a "marvelously effective communications system"); the other (deep-voiced Jackson Beck), as narrator, ominously setting the stage for each new episode.

At the start of the program each day, the two voices, chanting in a rising fever of excitement, joined in a melodramatic duet that has become immortal:

McCullough: Kellogg's Pep—the super delicious cereal—presents:
Beck: The Adventures of Superman! Faster than a speeding bullet! ... (*Sound of shot*) More powerful than a locomotive! ... (*Sound of train*) Able to leap tall buildings at a single bound! ... (*Jet of wind, whistling up and under*) Look! Up in the sky!
Voice: It's a bird!
Voice: It's a plane!
Beck: It's Superman!

Without a stroke of music, with just that mix of dynamic sounds and especially the streaking wind, it made an indelible opening impression. Occasionally the voices varied—in the early years a woman (Miss Alexander) shouted "It's a plane," but that became too awkward on days when the script didn't call for a woman's part, so a male voice was substituted—but this opening was standard and Olympian. When Paramount's Max Fleisher produced a series of *Superman* cartoon shorts for theaters in the early forties, he animated the radio opening exactly. Even to this day, trivialists recite the litany with awe, not even wondering about the easily impressed fellow who was driven to awestruck shouting by what he presumed to be a bird.

Although his origins were interplanetary, Superman's earthly adventures were mostly mundane. There were plenty of gangsters; crime in Metropolis was rampant. (Narrator Beck often doubled as gravelly voiced gunmen, and occasionally had a running part as frog-voiced Beanie, the *Daily Planet*'s office boy, whose status seemed even below Jimmy Olsen's.) But the excitement always ran high. To demonstrate, and as proof that the show's inventiveness never flagged, let us examine some of the various problems Superman faced during the first half-dozen months of 1945, fully five years after the show's birth.

Supe started the year with a trip to South America to wipe out a Japanese battalion secreted there in headhunter country. Immediately afterwards, escaping gas ignites in a "space shell" invented by Perry White's eccentric, rhyming cook Poko and the missile, with Poko and young Jimmy Olsen trapped aboard, blasts off through the roof of a barn outside Metropolis and hurtles to a landing somewhere near the North Pole. They are discovered by a pair of friendly—and English-speaking—teenaged Eskimos, whose entire village has been enslaved by vicious Nazis who have established a secret Arctic base. Superman, flying north in an effort to locate the space shell, spots a Coast Guard cutter sinking in the seas above Iceland, and rescues the ship with his bare hands. It is of course the Nazis' design to use explosive-filled icebergs to destroy U.S. ships, a plan which the Man of Steel scuttles.

The next adventure is a classic: the intrusion of Batman. Dick Grayson is found unconscious in a small boat floating in Metropolis Bay, and Superman divines that he is the Caped Crusader's young partner Robin, The boy confides in anxious tones that Batman has disappeared from "our cottage"; that gangsters have fired shots at him. It is a chilling moment later when the two new friends discover Batman—a wax dummy in a store window! It seems he has been hypnotized and glazed as part of an evil plot to ship America's best minds abroad as waxworks; happily the process is not fatal.

After Superman melts that scheme, he learns from office-boy Beanie's older brother, a wounded war veteran named Joe, that Beanie and Jimmy Olsen have been kidnaped after playing around with some screws that have a base of pure gold! (In this exploit nearly all the characters get to use the cardboard walkie-talkie that figures as a premium.) After the crooks who have captured Jimmy and Beanie nearly drown the two boys in a car hurtling into a river, the scene shifts to Montreal, when Jimmy and Lois Lane—forever snooping—nearly suffocate when the bad guys lock them in a mausoleum. Ever-vigilant Superman is the rescuer each time and he learns that the gold-thief villain has designs on Fort Knox (anticipating Goldfinger's similar scheme).

In the next adventures Superman saves a boy king from assassins, then unmasks a Japanese secret weapon, then saves Lois from an escaped convict in a flood-stricken town, then clashes with the Man Without a Face, then is weakened by a Kryptonite stone from which the immune Batman saves him. No bird or plane could possibly cover so many feats of action and excitement: these certainly were jobs for Superman—on radio as compelling a costumed hero as ever he was in print.

Few of these treasured programs still exist today, but a fascimile manages to continue somewhat the greatness of the old series. Bud Collyer, Joan Alexander, and Jackson Beck lent their voices to the recent animated *Superman* cartoons made for television, assuming their old roles and, while these short playettes can hardly approach the charm and vigor of their radio cliffhanger predecessors, one could close one's eyes and have those voices stir the memory . . . and be thankful that there were still jobs around for Superman. Bud Collyer's death shortly after dubbing his parts was a sad reminder that even men of steel are mortal.

Considering the rich variety of source material, surprisingly few costumed heroes from the comics joined Superman on radio. Not even Batman was to have a radio show of his own: his triumph on television came in a later epoch.

Some bright-costumed figures tried hard, though. The Blue Beetle started each show, amid police whistles and organ sirens, with this overwhelming exposition: *"The Blue Beetle—Sweeping down upon the underworld to smash gangland comes a mysterious all-powerful character who is a problem to the police but a crusader for law—in reality Dan Garrett, a rookie patrolman, loved by everyone but suspected by none of being the Blue Beetle! As the Blue Beetle he hides behind a strange mask and a suit of inpenetrable blue-stained armor, flexible as silk but stronger than steel!"* Unfortunately, his adventures often generated less excitement than this heavy introduction, and Beetle expired after a brief radio lifespan in the early forties. Interestingly, he carefully avoided victimless crimes: a mere case of missing jewels was "out of the Blue Beetle's line; no unfortunate individual is involved."

Another cop with a spare secret uniform was the Black Hood (*"Criminals beware, the Black Hood is everywhere!"*), who started each of his programs by snarling a vow in his heaviest New Centurion style: *"I, the Black Hood, do solemnly swear that neither threats nor bribes nor bullets nor death itself shall keep me from fulfilling my vow to erase crime from the face of the earth!"* The show, in both writing and acting, was a cut above average—the playful interlude in which Hood and his girl laughingly toy with a voodoo ring ("Abra cadabra! Alikazam! Make a wish, boots skit a-rattrap! Sca-*ram!*") is an example of its refreshing style—but the premise, derived from its comic-book origin, adhered closely to radio conventions: "The Black Hood, who is really patrolman Kip Burland, a fact known only to newspaperwoman Barbara Sutton . . ."

The Avenger had a secret identity and costume of sorts, if you so count the invisibility that enveloped the Shadow, upon whom this crimefighter was largely based. (He did not have a comic book.) Actually famous chemist Jim Brandon, he had developed two remarkable aids for his war with the underworld: "a telepathic indicator, by which he is able to pick up thought flashes, and the secret diffusing capsule, which cloaks him in the black light of invisibility." Just like the Shadow, Jeff has a girl, "the beautiful Fern Collier," who is the only one who shares his secret, and he barks out a similar introductory challenge: *"The road to crime ends in a trap which Justice sets! Crime does not pay!"* Not enough for the Avenger, apparently, for he soon dropped his radio career and returned to biochemistry. Some of the puzzles he solved while crimefighting were quite ingenious.

One young radio crimefighter wore a prep school uniform. Dick Cole of Barr Military Academy started each adventure with a rousing chorus of his school song (*"As we travel through life / We'll follow our star / We'll always be near to Barr"*), followed by an announcer's reminder that "you've known Dick Cole in *Blue Bolt* magazine and *Foremost Comics* for a long time." Dick, a Frank Merriwell updating with the same impossibly noble stance, still made for interesting listening as he and his devoted roommate Simba got themselves involved in platonic girl trouble (extricating themselves necessitated dressing an underclassmate in drag), or participated in war games or class plays, or poked around in haunted houses (the sort of ghostly buildings that invariably were the refuge of crooks determined to scare away intruders). Generally, though, Dick's villains were of a tramps-and-gypsies level of heinousness.

The comic-strip cop who lasted the longest on radio was that most legendary of policemen, Dick Tracy. Unlike the Republic movie serials, which hardly borrowed anything beyond Dick himself from Chester Gould's original, the radio series surrounded the square-jawed investigator with all his old newspaper friends: Tess Trueheart, Pat Patton, Chief Brandon, and the inevitable Junior. But the character best realized from the strip itself was the Shakespearean thespian Vitamin Flintheart, Tracy's friend who often found himself on the perimeter of crime. Sounding every bit like an outraged Jack Barrymore, with any time a good time for flamboyant oratory, Vitamin warmed every episode in which he appeared.

Like its strip source, the radio series—which began in 1935 and in various forms lasted a decade—had its share of grotesque villains, and portrayed Dick's use of police tools in his war against crime with almost documentary vigor. (Each show started with Tracy identifying himself through a crackling police radio, reporting the name of his current case, and barking *"Let's go, men!"* He was "the protector of law and order," and he worked with a top *team.*) So high was the thirties' sense of police realism that you knew, if a rookie cop announced proudly that his wife had just given birth, he would be killed by a hail of gangland bullets in the next few minutes. And you knew, too, that everything would come out *bizarre.*

Like the time Tracy and a prison warden wait grimly in the warden's office for a notorious criminal to be executed, a criminal who has shouted that no electric chair could ever kill him. The lights flicker momentarily . . . and then again . . . and an assistant rushes to the warden with the news that the electrified criminal has broken free from the chair and is rampant! A chilling moment in a fine action series.

(The current decline in America of the electric chair and of executions in general makes it hard to believe how many of radio's condemned criminals managed to "cheat" death devices. Nearly all of the crime shows had an episode where some drug or suspended animation potion—smuggled into the prison, often by quite fanciful means—would allow one to survive the electric chair's voltage. These restoratives were erratic, though; generally their subjects came back to us quite mad and only briefly. In one such drama a scientist began reviving excuted criminals in wholesale lots, but there were variants to the theme. In one *Shadow* adventure, a condemned murderer threatening to "come back" had already been spotted in two places at the same time before his arrest. When, after his execution, he is seen again, it doesn't take too much brilliance for the alert listener to suspect he was one of twins.)

Crime often went West as well. Bobby Benson and his B-Bar-B Ranch pals solved as many cactus mysteries on the air as they ever did in their comic book. Tom Mix handled everything from rustlers to Japanese spies on his spread; he was one of a very special group of real people who have inspired both radio adventure shows and comic magazines. Roy Rogers and Gene Autry on the air did everything their print counterparts did, and sang besides.

The most renowned of all the western radio heroes, however, unlike Roy and Tom and Gene and Bobby, was deliberately set in a harsh pioneer period past. *"Return with us now to those thrilling days of yesteryear . . . "* The monastic Masked Rider of the Plains, the Lone Ranger, allowed nothing to distract him from a humorless, impassioned defense of law and order. Fran Striker's great radio creation became an extremely successful comic-book and newspaper-strip series, and, as well, generated an intriguing spin-off: his grand-nephew Britt Reid, as the masked Green Hornet, carried the family's crimefighting traditions into the urban centers of today and into his own comic-book line as well as his own radio show. Both Britt and his uncle made it to television, as well.

"He hunts the bigest of all game . . . Public enemies . . . " So the legend swirled around the Green Hornet's sleek car, Black Beauty, racing through never-clogged night streets, but the champion challenger of crime was actually another cloaked figure—the shape known as the Shadow. At first just an identity-less voice from the shadows narrating murder stories ("Who knows what evil lurks in the hearts of men? *The Shadow knows!"*), with the stories borrowed from a Street and Smith Pulp magazine, the early program became so successful that it spawned a *Shadow* pulp of its own. Gradually the magazine narrator drew about himself a character of his own, a cloaked crimefighter who began to intrude personally on his narratives, in a shadowy war against evil.

He had many civilian identities: *one* of several was that of millionaire Lamont Cranston. By the mid-thirties Lamont was fully established as the Shadow's radio alter-ego. (Orson Welles was one of the early portrayers, with Agnes Moorhead at his side as Margot Lane, but for most of us clinging to the radio on Sunday afternoons while growing up, Brett Morrison, who played him for more than a decade, was the *real* Lamont.)

The Shadow earned his name in the pulp series, written by "Maxwell Grant," mainly because he stayed out of the range of street lamps, but the radio show added one magnificent refinement. *"Several years ago in the Orient Cranston learned a strange and mysterious secret: the hypnotic power to cloud men's minds so they cannot see him."* Not just content with blending into the darkness as did the pulp Shadow, the radio version was *truly* unseen and, when we heard his voice cackling through a filter mike (*"The weed of crime bears bitter fruit!"*) we knew he was crime's invisible foe. A successful comic-book series adopted the radio format entirely, suggesting his invisibility by printing him, garbed in cloak and low-brimmed hat, in blue gravure. Being hypnotically unseen, however, the Shadow could actually wear *anything*.

Unquestionably the Shadow's adventures were the most grotesque on radio. Because of the closeness of her relationship to Lamont—at times her duties were vaguely secretarial, but the show's introduction stated explicitly she was "friend and companion"—Margot Lane was assaulted by maniacs on a nearly weekly basis. Horrors were piled on with heavy hand, as a sampling of episode titles can surely attest: "Hypnotic Death." "Death Is Blind." "Appointment with Death." "Guest of Death." "Traffic in Death." "The Voice of Death." "Seance with Death." "Murder from the Grave." "The Phantom Voice." "Prelude to Terror." The Shadow hardly ever pursued ordinary crooks, but plunged after twisted, bizarre madmen and monstrous fiends. It was not listening for the squeamish.

The *Shadow* stories were shot full of adrenalin. When, in an early, Orson Welles episode, the Shadow was pitted against "the Creeper," events were no more than typical: a mad fiend has kidnaped people and chained them down in the vast tunnel system where he lives, his motive being no more than a desire to end his own loneliness. After the standard-operational attack attempt on Margot, he thinks to blow up the cavern with everyone in it to avoid exposure, but the Shadow, by "projecting his voice" (a doubly neat trick for a man who's invisible) forces the Creeper to detonate himself only in an otherwise harmless section of underground. But, as this very routine plot moved to its climax, one could count so many shrieks, screams, hysterical threats, vows of vengeance, cries of "kill!", quivering pleas for mercy, maniacal laughter, villainous bravado, and attempts at murder, that the ashen listener found himself all over gooseflesh and palpitating heart. This is the nervous level on which the *Shadow* show remained through most of its two-decade radio life, subdued only slightly in its last years.

One *Shadow* adventure, because it had a comics theme, will be especially interesting to readers of this book. This was the radio episode called "The Comic Strip Killer." Several people have toppled over dead, always in stadiums and parks and crowded areas. They were injected with a barely traceable new poison. Lamont thinks the pattern of the murders resembles recent events in Jack Prescott's popular crime comic strip, featuring the evil-

343

faced Hypo, a killer-for-hire who has "traded the old-fashioned automatic for the modern hypodermic needle."

Lamont and Margot visit Prescott, who turns out to be mild-mannered and pleasant, but harried almost to the breaking point by his deadlines. The news that someone has taken his creature to heart and imitated him only strengthens Prescott's hope to "get out of crime comics," to get away from "monsters and ogres." The cartoonist reveals that he has gotten much of his up-to-the-minute research information about drugs from Dr. Murray Schumacher, a biochemist. But this is all the help he can give. As Lamont and Margot leave the studio, they are stopped by Prescott's gaunt handyman, Harry Borden, who was the physical model for Hypo. He warns them not to disturb the artist further. He is very sinister.

The next day Hypo strikes again—and this time the victim is Jack Prescott. Not killed, he is carried delirious to a hospital, moaning: "It's all my fault . . . I've created a monster with my pen who is spreading death in the streets . . . ! I'll never draw Hypo again . . . "

Margot visits Dr. Murray Schumacher, and finds him a strange bird indeed. Eccentric, crippled by asthma, the toxicologist gloats that "poison is one of the most interesting, beautiful things in the world. It kills the undesirables—and when the undesirable is eliminated there remains only beauty." While he tries to dig up a copy of his monograph, *Timetables for Death*, on how quickly different poisons take effect, the frightened girl takes the opportunity to leave.

Margot pays another visit to the cartoonist's studio, breaking in to look for old *Hypo* strips. The handyman Harry catches her and becomes hysterical. Margot suddenly realizes that Harry is the killer. "You modeled for Hypo—you began to think and act like him. And tried to *kill* like him!" Harry begins to throttle her.

Into the room steps Jack Prescott, who has somehow gotten out of the hospital. He is dazed . . . and begins to mutter maniacly. *He* is *Hypo*. "Notice how I move around the room—swiftly, noise-lessly, like Death itself." He attacks Harry, and is about to murder Margot when the invisible Shadow intervenes.

Later, Lamont explains that Harry's assault on Margot was his way of protecting his master: he had known all along that Prescott was the killer, and had even given him a mild dose of the poison in a desperate effort to end his reign of terror. Schumacher, with his crippling asthma, could scarcely have been the active, swift-striking Hypo. It had to have been Prescott, Cranston reasoned, victim of—and can the Shadow here be thinking of more than one comics artist?—an "overwrought imagination and exhausted brain."

The Shadow lasted until the middle fifties. I know, because in its final year, while I was still in high school, I submitted a script (based on a story created in collaboration with Charles Collins) to the program's producer, and to my surprise it was accepted. The script was broadcast as "Smuggler's Secret," and—upon sober reading today—is ample demonstration that radio was slipping into its twilight.

The setting: Chinatown. Lamont and Margot (always spoken as "Margo" on the air but for obscure phonetic reasons spelt otherwise) are there to meet famed Asian explorer and author George Randall. He steers them into a curio shop; he's clearly troubled.

Lamont: (Sharply) Margot! Look out that window—what do you see?
Margot: It's the black coupeé!
Lamont: The same car that was following George outside! Down, everyone!
Sound: (Scuffle, smashing of glass, three rifle shots. Margot screams.)

George is killed. Later his brother Ted confides a strange fear to Lamont.

Ted: Mr. Cranston, have you ever heard of the rGyal-po? *(Pronounced "REE-GEE-AL-PUH.")*
Lamont: No, I can't say that I have. Sounds Tibetan, though.
Ted: It is. Chinese Tibetan, at any rate. The rGyal-po was the king of fiends, one of the eight classes of Tibetan gods. Folklore has it that he's thoroughly evil, with all the black arts at his fingertips.
Margot: But what has this to do with George?
Ted: I'm coming to it. You see, this fearful god has a sort of cult—or organization—around him, composed of the most skilled and powerful sorcerers and necromancers. *(Pause)* I thing George had discovered a modern-day reincarnation of the cult of rGyal-po.
Margot: Why, that's crazy!

Not all that crazy, for right on cue a timely warning from the cult, tied to a stone, is hurled through the window. Still later, eager to follow any clues, Lamont as the Shadow visits the suspicious proprietor of the Chinatown curio shop where George met death.

The Shadow: (Weird Laugh)
Len Yo Choo: Who—who is it? Who is there?
The Shadow: It is I, Len Yo Choo . . . the voice of your ancestors.

Len Yo Choo: Where are you? I cannot see you!

The Shadow: Since when does one see the shade of one's fathers, condemned to remain earth-bound because of your sins!

When he thinks he is alone, the superstitious, terrified Chinaman phones a rundown waterfront hotel managed by one Wharf Annie, begging to talk to "the boss." Lamont, disguised as a seaman, gets a room at the hotel. But tough Wharf Annie tells her stooge she thinks she's recognized him.

Annie: Look! This picture in the true crime magazine!

Charlie: Say, without those rags he's wearing, it's a spitting image! What was he sent up for?

Annie: Don't be a fool, Charlie, he's no crook! It says: "Amateur Detective Exposes Spiritualist Racket." This bird's Lamont Cranston!

Lamont is knocked out, tied up, dropped in the ocean. Meanwhile, Margot returns to the curio shop by night just in time to witness Mr. Choo being shot.

Margot: Mr. Choo! He's dead!

Ted: In Asia, I was renowned for my marksmanship, Miss Lane.

Margot: Ted! Ted Randall! It's you! What—what are you going to do with—with that pistol?

Naturally the Shadow intervenes—Lamont had merely pretended to be knocked out back in the old hotel, and used the Houdini trick of tensing his legs so that he could wiggle out of his bonds later.

Margot: So Ted Randall was behind it all! I never suspected! *He* was the head of the cult of rGyal-po!

Lamont: There wasn't any cult! At least not in modern times. Ted invented that fantasy just to throw us off the track—steering us away from his real activity.

Margot: Which was?

Lamont: It seems that while Ted was in the Orient, he started a side business—smuggling drugs from China . . .

A few months after this script was broadcast, the Shadow—radio's oldest and most venerable cloaked adventurer—ceased operations, and I, full of misguided pride and innocence, did not realize *my* contribution to his demise. Actually, however, it took more than bad scripts; the world itself was changing. High-intensity street lamps, the new architecture of square-glass city blocks and high-rise buildings, were making it impossible for the Shadow to lurk anywhere except in the hearts of men.

All of radio was vanishing, the afternoon adventure programs giving up the ghost in the face of the endlessly rerun features and movie-serial chapters provided on early television matinees. Radio, once so energetic and loved, crawled into a corner, confined itself to piping out music and news to be listened to in cars. Senility set in. Worse yet, nothing of its golden past had been adequately documented or even preserved. Its programs, its great moments, the social history of a nation, were gone, swept into studio trash bins, in large part not saved. Not only had an era ended, it had buried itself.

All this was lost to me; as a child growing up to the blood-and-thunder of adventure radio I thought its thrills would never end. Like ghosts, some shows—*The Shadow, The Lone Ranger,* and *The Green Hornet* among them—are occasionally revived, but they are presented as antiques and curiosities with no more vitality than a rerun. And, alas, so few of the old shows were preserved that these revivals can be nothing more than tokens of the past. Just like the comics of that golden long-ago—whose heroes often crossed over into radio—the shows and scripts crumbled and no one really cared. So perhaps there will be no future historians of the world I hugged close to me when I pressed my ear against the large speaker, a world of heroes and villains and fantasy and high adventure where the command was sometimes "Kill!"—as I shuddered and listened.

INTRODUCTION TO

THE SECOND BANANA STRIKES AGAIN!

LOOKED at soberly, costumed superheroes range from impossible
to absurd. The impossible ones can live a long time and attract
many devoted fans who will recall them fondly all their lives. The
absurd ones can do the same, but fewer of them last as long and
hardly any are really memorable to the majority of comic-book
readers.

Ron Goulart does not belong to that majority. His favorites are
the also-rans, the has-beens that never were, the born losers, the
flop-oriented creations who either had brief careers or never made
it up from the back of the book—or both. Here you will learn of
the heroes who became superpowered by being caught in torna-
dos—there were more of these than any rational person might
think—and of the world's only comic-book hero who fought crime
in drag. At least, we hope there was only one.

Ron Goulart lives with his wife and two sons on two and a half
semirural acres in Connecticut. He migrated east from California
five years ago and abandoned his advertising copywriting career
to do freelance writing, mostly of science fiction, but including a
sizable number of parodies and mystery novels. He has written
several novels about a Hollywood private eye named John Easy,
none of which has won an Edgar Allan Poe Award from the
Mystery Writers of America—but the MWA did give him an
Edgar for *After Things Fell Apart*, a science-fiction novel. Ron also
wrote the Nostalgia Book Club selection *Cheap Thrills*, an informal history of the pulp magazines.

His stories, articles, and parodies have appeared in most of the
science-fiction magazines and in such varied markets as *Playboy,
Sports Illustrated, Police Gazette, Mad, Crawdaddy,* and *Saturday
Review*.

"I began writing when I was six, though my original ambition
was to be either a cartoonist or a comedian," Ron writes. "I had
a standup comedy act when I was in high school and toured lodge
halls and Scout picnics along with two accordion-playing brothers
and some girls who tapdanced. I still draw a little, but I haven't
stood up and told a joke in several years."

CHAPTER 13

THE SECOND BANANA STRIKES AGAIN!

by RON GOULART

In *All in Color for a Dime* I did a nostalgia piece about the second banana superheroes, about the obscure, second fiddle, short-lived, and out-and-out-flop mystery men of the past. In it I confessed a preoccupation not with the monumental and famous superheroes of two or three decades ago, a few of whom are still with us, but with the loser and the near-miss hero. The kind of superman who lasted maybe three issues before either he or his magazine went out of business and the masked man who, even though he may have held on for a few years, never got more than eight pages at the back of the book. In the time since then I've occasionally thought, sometimes prompted by a reviewer or by someone who asked me something like, "How come you never mentioned the Blazing Scarab?", that there were still several hundred other second-rate superheroes I should have celebrated and didn't. This new piece then is an attempt to make amends, another look at that 30-years-back era which people in a newer generation than mine call the Golden Age of comics. A recollection of some more of those forgotten superheroes who never quite got anywhere.

When superhero comic books began to proliferate in the late 1930s, the writers', artists', and editors' main source of inspiration was each other. After that they turned to nature, swiping heroes from the elements, from birds, animals and insects. Air, water, and fire were a particularly rich source of heroes. Fire inspired the Human Torch, as well as one of the more interesting second banana supermen, the Flame. The Flame first appeared in *Wonderworld Comics* in the middle of 1939 and for a year or so was among the best drawn of the superhero strips. The feature was the work of the late Lou Fine, then a laborer in Will Eisner's shop. Unlike many comic-book men, who were content to steal from Caniff, Raymond, and Foster, Fine ranged farther afield. He borrowed, imitated, and assimilated the work of commercial illustrators like Leyendecker and Dean Cornwell and European cartoonists like Heinrich Kley. Since Eisner was well aware of the value of good packaging, he also got Fine to do the covers of the various comic books his shop put together for the Fox, Fiction House, and Quality lines. With few exceptions the other artists in the Eisner stable couldn't deliver anything like what the Lou Fine covers promised.

According to the origin story of the Flame, which they didn't get around to printing until six months after his debut, he came by his superpowers in Tibet. The Flame was the son of a China missionary named Charteris, who saved him from an impending flood by putting him, like Moses, in a basket. The basket floats finally to "a country overrun with exotic flowers and plants growing in wild confusion." This, it turns out, is Tibet. The baby Charteris is taken in hand by priests at the nearest Buddhist lamasery and eventually taught "the sacred secrets of the gentle lamas," plus gymnastics, magic, and finally "the power over flame, the greatest mystic secret of the grand high lamas." After getting all this from the lamas, young Charteris returns to America, vowing "No evil shall live!" He dons a yellow-and-scarlet uniform with a stylized flame embroidered on the chest. His power over flame was a somewhat vaguely defined ability, enabling him to do such things as materialize in fireplaces, furnaces, and even out of the top of a cigarette lighter. He was immune to fires and explosions and could occasionally set people to burning. For this last trick he'd use his flame gun, exhorting it to "do your stuff!" The plots of the Flame's adventures usually made little sense, but the stories were full of leaping action, lovely girls in jeopardy, and, often, settings of Ruritanian complexity. The episodes were more like advertising trailers for scripts somebody was going to get around to writing. After Lou Fine went on to better things, or at least to better page rates, the Flame was rendered by divers hands, among them Larry Antonette and Al Carreño.

Lou Fine next turned out a number of superheroes for E. M. Arnold's Quality magazines, where most of the books had explosive titles like *Smash, Crack,* and *Hit.* For *Smash Comics,* commencing in the summer of 1940, he did the Ray. Comics hadn't yet reached the level of sophistication they would in later decades and the pen name he used on the feature was E. Lectron. The Ray was in some ways similar to the Flame, except that he showed up out of flashes of light and crackles of electricity. His daytime job was that of newspaperman. He became the Ray in a work-related accident. "Happy Terrill, reporter, while hunting a 'scoop' in the stratosphere, was struck by a bolt of lightning . . . and became transformed to the amazingly powerful RAY!" During the year or so Fine worked on the strip the Ray alternated between adventures with everyday crooks and murderers and encounters with gothic monsters and fantasy pirates and wizards. Fine was also the original artist on Dollman, the hero with the dubious ability of being able to shrink down to teenie-weenie size. Just the right size to get stepped on.

Many superheroes were around for so short a time that today they inspire no nostalgia at all. If you were away from the newsstand for a week or two with measles or the mumps you missed them entirely. One such hero was Airman, who appeared twice in a comic book with the catchy title *Detective Eye* and twice in a magazine with the even catchier title *Keen Detective Funnies.* He had his brief career in the summer of 1940. At that point in time comic-book villains weren't much used to encountering flying heroes. When Airman swooped down on them they'd exclaim, "Who's dis guy dressed like a bird?" Though he resembled the more enduring Hawkman, Airman policed a different beat. His practice was limited to "crime on the high seas." When, at the end of a successful case, his girl friend asked him to come back home, Airman replied: "As for going back to the city, I think those who sail the sea need the service of the Airman in the cause of justice! I'm sorry, Ellen, but it's goodbye for a while!" And he flew away.

Another elemental and short-lived hero was Tornado Tom, who made it through five issues of *Cyclone Comics.* While Tornado was appearing in *Cyclone,* by the way, an avenger known as Cyclone was appearing in *Whirlwind Comics*. Tornado Tom, drawn by Jon Small, was around for so short a time that he never even got a costume. He did his superhero work, which usually consisted of beating up and choking labor agitators and spies, wearing an old work shirt and a pair of farm pants. Tom is another hero who came by his powers accidently. One day, like Judy Garland in *The Wizard of Oz*, he is carried away by a Midwest cyclone and "whirled above the earth for hours." He is finally deposited in another state, unhurt and with a strange feeling of power. He discovers that the cyclone, in some remarkable way, has imparted something of its strength and violence to him, making him the physical match for a dozen ordinary men and capable of great speed. Being whirled across state lines has also given Tom amnesia. In between heroics he tries to find out who he is, remarking, "I may have a mother waiting for me to come home." He went out of business without ever finding her.

A year after Tornado Tom had faded away another cyclone snatched up a teenage boy and took him for a spin. "I was picked up by the whirling twister. I never found out what really happened, but a strange feeling came over me . . . and as I collected my senses, I found myself a strange being . . . part of the cyclone itself . . . and able to control it at will." The cyclone not only does that, it ages the boy a good ten years, dresses him up in a crimson-and-black uniform, and inspires him to call himself the Twister. This character, first drawn by Paul Gustavson, survived through seven 1941 issues of *Blue Bolt Comics*.

Birds were an especially good source of costume heroes. Besides Hawkman and Airman, the early 1940s gave us such bird-oriented figures as the Raven, the Eagle, the Black Condor, and at least two separate owls. There was the Black Owl in *Prize Comics* and the just plain Owl in *Crackajack*. *Prize* was a venture of the venerable Munsey pulpwood-publishing outfit and so originally the Black Owl had some of the sedateness in dress and action of the pulp-magazine masked men. By day a seemingly cowardly playboy, he kept on his playboy tuxedo when he switched identities, adding an owlish mask and a cape. As the Black Owl progressed he updated himself and began wearing a tights-and-trunks costume. He changed artists frequently, being drawn by someone calling himself Pete Nebird, then by George Storm and Jack Binder. In 1943 he apparently decided to devote himself fulltime to being a playboy again. He turned his costume over to a fellow named Walt Walters, who was already the father of a pair of innocuous boy superheroes known as Yank & Doodle. Imagine living downstairs from that bunch.

The other Owl was the work of Frank Thomas, who was essentially a humorous cartoonist. This gave his Owl a wacky and not quite serious look that wasn't present in the majority of mystery-man strips. When the Owl wasn't fighting crime in his purple costume, which he referred to as his work clothes, he was Nick Terry. Terry was another of those comic-book cops who, impatient with due process, played vigilante in their off-hours. The Owl wasn't as adolescent as many of his hero peers. Though he flew a showy Owlplane around the night skies, when it came time to add a sidekick he chose not a boy wonder but a pretty blonde named Belle.

The insect world, too, inspired a good many heroes. The Green Hornet was the most prominent of these. Actually the Hornet was too conservative for comic pages, which is why he did much better on radio than in funny books. He preferred driving an automobile to bounding over rooftops, for a costume he ignored capes and boots to fight crime in a slouch hat and an overcoat. Much more flamboyant and irrational was the Blue Beetle. He came along in the summer of 1939, the star of a Fox magazine called *Mysterymen Comics*. The Beetle was one of the few superheroes who acquired his powers through attention to his diet. Blurbs continually reminded us he was "given super-energy by vitamin 2X." He wore a special costume of blue chainmail, making him "almost invulnerable." While some heroes had crack scientists for mentors, or at least mad doctors, the Blue Beetle settled for a druggist. Apparently it never occurred to him to buy up 2X in quantity, so every time he wanted to become super he had to drop into the neighborhood drugstore to get his prescription refilled by Dr. Franz. In everyday life the Beetle was an impatient rookie cop named Dan Garrett and I have the impression that he left his hero costume hanging in what the scripts referred to as "the back room of a drugstore." It's also possible that the Dr. Franz drugstore was a chain operation, since Dr. Franz would be a thin man with glasses in one issue and a fat fellow with a beard the next. Once powered by 2X, the Blue Beetle would run around for eight or ten pages, cracking skulls and attempting wise cracks, while he hunted down such villains as the Wart, Scrag, the Eel, Mr. Downhill, and a crazed scientist called Doc. The Beetle was especially fond of lying out flat on roofs and ledges, then dropping down on surprised thugs. Now and then he would scare his foes with "the sign of the Blue Beetle," a little blue scarab he would leave on desks and table tops or, when in a whimsical mood, lower into a room on the end of a string.

Among the other strips inspired by the insect world were *The Wasp, The Red Bee, The Black Widow* and *Alias the Spider*. The hero of the last-named, drawn by Paul Gustavson, appeared in issues of *Crack Comics* in the early 1940s. Back then none of us had encountered the word *alias* before. We figured it was the Spider's first name and that his friends probably called him Al.

Reflecting as they did an assortment of American and boyhood dreams, there were naturally superheroes whose careers were intimately bound up with machines and gadgets. Several heroes of the period worked with super-engines of one kind or another. The Red Torpedo tackled underwater evils in an invention of his own, "a torpedo that a man can navigate." A hero whose name escapes me knocked Germans and Japanese out of the air in a super flying bomb he dubbed the Blue Tracer. Airboy flew around in a special plane which could flap its wings like a bird. There was even a train engineer hero, Runaway Ronson.

Probably the best of the gadget-freak characters was Skyman. He appeared in the spring of 1940 in *Big Shot Comics*, accompanied by a, for then, very advanced airship called the Wing and a stasimatic raygun. The stasimatic paralyzed opponents by "temporarily suspending their blood circulation." The Wing was an incredible plane which could fly on its own and follow the Skyman like a pet dog. The early adventures were written by Gardner Fox, who was adept at jumping over rough spots. When the Wing had to do anything difficult Fox would insert captions like: "By an amazing scientific device known only to himself, the Skyman causes his plane to remain suspended above the house . . . and swings downward by rope." The Skyman wore an upper-class costume, the white pants, crimson jersey, and polished boots of the polo player, topped by a blue aviator's helmet. For most of his ten-year career Skyman was drawn by Ogden Whitney. Though Whitney never excited a cult or inspired a school of imitators, he was an excellent artist. He was very good at drawing the figure in action, an ability shared by a good many, but he was also an expert at doing the figure at ease and in repose. This is a much harder thing to do and in some *Skyman* episodes Whitney seems to be showing off with people lounging, leaning, slouching, slumping, and sprawling all over the place.

In addition to the heroes who were intimate with machines there were those who were actually machines themselves. Notable among these mechanical men was Bozo the Robot, who flourished in *Smash Comics* in the late thirties and early forties. Bozo looked like an animated oil furnace with a pot on top of it and was the invention of Hugh Hazzard, who sometimes rode around inside him. Besides building robots with highly compact inner workings, Hazzard was devoted to carrying on "his war against all that is evil." Hazzard and his iron man were particularly good at rooting out spies and subversives. After turning enemy agents over to a firing squad or similar violent retribution, Hazzard, inside Bozo, would observe, "That should serve as a warning to others who have in mind acts of sabotage against this great nation." For all of the four years he lasted, Bozo was rendered in suitably tinny style by George Brenner. In my youth I was puzzled as to what exactly Brenner was attempting, but now I realize he was trying desperately to imitate Alex Raymond and falling considerably short of his goal.

The superman fever spread rapidly in the early forties, striking characters you wouldn't ordinarily have expected to take to wearing costumes and performing strange deeds. We thus got masked and costumed doctors (such as Dr. Nemesis and Dr. Mid-Nite), masked and costumed commandos (Commando Yank, Americommando, *et al.*), masked and costumed aviators (Phantom Eagle, Masked Pilot, Sky Wolf), masked lawyers (the Mouthpiece), and a whole clutch of masked detectives. These mysterious detectives included the Spirit, the Clock, and Midnight, who eventually came to look as though he was patronizing the same seedy tailor who supplied baggy suits to the Spirit. Speaking of haberdashery, my favorite suit was the one worn by the Voice in *Popular Comics*. It was made out of cellophane and when he slipped it on he became invisible. Because he usually got ready in front of his pretty girl secretary he always put the cellophane suit on over his other suit.

A highly visible phantom detective was the Face. He did his avenging while wearing a rubber mask that made him look "grim and fantastic ... weird and gruesome ... his pallid features fearsome as a tormenting dream." In reality, as the captions in *Big Shot Comics* put it, he was Tony Trent, well-known radio com-

355

mentator. Trent didn't only report the news, he took part in it. If an item on his news broadcast annoyed him he'd take off after the show to investigate. He attacked everyone from murderers and jewel thieves to wholesalers who peddled tainted meat to orphanages. Like some of the playboy avengers, Trent wore his tuxedo while tracking down crooks as the Face. His mask, which looks to have been inspired by the Fredric March version of Mr. Hyde, was highly effective at scaring people, especially guilty parties. Women reacted to the sight of the face by screaming, "Eeee! Eeeee!" Pullman porters exclaimed, "Oh mah heavens!" and even hardened criminals were likely to cry out, "Gorsh—it's awful!" The author of the Face's initial exploits was the prolific Gardner Fox, the artist was Mart Bailey.

For all their eccentricities of dress, there were very few comic-book heroes who went around in drag. One exception was Madam Fatal. Ostensibly a little old lady in spectacles and sensible shoes, Madam Fatal is really famous character actor Richard Stanton. Stanton originally gets himself up as a grandmother type so he can track down the man who kidnaped his daughter. After catching him, in the first issue of *Crack Comics*, Stanton is reluctant to drop the role. He confesses to his parrot: "The actor's disguise of Madam Fatal has served its purpose, but this is not enough. For I've decided that as Madam Fatal I'll go on fighting crime and lawlessness as long as I can!!" This turned out to be a little over a year.

Since comic books were more eclectic, less rigid in format, in the late thirties and early forties, they generated a wide variety of heroes and attracted artists with highly personal, though not always good, styles. The science-fiction strip was a genre especially given to eccentric art and plotting. The prince of the eccentric and highly individual SF artists was Basil Wolverton. His major strip creation was *Spacehawk*, which began in the spring of 1940 in *Target Comics*. I wasn't aware of it at the time, but *Target* had the same publisher as the *Saturday Evening Post*. Meaning Curtis was simultaneously giving America the work of both Basil Wolverton and Norman Rockwell.

Spacehawk was a burly fellow, though part of his bulk was probably due to the thick green space suit he never took off. He had most of the abilities of your run-of-the-mill superhero (he was, for instance, indestructible and he could fly) and his turf consisted of the entire solar system. In the early 1940s, unhampered by a real-life space program, you could lay out and populate a planet any way you wanted. The decor of most Wolverton planets was dominated by rocks and vegetable-market foliage. His version of Saturn reminded you of the Grand Canyon with giant cauliflower and asparagus growing all over it. Neptune was similar, with more rocks. Wolverton's alien races were a mixture of the vegetable and the phallic, usually resembling cucumbers and gherkins. Since he had obviously grown up on the pulp SF magazines of the twenties and thirties, Wolverton made sure Spacehawk encountered a sufficient number of bug-eyed monsters and sparsely clad blonde girls. He was also very good at gadgets, especially the kind that required lots of nuts and bolts. His spaceships had the bulk and feel of ocean liners, the control rooms were as cluttered with pipes and dials as an apartment house basement. He was fond of all the intricate, time-consuming pen-and-ink techniques, such as cross-hatching, which brightened the work of newspaper cartoonists like Winsor McCay and Frank Miller. A Wolverton splash panel with a spaceship sailing over a stretch of Saturn or Neptune gives you a condensed history of 50 years of pen-and-ink rendering techniques. I wasn't surprised to read, in a recent interview with Wolverton, that during this period it took him a full day to do a page. Wolverton is basically a funnyman and *Spacehawk* is one of the few supposedly straight features he ever did. Maybe it's Wolverton's never-quite-restrained sense of humor that gives the strip its unique, slightly cockeyed, look.

An artist of even more bizarre talents was Henry Fletcher. He surfaced briefly in the late thirties, infesting the pages of the Fox and Fiction House comics magazines. His work resembles nothing else ever drawn by anyone, man or beast. If you haven't seen it, you can't imagine it. Suppose Wolverton and Grandma Moses collaborated on penciling a strip and then an exceptionally bright chimpanzee inked it. That's what Henry Fletcher's work looked like—sort of. Fletcher's major creation appeared in about a dozen and a half issues of *Fantastic Comics*. It was called *Stardust, the Super Wizard*. Stardust, who dwelled someplace out in space, wore a gray-and-yellow circus-acrobat-type costume. His most outstanding feature was his neck. Stardust's neck was twice as wide, and almost as long, as his head. That neck alone would have been enough to scare the racketeers and subversives Stardust was continually after. He, however, had superpowers and supergadgets as well. He could fly, he could read minds, he could, somewhat like the Holy Ghost, send his voice to speak to people out of a flash of light. He owned a universal soundplate, a panoramic television unit, and a tubular spacial. The best thing about Stardust, though, was the writing. Fletcher wrote as he drew. "Stardust, whose vast knowledge of interplanetary science has made him the most remarkable man that ever lived, devotes his abilities to racket-busting," a typical caption tells us. One of Stardust's boy helpers exclaims, "Holy mackeral! World-invaders from the eastern hemisphere are preparing to shoot enormous shells across the ocean to America, and those powerful magnets will be used to draw shells to vital points!"

Another pioneer comic-book science-fiction hero was Dick Briefer's Rex Dexter of Mars. Rex worked mainly in *Mysterymen Comics* from mid-1939 through mid-1941. His chief occupation was "rocketing through millions of miles of empty space daring the terrors of unknown worlds." Dexter, in his short career, came up against some pretty unsettling terrors. He battled giant plants, protoplasmen, flying octopuses, Mercurian slavers, walking germs, and Cranians, who had heads where other people have hands and a fist where you'd expect the head to be. Briefer, though no great draftsman, had a loose, fast-moving style.

Somewhere between full-fledged superheroes and average civilian characters were the magicians. Many early comic books, like vaudeville shows, wanted to have a magician on the bill. One of the earliest original-material magazines, Major Nicholson's *New Adventure*, featured a magician hero with the failure-oriented name of Nadir. Nadir was a moustached fellow in a turban. Though he employed "certain secrets of the far east" in his fight against crime he didn't have much in the way of spectacular mystic powers. Much more impressive was Zatara, who came along in *Action Comics* a year later. He looked even more like Mandrake than Nadir, right down to a giant minority sidekick named Tong. Zatara could do just about anything and there was no pretending his tricks were merely hypnotic illusions. He really could move buildings, turn crooks' guns into snakes, turn the crooks themselves into pigs, and then project his astral body to the moon. At first Zatara's magic words were merely nonsense patter—"Agga djin!" or "Gurgo hlath!" He then discovered the little-known magical principle that saying words backwards had a powerful effect. "Emoc nwod!" he'd order and something or

Zatara spoke his words backward (often with unintentionally humorous results) in order to work his magic. His magic wasn't strong enough to bring him back in a strip of his own during the super-hero revival of the sixties and seventies, but his daughter made it. Zatara never made it past supporting feature status. © 1945 Worlds Best Comics Co.; renewed 1973 National Periodical Publications, Inc.

somebody would come down. His reversed commands always had a nice ring, as when he told someone who'd just lassoed him to, "Ossal flesruoy!"

The first two or so years of *Zatara* were drawn by Fred Guardineer, who had a strange flat style, full of angles and patterns, ideally suited to odd and magical adventures. In later years Guardineer said he would have much preferred doing cowboy strips, but in the early forties they made him the number-one drawer of magicians. For *Big Shot* he did Marvelo. This "monarch of magicians" had Zatara's moustache and Nadir's turban, plus an Oriental dwarf for a companion. Over at Quality Guardineer drew Tor and Merlin, who resembled Zatara and Marvelo as well as each other. Among the other magicians practicing in those years were Zambini, Yarko, Sargon, Norgil, El Carim, Balbo the Boy Magician, and Ibis the Invincible. This last sorcerer, who was featured in *Whiz Comics*, always puzzled us. With a name like that, we thought, you shouldn't be able to see him.

The comic books of the forties were basically a boys' medium. The few lady supercharacters appearing in the magazines must have been intended not for little girl readers but for the boy readers who were nearing puberty. There were Phantom Lady, Wildfire, Pat Patriot, Futura, two different Miss Americas, Liberty Belle, and Lady Fairplay, who thrived in only three issues of a magazine with the splendid title of *Bang Up Comics*. One of the best of the mystery-women characters was Lady Luck. The feature started in the weekly syndicated *Spirit* booklets, then moved into *Smash Comics*. While several artists worked on it, the most distinctive was Klaus Nordling. Nordling, who still works with Eisner on advertising comics, wrote and drew *Lady Luck* for several years. The Nordling version, reflecting his sense of humor, had the look and sound of some of the better screwball-mystery movies.

As Proust found out, reminiscing is difficult to confine. I've reached the end of my space without getting around to such notable second banana heroes as Captain Battle, Ultra Man, the Jester, Sparkman, the Triple Terror (triplet superheroes), Quicksilver, the Fox, Wildcat, the Red Panther (the only costumed superman who worked the African jungles), the Comet, the Cloak, and Powerman. As a matter of fact, I still haven't mentioned the Blazing Scarab.